Essaying Montaigne

STUDIES IN SOCIAL AND POLITICAL THOUGHT
Editor: Gerard Delanty, *University of Liverpool*

This series publishes peer-reviewed scholarly books on all aspects of social and political thought. It will be of interest to scholars and advanced students working in the areas of social theory and sociology, the history of ideas, philosophy, political and legal theory, anthropological and cultural theory. Works of individual scholarship will have preference for inclusion in the series, but appropriate co- or multi-authored works and edited volumes of outstanding quality or exceptional merit will also be included. The series will also consider English translations of major works in other languages.

Challenging and intellectually innovative books are particularly welcome on the history of social and political theory; modernity and the social and human sciences; major historical or contemporary thinkers; the philosophy of the social sciences; theoretical issues on the transformation of contemporary society; social change and European societies.

It is not series policy to publish textbooks, research reports, empirical case studies, conference proceedings or books of an essayist or polemical nature.

Discourse and Knowledge: The Making of Enlightenment Sociology
Piet Strydom

Social Theory after the Holocaust
edited by Robert Fine and Charles Turner

The Moment: Time and Rupture in Modern Thought
edited by Heidrun Friese

Essaying Montaigne
John O'Neill

The Protestant Ethic Debate: Max Weber's Replies to his Critics, 1907–1910
edited by David Chalcraft and Austin Harrington
translated by Austin Harrington and Mary Shields

Essaying Montaigne:

A Study of the Renaissance Institution of Writing and Reading

JOHN O'NEILL

LIVERPOOL UNIVERSITY PRESS

Second edition published 2001 by
Liverpool University Press
4 Cambridge Street
Liverpool
L69 7ZU

First edition published 1982 by
Routledge & Kegan Paul Ltd.

British Library Cataloguing-in-Publication Data
A British Library CIP record is available

ISBN 0 85323 996 7 cased
     0 85323 507 4 paperback

Typeset by Northern Phototypesetting Co Ltd, Bolton
Printed in Great Britain by Bell and Bain Ltd, Glasgow

Contents

For my children
Brendan, Daniela, Gregory
Souvenir de Pully, Lausanne 1977–78

'. . . essays in flesh and bone'
(III:5, 640)

Preface to the revised edition

It is quite in tune with Montaigne that one should revise one's work in the light of more thought and changes in historical fortune affecting publishing itself. Twenty years ago, academic publishing began to experience those changes in production formats, costing and marketing with which we are now more familiar. *Essaying Montaigne* (1982) has survived its fate and happily is now ready to take on a new lease of life in the spirit of Montaigne's own perennial *Essays*. The original impetus for my work was Maurice Merleau-Ponty's beautiful essay, 'Reading Montaigne' (*Signs*, 1964). The subtlety of Merleau-Ponty's exploration of the ambiguous self in Montaigne and his larger phenomenology of embodied thought provided me with an early and lasting model of the carnal practice of literature. It is one I have preferred to the rival practices of literary deconstruction launched by Derrida whose *Grammatology* (1974) fixes upon Rousseau. The reader must choose between Montaigne and Rousseau, as I have done here and in other works of mine on literary criticism, psychoanalysis and cultural studies. I have, of course, defended my preference for Montaigne's practice of 'essaying' through elaborate commentary upon rival readings, which the *Essays* have inspired for centuries with no sign of exhaustion in our own time. Indeed, the classical status of the *Essays* proves itself over and over in their contemporary relevance. I have grounded the *Essays* in the ethical relation of friendship as a rule for personal, familial and political relationships. I have rejected the contemporary psychoanalytical bias towards the absence and lack as the driving forces in relationships unless a counterweight be given to presence and recognition in social and political life. I believe that Montaigne discovered in the practice of the essay form a technique of the self – that is both personal and civic. The reason I pay such close attention to other critics of the *Essays* is that I am concerned to defend them against any reading that enslaves Montaigne's own reading/writing competence in the name of the current machinery of writing that runs on after the death of the author.

To the Reader

Montaigne's *Essays* speak to us in a voice so direct that the reader must consider from the start how to accommodate their intimate appeal. The reader is no more released from the world by the *Essays* than was their author in writing them. The room in which the *Essays* were written, and wherever they are read, is therefore not apart from the world; it becomes the setting of one of the world's great friendships to which we lend ourselves in a lesson of freedom, family and good sense:

To the Reader
This book was written in good faith, reader. It warns you from the outset that in it I have set myself no goal but a domestic and private one. I have had no thought of serving either you or my own glory. My powers are inadequate for such a purpose. I have dedicated it to the private convenience of my relatives and friends, so that when they have lost me (as soon as they must), they may recover here some features of my habits and temperament, and by this means keep the knowledge they have had of me more complete and alive.

If I had written to seek the world's favor, I should have bedecked myself better, and should present myself in a studied posture. I want to be seen here in my simple, natural, ordinary fashion, without straining or artifice; for it is myself that I portray. My defects will here be read to the life, and also my natural form, as far as respect for the public has allowed. Had I been placed among those nations which are said to live still in the sweet freedom of nature's first laws, I assure you I should very gladly have portrayed myself here entire and wholly naked.

1

> Thus, reader, I am myself the matter of my book; you would be unreasonable to spend your leisure on so frivolous and vain a subject.
> So farewell. Montaigne, this first day of March, fifteen hundred and eight.[1]

From the very beginning, Montaigne requires a reader who will not simply lean upon the preface for an easy sense of the essays to follow. How is the reader to intrude upon this domestic and private activity; how can he, without a family acquaintance, trade upon the *Essays* as a convenient access to Montaigne's life? To compensate for this lack of direction, however artfully, may not (as I intend to show) save the reader from the rebuff of being clever by too far on behalf of so selfish and indulgent a writer as Montaigne set himself to be. The reader, after all, is warned that the author's purpose is nothing more serious than an easy nakedness sported on some exotic isle. What has cost Montaigne so little is hardly to be worked for in the sublimation of learned reading.

We cannot search for Montaigne in the *Essays* in the same way that his family and neighbours might have looked for the original. But, of course, not even his family, any more than Montaigne's neighbours, saw in him the man who was writing the *Essays*:

> In my region of Gascony they think it is a joke to see me in print. The farther from my lair the knowledge of me spreads, the more I am valued. I buy printers in Guienne, elsewhere they buy me. (III: 2, 614)

Montaigne's consubstantiality with the *Essays* in no manner precedes his own reading of them. We must disregard this aprioristic fiction upon the way an author comes to terms with the gradual inscription or textualisation of his moods, thoughts and temperament collecting in his own fiction or self-portrait.[2] We therefore cannot grasp Montaigne's authorial self apart from the constant crossfertilisation between his reading and writing. Montaigne reads with his body. By the same token, Montaigne's reading and writing is an act of carnal inquiry, often moody, lazy and dependent, but also witty, strong, humorous and gay. Montaigne is therefore a religious writer in the only sense that is proper to him; or to the word, namely, as a loving effort to keep body and soul together in family life. To achieve this, Montaigne had to rework his beloved authors, to shift from his first Latin tongue into his local Gascon; and always to communicate as though with a friend or neighbour: 'you and one companion are an adequate theater for each other, or you for yourself. Let the people be one to you, and let one be a whole people to you' (I: 39, 182). It is from this perspective, too, that we can understand Montaigne's continuous conversation with his heroes from the past. He knew, of course, that his own society provided no pedestal for them, and certainly not for their imitators – at least not before their 'replay' in the French Revolution.[3]

Montaigne read himself in the double history of the classics and the *Essays*. He learned to speak again, to reinvest conversation with the trust it needs, while simultaneously testing its fidelity in the most audacious enterprise of self-inquiry. Therefore Montaigne's additions to the text of the *Essays* represent nothing but the ordinary revisions of living thoughtfully, without any escape from the limited horizons of carnal inquiry. Within this perspective, one can only see where one has been, or where one is going, by stopping to take a look, to rearrange things a bit, and then to move on. As carnal inquiry, writing is inseparable from reading, and each has its life in the other.[4]

A writer begins with a model of other writing which he nevertheless cannot imitate if he is to become a writer. The problem of beginning is therefore a problem of how the essayist founds his own literary authority so as to animate the tradition that weighs upon him like the community of the living dead. For it is in this literary community that the great writer seeks his place in order to remain alive in those who will continue to read him as much as any in his own lifetime. Montaigne is obsessed with this dead community, the corpse of literature. He cannot refrain from celebrating its achievements; he seeks every opportunity to humble himself in its repetition, in its visible and invisible uses, always acclaimed with an innocence that nevertheless harbours a necessary literary subversion. The anxiety of literary origins[5] is therefore essential to a writer's authority. For this reason, the preface cannot possibly constitute the literal beginning or start of any writer's life.[6] It is rather an activity that must inhabit his work, without ever being settled in any particular address or place, as in an introduction or in Montaigne's preface To the Reader. This is because the essayist must draw on his beginning throughout his literary life – not because he cannot get beyond it, but because the *Essays* continuously renew their sources so that any beginning is never wholly autonomous, and therefore never strictly methodic.

What, then, is the activity that Montaigne inaugurates in his preface? How are we to understand the role a preface plays in the relation between author and reader and what each of them may hope to gain from the preface with respect to the *Essays*? The preface will come first. In view of the way it faces the text, the work of the preface might be thought to consist in disposing the reader to the author's intentions:

> That is the introduction. Writing one allows a writer to set the terms of what he will write about. Accounts, excuses, apologies designed to reframe what follows after them, designed to draw a line between deficiencies in what the author writes and deficiencies in himself, leaving him, he hopes, a little better defended than he might otherwise be.[7]

Montaigne, as we see, invokes his own inadequacies in his introduction in order to alert the reader not to trust the presumptive literary authority of a published work that will be found to exploit nothing but a selfish resource. Nothing is to be found in the organisational features of the *Essays* that will allow the reader to absorb them in any such principled way as a treatise in philosophy, morals or politics would permit. Since the author has no such quarry, he abandons glory, and so counts upon losing rather than winning the ordinary reader. The fate of an author depends upon his reader. But the reader is one who is just as likely to resist as to welcome the author's self-indulgence. For this reason, both the author and the reader will look to prefacing for the collection of their literary intentions so as to preserve each of them against the dispersal and distractions that otherwise invade their ordinary lives. Indeed, it is difficult for either the author or the reader to avoid the mutual conveniences of prefacing in this fashion. A preface tempts an author to adopt it as the occasion for providing himself with an ideal reader[8] through suitably rhetorical appeals to the reader's seriousness or to kindred concerns. The reader, in turn, looks to the preface for assurances that the author's intentions are clear and forthright and that his investment as a reader will not come to fault and ruin.

Thus, the preface needs to come first in order to make a double appeal to the reader's seriousness and to his uncommitted life. In this, however, there is a risk of mutual bad faith. For a preface may tempt the author to a wilful use of the reader whose literary competence he needs for the fulfilment of his writing. The reader, too, may look to the author for such direction in order to obtain a preview of his task in the hope of escaping the responsible labour of reading. Yet, surely, the preface will itself presuppose the reader's willingness to free himself from prejudice and convention, to prefer truth to appearance and to love inquiry more than self-deception. In other words, the writer's preface must also appeal to the reader's creativity and willingness to bring his own literary competence to share in the appropriation of the author's text.

A preface, then, brings together the work of the reader and the writer in order to secure what the text needs from each of them separately if it is to fulfil its proper discourse. Prefacing, as Hegel observes in *The Phenomenology of Mind*, is a work of mutual self-consciousness through which the writer and the reader engage their common need and recognition of one another in the labour of truth. The preface cannot conscript the reader's attention, his commitment or fascination: it must recognise in these things the peculiar literary consciousness of the reader who engages himself in the exploration and recomposition of the author's text:

In the case of a philosophical work it seems not only superfluous, but, in view of the nature of philosophy, even inappropriate and misleading to begin, as writers usually do in a preface, by explaining the end the author had in mind, the circumstances which gave rise to the work, and the relation in which the writer takes it to stand to other treatises on the same subject, written by his predecessors and contemporaries. For whatever it might be suitable to state about philosophy in a preface – say, an historical sketch of the main drift and point of view, the general content and results, a string of desultory assertions and assurances about the truth – this cannot be accepted as the form and manner in which to expound philosophical truth.[9]

The preface is the dialectical centre of the relation between the reader and writer. It is not possible for the author to use the preface ahead of his work, any more than a reader can use the preface to keep ahead of the work of reading. The preface is rather a place of inspiration, drawn upon repeatedly in the effort to bring the work to fulfilment. A preface, therefore, serves to rescue writer and reader from the inevitable failings of the text without, however, being able to address the accomplishments which it generates. A preface is neither before nor after.[10] This is because we have no hope of bringing speech, or thought or writing, to completion – but only to an essay. In prefacing, the writer and reader can only essay an essential beginning as an irony upon their respective proportion of knowledge and ignorance which together bring the text to life.[11]

It is here precisely that Lukács finds the proper sense of the essay form. To overlook its essential irony, obliges forceful critics like Wilden, whom we consider later,[12] to locate the literary autonomy of the *Essays* outside of Montaigne in his dependent friendship with La Boétie. Unlike Lukács, Wilden makes no allowance for the autonomy of the essay as a medium of the work of the intellect at grips with life. He thereby misses the intrinsic irony and humour of the *Essays* which, as Lukács observes, make Montaigne and Socrates natural allies in the very sense that Montaigne and La Boétie also were natural friends:

> Perhaps the great Sieur de Montaigne felt something like this when he gave his writings the wonderfully elegant and apt title of '*Essays*.' The simple modesty of this word is an arrogant courtesy. The essayist dismisses his own proud hopes which sometimes lead him to believe he has come close to the ultimate: he has, after all, no more to offer than explanations of the poems of others, or at best of his own ideas. But he ironically adapts himself to this smallness – the eternal smallness of the most profound work of the intellect in face of life – and even emphasises it with ironic modesty.[13]

Thus it cannot be the case that Montaigne's preface comes before the *Essays*, for then it would stand both the author and the reader outside of the sense each brings to the *Essays*. If the preface To the Reader were literally first, it would have to rely upon Montaigne's ability to read his own writing in the same way as any other reader. Rather, Montaigne would have to be able to parody his reader's work, whereas he needs the authentic and inviolate competence of the reader for the amplification of the *Essays*, for their power and interest, for the difference each essay makes in the articulation of Montaigne's literary life.

> Thus the author writes in order to address himself to the freedom of readers and he requires it in order to make his work exist. But he does not stop there; he also requires that they return this confidence which he has given them, that they recognize his creative freedom, and that they in turn solicit it by a symmetrical and inverse appeal. Here there appears the other dialectical paradox of reading; the more we experience our freedom, the more we recognize that of the other; the more he demands of us, the more we demand of him.[14]

If Montaigne's preface To the Reader were in any real sense a key to the *Essays*, it would undo the essayist's discourse by destroying the reader's future, and with it the waiting and ignorance generated by the *Essays'* otherness in the reader's life. By the same token, the essayist himself would be deprived of his art, which is the probable effect of his work upon the lives of others who are responsible and co-creators of his work.[15] At the very worst, if the preface were outside of the *Essays*, it would destroy the objectivity of the various essays since without a reader to live their themes and contents the *Essays* would remain a dead word. A preface must respect equally the labour of the author and the reader in bringing to sense the text that follows. Thus the preface cannot hope to clarify the text on behalf of the reader, as though the meaning of the *Essays* lay in any clarity of language and could be secured by guaranteeing the reader's ability to sustain its sense from the first world. Nor should the reader require from the author such a beginning, for then the writer's labour would also be superfluous to what follows. Nothing 'follows' the *Essays* – despite the critics – neither their beginnings nor their ends – except through what the writer and reader bring to the essay through their own literary skill. In short, the critics who look to the order and composition of the *Essays* ignore that covenant between the reader and the writer which brings to language that living competence upon which spoken language rests, that meaning is not trapped in words, sentences and characters, but merely gathers in words to overflow them, falling back upon living which is the true source of the density and particularity of reading and writing. Thus Montaigne's preface To the Reader inaugurates a course of writing whose necessity it defers in the fiction of beginning.[16] The preface cannot possibly exhibit the whole life of the *Essays*. Rather, it is itself subject to the very necessity of writing which it seems to deny. The preface has the air of a deliberate beginning; it speaks as though Montaigne might have written otherwise, or not at all, had he thought better. But, of course, nothing separates the page of the preface To the Reader from the rest of the pages in the *Essays*. The preface, then, as a representation of the scene of writing, is equally as subordinate to the process of writing as any of the essays which follow it:

> But what about comments on prefaces? Where does such a topic taken up at such a point leave the writer and the reader (or a speaker and an audience)? Does that sort of talk strike at the inclination of the reader to discount or criticize prefacing as an activity? And if it turns out that the preface was written in bad faith, tailored from the beginning to exemplify this use that will come to be made of it? Will the preface then be retrospectively reframed by the reader into something that really isn't a preface at all but an inappropriately inserted illustration of one? Or if an admission of bad faith is made unconvincingly, leaving open the possibility that the disclosure was an afterthought? What then?[17]

The preface is never a real start because the writer is already inside his work long before he can displace its beginnings and ends. Or rather, the preface is a real start in that it represents a concession to the hard fiction of organisation. The *Essays* treat their beginning paradoxically, thereby requiring a coproductive reader who is prepared to essay his own literary ability. Although in his preface To the Reader, Montaigne speaks as one seeking to be remembered among family and friends, who will not have to construct for him any epitaph beyond reading him from the *Essays*, to read them with the skill they require is to witness in him the pleasure of writing: 'Thus, reader, I am myself the matter of my book; you would be unreasonable to spend your leisure on so frivolous and vain a subject'. Nothing is contradicted by Montaigne's denial (*Verleugnung*) of the necessity of the *Essays*. Montaigne's pleasure in writing, which he translates into the scene of an exotic country where 'in the sweet freedom of nature's first laws, I assure you I should very gladly have portrayed myself here entire and wholly naked,' is forthright. At the same time, this literary pleasure is compromised in the recognition of the writer's concession to prevailing standards of public decency. The preface To the Reader, then, announces a possible split in the *Essays* between the writer's production of a literary desire and a comfortable reading unless the reader seeks out the pleasure of reading, in an alliance with the writer's incarnate union of book and self. At the same time, the *Essays* are not simply a fetish of Montaigne's subjectivity.[18] The *Essays* are Montaigne's happy credo – into which he can pour himself while simultaneously standing at a Sunday distance from them. They accumulate from a working pleasure in reading and writing and from the joy of finding a reader capable of exercising his own literary competence with the *Essays* as a continuous bodily inscription. Such pleasure lies outside of any literary organisation, hence Montaigne's topics and titles in the *Essays* serve only as strategies of pleasure, taking a page from a book or a poem in order to go on writing a book or a poem in order to go on reading a book or a poem. And so the *Essays* find readers who find readers like friends seeking one another. By word of mouth.

In essaying Montaigne we want to show how it is that any reading of the *Essays*, if it is to be faithful to their friendship, must preserve a certain literary equality between the reader and the writer. What we have tried to exemplify throughout our work we now set down as beginnings, subject to the prefatory limits we have introduced so far. In this spirit, we propose for consideration and, as it were, in defence of the reader, that the reader/writer exchanges essential to the *Essays* constitute a set of practices that may be given a regulative formulation.[19] These practices aim at a literary covenant which fulfils the exchanges between writer and reader in such a way that neither is made the slave of the other.[20] The writer requires the freedom of the reader, and, indeed, both expects and sustains the reader's literary competence. In turn, the writer expects not to be subject to omnipotent meta-readings that discover his meaning, style and composition in every way but one known to himself.[21] So much of what passes as literary interpretation is in our view nothing but literary decomposition. It requires equally mindless authors and readers in order to service its own critical act. By the same token, we are not arguing for neutral commentary. We are arguing against criticism that makes the critic, the reader and the author passive subscribers to meaning as the product of notions of clarity and organisation borrowed from a simplistic sense of scientific communication. The issue here, which we shall take up at length later on,[22] is put very well by Geoffrey Hartman:

> Every item in the interpreter's ethos should be submitted to a methodical suspicion. If he stresses objectivity, one should ask whether he is not overreacting to his fear of private compulsions, and using textual study as self-discipline. Nothing wrong with that, but let it be thought. If he stresses too much the integrity of the text, one should wonder about the streaminess or pseudo-continuity or his mental life. The text-fetishist may be deeply concerned with excluding the influence of strange ideas – usurpations from within him as well as from anthropology, psychology, etc. Similarly, if we find too great an emphasis on unity, we can expect a fear of ambivalence, or of split states of consciousness. The unitive or reconciling critic often harbors a love–hate of literature: his devotion to 'unity' may become a demand for 'totality' and turn against art in the name of a more comprehensive (religious or political) vision. The greatest advances in interpretation have occurred, moreover, by showing that a false unity has been imposed on an author: in his work there may be another work trying to get out.[23]

The writer, then, faces the problem of how it is he can provide for the reader as an authentic interlocutor, as a genuine dialogic partner who is not simply his own creation:

> *Socrates:* Any one may see that there is no disgrace in the mere fact of writing.
> *Phaedrus:* Certainly not.
> *Socrates:* The disgrace, I assume, begins when a man speaks or writes not well, but badly.
> *Phaedrus:* Clearly.
> *Socrates:* And what is well and what is badly – need we ask Lysias, or any other poet or orator, who ever wrote or will write either a political or any other work ... poet or prose writer, to teach us this?[24]

The dialectic proceeds by questions and answers so as never to pass from one assertion to the next without being assured of the interlocutor's assent. The art of the dialectician is to act so that this assent can never be refused.[25] This method of dialogue is essentially oral and requires at least two persons. How is it that Plato believes that it can be practised in a written dialogue where the same person, the author, constructs both the questions and the answers? Does his own assent give him the right to pass on the other's agreement? What makes Plato believe he can be sure that any other reader would reply as he does? In so far as the writer is not concerned merely to win over and conscript his reader, he is concerned to have him as an equal. Thus his starting points are not intended to engage a war of opinions; they are rather subjunctive alliances for the sake of exploring what hitherto had been shared terrain. By the same token, the conclusions that are reached are not meant to be absolute, but only what now seems reasonable as a shared experience. But as soon as we think, of any text, from an essay of Montaigne[26] to a novel or poem, we realise that our problem is overstated. No text can be given the kind of closure that shuts out the reader's work required to bring out its meaning. No author has his thoughts all to himself; none can control his comments, asides and evaluations so that they preserve his text from the indeterminacy that is the very opening for the reader's response.[27] The reader–writer relation therefore involves a literary covenant whose ethical principles might be formalised as follows:

The Literary Covenant

(i) The reader and the writer are both competent speakers of the natural language in which the text is written;

(ii) The reader and the writer both share the requisite *semantic knowledge,* idioms, linguistic and stylistic conventions required for the production (writing) and consumption (reading) of texts;[28]

(iii) The reader and the writer share a certain *literary competence* which is affirmed in the reader's response to the writer's invocation;[29]

(iv) The reader and the writer share in the *pleasure of texts* (the joy of reading and writing);[30]

(v) The reader and the writer participate freely in *making sense together as a personal and historical institution.*[31]

In essaying, Montaigne discovered a literary instrument for turning common sense into good sense. The essay is, then, an experiment in the community of truth, and not a packaging of knowledge ruled by definitions and operations. The essay is a political instrument inasmuch as it liberates the writer and reader from the domination of conventional standards of clarity and communication. The essay is a basic expression of literary initiative, authority, style and gratuity accomplished against the limits of received language. It exercises the reader and the writer in the practice of the antinomy of speech (*la parole*) and language (*la langue*), making sense together somewhere between communism and solipsism. The essay is not a literary technique; that would make it an instrument of the dominant culture of ready communication. Literacy is a bodily art of expression and understanding which requires the free subscription of writers and readers whose encounter with tradition requires that their own lives be the material and resource of the literary artifacts they produce. In the literary community, autonomy is membership in a continuous re-articulation of the tradition that has sedimented in us our natural being:

> True history thus gets its life entirely from us. It is in our present that it gets the force to refer everything else to the present. The other whom I respect gets his life from me as I get mine from him. A philosophy of history does not take away any of my rights or initiatives. It simply adds to my obligations as a solitary person the obligation to understand situations other than my own and to create a path between my life and that of others, that is, to express myself.[32]

The essayist, then, does not indulge himself in the pleasure of writing apart from any consideration of the reader who then needs the intermediary of the critic to bring the two together. Inasmuch as the essayist is concerned with 'making sense', or with the very makings of sense, he seeks a reader open to a similar experience of the acquisition of meaning. The essay is therefore a literary exemplar[33] of that equality of condition between readers and writers that makes literary authority and literary institution essential to our political life. The *Essays* hide nothing. They are entirely readable. But this is not because they are easily seen through, or because they reward anyone who digs beneath their surface. The *Essays* are talkative. This is not because Montaigne has nothing in mind and is therefore open to any reader with just as little purpose. The *Essays* converse because that is the only way we can bring our thoughts together. There is no straight line through the *Essays*. This is not because they are lacking in organisation, as some of the critics whom we shall consider claim on behalf of their own impotent readings. It is because the very nature of the literary artefact, exemplified in the essay, is that it cannot be given ahead of its own course of work.[34] But that means that the essay requires endless reworking by the author and reader alike, to furnish its alterations, its revisions and options.

CHAPTER 1

Society and Self-study:
the Problem of Literary Authority

Montaigne is said to have withdrawn from public life in order to find himself in the *Essays*. But if this were true, then Montaigne would have indulged a greater vanity than any he had encountered in public life. Fortunately, he knew himself better than to attempt the life of a literary recluse. For he knew that he was by nature given to society and friendship. Indeed, he considered himself nothing apart from France, and less than half of that beautiful friendship with La Boétie, whom it was his sorrow to survive:

> There are private, retiring, and inward natures. My essential pattern is suited to communication and revelation. I am all in the open and in full view, born for company and friendship. The solitude that I love and preach is primarily nothing but leading my feelings and thoughts back to myself, restraining and shortening not my steps, but my desires and my cares, abandoning solicitude for outside things, and mortally avoiding servitude and obligation, and not so much the press of people as the press of business. Solitude of place, to tell the truth, rather makes me stretch and expand outward; I throw myself into affairs of state and into the world more readily when I am alone. (III: 3, 625)

What we know of the political and religious conflicts of his times, and how they troubled Montaigne, makes it reasonable to assume that he needed to retire from the violence and treachery of political life to find himself. When we recall how dearly he loved La Boétie, we might well believe that the rest of the world could only disappoint him, and that he would yearn for the seclusion of his study to cultivate his love of the virtues impressed upon him by his friend. But we know that Montaigne served his king faithfully, that he loved La Boétie and died a Catholic. In short, we know that despite the troubles of sixteenth-century France, despite

13

the bitter religious struggles between Catholics and Protestants, and the terrible strains that these events placed upon men's principles, corrupting their thoughts and deeds and brutalising their actions, Montaigne nevertheless gave himself to public life and preserved in himself the capacity for self-inquiry. If this is so, and it is to this that the *Essays* are a testament, then we cannot understand the motive and accomplishment of self-study as a literary practice that in any sense puts aside the world. For Montaigne is the same man in writing the essays as he is in travel, or in love, or as the Mayor of Bordeaux or the friend of La Boétie; the same man in doubt as in belief, in passion as in reasoning. It is these bonds which underwrite the literary authority of the *Essays*.

Montaigne did not have two lives, one in public and one in private. The world is not ordained to such perfect Stoicism. Reason and passion are too mixed in us for us to choose all our entrances and exits. Often we are committed ahead of our choices and this is our alliance with the world's fools, our essential folly upon which we have no external stance. Thus we must learn that self-study, like any other conduct of ours, is entirely beholden to the events and places of this world and needs the company of our fellow men for its reflection. A thoughtful man is not another kind of man, even to himself; though we may well associate his reflections with the seclusion of his study and the quiet voice of his soul's conversation, in reading and writing. But a thinking man is not self-possessed. For this would make no sense of the path of thought, of the 'essaying' of experience which is only brought together by good sense and that sound judgement through which a man begins to know himself.

Montaigne invented the *Essays* because he knew that self-knowledge is not gained by standing outside of ourselves metaphysically.[1] We find ourselves only by travelling the road of our own lives and so coming to know better our own strengths and weaknesses, our likes and dislikes. By testing the variety of our moods and the differences cultivated by other men, we may learn from life's journey what it is we wish to call our own. Montaigne's *Essays* are embarked upon life. They hug the shores of society and custom. Undistracted by metaphysic speculations, they push on steadily in a bodily odyssey, seeking to bring home good sense and sound judgement, avoiding the sirens of fantasy and despair. Montaigne learned from his body to know himself: 'I study myself more than any other subject. That is my metaphysics, that is my physics' (III: 13, 821). In other words, he never allowed himself to become the place of the separation of reason and passion. Of course, Montaigne knew very well that men are infinitely capable of locating their ideal self beyond themselves in metaphysical abstractions, in literary and rhetorical flights, as well as in military and civil extravaganza. Indeed, the history of man is nothing but the history of man's fantastic ability to separate himself from himself. No other creature is as subject to self-flight as man in his imagination; he is as much carried off by reason as by passions for both result in the strangest deeds. We are overwhelmed by sorrow, anger and jealousy, driven by fear and pride, by lust and envy. And in these passions we are as unrecognisable to our friends as we are to ourselves once our passion is spent. Thus Cambyses, King of Persia, murdered his brother because of a dream and Aristodemus, King of the Messenians, slew himself because of the ill omen of his howling dogs: 'Inquire of yourself where is the object of this change. Is there anything besides ourselves in nature that feeds on inanity and is subject to its power?' (III: 4, 637–8).

Man is everywhere and nowhere. How then should a man keep himself together? Montaigne tells us that his thoughts, like anyone else's, roam at will, carried off by the wind, leaving him quite incapable of catching up with them or of keeping them in any orderly pattern. He complains of poor memory, aggravated by desultory reading habits which seem to surrender him to the flux of things, hurrying him towards death. With such a disposition, how is a man to acquire character and identity, how should he leave a mark, a place in the memory of his friends and family? At best, his place in the world will be marked by a monument upon which others will be left to write what might be said of him in any lasting way. We are in flight from ourselves and the image of our flight is the bird of death. We are time's body,[2] separating from ourselves from moment to moment, just as we are never here in our thoughts but always elsewhere:

If others examined themselves attentively, as I do, they would find themselves, as I do, full of inanity and nonsense. Get rid of it I cannot without getting rid of myself. We are all steeped in it, one as much as another; but those who are aware of it are little better off – though I don't know.

The common attitude and habit of looking elsewhere than at ourselves has been very useful for our own business. We are an object that fills us with discontent; we see nothing in us but misery and vanity. In order not to dishearten us, Nature has very appropriately thrown the action of our vision outward. We go forward with the current, but to turn our course backward toward ourselves is a painful movement: thus the sea grows troubled and turbulent when it is tossed back on itself. Look, says everyone, at the movement of the heavens, look at the public, look at that man's quarrel, at this man's pulse, at another man's will; in short, always look high or low, or to one side, or in front, or behind you.

It was a paradoxical command that was given us of old by that god at Delphi: 'Look into yourself, know yourself, keep to yourself; bring back your mind and your will, which are spending themselves elsewhere, into themselves; you are running out, you are scattering yourself; concentrate yourself, resist yourself;

you are being betrayed, dispersed, and stolen away from yourself. Do you not see that this world keeps its sight all concentrated inward and its eyes open to contemplate itself? It is always vanity for you, within and without; but it is less vanity when it is less extensive. Except for you, O man,' said that god, each thing studies itself first, and according to its needs, has limits to its labors and desires. There is not a single thing as empty and needy as you who embrace the universe: you are the investigator without knowledge, the magistrate without jurisdiction, and all in all, the fool of the farce.' (III: 9, 766)

The *Essays* are at once Montaigne's recourse from time and themselves the creature of time, as we know from the cumulative editions of the text.[3] But the growth of the *Essays* is not due to Montaigne's lack of method or of art, nor to a patchwork attempt to appear more methodical and artful than he had earlier thought possible. True thought is no more ahead of itself than life is outside itself. Therefore thought is like our living, and finds its way from day to day; and not without us. For this reason, we cannot subject our reading of the *Essays* either to a principled Stoicism or a dogmatic Christianity, and far less to any radical subjectivism. The *Essays* are a daily resolve, like the body's needs, or like love and friendship, which we cannot serve in principle, but must attend to here and now, according to their seasons. The *Essays* are Montaigne's body, his constant companion, the double of his life. The *Essays* are therefore not articulated according to any philosophical or artistic principles, though they establish an unrepentant claim upon literary authority or moral truth.

If Montaigne concentrates upon himself, it is with a steady attachment to his friend La Boétie, to his family and to his city, and to the voices from the past with whom he conversed in his library. He considered himself a small note in the collective and largely anonymous history of mankind, of which literature and art yield us only a fractured sounding. What is mature in Montaigne is not his scepticism or his relativism, it is rather his ability to hold life's attachments at a distance in order to consider how it is we are nevertheless beholden to everything and everyone around us.

In an exemplary reading of Montaignie's last essays, Merleau-Ponty has argued that it is not enough simply to say of him that he was a sceptic.[4] For scepticism has two aspects. It means that nothing is true, but also that nothing is false. That we cannot conclude that scepticism abandons us to an utter relativism of truth. Rather, it opens us to the idea of a totality of truth in which contradiction is a necessary element in our experience of truth. Montaigne's scepticism is rooted in the paradox of conscious being, namely, to be constantly involved in the world through perception, politics or love; and yet always at a distance from it, without which we would know nothing of it. And, as Merleau-Ponty adds, 'it could not possibly be otherwise. To be conscious is, among other things, to be somewhere else'. Thus the sceptic only withdraws from the world, from its passions and follies, in order to find himself at grips with the world, having, as it were, merely slackened the intentional ties between himself and the world in order to comprehend the paradox of his bodily being-in-the-world. Whenever Montaigne speaks of man he refers to him as 'strange', 'monstrous' or 'absurd'. What he has in mind is the paradoxical mixture that we are of mind and body. But the variety of human practices produces in Montaigne something more than anthropological curiosity or philosophical scepticism. Because of the mixture of being that he is, the explanation of man can only be given by himself to himself, that is, through essaying the problematic being that he is. Man does not borrow himself from philosophy or from science. He is rather the treasure upon which all the sciences draw. Nevertheless, man has to make his own fortune, and in this the folly of a treasure laid up in heaven is no worse, nor, for that matter, any better than the treasures of Eldorado. The enthusiasm of religion is a mode of our folly and our folly is essential to us: 'When we put not self-satisfied understanding but a consciousness astonished at itself at the core of human existence, we can neither obliterate the dream of another side of things nor repress the wordless invocation of this beyond'.[5] Montaigne, nevertheless, speaks as though we should remain indifferent to the world and in love or politics never allow ourselves to play more than a role: 'We must lend ourselves to others and give ourselves only to ourselves' (III: 10, 767). And yet we must adopt the principles of family and state institutions, for they are the essential follies of our life with others. To attempt to live outside of the state and the family reveals the abstraction of the Stoic distinction between what is internal and what is external, between necessity and freedom:

> We cannot always obey if we despise, or despise always if we obey. There are occasions when to obey is to accept and to despise is to refuse, when a life which is in part a double life ceases to be possible, and there is no longer any distinction between exterior and interior. Then we must enter the world's folly, and we need a rule for such a moment.[6]

But this need not involve us in a desperate attempt to achieve certainty. It would only do so if we assumed the standpoint of a finished truth towards which we could move from doubt only by a leap. But that would be to exchange our human nature for some other existence, whether animal or angel. If we abandon such a notion, then, as Montaigne realised, we come back to the ground of opinion, to the fact that there is truth and that men have to learn doubt: 'I know better what is man than I know what is animal, or mortal or rational' (III: 13, 819). Scepticism with respect to the passions only deprives them of value if we assume a total self-possession, whereas we are never wholly ourselves but always interested in the world through the passions which we embody. Then we can understand the passions as the vehicle by which truth and value are given to us, and we see that the critique of the passions is the rejection of false passions which do not carry us towards the world and men, but instead close us in a subjectivity we have not freely chosen.

While it is the evil of public life to associate us with opinions and projects we have not chosen for ourselves, Montaigne found that the flight into the self only reveals the self as openness towards the world and men, so that, among other things, we are for others; and their opinion touches the very core of our being:

> The fact of the matter is that true scepticism is movement toward the truth, that the critique of the passions is hatred of false passions, and finally, that in *some* circumstances Montaigne recognized outside himself men and things he never dreamed of refusing himself to, because they were like the emblem of his outward freedom and in loving them he was himself and regained himself in them as he regained them in himself.[7]

Montaigne wrote in order to remain in men's eyes what he had been in the eyes of La Boétie. The difference is that, having survived his friend's regard, he had then to reflect himself in truth and honesty to the mark of that unparalleled friendship. Moreover, what he could do in keeping the memory of La Boétie, or of his father and the Château de Montaigne, he could not so easily do for himself. The essay 'Of Friendship' stands as a lasting monument to La Boétie, drawn in a few simple strokes, using no unusual materials except the love in which he held him. In the same manner, The 'Apology for Raymond Sebond' stands as a towering memorial to Montaigne's love for his father and the gratitude he felt for his youth and education fostered by him. And, as we know from the preface To the Reader, Montaigne hoped that the *Essays* might likewise stand as a memorial to one who loved himself enough, as friendship and family require, to have essayed himself day by day in the hope of remaining lively to their memory.[8] This is not to say that Montaigne bothered himself with the convention of a funeral address. Indeed, we can see all the more in such a contrast the laboured invention of the *Essays* which remain as essentially unfinished as the author they generated, drawing him closer to the life that ebbed in him without weakness or regret. The transcendence that might have concentrated in a moment of friendship opened into the field of writing and reading, the resort of each day in his life, rooted to every moment in which the ordinary occasions of living, however small or seemingly off the track, offered something of the self's reflection. And it is in the field of writing and reading that the author and the reader of the *Essays* experience a doubling of themselves that they must learn to handle according to the responsibilities of friendship. There is also an incredible dispersion to be risked in these activities unless, as Montaigne found, they can be brought to a measured order, as a watchful practice that strengthens solitude and society, while fearing to fall into emptiness and its crowded consolations.[9] Day by day, Montaigne acquired the powers of the essayist to labour between what he owed to friends and family, and to the state, and what he rightfully owed to himself. Thus he ordered his introspection into a theatre of the embodied self, observed in the past history of mankind and noted in his present activities with a passion that put life over death so long as Montaigne could write.

Like Rembrandt's self-portraits, the *Essays* constitute a definite and eternal moment of carnal knowledge.[10] They hold time together as a human achievement, ruled not by vanity and dispersion but by the resolve to cultivate the bottom nature in ourselves. Human time is therefore our very chance of at any moment becoming ourselves. But as Montaigne discovers, such occasions are lost upon us without sound ignorance and good judgement. Good sense and sound judgement is knowledge of things well digested. We cannot be sure that we shall live up to our bookish knowledge nor that it will stand us in the trials of living. Much of our speculative knowledge is unserviceable and makes unseasonable demands on us. Life always thrusts us back upon ourselves. And so we must learn from our own habits, moods, likes and dislikes, our conduct at table, in marriage, in love, and in politics, who we are. In this, the *Essays* reveal that we cannot overlook the slightest detail, the least discomfort, the smallest joy, for we are nothing beyond these things. Good sense and sound judgement cannot be acquired like property. They are more like our habits and complexion, a natural possession dependent upon the occasions of living and lively example, rather than upon bookish pre-cepts. Therefore Montaigne believed that history, law and travel will teach us more of what men and ourselves are capable than the pursuit of philosophy and science.[11] Our body, too, will teach us much of what we need to know, or rather how we must suit our knowledge to our needs. That is to say, in so far as we ques-tion our living, inspecting how well things suit us, and how well our conscience and self-love prosper from them, we make life our own activity and not a passive indulgence. The goodness of life is not made our own without the effort and judgement we bring to its conduct and enjoyment.

Man is always elsewhere. His thoughts and passions, his dreams and imagina-tion transport him ever beyond himself. In this, the poet and the traveller, the philosopher and the general are driven equally by man's restless nature:

> Our thoughts are always elsewhere; the hope of a better life stays and supports us, or the hope of our children's worth, or the future glory of our name, or flight from the ills of this life, or the vengeance that threatens those who cause our death:

> On ocean rocks, I hope, if the just gods
> Have power left, you'll drain your cup of pains,
> And often cry out Dido's name
> I'll hear: the news shall reach me ... mongst the shades.
>
> Virgil (III: 4, 633)

Thus we need to find bodily anchors for our lives, and we shall be lucky indeed if, like Montaigne, we can find faith or a friend, customs or examples of good sense by which we may order our living. A man is just as easily lost in metaphysical speculation as he is in dreams of military glory, for there is no other creature in nature so disposed to live beyond his means. But then we should gain nothing by retiring from life in order to find its rule. For we would only succeed in surrendering ourselves to ourselves and thus find no stable point at all. On the contrary, we need a certain and steady attachment to life in order to find our true self. For truth and goodness are neither wholly within us nor entirely outside us. And so transcendence is not achieved by aspiring above or behind this life; it is rather the accomplishment of love, service and friendship which answers to our bottom nature. Thus Montaigne's *Essays* are, in the first place, written out of love for his friend La Boétie, and then, gradually, they become a method of self-love and self-understanding through which Montaigne's literary labour achieves self-mastery. It becomes essential to the *Essays* that the good they are in search of not be reduced to a literary art, nor to the steady accumulation of commonplaces. At the same time, the literary authority that is acquired through the method of essaying is deservedly honoured by embellishment and the services of writing and reflection. Therefore Montaigne is obliged both to disclaim any art in writing the *Essays* and also to claim them as his own body. For in the *Essays*, just as in the friendship of La Boétie, he is never more himself than in giving himself to what each needed from him.

Montaigne is never tempted by the privacy of self-knowledge. He knew too well that we are beholden to our parents and teachers, our friends and enemies, our neighbours and ancestors for what we can know:

> No pleasure has any savor for me without communication. Not even a merry thought comes to my mind without my being vexed at having produced it alone without anyone to offer it to. *If wisdom were given me on this condition, that I keep it hidden and unuttered, I should reject it* [Seneca]. The other raised it a tone higher: *if such a life were granted a wise man that, with an abundance of all things pouring in, he could have full leisure to consider and contemplate everything worth knowing, still, if his solitude were such that he could never see a human being, he would abandon life* [Cicero]. I like the idea of Archytas, that it would be unpleasant to be even in heaven and to wander among those great and divine celestial bodies, without the presence of a companion. (III: 9, 754)

Only a fool relies totally upon himself in the business of life. Knowledge that we have not truly made our own ill suits us as much as an uncomfortable shoe, and neither will take us far. Life tests our foolishness as hard as any journey tests him who has not well prepared for it by knowing his own strengths and weaknesses. He who does not know himself well enough to provide for his corporeal needs will also be ignorant of the things around him, and misjudge them to his ruin. Foolishness, like an uncomfortable shoe, or an undigested meal, does not carry us far in the way of our purposes. All the same, we cannot hope to he wholly provided for in this life. Such a dream merely suspends us irresolutely, or else pitches us into fantasies of omnipotence. We must trust to our sense of truth and goodness and find in the common round of these things a grace to which we must remain open.

The friendship of La Boétie was just such a grace, for it allowed Montaigne to formulate the project of knowing himself as La Boétie knew him. But then Montaigne's project can hardly be said to have been ruled by scepticism, since it was born in the certain goodness of being loved and understood. Moreover, Montaigne's love of La Boétie is not tied to his friend's gaze or the need of his presence. The *Essays* are generated in the absent presence of his friend, like a lover's passion for seeing and hearing things to tell his lover once they meet. Friendship, or love, is therefore the incarnate place of the *Essays*, and not a lack or a dependency from which nothing grows:

> In true friendship, in which I am expert, I give myself to my friend more than I draw him to me. I not only like doing him good better than having him do me good, but also would rather have him do good to himself than to me; he does me most good when he does himself good. And if absence is pleasant or useful to him, it is much sweeter to me than his presence; and it is not really absence when we have means of communication. In other days I use an advantage of our separation. We filled and extended our possession of life better by separating: he lived, he enjoyed, he saw for me, and I for him, as fully as if he had been there. One part of us remained idle when we were together; we were fused into one. Separation in space made the conjunction of our wills richer. This insatiable hunger for bodily presence betrays a certain weakness in the enjoyment of souls. (III: 9, 746–7)

The *Essays* are to Montaigne and to his readers what Montaigne wished to be to La Boétie – a friend. Therefore the *Essays* are not merely Montaigne's 'things', but rather serve him only as he would have wished to serve La Boétie. Just as the *Essays* are the work of a friend, or rather a work between friends, they are themselves the generative place of Montaigne's own friendship with his readers.[12] Hence they do not offer idle reading, and are not reached through their surfaces.

We cannot expect to encounter them unless we have addressed our own motives for placing them in our lives. For this reason, so much of the commentary and interpretation of the *Essays* is alien to Montaigne because it seeks to make him dependent upon his critics.[13] Some will find him less orderly than he might have been, or too slavish and self-deprecating. Others will claim for him more than he claims for himself, speaking of him as a philosopher, a poet, a statesman, and a true Christian. Throughout our study we shall address the question of essaying the *Essays*. For now, we must hold our reading to the rule of friendship, finding in Montaigne a man who is neither ahead nor behind his times, a man neither more nor less than he shows himself to be.

Since Descartes, we have been inclined to believe in the absolute clarity of thought and speech.[14] Thus, as readers and listeners, we make ourselves the passive subjects of science and its syllogisms. In everyday life, however, we are less passive as speakers and listeners, and more inclined to collaborate in making sense.[15] The *Essays* are unwelcome to a passive reader. They require that the reader share in the author's activity, happily recognising the artfulness with which the author provides for such collaboration. In the rhetorical tradition familiar to Montaigne, reading and writing, as well as speaking and hearing, were considered ethical relations in which the proper edification of the writer and reader, of the speaker and listener, was the principal art and enjoyment. It is only in the post-Cartesian tradition of scientific discourse that the author treats himself as the neutral medium of nature with which the reader seeks a direct contact. From the standpoint of scientific discourse, once language is subordinated to the clear and distinct formulations of mathematics and logic, the rhetorical influences between the author and the reader are merely distractions, if not positive distortions of commonly available truths of nature. Montaigne would, of course, have favoured the rational empiricism of Galilean science over the scholastic abuses of Aristotle. Nevertheless, what he wanted to keep from the rhetorical tradition, was the Socratic conviction that truth, while it must not be tailored to suit men, nevertheless cannot be found apart from them. The *Essays* are a persistent attempt to explore this middle ground of truth.

To the modern scientist, Nature is indifferent to speech about it, and contains no voice or spirit capable of angry or joyous response. But where Nature is thought to be divine, either in a single person, or in its many gods and goddesses, then it is incumbent upon man to listen to Nature's voice, and to adjust his own speech in the interests of harmony. Indeed, the religious man will be content to call upon the name of God, and his only concern will remain in the righteousness of his prayers. Now between God and Nature there lies Society. It is a conceit of modern social science that Society can, on the model of Nature, be indifferent to talk about it. Rather, all men hold themselves socially responsible in their talk.

This is nowhere clearer than in religion and politics, where talk may cost a man his life. But it is just as true in the smaller settings of social life where our talk may delight, anger, praise, shame, bind and release. Nothing was clearer than this to Montaigne, as he so often testifies in the *Essays*.

Once we distinguish the domains of Nature and Society, it is especially difficult to speak of truth in regard to social discourse. To many minds, Society is the enemy of truth, obliging us to adopt masks, to suit our speech to the occasion, and, above all, to avoid the extreme folly of telling the unvarnished truth.[16] It is only outside of Society, in Nature and its associated nakedness, that men set aside their masks and deceits, in order to reveal their true thoughts and feelings. Or else, men must empty themselves in prayer until only the name of God echoes in their hearts. None of this tempts Montaigne. He chooses to say his part among men, without trusting foolishly to their goodwill, and without the benefit of any higher concern than the ways of men to men.

> I dare not only to speak of myself, but to speak only of myself; I go astray when I write of anything else, and get away from my subject. I do not love myself so indiscriminately, nor am I so attached and wedded to myself that I cannot distinguish and consider myself apart, as I do a neighbor or a tree. It is as great a fault not to see how far our worth extends, as to say more about it than we see. We owe more love to God than to ourselves and we know him less, and yet we speak our fill of him. (III: 9, 720)

As a lawyer and politician Montaigne knew very well the weight of words and the price of men. Moreover, it would be quite mistaken to think that Montaigne imagined his private and domestic conversation to have removed him from the world and its critical comment. This is a separation that is hardly open to public men; and much less so in times of civil and religious quarrels. Nor should we overlook that the problem of 'lying' exercised Montaigne as a humanist concerned with the veracity and reliability of historical narratives. The vanity of the sciences – a frequent theme in the *Essays* – had been the subject of Pico della Miran dola's *Examen vanitatis doctrinae gentium et veritatis Christianae disciplinae* (1520) and of a satirical attack by Cornelius Agrippa in his *De incertitudine et vanitate scientiarum* (1531). These, as well as similar arguments from Sextus Empiricus, were well known to Montaigne. In this connection, we might also consider Montaigne's comments upon his short way with many of the books he read. They, too, should be seen in the light of humanist attempts to develop critical practices in the reading and writing of history. Here, surely, is another source of Montaigne's Pyrrhonism.[17]

Montaigne spoke selfishly but not privately. He spoke of himself not to hide his speech but in order to defend speech. Montaigne read and wrote at a time when it was impossible to presume upon these activities. He did not prattle on about himself in the hope that the *Essays* would escape judgement as the pastime of an old man in retirement from the troubles of his day. He spoke in defence of speech as the fundamental bond of human society. He read and wrote in order to reveal the family of man from which each of us borrows, and which each of us recreates in himself. Montaigne spoke selfishly in order to ground his speech in the family, in friendship and in the incarnate words of living thought. It is only in these contexts, where thought, speech and embodiment overlap, that Montaigne is concerned with literary truth and falsity. Thus Montaigne's writing speaks to us as though in a conversation or a letter; and he is for ever telling us stories which engage us precisely because of their lively and artful proportions of brevity and fullness. Stories and anecdotes are frequent resources of the *Essays* precisely because they are inter-sensory instruments of human speech and community. They cannot be told without being shared; what they tell are the lessons of truth and falsehood. Stories are man-made while at the same time they too make men.[18] They are therefore essential to the task of the *Essays*. The stories are frequently inconclusive; they approach their topic obliquely and always require the reader to work against received opinion, occasionally even leaving him to finish things for himself. Similarly, the topics of the *Essays* rarely yield themselves from their titles. Thus so many readers have been challenged to reveal Montaigne's practices in the composition of his essays taken singly, as well as in the overall structure and editing of the *Essays* as a whole. As we shall see, every facet of Montaigne's use of language, grammar, style and imagery has attracted the attention of some reader or other. Very often Montaigne's treatment of a topic is a declamation (*declamatio*) which requires of the reader a response to the author's talent and literary power.[19] The challenge to the reader is to find the same amusement and pleasure that the author experienced in its composition. It is not a question of the literal truth, but of the truth of literature that we enjoy such exercises and thereby something of the truth that always eludes us, except as we write after it. The same applies to our understanding of Montaigne's fondness for the paradox, 'a desperate thrust' whose perversity is allowed only because it introduces the reader as an actor into the illumination of the contradictions of human being and experience.[20]

Starting from the biblical conception of a cosmos inhabited by the plenitude of divine purpose, it is possible to view the world's discourse as the progressive accumulation of found truth, as a recollection, a summa, an anthology. Within an immutable creation, knowledge elaborates truth into a garland of thought. But Montaigne started work on the *Essays* when such a divine closure had well begun to crumble; the cosmos had been displaced by Copernicus and Christianity shaken by Luther. The *Essays* display this shift in the ground plan of European thought. They begin with patient inventories of experience, without much questioning the framework they trade upon. Gradually, however, the inventory is questioned, the cumulative powers of discursive rationality are tested upon intrinsically open-ended issues. The world is no longer the enclosure of a divinely guaranteed rational inquest. Reason must essay itself, no surer of its ends than any other voyage of discovery. Lacking any divine proportion, reason and nature become essentially fields of self-inquiry. Thus the human senses seem marked only by their variability rather than any proper object. Our reasoning, too, is characterised by a discordance that is relieved only in municipal rather than universal laws. We can therefore find no order by following up divine teleologies. Reasoning has no privileged matter and no privileged end. Reasoning, therefore, must content itself with its own practices as the material for inquiry into its seemingly competent production of evidence, generalisation and the like. Thus essaying is the proper instrument of such inquiry, since it avoids an a priori construction in favour of a situated practice of reflexive analysis engendered in the course of an exemplary inquiry – as in 'Of Coaches' or 'Of Cannibals' (see Chapter 10 below). Socrates is the figure of such reasoning and Montaigne is surely his rival. Neither of them abandoned the marketplace of ideas, custom and belief in favour of tidy reconstructions. The *Essays* only achieve self-consciousness in order to tie unreflected custom to reflexive convention that is neither above nor below human practice.

Hence Montaigne can speak of the gratuity of writing the *Essays* in the same way that Socrates could downplay his midwifery. The discourse of the *Essays* no longer turns upon a divine plenitude; it forsakes any such coincidence. What is happy in the *Essays* is rather due to that same good fortune that may supervene upon any artistic work. Montaigne's use of paradoxy reflects the general shift in the Renaissance from the sterility of logical structures repeated without any sense of ultimate reference to the rhetorical integration of style, form and matter. The paradox brings together the writer and the reader in a highly controlled but seemingly effortless marriage of thought and expression – itself a paradox. The enjoyment of paradox requires that the reader sacrifice his ordinary enjoyment of reading in favour of its surprises, which in turn need to be all the sharper, since the reader is learned in paradoxes.[21] Thus Montaigne warns Margaret of Valois that she does best to exercise her mind on the Apology's ordinary paradoxes, and to be most careful in risking the ultimate paradox of self-essaying which, in laying bare the soul, may win or lose everything:

> You, whom I have taken the pains to extend so long a work contrary to my custom, will not shrink from upholding your Sebond by the ordinary form of argument in which you are instructed every day, and in that you will exercise

25

your mind and your learning. For this final fencer's trick must not be employed except as an extreme remedy. It is a desperate stroke, in which you must abandon your weapons to make your adversary lose his, and a secret trick that must be used rarely and reservedly. It is great rashness to ruin yourself in order to ruin another. (II: 12, 418–19)

If the *Essays* succeed in disarming the reader in the same way their author has bared his soul, everything is won. But if the author's nakedness proves only to be a weakness in the reader's eyes, then everything is lost. Then it is really wiser to seek self-knowledge in the moderate practice of custom and belief, and to resist any such desperate exercise as the *Essays*.

There was a considerable prejudice in Montaigne's circle against the trade of the writer. The Pléiade poets knew very well that misery was a more likely product of writing than the glory they hoped to find in poetry. Du Bellay, himself a military man, had to protest the opinion that poetry was beneath the exercise of a nobleman. In certain respects, Montaigne resolved this problem by determining to write a singularly different kind of book. In fact, what he did was to reinvent the book as a self-essay, open-ended, without authority or reception, except as it could find similarly self-essaying readers. From this perspective, the *Essays* do undergo a certain 'evolution' in that Montaigne has to come to terms with his own initial prejudice against writing. The *Essays* are Montaigne's glory. It was still true in the Renaissance that a writer no less than an artist could dedicate himself to the pursuit of glory. Montaigne did not fool himself in this. He knew very well that fortune and convention alike conspired in the arbitrary award of honour and fame for deeds repeated a thousand times away from the glare of public attention or the accident of historical records. He knew, too, that it is hard to make even a name[22] for ourselves that others will not carry just as well, but for quite different ends (II: 16, 475). The pursuit of glory involves us in the same paradox of publicity whether we seek fame in war or in the peaceful art of writing. Both are public events, different only in the source of their declaration. And even the numbers involved by war, until recent times, are not as great as those populations who may be reached by writing, especially when we consider the influence of literary tradition. The popularity and publicity of glorious deeds, then, are tied phenomena. What might distinguish war from writing is that the author seeks, as did Montaigne, to dedicate his work to a friend or to his family. Although at first the literary public seems to be more anonymous than the friends, families and nations joined together in war, the tyrant fears literature, since it joins friends and creates a public not so tightly drawn to the ambitions of state. The literary public is therefore both a resource and a goal of creative writing, necessarily relied upon for the way it already exceeds the tyrant's grasp, yet needing to risk articulation in order to become the realm of liberty in which the writer is properly glorious. When Caesar wrote, he wrote of Caesar. His pen was in the service of his sword. To the extent that he revealed himself, he did so inadvertently; or by requiring a Suetonius. One is not free to read Caesar's *Commentaries* in the same way that one ambles through the *Essays* – as many a schoolboy can still recall from his 'forced marches' through the Gallic wars.

Whatever he says about his memory – in any case, rote learning is the enemy of true education – it is clear that Montaigne shared from his youth in a widely ranging classical culture. He tells us how much he owed to his father on this account. Moreover, he is aware that his education from the very beginning culti-vated those inextricable exchanges between culture and embodied character that are the distinguishing mark of the *Essays*. Montaigne's classical education is the practical resource of his humanist aspiration to balance authority and creativity:

> The subject, according to what it is, may give a man a reputation for learning and a good memory; but in order to judge the qualities that are most his own and most worthy, the strength and beauty of his mind, we must know what is his and what is not his, how much is due him in consideration of the choice, arrangement, embellishment, and style that he has supplied. (III: 8, 718)

We can hardly criticise Montaigne for working in the only materials he had at hand. His culture is classical, opening gradually to the discovery of the new world. But his use of the classical tradition is rarely, even from the earliest essays, scholastic in the worst sense of professional pedantry, abstract moralising and blind authority. These are rather the risks of much contemporary interpretation of Montaigne, concerned with the endless mining of his sources, borrowings and the like, as though any artistic work did not have its origins in a faithful depar-ture from its sources. What is at fault in such inquiries is not the information they yield. That may well be useful, provided one has a sensible question that is ser-viced by it. Montaigne was certainly not ignorant of the philological standards of Budé, Estienne and others of his day.[23] Nor would he have thought of challenging the glory of such scholars on these grounds. Rather, their very accomplishments left him with his own problem; namely, how to distinguish himself. For Mon-taigne was not uncommon in that he did seek glory. What is peculiar to him is that he set himself this challenge as an essayist. Montaigne challenged the stan-dards of his day in that he eschewed military and political glory and, while cling-ing to his status as a gentleman with little taste for the middling professions of law and theology, sought to risk the contemptible practices of a 'scribbler' in order to discover himself a writer, if not a political innovator.[24] The accumulation of painstaking scholarship on Montaigne's *Essays* is curious in the light of Montaigne's own strictures on making books about books. It is an industry that defies Montaigne's complaint that the world is full of interpreters but still lacks authors, To understand this – the problem of literary truth and sincerity – as well as the problem of the accuracy of historical writing, just mentioned – requires some remarks upon the theory of poetry from Greece and Rome to the Pléiade poets.[25] Although Friedrich[26] rejects any strong relation between Montaigne and the Pléiade, I think even a brief discussion of the principal aspects of their work is enough to show that Montaigne shared their problems – even though here, as in everything else, he has his own way. All writing is so easily identified with fiction, and poetry particularly so, that it becomes a question for practitioners to ask about the authority or the truth and sincerity of any author's work. In the pagan and Christian traditions the poet was conceived as the medium possessed by divine truth which he either imitated or falsified.[27] He might, of course, claim that because of the ultimate mystery bequeathed to him, the poet could only give a likely version, fashioned to accord with simple human understanding. How far to go in this direction was the particular responsibility of the poet. In its exercise there arose, then, the problems of creativity, sincerity and truthfulness.[28] A great poet might achieve a 'poetic truthfulness' even while offending the standards of historical and logical truth. Plato and the Church Fathers could be appealed to for the argument that poets are mostly liars. This, of course, did not mean that the ancient poets were thrown out. It was teaching which simply reinforced the growth of independent reading and writing; it encouraged the need to develop one's judgement, as Montaigne reminds us so tirelessly. It also explains in part his preference for historical writing, such as that of Froissart, Commincs and Guicciardini. This is not to say that humanist historiography did not raise the same questions of literary authority and moral purpose as poetry.[29] History could show how men misjudge events, or the difference between impassioned action and a reasoned account of events. It might also show how man can none the less rely upon nothing else but his own reason, and that historiography itself is a practice necessary to the humanisation of a world subject to fortune, if not chaos.[30] So many of Montaigne's own observations of historical and political events fall in this line.

Poets, and historians, for that matter, risk shame; but they also court glory, even when they disclaim it.[31] We may include in this company writers and lovers, concerned only with themselves, yet yearning for immortality. Montaigne's disparagement of his own writing is well enough known, while at the same time we observe his pains to revise and publish the *Essays*, as a domestic monument at least:

> It is not for show that our soul must play its part, it is at home, within us, where no eyes penetrate but our own. There it protects us from the fear of death, of

pain, and even of shame; there it makes us secure against the loss of our children, of our friends, and of our fortunes; and, when the opportunity presents itself, it also leads us on to the hazards of war. *Not* for *any profit, but for the beauty of merit itself* [Cicero]. This profit is much greater, and more worthy of being coveted and hoped for, than honor and glory, which is nothing but a favorable judgment that people make of us. (II: 16, 472)

Like the Pléiade poets, Montaigne knew that his literary enterprise was half impossible. It needed an honest recognition from a dishonest society; and those simple men, whom Montaigne admired most, hardly needed the *Essays* for their reflection. The question arises, then, why, if they are so unlikely to please anyone, do poets and essayists write? What difference can it make to be read once a writer is dead?

> And if no one reads me, have I wasted my time, entertaining myself for so many idle hours with such useful and agreeable thoughts? In modeling this figure upon myself, I have had to fashion and compose myself so often to bring myself out, that the model itself has to some extent grown firm and taken shape. Painting myself for others, I have painted my inward self with colors clearer than my original ones. I have no more made my book than my book has made me – a book consubstantial with its author, concerned with my own self, an integral part of my life; not concerned with some third-hand, extraneous purpose like all other books. (II: 18, 504)

Montaigne's defence of writing is here very much in the style of the Pléiade. We can understand that he might have little profit from the merely agreeable (*dulcis*) pleasures of writing. Yet how can writing be both agreeable and useful (*utile*)? This double objective subscribes to the Horatian standard for poetry: *Omne tulit punctum qui miscuit utile dulci lectorem delectando pariterque monendo.* ('He has won every vote who has blended profit and pleasure at once delighting and instructing the reader.')[32] Horace's prescriptions for holding a reader were never taken to heart more than by Montaigne, both in the composition of his own essays and in his educational theory. Here, especially, we come upon one of the central images of the classics and of the Pléiade – the metaphor of the bee, the flowers and the honey.[33] The bee symbolises that combination of industry or usefulness and sweetness of which it is the aim of a writer/reader to seek from art:

> For all good poets, epic as well as lyric, compose their beautiful poems not as works of art, but because they are inspired and possessed. And as Corybantian revellers when they dance are not in their right mind, so the lyric poets are not in their right mind when they are composing their beautiful strains: but when falling under the power of music and metre they are inspired and possessed;

like Bacchic maidens who draw milk and honey from the rivers, when they are under the influence of Dionysus, but not when they are in their right mind. And the soul of the lyric poet does the same, as they themselves tell us; for they tell us that they gather their strains from honeyed fountains, culling them out of the gardens and dells of the Muses; they, like the bees, winging their way from flower to flower. And this is true. For the poet is a light and winged and holy thing . . . .[34]

Plato, Seneca, Horace and Lucretius, all provided Montaigne with the idea that the labour of the writer and of the reader results in a pleasure that is finally all his own. At first there is the labour upon what is not ours, which we may even fail to incorporate in any way, so that we have to give it back undigested, and at best well imitated. In view of the Renaissance respect for antiquity, the problem of imitation was serious. Here, however, Montaigne could also follow Seneca's recommendation that an author is properly one who mixes reading and writing so that each fertilises the other: 'We should follow, men say, the example of the bees, who flit about and cull the flowers that are suitable for producing honey, and then arrange and assort in their cells all they have brought in.'[35] Thus one cannot separate the anxiety of self-study from the pains and pleasures of the search for literary authority. I believe that this is an essential rule of interpretation in essaying Montaigne.

At first sight the *Essays* escape any strict definition. They so easily accommodate to the shape and flow of everyday events, whatever their degree of seriousness, and hardly anything seems beyond their reach. Indeed, they seem to profit from a simultaneous freedom and restriction through their commitment to record the ordinary events of living. Montaigne's decision to observe the plain events of an ordinary life without placing upon them any elaborate design gave him the freedom to explore a neglected terrain. By the same token, it enabled him to tie any transcendental or exotic thought to the incarnate grounds of common sense. From the same commitment, it turns out that Montaigne had to deal with those extraordinary events, cruelties and injustices that in fact make up part of ordinary living. Moreover, because he did not start from any abstract principles, he was able to speak forthrightly upon what is unnecessary institutional evil and nonsense rather than merely popular ignorance or common human folly. Custom and common sense are Montaigne's emblem. He defends them in every way. Yet he never hides the comedy they involve us in. Because of his ability to see what is good and what is evil in custom, he can rely upon them as an ultimate weapon in exposing the arrant nonsense and pretence of social institutions and offices that set custom aside as though it were mere blindness. The more he was able to circumscribe the *Essays* to the field of his daily living, the more Montaigne found he was able to achieve sincerity with what is required in order to be faithful to the record of ordinary events.

In keeping to ordinary things, the *Essays* stay closer to life than to ceremonial literature. That is to say, they treat of things from within their ordinary concerns and without first mounting any elaborate schema to service philosophy, theology or literature. This means that Montaigne is able to avoid the extremes of either subjectivising his literary task or else pushing it towards anonymity. He is able to display his writing and reading as a course of work, capable to a certain point, subject to revision without radical alteration, and always achieving its purpose as far as it goes. The *Essays* feed upon themselves in the sense that they improvise the skills of reading and writing required for composing their material at hand. But they never pretend to absolute literary autonomy. The essayist wishes to be seen and heard as a craftsman, not as the medium of art for art's sake. Here, as elsewhere, we encounter the problem of literary authority. The artist's temptation – what leads him on and what may lead him astray, or into sheer imitation – is the museum, the tradition of writing or painting or thinking that precedes him, seduces him and makes him want to continue its past.[36] To survive, the artist must concentrate upon his own work, this essay, or this canvas. Only this matters, and yet it must also provide for the movement from work to work, essay to essay, which is the artist's life. Montaigne is never very far away from his books, from his philosophers, historians and poets. He moves among them like a bee among the flowers, alighting here and there, a buzzing, busy presence borrowing what he needs in order to remake himself in the *Essays*. Thus he combines work and plea-sure, leaving for his readers the same bodily and spiritual re-creation; provided they are capable (*suffisant*). When he speaks of his nonchalance, and even of his ignorance, Montaigne speaks of that necessary creative ignorance without which the thinker, writer or artist could not get under way. This, of course, is not a com-plete ignorance since the work of art, once it is under way, must connect with its own conventions, and seek a public for its intelligibility or its visibility. Mon-taigne therefore works at the *Essays* indirectly, and only gradually, with here and there a quick sally centring upon its own vocation, he requires his reader, like a friend, to undertake the same break with convention in order to experience him-self in re-creation. To achieve this, Montaigne employs paradox and a style that awakens the reader's instincts, or his bodily ties to language and community, whereby the author and reader discover their mutual incarnation in the pleasure of literature. To achieve this, Montaigne shifts from the impersonal to the per-sonal voice, from the past to the present, from obiter dicta to the testimony of his own eyes, ears and body, and by means of these shifts he heightens the literary covenant between himself and I his reader.[37] By requiring of him his own literary competence, the *Essays* exercise the reader, and do not simply subordinate him

31

before an exaltation of literary language. Montaigne's literary style is therefore essential to the liberty of discourse and friendship, which excludes tyranny. It requires, too, the solitude represented by his library tower. There he fostered the silence that permits men to choose their words. By contrast, the tyrant – at times played by the literary critic – monopolises talk, fearing the liberty of discussion; or else he subordinates the arts to his pleasure, denying them any more serious revelation. Montaigne understood as well as anyone the politics of language. Hence his deceits, paradoxes, humour and self-parody. Hence, also, his insistence upon the publication of his private thoughts, since thoughts without hope of a public cannot be free. For the same reasons, the *Essays* take their time, walk when they want to, and run when they like; always free to turn to any side that attracts their author, yet never losing themselves for want of their own direction. Moreover, the *Essays* display their liberty in the ordinariness of their topics, in their essentially anthropological centre and their avoidance of the conceits of theological or philosophical alienation. For this reason, the *Essays* are an essential part of the political culture of Montaigne's times; and not at all an idol set outside of them.

CHAPTER 2

Literary Anxiety and the Romance of Books

Montaigne loved books and gave up his life to writing one of his own. Yet he speaks disparagingly of many books; and especially of his own. This has permitted several critics to imagine that Montaigne did not have his heart in the *Essays* and to argue that he gave to them only the residual energy of a sick man, one withdrawn from society and essentially incapable of action. Nothing could be less true. The *Essays* are the living incarnation of thought and sensibility, the embodiment of a literary spirit whose hold upon this life never slackened, even in the worst of its experiences. But to show this we need to understand something of the background of literary anxiety and then we shall be able to gain better insight into the joy of reading and writing that is the real force behind the *Essays*.

Montaigne knew very well that the essay was a slight literary form. To many it was nothing but a schoolboy's exercise.[1] Even today, the essayist is regarded as a self-indulgent thinker, announcing in his titles topics he has no intention of treating with any thoroughness, because of a prior resolve to manage things on behalf of a moral conclusion, or merely for the sake of an aesthetic display. Thus Montaigne could speak of his essays as trivial things, a mishmash, the work of an undisciplined mind, betraying a character of little interest to anyone but their author. Are the *Essays*, then, nothing but self-indulgences that only a foolish reader would want to search for any wisdom? Fools generally keep their own company, and it is unlikely that Montaigne's modest evaluations of his work were designed to prevent the exploitation of witless readers. On the contrary, he explicitly challenges the reader to find the sense of the essays for himself. This is not because Montaigne deliberately concealed their aim, as a sort of game between himself and the reader. Such a notion would imply a kind of manipulation, or an inequality between Montaigne and his readers that would have distracted him from his own self-inquiry, as much as such a game would have at best challenged the reader's wits but not his wisdom. Modesty is not the same thing as a confession of inadequacy. Thus, if Montaigne was a modest man, it was not in order to serve up his faults to pander to his reader's ability to discern literary failings, imagining thereby to improve his own moral ability. The modesty of the *Essays* does not lie in Montaigne's modesty. To imagine this is to confuse an ethical invocation with its substantive achievement, as though modesty were at once the origin and fulfilment of the ethical life. Modesty is rather a literary trope, announcing an inquiry or enterprise which deliberately brings its author to consciousness of his limits.[2] There is, of course, nothing modest about the stakes in this enterprise. Montaigne is in search of Michel de Montaigne. Montaigne's signature to the *Essays* is neither modest nor immodest. It is the self-standing achievement of the *Essays*. It might be argued that Montaigne was uncertain of himself as a writer, and that therefore he took pains to forestall the criticisms of more accomplished writers, historians and theologians. It has also been said that Montaigne's pretension to nobility made him hesitate to succeed as a writer. But if Montaigne had preferred status to achievement, he would surely not have chosen poor writing as evidence of his rightful place in the world. The truth is that Montaigne loved writing, and that he valued the company of good books and poetry. But, most of all, he valued writing because it offered him the one chance he could see in this world of finding Michel de Montaigne. In other words, Montaigne was in search of himself and not the tribe.

Nevertheless, Montaigne does seem to deprecate his enterprise, and to be at particular pain to forewarn his reader against attaching any significance to what he reads in the *Essays*. What should we make of so many disclaimers? It is easy enough to discount them. There is, after all, the glaring evidence of Montaigne's careful additions to his text. Yet how could any one passage be an improvement upon another, coming from the pen of the same author? How is the reader to treat more seriously than the author himself any passage more or less wise than any other to be read in the *Essays*? How is the reader to trust his own judgement in the face of the *Essays* any more than the views of their author? Once he has turned the pages, is not the reader surrendered to the subtle appeals of Montaigne, so that there is nothing more to be preferred between them? Such questions cannot be settled through a simple appeal to Montaigne's modesty. Indeed, Montaigne's modesty might well be irritating to a reader who finds its display paradoxical, if not downright manipulative – perhaps even a cover for mediocrity. We cannot go far with this line of argument since it requires the notion of a reader prepared to anger or to bore himself with Montaigne's inferior 'Book of Hours'. In turn, it supposes that Montaigne had nothing else in mind than fashion such a reader for himself and to seek him out as a friend. Could Montaigne have wished to be remembered in this way?

Montaigne speaks of the difficulty he experiences in giving shape to his thoughts. He complains of their fleeting nature and their vagueness. Thoughts come upon him suddenly and do not stay; they lie upon him like an ill humour. It is he who is in the grip of ideas, labouring at them to give them some sort of shape and definition. Montaigne is no Cartesian. For him ideas are not the clear and distinct constructs of a disembodied mind proceeding in accordance with logical or mathematical rules. There is an embodied state of ideas to which any thoughtful man is beholden. To begin with, our ideas are no clearer than any mood or passion of ours. Indeed, even our passions are not given to us without devotion. Thus jealousy, or envy or voluptuousness, require all our strength and imagination, and may even demand that we develop great cunning if not intelligence on their behalf. By the same token, we cannot devote our minds to serious thought without passion and labour. Montaigne is beholden to thought's embodied way. It is not because he was a pre-scientific mind that he found thought difficult. Nor was he hesitant because he was not a trained philosopher or theologian. Above all, it is not because he was weak in character, easily distracted and secretly given to failure in order to preserve face as a gentleman of leisure. We shall consider all of these arguments later on. Montaigne found thinking difficult because he rejected the easy assembly of philosophy and theology careless of man's embodied state, and because he could not ignore that the practice of science in his day only made itself foolish in its pronounced omnipotence. The thinking self is not outside of thought's embodied practices, and the same is true of the reading self or of the self in pursuit of writing.

Montaigne's *Essays* are the consequent exploration of the exchanges between sources, texts, language and the self that inhabits them in order to explore its own dimensions. For this reason, we must locate Montaigne's bodily troubles in writing and reading as natural effects of the romance of books. Whereas other critics have seen faults in Montaigne's methods of reading and composition, with the purpose of displaying their own higher morality in these matters, we shall argue that it is precisely in the way that the essayist works that he gradually establishes himself as the most serious of all writers, the one most concerned with the bodily regime of literature and its lively uses. It is in the light of this problematic that we must approach Montaigne's defensiveness with regard to his choice of the essay form. For, after all, he did not choose to write history or poetry. Montaigne wrote essays. He did not write poor history or bad poetry. He wrote in his own fashion, rather than forgo writing because he held any previous model or genre of the art in too high esteem. Moreover, Montaigne wrote conscious of his own incapacities, quirks, mannerisms and modes of thought and speech. Therefore writing was as essential to him as it was to Petrarch or to Rabelais; it was a daily undertaking that he could no more go without than any other bodily function. He lived the *Essays*, and waited upon them, like the very days of his life, for the trail of meaning that life acquires only over its course, and in no other way than at its own expense:

> Who does not see that I have taken a road along which I shall go, without stopping and without effort, as long as there is ink and paper in the world? I cannot keep a record of my life by my actions; fortune places them too low. I keep it by my thoughts. Thus I knew a gentleman who gave knowledge of his life only by the workings of his belly; you would see on display at his home a row of chamber pots, seven or eight days worth. That was his study, his conversation; all other talk stank in his nostrils.
>
> Here you have, a little more decently, some excrements of an aged mind, now hard, now loose, and always undigested. And where shall I make an end of describing the continual agitation and changes of my thoughts, whatever subject they light on, since Didymus filled six thousand books with the sole subject of grammar? (III: 9, 721)

A writer comes to experience language, as a sculptor must know the stone or wood or metal in which he works. He must learn the challenge it offers him to achieve any given expression within the limits of himself, his body and his material. A writer, then, cannot simply complain of the vagueness of language, for he can be just as limited by its clarity. Language is man's bodily punishment. The variety of tongues is a testament to human distractedness. But the deepest separation in man is not between men, as painful and dangerous as it is, but the separation within a man from the word of his life. This separation is not due to the intrinsic opacity of language, or to the struggle of the senses against the soul's reason. These merely represent our self-alienation. For one whose declared task is to essay himself, the limits and dangers of language are no different from the limits of any artist's materials. The subtle mystery remains that Montaigne, Saint Augustine or Petrarch can seek himself in words, or in stone, as well as in prayer or solemn assembly:

> I am not so fortunate in what I achieve as passionate in my work, being much more a lover of learning than a man who has got much of it. I am not so eager to belong to a very definite school of thought; I am striving for truth. Truth is difficult to discover, and, being the most humble and feeble of all those who try to find it, I lose confidence in myself often enough. So much do I fear to become entangled in errors that I throw myself into the embrace of doubt instead of truth. Thus I have gradually become a proselyte of the Academy as one of the

big crowd, as the very last of this humble flock: I do not believe in my faculties, do not affirm anything, and doubt every single thing.[3]

Montaigne chose the essay form because it offers an analogy to the open form of life and the constant question that life is to a living being whom death awakens to life. Death sets a limit to life's questions and answers. Whatever mortal man undertakes must therefore seek a limited form; it must hold under way, yet not be tempted by permanence and complete closure. In the essay, the writer tests himself and his topic within a space subject to the limits of thought and speech that are reflexively present in the very style and compass of the essay form. Gradually, Montaigne became convinced of his power to combine the resources of paradox, plain style, conversational intervention and intimate bodily and familial reference, so as to make his own essaying consubstantial with the daily act of living. Every habit of living, eating, drinking, writing, reading and thinking is examined in the *Essays*, the way we might examine our face in the mirror, finding ever so familiar what seems strange at first, while at the same time its familiar aspects slip into the unfamiliar, without us ever resolving their proportions in the mirror of reflection. It is therefore natural that the body should provide the bridging metaphors for the recreation offered to it through the *Essays* own procreation. Rabelais and Montaigne offer striking comparisons in this regard.[4] *Gargantua and Pantagruel* is an obvious feast for the reader who is reminded at once of the alimentary, excretory and reproductive processes that bring life to the mind and the body.

In the first prologue, Rabelais compares his book to the *Sileni*, those tiny boxes decorated with grotesque figures but containing precious objects. Beauty and ugliness, frivolity and seriousness are here combined according to the Platonic theory of the coincidence of appearance and reality. In the same prologue, Rabelais engages the reader's attentiveness by warning him that he has to look for the marrow in his book, the reward for his efforts. At the same time, he taunts his reader with the nonchalant claim that his book has served only his own pleasure in writing it, suggesting that the reader may find the cupboard bare by the time he goes through the book (I, 9).[5] Thus we find Rabelais offering his book to the reader as food and drink, a pastime repeating the gesture of communion through consubstantiality, but jovially and with no religious tone. The preoccupation with eating and drinking represents a constant reminder of the unified source of life and creativity – of intake and inspiration. Pantagruel's endless thirst is the mark of his unsatisfied creativity, his capacity for assisting at the symposium on love and spiritual creation. Just as food, hunger and thirst are the necessary paths to the contemplative and erotic life, the needs of excretion and copulation serve to restore the soul to its ordinary condition of embodied living. Rabelais's playfulness with the imagery of copulation is due not so much to any ribald pre-occupation with sex as with the writer's discovery of his own literary powers, and therewith the endless (fantastic) generativity of language – witness its explosion in the description of Diogenes and his tub – and the sheer folly of trying to restrain it. When Pantagruel is tempted to save some of the odd words from the sea of frozen words, Panurge restrains him: It was folly, he argued, to hoard a commodity we were never short of; all good, jovial Pantagruelists always had plenty of gullmaking words in their gullets.[6] Rabelais discovered writing as the power to re-create himself. By putting words into their mouths, he animates his characters, whose lives in turn amuse and delight those who remouth his words in reading – and thereby enjoy the feast of literature. Thus Rabelais, too, thought of the book as another body and recommended it as food and wine:

> For this reason, all worthy tippers, and all good goutridden poxicrats, insist upon enjoying, to the last drop, the tonic wine of joyous books. Quoting from them when they foregather, discussing the high mysteries treated in them, our bibbies and scrabbies acquire as singular a mastery as Alexander the Great, when he studied Aristotle's capital works of philosophy.
>
> God help us belly to belly, what swilling reprobates, what lecher rap scallions!
>
> Therefore, fellow-topers, let me give you a piece of timely advice. Get in a large supply of such books, whenever you come upon them in a book shop. Do not content yourselves with merely shelling these beans in their pods; toss them down as you would an opiate cordial. Incorporate them within yourselves. You will soon discover the advantages they reserve for all good shellers of beans.[7]

What Montaigne wishes to convey by disclaiming so much of the *Essays* is his artistic intention of having fashioned his book upon the living matter of his own life; he is adamant that he has not scribbled down the *Essays*, stuffing them with empty words. The visceral metaphors culminating in the supreme assertion of the consubstantiality (the heart of the mass) of the *Essays* and their author are intended to overcome the literary and artistic separation of appearance and reality. This, too, is the burden of his pedagogic concerns; so that Montaigne weans the *Essays* as he would a child, to insert them into a life of action and society. The worst that could happen to a man is that other men should be able to drive a wedge between his speech and his deeds. The best of outcomes is a life of action, based upon sound sense and lively reflection that feed rather than starve a man's life in society. We need to read the *Essays* much as Montaigne read the books from which, like a bee, he made himself and his own book. That is to say, we need a notion of literary joy that is broad enough to furnish an understanding of the

intellectual and sensual conduct involved in reading and writing. We shall therefore try to connect the writer's intelligence with the author's pleasure in reading
and writing. Unless we do so, we shall fall into undermining Montaigne's literary
authority through the documentation of his sources, an exercise that for the most
part represents an unreflexive display of the scientific colligation of influence.[8]
Such critics merely impute to Montaigne the dull labour exhibited in their own
allegiance to conventional scholarship. The result is that, having missed the joy
in their own work, they are deprived of anything but a gloss upon Montaigne's
love of literature.

It is essential that we discover in the practice of literature our own bodily and
sensuous activity. The problem is that we are biased towards the objectivity of
texts, attributing to them our own powers as disembodied readers, and in the
worst of cases, banishing from the text any trace of its author's hand. This is not
to deny that a work in some sense transcends its author's aims, even though it has
no existence apart from them. But here we are really referring to the results of the
author's literary consciousness and his skills with language which are already
transcendent, or social accomplishments that guarantee a public quality to his
work, however intimate its nature. Without these public skills, an author could
never invite his readers into the pleasures of the text, and without a reader
an author must doubt his own capacity for literature. In other words, if the
author cannot be found in his work, then there is no relation between the writer
and the reader. For the reader has a right to such an encounter in virtue of his
acquisition of a similarly public literary consciousness and skill whereby he
comes to the title of reader. Classical literature continuously renews this bond
and for that reason it has a permanent claim upon the literary consciousness
and sensibility of all who enjoy the community of reading and writing. Critics
too often engage in interpretation as though the possibility of finding out an
author diminished his creativity. In fact it is the mark of his ability to bring his
singular condition into an instance of universal literature. To recognise an author
is really to share the pleasure in his style as a successful mediation of public
and private life. This pleasure is created out of the tension between the commonplaces of the language and the genre in which the writer works (to which the
reader is accustomed) and what he requires of himself to reawaken his reader.
We may therefore speak of a literary fortune involved in the reader's quest for
communion with a distant, yet surrendering author. By contrast, the critic
remains a literary eunuch so long as he fails to connect the bodily competences
that are the instruments of literature with the joys of initiation and surrender
in the play of writer and reader.

Montaigne knew, as does any writer, that writing is as much subject to the play
of fortune as any other action.[9] Consider the following passage which we shall

analyse in some detail for the sake of the light it throws upon the contingencies in the reader–writer relationship with the text, art or music:

> Now I say that not only in medicine but in many more certain arts Fortune has a large part. Poetic sallies, which transport their author and ravish him out of himself, why shall we not attribute them to his good luck? He himself confesses that they surpass his ability and strength, and acknowledges that they come from something other than himself and that he does not have them at all in his power, any more than orators say they have in theirs those extraordinary impulses and agitations that push them beyond their plan. It is the same with painting: sometimes there escape from a painter's hand touches so surpassing his conception and his knowledge as to arouse his wonder and astonishment. But Fortune shows still more evidently the part she has in all these works by the graces and beauties that are found in them, not only without the workman's intention, but even without his knowledge. An able reader often discovers in other men's writings perfections beyond those that the author put in or perceived, and lends them richer meanings and aspects. (I: 24, 93)

Montaigne is conscious of the artistic phenomenon of achieving a grace and beauty beyond what the writer has striven for; and he observes that this difference is the happy find not of just any reader, which would make the artist a mere literary medium, but of an 'able reader' (*un suffisant lecteur*). The latter is both the reader/viewer, listener and the artist/reader for, inasmuch as the artist is also an able appreciator of his own work, we may in part allow that his reflective experience cycles back into his work over its single course, and from work to work. '. . . the joy of reading appears to be the reflection of the joy of writing, as though the reader were the writer's ghost.'[10] Thus Montaigne is not saying that it is pure chance that supervenes in the happy artistic achievement. It is rather that the artist must be open to a certain dispossession by the flow of words, colour, sound, movement and material in which he is working. In the poet the initial dispossession may precede the act of writing, while in the painter it is the work of painting that grasps him. But these are utterly relative distinctions. It is more probable that the artist alternates between periods of inspiration and restless brooding, with breaks for intense work within which he is seized by his materials in ways that are proper to their artistic expression. We sometimes speak as though the artist's hands were the instrument of a prior creative impulse; we think of the brush, the pen, the piano, the chisel as the trademarks of the artist's spirit. But this is a practice that separates the artist from the layman by separating the artist's soul from his body; the artist raises himself above us because he is able to suspend his body in the service of the soul's art. However, Montaigne rejects these distinctions. The artist is a man, a corporeal being. He cannot be ahead of himself, despising his body as the sluggish instrument of divine enterprises. What is true of all human action is equally true of art. We can only launch upon our embodied self. There may be a variety of outcomes open to us, but these are not given to us through any previous survey. They are rather seen as interpretative possibilities, just as a painting or a text will lay open different points of view to those who encounter it. The originality of the artist's intention, like that of the doctor or the military commander, is an alibi, or an ex post attribution of the happy outcomes we find in fortune's intervention. Since the artist, however much he tries, cannot foresee what will be made of his work, he does best to follow his own path:

> I feel this unexpected profit from the publication of my behavior, that to some extent it serves me as a rule. Sometimes there comes to me a feeling that I should not betray the story of my life. This public declaration obliges me to keep on my path, and not to give the lie to the picture of my qualities, which are normally less disfigured and distorted than might be expected from the malice and sickness of the judgments of today. (III: 9, 749)

This is not to ignore Montaigne's dependence upon the literature of antiquity upon which he necessarily relied in taking his first steps towards that later vantage point from where he could see clearly the direction the *Essays* would take until the end of his life. For Montaigne, like any humanist thinker, the need to begin can only be conceived as an intertextual start that is overburdened with a sense of lateness. He is therefore tempted to deny any possibility of beginning because of the fund of antiquity. In this vein, a writer can at best thread things together, making a garland of his thoughts without worrying too much over where he found them, so long as they are pleasingly arranged. At worst, a writer is a mere scribbler who would have done better never to have started upon such a feverish activity. Scribblers have no sense of the anxiety of intertextual influences, and no amount of failure is enough to make them leave the writer's calling to those who practise it in awe, never sure they will not be overwhelmed by the need to surpass their posterity. Scribblers suppress the literary tradition in order to reduce the problem of beginning to an effortless start, confounded with the ulterior motives of social success. A writer can never be sure, in his own eyes, that he is not a scribbler. A scribbler has no eye except for how others will see him who do not see very well what writing is.

Montaigne is anxious not to fall into writing a book about books. Yet the *Essays* so obviously draw upon books, and Montaigne makes it clear that life without books is unthinkable. How did he understand literary encounter? First of all, he insisted upon literature as a corporeal instrument of living. He therefore preferred authors whose writings revealed their conduct in critical biographical situations. At the same time, this criterion of literary interest ruled him not only as a reader but above all as a writer. That is to say, it constituted for him his very literary vocation, the challenge of inventing the essay as a living inquiry. This may help us to understand the curious patchwork of the *Essays*, which at times seem to sink under the weight of quotation, or to indulge in it without serious purpose. Quotation is a writer's risk. It is an embellishment of his own writing, if it sufficiently displaces its elevated sources, and a mark of dependence, if unredeemed by its context: 'Plagiarism is necessary. Progress implies it. It presses after an author's phrase, uses his expressions, erases a false idea, replaces it with a correct one' (Lautréamont).[11]

We need, then, a theory of literary influence[12] if we are to be able to make of Montaigne's reading practices anything more than the happy hunting ground of bibliophiles, statisticians and the poor but legal comparisons that dominate so much of literary criticism. In the case of great minds like Montaigne's, whose relation to other minds is completely self-conscious, there is even provision by the author himself for the conventional but unreflexive finding of his 'sources'. In part, we have raised this issue in terms of the classical doctrine of *imitatio*; and, of course, we have ourselves indulged the practices of locating Montaigne in terms of such conventions. The irony here is that scholarship makes a settled way of life out of what the author himself experienced in the anxiety of influence, Unless we are to engage in unconscionable pedantry vis-à-vis Montaigne, forgetting his hatred of it, we need to treat literary history, within which Montaigne is a major figure, making and made by it, as indistinguishable from literary influence. To adapt Harold Bloom's words ever so slightly (anxiously), literary history is indistinguishable from literary influence, since great writers/readers make literary tradition *by misreading* one another in order to clear imaginative space for themselves.[13]

It is clear from Montaigne's comments on his own reading habits that he felt the weight of the past, as did all Renaissance writers. But the melancholy of this awareness is turned, as we shall argue from the practice of Petrarch and Montaigne, into a romance of books in the life of the writer. Like Rabelais, Montaigne's critique of the abstractive character of scholasticism arose from his rhetorical and poetic interest in the artful marriage of things (*res*) and words (*verba*), which would move the reader to rediscover in himself the experience which first moved the writer. In view of the weight of previous literary experience, there arose the problem of *inventio*, or the ratio between found and original material. A prospective author began by recalling the precepts and examples of tradition, assembling its 'topics', the analogies of moral philosophy, the proverbs and sayings of ancient wisdom. This, however, might be done without any spark from the writer or speaker, moving on a wholly logical level, without any ability to generate those imaginative connections that constitute real poetry – to combine proof, pleasure and moral judgment. Thus Montaigne contrasts the logical arrangements of books (other than his preferred historians and poets) with the natural inventiveness of his own mind – which ultimately called for the discovery of essaying:

> Books are for my mind one of the kinds of occupations which entice it away from its study. At the first thoughts that come to it, it stirs about and shows signs of vigor in all directions, practices its touch now for power, now for order and grave, arranges, moderates, and fortifies itself. It has the power to awaken its faculties by itself. Nature has given to it as to all minds enough material for its own use, and enough subjects of its own for invention and judgment. (III: 3, 621)

Here there is a profound change in Montaigne's relation to the Renaissance rhetorical tradition. While employing its terminology, he shifts its problematic into the internal workings of experience and the writer's task of finding a method of expression on his own grounds. The writer must now hunt after his thoughts, rather than sit at home borrowing them from books without any struggle. A writer must come to terms with the autonomy (virtue) of language. So long as the word is divine, then there are no writers; only copyists, however beautifully they illuminate their sacred manuscripts. The Renaissance humanists, faced with the enormous authority of the classical tradition, easily fell into an imitative response guided by the conviction that there was little new to be said that might seriously rival the ancient philosophers, poets and historians.[14] Montaigne's *Essays* are studded with such knowledge, and full of reflections regarding the problem of originality and independence with regard to the classical sources.[15] Moreover, as a writer, it was much more difficult, if not impossible, to separate thought and practice, as some do in matters of religion. Yet, in a way, such an accommodation was open through the humanist and nominalist separation of language and being, which assigned ontology to the Creator and left to man the creativity of language and meaning, or the 'middle ground' of communication, and perception, expression and sensibility. It was this middle ground that the writer had to exploit, and Montaigne's sense of this is not different from the practice of the humanist poets and historians whom he admired.

Here, Petrarch is surely a mediating figure, emphasising that the classical authors are to be followed only in so far as they resonate, literally and pleasurably, with the reader's own experience:

> It is he who gave the man of letters for the first time in the modern era a place in society not merely respected but honored; whether or not he had an 'influence' on Montaigne and so on through Rousseau down to our contemporary

commentators and essayists is irrelevant; without his example it is unlikely that they would have had a hearing.[16]

Petrarch is also important for his determined efforts to revive the force of the rhetorical doctrine of *imitatio*, in which the relation between past literary achievements and the author's self is the central issue.[17] An author must know himself well before he borrows from others. For unless he is sure of his capacities, he will fall into slavish imitation. The problem is to come close without being identical, as a son will do well to resemble his father, but will never really grow up if he tries to be like him in every way. In this respect, an author's identity requires the resources of tradition in order to exploit its infinite possibilities, as the bee makes honey from many flowers and not just one: 'we write as bees make honey, not conserving the individual flowers but converting them at the honeycomb, so that from many and various things one thing is produced, and that different and better'. The classical doctrine of *imitatio*[18] therefore results in a practical sense of the writer's identity and of his freedom, exercising choice and responsibility towards his cultural past instead of resting upon the authority of received opinion. Thus Quintilian recommended a critical approach to past sources in terms of the principle of appropriateness and a recognition of the author's own personality in achieving his purposes. Inasmuch as he learned to recognise the virtue of different modes of discourse, the humanist reader acquired a critical and comparative sense of the historicity of reason.

For Petrarch, like Montaigne, man is at the centre of a world in which Nature is by and large irrelevant and God unreachable. More precisely, Petrarch was concerned only with the moral and psychological world of man unable to escape his involvement with God and with Fortune, which seems to act upon him independently of God. To the extent that man can remedy his Fortune, he comes closer to God. In his *Secret Conflict of My Cares*, Petrarch insisted upon the reality of suffering and misery as active human capacities and not mere illusory evils, as witnessed to by his own experience.[19] The reality of human misery cannot be altered by philosophical analysis. The soul must be moved towards its good through exhortation, or the eloquent remedy of Petrarch's own writing.

> Everyone who has become thoroughly familiar with our Latin authors knows that they stamp and drive deep into the heart the sharpest and most ardent stings of speech, by which the lazy are startled, the ailing are kindled, and the sleepy aroused, the sick healed, and the prostrate raised, and those who stick to the ground lifted up to the highest thoughts and honest desire.[20]

Indeed, Petrarch paid little attention to the machinery of pastoral theology and the administration of penance. His task was rather to write so as to cure souls.

Plato's *Phaedo*, Aristotle's *Nicomachean Ethics*, Seneca's *Epistles*, the *Tusculan Disputations* and the *De Finibis* of Cicero were all resources upon which Petrarch, like Montaigne later, could draw in his concern with the problems of selfhood, But it is especially in the *De remediis utriusque fortunae*[21] – a physic or medicine whereby the reader might learn to handle himself in both prosperity and adversity – that Petrarch undertook, 'for ordinary readers and not philosophers', to explore the mutability of the human soul. The comparison with Montaigne's *Essays* is hard to resist,[22] as is the underlying continuity with Boethius in the *Consolation of Philosophy*. Chaucer found no philosopher so 'bone of the bone and flesh of the flesh' as Boethius, a phrase that Montaigne applies to his own essays to speak of the necessary candour in self-study. These and other comparisons abound,[23] but it is especially Petrarch's self-consciousness as a writer and reader that makes us think of him as a forebear of Montaigne, even if we did not know that both drew upon Seneca for their basic reflections upon the reader's life:

> Be careful, however, lest this reading of many authors and books of every sort may tend to make you discursive and unsteady. You must linger among a limited number of master-thinkers, and *digest* their works, if you would derive ideas which will win firm hold in your mind. . . . Food does no good and is not assimilated into the body if it leaves the stomach as soon as it is eaten. . . . And in reading of many books is distraction. Accordingly, since you cannot read all the books which you may possess, it is enough to possess only as many books as you can read. 'But,' you reply, 'I wish to dip first into one book and then into another.' I tell you that is the sign of an overnice appetite (*fastidientis stomachi*) to toy with many dishes; for when they are manifold and varied, they cloy but do not *nourish*.[24]

Petrarch and Montaigne both struggled with the problem of irresolution alternating with wild flights of fantasy that threatened to make their solitude less calm than the world within which it promised a retreat. It is noticeable that, in the very second essay of Book One, Montaigne already treats Sadness as a theme. Although he keeps it at a distance – as an Italian passion, or by means of historical examples – it is significant that he makes it a topic at all. Between his first and last touches to the essay, Montaigne recognises that he needs to keep on top of this malignant tendency, and above all to seek its best remedy in discussion. The problem of solitude is that a man easily loses his sense of things, that distinctions too easily crumble. Just as love serves Petrarch as a metaphor for these reversals of the inner and outer world, so Montaigne's reflections upon the reversals of war serve the same meditation. There is, however, a structure of reversal contained in the metaphors of love and war and it extends, I think, to writing, where love and war come together for Petrarch and Montaigne. Petrarch wished to leave a monument of his love for Laura, like those triumphant columns that dotted Italy, standing since ancient times. This in fact is the literary achievement of the Renaissance, namely, to have found a way of grafting upon the ancient models an equally lasting literature, while at the same time building upon personal resources.[25] Petrarch's *Sonnets and Songs* are fashioned out of himself and the region of the Vaucluse, just as Montaigne created the *Essays* from himself and the Perigord. Moreover, Petrarch's love for Laura, like Montaigne's love of La Boétie, grew with his strength as a writer beyond anything in the power of mere youth, and even more proportioned to its age:

> (That fire is dead, in a small marble press.
> Ah, if with time, it had my oldest age.
> As in the past, until my oldest age.
> Armed with my rhymes that now I leave alone
> My grey-haired style would have broken a stone
> With words, and made it weep from tenderness.)
>
> (Sonnet 304)[26]

Irresolution, then, is not such a sentimental notion in either Petrarch or Montaigne.[27] First of all, it is a risk that arises from the constant variety and contradiction in our passions, moods and opinions. Second, it tempts us in the face of Fortune which is always at work to overturn men's hopes, if not their achievements. There is nothing men can be so sure of that may not turn against them. In the face of Fortune, men do well to aim at moderation. Thus they both chose to become writers, the better to confront what Montaigne called his scar of irresolution:

> So I do not want to forget this further scar, very unfit to produce in public: irresolution, a most harmful failing in negotiating worldly affairs. I do not know which side to take in doubtful enterprises:
>> Nor yes nor no my inmost heart will say.
>>
>> Petrarch
>
> I can easily maintain an opinion, but not choose one. (II: 17, 496).

It is quite wrong, in view of the tradition of melancholy, to argue that Montaigne wrote because that is the easiest thing for sickly persons to do.[28] Rather, it is only through the strenuous efforts of writers like Petrarch, Montaigne and Richard Burton that we know of the dangers of irresolution and of the paradox of activity required by a retired life if it is to avoid ruin. In solitude, a man can no more be sure of himself than in the midst of battle. The moment he succumbs to that temptation he risks Fortune's reversal.

Acedia, ... had a continuous reference to man's religious activities; it was a theological vice – Petrarch's *accidia*, on the other hand, has nothing to do with the
religious life; it is a 'humanistic' vice, caused by reflection on *fortuna* and the
unstable *humana conditio*. Its evil effect, similarly, consists not in cutting man
off from the grace of God, but in hindering him from achieving peace of mind,
the *conditio sine qua non* for a great and unified personality. While the medieval
acedia endangered the achievement of the noblest and highest values in man's
spiritual life, Petrarch's *accidia* is an impediment to the humanist's noble and
fruitful work for self-development and self-expression.[29]

In practice, Petrarch and Montaigne were both men of letters and of politics,
drawing upon the paradoxical life of gregarious solitude that others before them,
like Seneca and Cicero, had forged in the face of the same uncertainty. Their ability to don the masks of occasion and nevertheless to preserve something of themselves is expressed in the lovely image of the bee borrowing from the flowers the
nectar that otherwise cannot become honey. Thus Petrarch and Montaigne each
experienced the need to synthesise and to incorporate a fragmented world, to stay
with it for the moments that they needed but could not prolong, except through
their own literary re-creation. Hence they had to place style above each moment,
to affect a nonchalance that permitted them to recommit themselves in a world
increasingly relativized by their own humanist stance.

Although Montaigne does not directly address his favourite heroes from antiquity in the same way as Petrarch in the last book of the *Familiares*, the same
intense attachment unites them. Moreover, Petrarch had a knowledge of anachro-
nism and a care for the proper establishment of texts (Livy, Virgil), which makes
him the precursor of later humanist standards of historical scholarship.[30]
Petrarch's collection of biographies, *De viris illustribus*, anticipates Montaigne's
use of moral sketches drawn from the Roman world, measured by a sense of loss,
though still compelling.[31] But it is unquestionably Petrarch's love of ancient
books and his collection of a private library which links him with Montaigne,
however nonchalantly he and Montaigne might speak of this passion: 'It shall
always be my aim and wish to be called illiterate' (Petrarch). Petrarch's reflections
On the Abundance of Books (*De librorum copia*) take the form of a dialogue between
Joy and Reason.[32] Joy observes that there is a great number of books. Reason comments on the various motives that lead people to accumulate books without any
intention of studying them. Joy again repeats that the number of books is large.
Reason observes – that the number of books outstrips their sensible use. Joy
repeats that the number of books is immense, and incalculable. Reason continues
to speak of the great Alexandrian libraries of Ptolemy Philadelphus, King of
Egypt, and such private libraries as that of Serenus Sammonicus. Joy confesses

that she posseses countless books. Reason admonishes her against the countless errors to be found in so many books and against the slavishness in subjecting one's mind to one's library. Joy replies that she has a good number, an abundance of books. Reason argues that it is better to possess integrity and goodness than books which can do harm as well as good, or else the possession of books would make a man famous. Joy replies that she owns books that are an aid to study and that she possesses many different and outstanding books.

To each of Reason's arguments about the dangers of books, Petrarch unrepentantly answers with the joy of reading, the passionate life of the man of books, aware of his misfortunes and disappointments in reading, yet beholden to books as friends and his very food. And on another occasion, in the dialogue *On the Fame of Writers (De scriptorum fama)*, Joy confesses that she not only reads but writes as well, and asks Reason for an opinion on this. Reason replies that writing is a common disease that spreads day by day. Joy answers: I write. Reason continues to argue that writing should only be undertaken by those concerned with clarity and charm of expression, able to pass critical appraisal. In practice, however, everyone claims the privilege of writing and seeks no wider audience than the company of scribblers like himself. Joy answers: I do write books. Reason suggests that Joy would do better to practise the best things she has read rather than to puff up with noble advice, which she is incapable of practising. Joy replies: Books I do write. Reason then argues that she might be better employed in a gainful trade, in which there are many good minds, whereas, surprisingly, there are so few good minds among those who write. To this Joy answers: I write ardently. Reason then claims that those who wrote nothing were more ardent for they knew that nothing made by man can survive for ever. Joy insists: I write much. Reason answers that since there have been authors who wrote countless books which we would marvel to have read, let alone write, Joy's prospects from writing must surely be dimmed. Joy stands firm: I write, and this is my only enjoyment. Reason then offers to understand this providing the compulsion to write is ruled by the need to escape boredom through remembering the past. But Reason is contemptuous of those who write simply because they do not know how to control the urge to write. Joy confesses: The urge to write is enormously strong. Reason continues to suggest that writing is a sickness, the beginning of madness, a species of melancholy. Undaunted, Joy replies: I have written much and I am still writing. Reason is prepared to approve if the purpose is to improve future generations but not if it is simply to seek reputation. Joy says: Much I have written. Reason explodes at this folly which achieves nothing but to make paper more expensive. Joy, however, remains steadfast: I write and hope to become famous by writing. Reason returns to the argument that writing is the least useful of human activities; only a few have excelled in it and many have ended their days in idiocy and poverty. Writing is like chasing the wind. Joy answers: I write nevertheless, yearning for fame.

Petrarch knew very well the utilitarian arguments against reading and writing. He nevertheless persisted in the joy of writing, as necessary to him as life itself. No one is put off from living because of its pains and evils. Everyone hopes to do better but is lucky to stay within the common lot. Writers are not different from other men in wanting to be different and are even more like them in failing. Anyone who writes will learn to cling to writing, as another who lives will cling to life, whatever it costs him or her and will persist in it to the very end. Thus Petrarch confessed to Boccaccio what Montaigne confessed of himself as an author:

> Constant toil and application are the food of my spirit. When I begin to seek rest and to work but slowly I shall soon cease to live. . . . No burden is lighter than the pen, none more delightful. Other pleasures are fleeting and injurious: The pen brings joy as one takes it up and satisfaction as one lays it down; and it serves not only its owner but many others, often those, even, who are far away, sometimes those who will live a thousand years hereafter. Confidently I declare that of all earthly pleasures none is nobler than literary activity, none more enduring, none sweeter, none more faithful, none that he who engages in it can obtain so readily, or with so little trouble . . . On this, therefore, my mind is fixed. . . . I do hope that death may find me reading or writing, or, if it should so please Christ, in tearful prayer.[33]

It is generally observed that the Renaissance is characterised by an extravagant sense of the mutability of things, above all, of man, himself.[34] Like Petrarch before him, Montaigne discovered in writing and reading how, so far from being diverted, the experience of mutability achieves reflexivity, so that each activity becomes an instrument of alternating despair and optimism. The author can find in himself no settled habit, no intransigent nature that can save him from sudden starts of joy and fatigue. The reader, similarly in search of himself, cannot be marginalised subjected to the repetition of stale and unsituated verities from which everything he experiences excludes him. Such a reader cannot be satisfied with the expected truths of fixed characters paraded upon a well-known scene.[35] Petrarch and Montaigne each read from a sense of the lack of continuity in himself, from the disquiet of consciousness with which Saint Augustine had struggled. Thus, in her dialogue with Reason, Joy confesses her possession of many kinds of books, as Petrarch himself lived many lives that could not be fitted to a single frame, except through the abiding confrontation with this experience in writing. In writing the self takes shape. Neither Petrarch nor Montaigne indulged the Renaissance passion for ideal 'institutes' of the state, or family (though

Montaigne's pedagogy may be an exception).[36] Neither engages any ultimate remedy for the mutability of self-consciousness other than the writer's essay of himself. In this, they permitted themselves a daily and necessary extravagance, hard for Reason to understand. Thus both Petrarch and Montaigne, like Horace earlier, were the most serious readers of their own writing. This is because, once they had surrendered writing to the mutability of their own experience, they could only achieve accumulation, weight and shape through constant returns or revisions, working against that work against the losses of living held together by memory and the joy of writing:

> Who is to carry the research beyond this point? Who can understand the truth of the matter? O Lord, I am working hard in this field, and the field of my labours is my own self. I have become a problem to myself, like land which a farmer works only with difficulty and at the cost of much sweat. For I am not now investigating the tracts of the heavens, or measuring the distance of the stars, or trying to discover how the earth hangs in space. I am investigating myself, my memory, my mind. There is nothing strange in the fact that whatever is not myself is far from me. But what could be nearer to me than myself? Yet I do not understand the power of memory that is in myself, although without it I could not even speak of myself. (Saint Augustine)[37]

CHAPTER 3

Rival Readings

In 'essaying' Montaigne we mean to stay as close as we can to Montaigne's reflective practices as a writer and a reader not only of the classics but especially of his own *Essays*. We consider Montaigne a rival reader of the *Essays*. This is not an afterthought, but an activity proper to the literary competence of an author. From this standpoint we are able to evaluate the less reflective practices of rival critics whose views on the style, composition and sense of the *Essays* will be considered at length further on. We do not, however, claim complete reflexivity for our own reading. We are concerned, none the less, to enter a claim upon the attention of the literary community for what we have to say on the bodily arts of reading and writing; and since this is not done otherwise than by means of critical appraisals, documentation and the like, we seek, where we can, to fault what we consider poor but conventional approaches to what Montaigne himself called his 'essays in flesh and bone'.

Since it is tiresome to chase down every reading of the *Essays* that we consider beside the point, it may be useful to avail ourselves of some of the ground cleared by Pouilloux's reading of the *Essays*.[1] His arguments are rather schematic and leave little room for his own constructive reading of the *Essays*.[2] But this we undertake for ourselves, in part at least, and will expand through more detailed analyses of rival readings of Montaigne in the following chapters.

Pouilloux begins by rejecting a dominant mode of reading the *Essays*, namely, the moralist reading, which consists of anthologising or rendering the essential thought of Montaigne in terms of a set of timely moral maxims.[3] Such a reading consists of treating the *Essays* as a pretext, subordinating them to the editor's recipes for predigested reading. No questions are raised regarding the initial problem of Montaigne's own use of quotations – the problem of *imitatio* and *inventio* – nor does the editor consider his own practices as an anthologist to be similarly problematic. It is assumed without question that there is literally an underlying essence of Montaigne's thought which can be reached with more economy, or with improved assembly, than Montaigne himself achieved. It is further assumed on behalf of the reader that the reader is interested only in the shortest way to the gist of Montaigne's thought. Basics are the morality of reading and writing; anything that obscures this is justifiably removed by the editor. Moreover, editors are obliged from time to time to repair the *Essays* in order to keep their original intention clear to all future reading publics. Reading, then, is conceived as an empirical task of finding the order and composition of the *Essays*, removing blemishes and other distractions, making clear the solid lines of development either in specific essays – we shall look in detail at the essays on coaches and cannibals, for example[4] – or in the *Essays* as a whole. Of course, as Pouilloux concedes, he cannot entirely ignore a certain amount of critical work necessary to establish the text of the *Essays* – especially in view of Montaigne's interpolations and successive editions. This is certainly a necessary task before the work of interpretation begins. Yet it is hard to preserve this distinction, since even Villey's great work on the archeology of the *Essays* requires the evolutionary hypothesis a little more than many of us would concede. We need to do more than introduce an easy philosophical rope – the shift from scepticism, to Stoicism, to Epicureanism – to establish what Montaigne experienced by the time he was a committed essayist. Similarly, nothing very much is decided by statistical counts regarding the influence of Montaigne's sources, since what is involved here is the whole problematic of a writer's relation to the tradition and his own literary authority. Those who comment upon the *Essays* cannot excuse themselves, as we shall show, from reflection upon how it is they in turn use sources, accumulate documentary evidence and make use of such organising metaphors as the sick writer, the absence–presence, the baroque manner, or the consubstantiality of author and *Essays*. These problems are central to any rival reading of Montaigne.

Pouilloux quite rightly rejects another conventional reading of the *Essays* – namely, the aesthetic reading – which consists of finding an order in the phenomenal disorder of the *Essays* by treating them as the reflection of the flux of the world or of the unstable model upon whom Montaigne based his self-portrait.[5] Pouilloux also sets aside the ideological reading[6] – which later we shall analyse at length in our discussion of Wilden's interpretation of friendship in the *Essays*[7] and Etiemble's account of the essay 'Of Coaches'. At issue here is the relationship between La Boétie and Montaigne. As we shall see, it bears upon the question of political independence in vital, yet seemingly opposed ways. Wilden's version of the enslaved friendship between Montaigne and La Boétie blinds him to Etiemble's argument that Montaigne is a clever critic of absolutism and colonialism. We need to be careful with each of these arguments since the *Essays* are far from containing any deliberately disguised political teaching.

We shall not, of course, suggest a purely sentimental source for the *Essays* when we speak later of their source in Montaigne's loss of La Boétie. For one thing, as we have shown, this would overlook the seriousness of the classical institution of friendship which requires more than the mere play of emotion. As friends, Montaigne and La Boétie had engaged themselves in a strenuous intellectual and moral practice which is not easily set aside with the absence or even the loss of the other partner; for it began even before the two men actually met. We can therefore discount the extreme suggestion[8] that Montaigne's essay 'Of Friendship' is largely a literary exercise, without denying that it trades upon the tropes of classical friendship.[9] It is because Wilden ignores the institution of friendship, with its important political functions, that he is able to make of Montaigne a transitional figure in the world between feudalism and socialism. He thereby completely overlooks Montaigne's ability to take a stand on the constitutional issues of his time. Wilden neglects that it is La Boétie's *Discours de la servitude volontaire* which furnishes the absent centre of the *Essays*, though here again we shall dispute Butor's interpretation of its significance. It cannot be denied that in view of La Boétie's early death, Montaigne is left to essay in himself this experience like so many others he never failed to set to his purpose.

We cannot allow either an aesthetic or an ideological reading to dominate the interpretation of the *Essays*. The ideological reading neglects the autonomy of the aesthetic features of the *Essays*, while a purely aesthetic reading overlooks Montaigne's experience of order and disorder as real historical and political affairs, which shaped the concerns of the *Essays*. It is common to these reading practices that they all rely upon the unquestioned interpretative resource of an underlying text which it is the task of the literary critic to extract, or illuminate, for a reader presumed to lack such competence – or better, for a reader who allegedly insists upon clarity in order not to lose the nuggets at the bottom of the pan.

Whether the apparent incoherence of the book derives from its fidelity to the mobile nature of the baroque world (aesthetic order), or from its prudent dissimulation of socially dangerous opinions (ideological order), one concludes by formulating its very incoherence as what provides its *unifying principle:* namely, the ontological unity of the universe, or the political and ideological objective in question. In each case, it is implicitly assumed that, at bottom, the book is the product of a single project enunciated within it; the *Essays* wish to attain the absolute beauty of a faithful painting, or to achieve the historical effectiveness of a collection of opinions capable of influencing contemporary conduct. In both cases, one affirms ends external to the book in order to be able to interpret it according to what one takes to be its nature. Thus reading is assigned the sole function of recovering a unifying principle and describing its modes of application, that is, *of extracting from the book its buried meaning.* These hypotheses only envisage disorder the better to destroy it even where it has a place, and to affirm even more, behind and despite it, an ideological unity. The figure of the book is thus a circle whose radius need only be known to calculate the rest of its dimensions, or a totality that is rigorously closed and interpretable.[10]

Pouilloux therefore rightly rejects that critical activity which consists of the practices of gratuitous assertion of figures of order and disorder, drawn from different fields of metaphor. These only facilitate the work of interpretation provided the critic – we consider Butor's practices at length[11] – does not place in question the literary resources he himself trades upon for interpretation. Literary criticism is otherwise not different from other conventions whereby we make sense of things; and it easily finds at hand what it needs to make of a text a basically moral, or political or aesthetic document. But nothing is resolved by these practices, since they stand under easy contradiction and are endlessly revisioned. Hence, with Montaigne as a guide, we might argue that it is necessary for the literary critic to make of any interpretative strategy a self-essay, to inquire into the conditions of its production of literary sense with respect equally to the established text and to the community of opinion it produces as 'a reading'. By the same token, the critic must be conscious of previous readings that constitute the text as a collective object whereby he has access in the first place to a literary tradition that his own activity supports and alters. Therefore the critic must have a keen sense of literary passage rather than any insistence upon literary essence:

> Those who commonly contradict what I profess, saying that what I call frankness, simplicity and naturalness in my conduct is art and subtlety, and rather prudence than goodness, artifice than nature, good sense than good luck, do me more honor than they take away from me. But surely they make my subtlety too subtle. And if anyone follows and watches me closely, I will concede him the victory if he does not confess that there is no rule in their school that could reproduce this natural movement and maintain a picture of liberty and license so constant and inflexible on such tortuous and varied paths, and that all their attention and ingenuity could not bring them to it. (III: 1, 603)

Finally, we might formulate a further principle of literary study, it being understood that we are condensing what we take to be Montaigne's practices as the first reader/writer of the *Essays*. In view, then, of the claims just mentioned, the critic must realise that what a text is can only be constituted with reference to what he can tell of it, and that this is not a simple descriptive activity. The literary critic will therefore talk about himself in search of how it is he speaks of other things. We may speak of this third formulation as the Socratic turn in the *Essays*. What we mean by this is that, as Montaigne came gradually to understand his own enterprise, he saw that what constituted the movement in the *Essays* from topic to topic was not the art of conversation as a remedy for distraction. What he saw was the need to examine how it is that the essayist can make reference to the accumulated knowledge and contradictory opinions of mankind, whether in philosophy, law, religion or custom, without transcendental irony. 'The essayist discovers that it is not his topics which constitute the interest he has in them, but how it is that he comes to formulate as a matter of course the questions they raise.[12] Montaigne's topics – by which we risk identifying him – are not what he writes about. The topics are a first condition for his writing without the anxiety they raise once he becomes a self-conscious essayist, namely, one concerned with the literary resources required for the production of questions and answers within a given linguistic community. If we avoid this level of critical reflection, we reduce the *Essays* to conventional formulae, assembling them, for example, in terms of simple tropes from the history of Western philosophy – scepticism, Stoicism and Epicureanism. The order of the *Essays* is then merely a derivative of the schemas practised by historians of philosophy. The *Essays* turn out to have been constructed by an orderly mind since they reflect the history of the Western mind, at least as we know it from textbooks, or from Villey.

Any reading of the *Essays* must be subject to Montaigne's own first reading – or to what we have called the 'Socratic turn' in the *Essays*. This involves a 'double reading' which might be formulated as follows:

(i) *topical reading*: here is what others say, think and do, including what I say, think and do;

(ii) *reflective reading*: how is it that others and myself come to say, think and do just what we observe them to do in (i) above?

In turn, these two readings are, as it were, mediated by an awareness of three levels of discourse (affirmation, distinction and dissolution) which function to preserve for the writer the question of the communal limits of the enterprise of self-essaying:

(a) discourse ruled by the common and ordinary traps of language (the ideological standpoint of an innocent speaker);

(b) discourse ruled by the search for logical distinctions (the philosophical standpoint of a scientific speaker);

(c) a discourse happy with the play on pronouns, words and metaphors (the aesthetic essays of a joyful speaker).[13]

These levels function simultaneously in the work of essaying, in exploring their mutual limits, and in each providing for the others' starting point. Because of their coexistence, criticism cannot dwell on any single level of reference that is not mediated by the return of a level of discourse temporarily out of play:

> These different orders are distinguished from one another according to their reference to understanding; from the dissolution of a naive knowledge, for the awareness of an alert knowledge, there arises the pleasure of writing down the humorous inanity of human ideas. But this itinerary does not in any way represent an evolution, an access to knowledge finally found and secure; it only traces the outline of a circle, the stages of a repetition in which a limit is recognized beyond which neither the ordinary man nor the philosopher, nor the writer can go, but which all three can point to and explore for the purer approach of a knowledge that remains relative. From this point, but perhaps only from this point, there can begin all the deliria of interpretation. By the same token, they will not reach grounded conclusions.[14]

It would, of course, completely falsify Montaigne's practice to imagine that the *Essays* are the result of a simple addition of topical and reflective readings. These practices are too subtly interwoven with the charm and surprise that mark the *Essays* to be grasped so simply. In other words, Montaigne like Socrates knows that he is unable to draw a distinction between his own speech and that of other men. Rather than remain silent on his own behalf, or to undertake to reform the community which motivates men's conduct, Montaigne chooses, like Socrates, to abide by custom and place whereby we act and are acted upon. It is not possible to talk, to think or to see without differences of opinion and perspective. The limit of difference is a further difference, and nothing permits us to make of good and bad, or before and after, any absolute difference that would guarantee the authenticity of thought and speech. Hence Montaigne is utterly opposed to any ultimate relativism, or to the myth of the Socratic daimon. To speak of oneself is to speak of others, to be caught up in the proliferation of personal, impersonal and interpersonal perspectives which generate that human community and conversation of which the *Essays* are a sound example.

The *Essays*, in our view, are not in obvious need of restoration or recomposition. This, however, has been the sense of so much of the scholarship to Montaigne. Very little of it has been concerned with the critical question, i.e. the question that criticism must raise on its own behalf, namely, how it is that the interpretative texts generated by the *Essays* can claim to deliver the original text, to suppress their own writing, treating it as a lens or temporary scaffolding whose purpose is only to reveal the original text, unmarked by the ravages of previous misinterpretation, including its author's own neglect. In Montaigne's case, this literary prejudice is all the more harsh, inasmuch as it neglects that Montaigne's own reading of the *Essays* is a first reading inseparable from his practice of writing. In other words, Montaigne makes it quite clear that his text is from beginning to end a resource interwoven with his desire to be a writer. The method of essaying is the very invention of Montaigne's desire to identify his life with his text, so that every discrimination of prior or ulterior motive is possible only within his text. We do not preserve Montaigne by preserving his text. Criticism with this intention merely expropriates the honour in which it claims to hold its classical authors. It is the backdoor to the Pantheon.

With the assurance of his literary vocation, Montaigne's writing is able to shift subtly between prose and poetry, and therewith to make his thought and style so interchangeable that the *Essays* resist his own correction as much as ours. Montaigne can speak of his consubstantiality with the *Essays* because he gradually came to bring together his thought and speech in a poetic fusion of sense and sound. He discovered a literary delight that is inseparable from reading and writing the *Essays*. This delight differs from the security to be found in Cartesian compositions of thought and expression, whose connoisseurs will be irritated at losing their way in the *Essays*. The fact is that *The Meditations* of Descartes and the *Essays* envisage different republics of reading. It is not that Descartes is clear whereas Montaigne is fuddleheaded. It is because of this notion that the *Essays* have so often found abridgers and organisers such as Charron, and a host of others whom no one now reads any more than one reads Montaigne's contemporaries who compiled moral lessons and memorials to themselves without ever managing to surpass the *Essays*. Montaigne's thought branches towards the light like a tree, creating shadows and supporting life of all kinds, rooting more deeply in the earth with the passing of time, withstanding those winds of change against which Montaigne first braced himself. One might have expected Montaigne to have preferred Cicero's steady pace to the crackle of Seneca. That he did not, means that he rejected the false sense of roots conveyed by Cicero's sturdy prose because he knew he could not be as sure of the man in Cicero as of the man revealed in Seneca's bodily flashes and sallies. These delighted him as any other companion whose mind shone on the tip of his words. By the same token, Montaigne, although he could speak loosely of his borrowings – making easy work for those who are content to compile them – nevertheless showed strong preferences in his choice of literary companions. He rarely cites a beautiful line or passage that is not also an occasion for reflection. Their variety is a further expression of the freedom of his mind and of the pleasure he took in reading – always avoiding pedantry. 'I think', says Gide, 'the great pleasure we take in Montaigne's *Essays* comes from the great pleasure he took in writing them, a pleasure we feel, so to speak, in every sentence'.[15]

With the opening preface 'To the Reader', as we have seen, Montaigne faces us with the paradox of the publication of an otherwise private and domestic document.[16] How, then, is the reader to understand his relation to Montaigne; is he needed or not? It is as easy to find remarks in the *Essays* that assure the reader of Montaigne's need of him as it is to find Montaigne insisting that he has written the *Essays* with nothing but himself in mind. Has the reader then to come to terms with the *Essays* for himself just as Montaigne had to; would this be what Montaigne had in mind for him? Given that we continue to read the *Essays* long after Montaigne's death, we are more likely to encounter ourselves in them, as did Montaigne in his own day, but not to feel bound to look more for him than ourselves. Perhaps Montaigne provides for his reader precisely by not concerning himself with him directly. He thereby allows for a certain anonymity to foster the approach of intimacy, while preserving in both the reader and the writer the essential liberty of the essay as an experience. Then, as Auerbach has shown in such detail,[17] the tight logical structure of even a single passage of the *Essays*, rhythmically condensed, yet sprung in anticipation of the reader's ability and pleasure, makes it impossible for us to consider that Montaigne ever seriously neglected his reader. Hence the effect of Montaigne's conversational style, his palpable presence in the warmth of his ideas and the place he makes for his reader in the quiet where he too must listen to the changing voices of his moods: 'The life of Caesar has no more to show us than our own; an emperor's or an ordinary man's, it is still a life subject to all human accidents. Let us only listen: we tell ourselves all we most need' (III: 13, 822).

Montaigne stands in no irony toward the *Essays*. He indulges no unnecessary fictions. Thus he does not have to give self-knowledge any speculative form or force it into any architectonic. He comes nearest to this dependent authority in the 'Apology for Raymond Sebond'. Here is an exercise of filial duty from which, judging by its disproportionate claim on the *Essays*, he seems hardly able to release himself. This is not to say that he does not succeed in the internal subversion of this obligation. The 'Apology' stretches towards a completion that its method exhausts without yielding its author, or else not in the same way that the later essays foster and release him. Thus Montaigne would have had little patience with the kind of literary criticism that produces nothing but a reader wholly dependent upon the factual status of the text before him, impressed upon him by the scholar's love of chronology and his anxiety to place himself in his own critical community. Rather, he wished to foster a reader competent to essay the intertextuality of the *Essays*, finding for himself their borrowings, their leaps and condensations, and so to make of reading an activity rather than the passive recognition of some grounded inquiry or object. The *Essays*, then, require a severe reader, one capable of finding origins in himself and himself in origins, in family, in custom and in folly:

> Here (and elsewhere) there is a difference between speaking about *reading* and speaking about the *reader*, since it turns out that the reader is read as much as he reads. In fact, every book, more or less consciously, more or less forcefully, tends to upset a given way of reading (or a habitual reading). Thereupon, the reader finds himself faced with an alternative: either he 'resists' and preserves, carefully and jealously, his way of reading – he thereby misses the novelty of the book he is reading – or else he 'goes along', lets himself be ready, and so really reads. Literary criticism encounters the same dilemma. In the first case, it pronounces what it believes to be the meaning of *the book;* an illusion of objectivity if it turns out that the meaning of the book is in fact imported by the critic into the book. In the second case, in describing a unique experience of reading, the critic finds he needs to invent a specific metalanguage for each book; the pleasure of subjectivity which has -the advantage that it clearly marks the transforming activity of the book. But such criticism cannot, by definition, be systematized. More precisely, it could only be systematized on condition that its own presuppositions were examined: that is to say, the critic would have to interrogate himself on the modalities of reciprocal action between the book and the reader and between the reader and the book: in other words, *on reading*. Criticism cannot, nor should it, envisage a *direct* access to objectivity; that would amount to suppressing the effect of the book. It should know how to transform itself but also how to control (or master) this transformation. However, this control (or mastery) derives from another 'discipline', that here I shall call rhetoric. In a word, rhetoric, so far from being an obstacle to the pleasure of reading, rather enables it. It does so in two ways: insofar as it presupposes the book will transform its reader and insofar as it regulates this transformation.[18]

We ought not to treat the negativity required by self-essaying as a mode of rejecting reality in favour of textual platitudes. Wilden's argument along these lines has recently been expanded upon by Regosin in terms of the Edenic myth which, I think, must also be countered in any interpretation of the literary impulse behind the *Essays*. According to this view,[19] the loss of La Boétie is experienced by Montaigne as an essential self-alienation which is then displaced as a literary void to be filled redemptively by the *Essays*:

> The Edenic moment, that mystical fusion in oneness that confers plenitude and confirms integrity dissolves: the metaphorical death as exclusion from the fullness of being leaves a fragmented, alienated soul, errant in the instability of

the world of becoming, seeking a means of return. A familiar falling away whose very terms compellingly recall the Adamic fall from grace through original sin and suggest a dialectic reminiscent of Christian conversation.[20]

Here, again, the language of interpretation is far in excess of the text of the *Essays* even where, as in the *Apology* or in Montaigne's more or less direct borrowings from Saint Augustine, we might expect to find some echo of the critic's view. What is worse, having taken the trouble to introduce this comparison, Regosin immediately remarks upon its foreignness to the *Essays*, though he seems to think that Montaigne was certainly influenced by Stoic notions of conversion (epistrophe), if not by Christian renunciation It then turns out that what Regosin does want to say is that it is the seventeenth-century absorption of Stoicism and Christianity that explains the moral tone of the *Essays*. His thesis then becomes the following one:

> The dramatic echoes of Christian *epistrophe* represent a stunning transposition, for the *Essays* secularize and concretize this essential religious concept. Nowhere perhaps is Montaigne more humanistic – in the rather broad sense of the emphasis on things human – and nowhere is he less traditionally Christian (one is tempted to say more un-Christian) than in this critical interchange of temporal and religious terms. What we find is the traditional circle of conversion except that the original state is not union with God, the death to the world not a spiritual renunciation which begins the return to divine sanctification, the reformation not a repristinization of God's image in man, not a refashioning by the celestial maker. Instead, in a purely human context where friendship functions as a kind of secular analogue to union with God, the individual becomes the source of his own recreation.[21]

Regosin's commentary is a perfect example of gratuitous interpretation. This practice consists of the attribution to a text of terms for which it in no way calls. These terms are then withdrawn as the absent terms organising the presence of a comparative term whose function can really only be located in the critic's own free practice. Nothing makes such devices necessary, except a kind of literary bricolage, or an uncertain display of the freedom of interpretation exercised without due consideration for its responsibilities. Moreover, Regosin shrinks from any definite use of his own terms – witness his appallingly weak use of humanism, and his irresolution with respect to Montaigne's Christianity. Things are no better with his use of the central metaphor of conversion[22] since every element in it is withdrawn. The last thing in the world that organises the *Essays* is the creation myth. Montaigne did not have to secularise his religious consciousness in order to become a writer. If anything, it was Montaigne's social consciousness that stood in the way of his becoming a writer. Thus the *Essays* often treat the paradox of the social presuppositions of this otherwise private activity. Montaigne began as a casual writer, if not somewhat slavish, as he himself observes. If there were anything in Regosin's thesis, Montaigne might never have written the 'Apology for Raymond Sebond' (II: 12) or else that single essay might have submerged the entire enterprise that got under way with his gradual discovery of writing as a method of self-essaying. Regosin fails to see that Montaigne is no different from a host of Renaissance writers concerned with literary creation. Montaigne believed that a man could make himself – witness the pedagogical essays – without any harsh Platonic or Stoical separation of himself from his own nature. Indeed, he believed that a man is himself if only he can come to circumscribe himself and shore himself up against the winds of extravagant fantasy:

> Once the great Renaissance shift away from orthodoxy had taken place, in religion, in political theory and practice, in geography and cosmology, in economics, there was opportunity for intellectual recombination, deliberate and random: Montaigne's stout corpus of essays is not only the record of one man's inner life but also a convex mirror reflection of the intellectual universe in which he lived. No stock adjective can characterize the speculative activity of Montaigne, or of the Renaissance: no scheme reduces to a single formulation their irregular, independent, and arbitrary activities.[23]

It is impossible to read the *Essays* without a sense of the literary tradition of paradox in which Montaigne worked; we otherwise risk making the *Essays* a work of indulgent inconclusiveness suited to Montaigne's allegedly subjective style. Renaissance thought is full of the paradoxes of faith and doctrine, of science, philosophy, the literary and visual arts. The Stoics received from Parmenides and Zeno the dialectical paradox that, despite appearances, the many are in fact one. Whereas the Sophists pushed such arguments to the destruction of truth, the Sceptics undertook the more painstaking labour of working their way through all philosophical claims, exploring their inconsistencies, weighing their oppositions. This is Montaigne's method in the Apology for Raymond Sebond. Yet he could also work in the Stoic tradition, seeking a moderate line with a single-mindedness that offered a bulwark against the rage for contradiction and confusion.[24] The Stoic duty of the pursuit of self-knowledge laid upon such learned men as Erasmus, or Henry Cornelius Agrippa, the duty of distancing themselves from all of their knowledge, natural and supernatural:

> the name of Cornelius in his Vanity of Learning was famous, not only among the *Germarnes*, but also other Nations; for Momus himself carpeth at all amongst the gods; amongst the Heroes, *Hercules* hunteth after Monsters;

amongst the divels *Pluto* the King of hell is angry with all the ghosts; amongst the philosophers *Democritus* laugheth at all things, on the contrary, *Heraclitus* weepeth at all things; *Pirrhias* is ignorant of all things; *Aristotle* thinketh he knoweth all things; *Diogenes* contemneth all things; this *Agrippa* spareth none, he contemneth, knows, is ignorant, weeps, laughs, is angry, pursueth, carps at all things, being himself a Philosopher, a Demon, an Hero [*sic*] a god, and all things.[25]

Renaissance writers were extremely conscious of the demands placed upon them by the various literary genres that they had inherited from the classical world. They might have inhibited their project of making these found forms resonate with humanist rebirth. In practice, the variety of literary kinds and the possibilities of exploiting their mixed forms seems to have contributed to the liveliness of Renaissance creation. For example, the adage is literally a commonplace, a quotation taken from an authoritative source, compressing a mass of human experience into a powerful phrase. Erasmus's *Adagia* deliberately exhibited a patchwork of ancient wisdom with the purpose of handing on an immense culture to which its users might apprentice themselves with more or less ingenuity. Of course, the commonplace book functioned for most persons merely as a source of borrowed culture considered as a social necessity. Montaigne's *Essays* often make such use of the adages. But gradually he crosses the adage with the essay in his own artful discovery of self-essaying. 'The essay is, really, in part a fulfillment of the implications of adage-making: by working from adages into a new context, it developed into a form of its own.'[26]

It is, I think, quite wrong to intrude upon Montaigne's conception of himself as an essayist anything so foreign as the divinity of creation.[27] However, this is argued by Regosin, despite the fact that Montaigne is anxious to associate himself with the language and doings of far humbler trades than that of the Creator:

> In the secular context that Montaigne delineates in the *Essais*, where he seeks to find and found being, the role he takes on and the action he sets out ring with distant echoes of divinity. He will not claim it (except in the terms noted earlier, at the close of *De l'experience)* nor will he speak of creation, but his authorship of the book of the self will recall the Author of the book of nature, the book of the ultimate self. Montaigne's insistence on writing as making, his view of the book as the concrete externalization of the self, his notion of consubstantiality, of the identicality of sign and referent, evoke God's function as metaphorical writer, his creation of nature as the invisible rendered visible, tangible, intelligible, the unequivocal sign of Himself. The parallel suggests that as God is to be found in this book, so Montaigne resides in his.[28]

Nothing could be more alien to the *Essays* than the suggestion that they stand to things considered therein as the book of nature. Nothing could be more erroneous than to suggest that Montaigne's conception of the exercise of reason and sound sense might consist in deciphering some divine code hidden in the nature of things. Nothing is more irresponsible than Regosin's suggestion that Montaigne should offer himself as a divine surrogate for attentive readers of the *Essays*. If this were the case, then the *Essays* would not, properly speaking, be any longer a literary phenomenon. Indeed, that is the risk courted by Regosin in mixing the metaphors of theology without any grounded theory of literary interpretation to delimit his borrowings in favour of the literary text rather than his own wordiness. If Montaigne drew upon the image of consubstantiality, he did so as much to rework the sense of that notion in terms of self-inquiry as to lend to the *Essays* a theological weight that could serve only to mystify his enterprise. Montaigne ordinarily keeps his distance from the central mysteries of the Church, content to pay them a Sunday visit but not to embroil them in the discourse of his day. Moreover, such a comparison would entirely throw out of balance Regosin's better appreciation of the *Essays* as the reader's friend. Here, of course, it is impossible to confound a necessary equality between the writer and the reader with the notion of their identity. This would ruin friendship, as it would, inicidentally, ruin Montaigne's sense of child–parent relation. Rather, what Montaigne exemplifies is the tolerance of the artist, parent and statesman for the independence of the persons and things around him, which he may have fashioned in some way, but always with an eye to their mutual freedom.

To insist upon the theological sense of Montaigne's consubstantiality with the *Essays* would also conflict with the more practical problems involved in the work of self-portrayal which Regosin rightly considers to be more than a figurative expression in respect of the *Essays*:

> In general, humanism's keen interest in classical life nourished the vogue of the portrait, for it found in antiquity both that broad affirmation of the individual and its expression as art in the medal and the portrait bust. The Florentine Alberti was responsible for reawakening interest in medallic art, and no less a figure than Erasmus introduced it to northern Europe, with himself as subject. In Italy medals and portraits of rulers and military figures reflected – the Renaissance preference for the life of action, its emphasis on personal glory and self-perpetuation; paintings of humanists expressed the esteem of learning and the sense that knowledge was a shaping force of virtue and character. Erasmus' interest in the portrait – and his own appearance – found a place in the cult of friendship that evolved from Cicero's *De Amicitia*. He and Thomas More

exchanged portraits as expressions of devotion and, more importantly, as surrogates for the self.[29]

Montaigne discovered in the *Essays* that his task was to model them according to his own living image, but with the distinctly literary problem of claiming that he could somehow surpass the limits of literary fiction, just as the painter had somehow to use illusion on behalf of reality. This problematic is simply short-circuited if we stress the consubstantiality of author and text or make of it a divine allegory. What the essayist is concerned with here is the artist's responsibility for his art as a moral appearance, in unrepentant offering of things as he sees them, without any other correction than the development of his artistic life. In this regard Horace's 'Epistles' are an important influence in Montaigne's shift towards the self-portrait. Here he found the art of the small essay tied to a personal standpoint and circumscribed by ordinary affairs which was to suit his nature. Although his borrowings remain in Latin, we should not miss their self-revelatory nature which begins to rework the otherwise impersonal beginning of the *Essays*.[30] With Horace, Montaigne learns that philosophy is best off out of school but well ingrained in our daily self-observation:

> The most beautiful lives, to my mind, are those that conform to the common human pattern, with order, but without miracle and without eccentricity. Now old age needs to be treated a little more tenderly. Let us commend it to that god who is the protector of health and wisdom, but gay and sociable wisdom:
>
> > Grant me but health, Laton's son,
> > And to enjoy the wealth I've won,
> > And honored age, with mind entire
> > And not unsolaced by the lyre.
> > Horace (III: 13, 857)

There is nothing behind the *Essays* for the reader to trade upon, any more than there is for the viewer before the self-portraits of Rembrandt or Dürer.[31] But this requires elaboration in a later chapter.[32]

In another move, Regosin sees in the *Essays* a tower built against the world, against the corruption and illness of the body politics; as though the condition of France would as surely have killed Montaigne as it did La Boétie:

> Montaigne repudiates the social world and what it represents, and maintains this posture throughout. He denounces that world to renounce it, he turns away from it through symbolic destruction that clears the ground for subsequent reconstruction. This movement is both the reiteration and the extension

of the paradigmatic death that accompanies the rupture of Montaigne's friendship with La Boétie.[33]

By submitting to this line, Regosin, like so many before him, risks wrapping Montaigne in himself; leaving him secluded, alienated, and suffering an irreparable loss which he repeats by rejecting everything else that belongs to the world, save a little corner of himself within which he is to reconstruct himself on the model of the *Essays*. Here we encounter the myth of *creatio ex nihilo*;[34] the fiction of a literary striptease that suits Montaigne less than anyone. Montaigne did not retire from the world in order to write the *Essays*. Indeed, he relied upon nothing else but his comfortable life, his charming château and the rich company of friends and books, as well as the continued assurance of his king and townsmen that he was needed by them. That is why, as Regosin himself sees, Montaigne was not tempted towards any expatriotism, however much he loved travel and however strong his excoriation of the civilised encounter with barbarism. What he needed to preserve in himself was the living tie to this world and the family that he loved but which he knew he must one day surely leave. The *Essays* are therefore plainly the work of a family philosopher.[35] That is why Montaigne is never tempted by the excesses of philosophy and theology. He no more set himself above himself than above his children, or servants or his wife. He kept an open house. He never forgot his own father's generosity in moulding him and he adopted it as the measure of any of his own instructions. Just as families are not kind to moral heroes. Montaigne hunted out any tendency in himself towards the extremes of pride and humility. But this means he had to try to mould himself within the limits of ordinary sense and reasonable folly.

With this in mind, we may see how easily the consubstantially thesis becomes excessive. This is the case, I think, with Glauser's brilliant reversal of the metaphor, whereby Montaigne is nothing but a creature of his own literary activity.[36] According to this view, Montaigne lacked any substance before he began to pour himself into the *Essays*. The essayist is then the paradoxical embodiment of what began as sheer fantasy. The *Essays* continued to clothe him so appealingly that Montaigne could never recover his protested nudity and originality. Having borrowed everything for fear of lacking substance, Montaigne became a creature of a literary style whose visceral metaphors gave him the illusion of embodiment. Apart from the light and warmth of the *Essays*, Montaigne was nothing but a cold creature wracked with sickly dreams and uncontrollable fantasies, haunting his life from his books, more like a vampire than a honey bee.

Having begun this way, it is easy enough for Glauser to feed everything into the consubstantiality thesis. Thus Books One and Two are stuffed with a life of action, politics and war with which Montaigne was otherwise unconnected, being too indecisive, self-indulgent and generally weak-natured ever to have found himself engaged in real life:

> A writer asserts himself in relation to his life as a man. There is a very clear separation between the mayor and the essayist and their dialogue creates the distance that generates the essays. Montaigne would rather deform his own life than the one taking shape in the Essays. He only acquires worldly graces through his work. His indifference towards the cares of society is transformed into a strange passion for his own company. These contrasts are devices of a writer. When he pretends to wants to resemble the craftsmen and labourers whom he imagines more happy than university rectors, he forgets, for the moment, that those whom he envies do not write the *Essays*, and are for that reason hardly worth envy.[37]

Relentlessly, Glauser argues that Montaigne never ceased to run away from the void in himself. Travel, writing and dreaming are the whole of his life and only in the *Essays* can he invent for himself any substance or any attachment to life and society. Even in old age, Montaigne persisted in recreating a youth, good looks, health and love he had never possessed. He is, in short, the most vain, the most empty and the most deformed of all men, dragging out his days as a literary Casanova. The *Essays* are nothing but the mirror of Montaigne's self-spectacle; once the mirror is removed nothing remains. Worse still, having dissolved himself in the mirror's illusion Montaigne has no qualms at drowning his friend La Boétie in the same pool of narcissism. All this is not achieved, however, without a burden of guilt. Thus Montaigne reaches the heights of literary sublimation in romanticising people at home and abroad in a pre-civilised age before the very invention of letters that now invent the innocence of barbarism as the measure of the guilt of literary culture.

Finally, Glauser rests his argument on the claim that the *Essays* are truly a literary illness,[38] alternating between misery and gaiety to suit the fictions of Montaigne's mind, unbridled by anything in the world. Indeed, had Montaigne not poured himself onto the paper, and mummified himself between the pages of the *Essays*, he would have left no single thing of substance. With no real ability for communication or friendship, Montaigne made himself consubstantial with the *Essays* in which he forged himself upon the world as an unforgettable immoralist:

> Having set out with the honest intentions of a man who also wished to be as true as possible, the work became, despite him, the distorting image of a sincerity that saw itself further and further compromised by the creation of the *Essays*. Sincerity – *sine cera* – turned into something else, became therefore

impossible, in the wax of the *Essays*. The honey all his own, of which he speaks, is nothing without the bee-hive capable of preserving it.[39]

How can the *Essays* have provoked such starkly opposed conclusions? Is there no middle ground? We, of course, could not mean by this that there is some way of withholding interpretation. Rather, what we have in mind is the question how it is we are to move among rival readings, attacking here and holding our ground there, much as Montaigne handled himself among the conflicts and controversies of his own day, thereby strengthening his friends and fortifying the republic of literature. Everything of Montaigne has been subject to that same re-inscription begun by himself in the text of the Bordeaux Edition of the *Essays*. Just as Montaigne was never content with the printed page, continuously altering a word, a punctuation mark, inserting lines, paragraphs and pages, so, too, everything around him was subject to the same re-inscription. Thus in his own day Christianity was being rewritten by Luther and Calvin, altering its ancient texts with novel readings that shook Montaigne's faith as it shook his France. The princes served by Montaigne had need of him, though not ultimately, because of the changes they were engaged in by rewriting principalities into the constitution of an absolute monarchy. Time, too, has covered the family home in Bordeaux with the graphics of local commerce, just as history has left of the seigneurial domain only a tower and a few bare rooms whose significance survives only through those who love them enough to continue that original re-inscription that was Montaigne's passion for writing. For this reason it is as impossible for us to recapture Montaigne as it was for himself. What we see in the text of the *Essays*, that is, in the marginal additions – are they additions and to what are they additions? – is Montaigne's own abandonment to the joy of writing. Imagine the sheer strength of the hand that so carefully illuminated the margins of the *Essays*, repeating a holy tradition of writing found now in the stream of human consciousness. It is only weaker minds, because less joyful, that insist upon re-inscribing the text of the *Essays* into the orderly schemas that are suited to our secular faith in science's assembly of clear thought. Such exercises are nothing but the worst democratisation of Montaigne's thought – neither popular nor singular. They make of Montaigne a mind without any distinction but its faults; they humble him in favour of minor professionals and the feeble breed of their students. They produce interpretations without heart: and merely add to books those books that make it impossible for anyone to understand the love of books. This is, of course, a jealous claim. It requires care because it risks intruding upon the friendship of Montaigne, making love's enemies where perhaps he might not have chosen. Therefore we need to recall Montaigne's own beginning. He had been young once and in his youth he had fallen in love with everything La Boétie had stood for, just as La Boétie had seen in him his own life had he lived it beyond a few years. It fell, then, to Montaigne to survive their friendship. And so he retired to his tower and his books to construct there a difficult memorial of their love. Montaigne might simply have tried to live in the past, thereby risking an idealisation of his friendship with La Boétie beyond anything in the ordinary convention of friendly expression. But then he would have dammed the stream of his own life, turning it into a pond in which nothing either of himself or of La Boétie might be seen. Fortunately, Montaigne's love of the past was not constrained by any such diversion. He continued to live his life, to marry, to have children, to take care of his domain as best he could, and while never far from the political life of his town and country, to engage in that double decentring of his life – in travel and in essaying.

CHAPTER 4

Writing and Embodiment

Montaigne's consciousness of being a writer develops as the deepest finding within his self-inquiry.[1] He is not concerned with any conventional introspection of his motives for writing. Such an address, as we have seen in To the Reader, is never more than a pretext that waits for its fulfilment in those sudden moments of comparison, of metaphor, and in asides dispersed throughout the *Essays*. As an essayist, Montaigne experienced what Barthes claims to be a modern literary experience:

> But in our literature, it seems to me, the verb is changing status, if not form, and the verb *to write* is becoming a middle verb with an *intégrant* past. This is true inasmuch as the modern verb *to write* is becoming a sort of indivisible semantic entity. So that if language followed literature – which, for once perhaps, has the lead – I would say that we should no longer say today '*j'ai écrit*,' but, rather, '*je suis écrit*,' just as we say '*je suis né, il est mort, elle est éclose.*' There is no passive idea in these expressions, in spite of the verb *to be,* for it is impossible to transform '*je suis écrit*' (without forcing things, and supposing that I dare to use this expression at all) into '*on m'a écrit*' ['I have been written' or 'somebody wrote me']. It is my opinion that in the middle verb *to write* the distance between the writer and the language diminishes asymptotically. We could even say that it is subjective writings, like romantic writing, which are active, because in them the agent is not interior but *anterior* to the process of writing. The one who writes here does not write for himself, but, as if by proxy, for a person who is exterior and antecedent (even if they both have the same name). In the modern verb of middle voice *to write,* however, the subject is immediately contemporary with the writing, being effected and affected by it.[2]

That is why Montaigne's language is visceral, visual, sonorous and sensuous: it explores its author's bodily being, listening and recording every change of mood, as lively in sickness as in health. Writing is, above all, a sane enterprise, that is to say, it is a healthy undertaking for both the mind and the body to be set in mutual exploration, from day to day, unrepentantly borrowing from each other whatever they need for their preservation from the corrosion of time and forgetfulness. For one who writes, it is only writing – others will speak of their own art – which can rescue the self from its humiliation and its emptiness, while offering it a resource that is not dependent upon anything outside of itself:

> I set forth notions that are human and my own, simply as human notions con-
> sidered in themselves, not as determined and decreed by heavenly ordinance
> and permitting neither doubt nor dispute; matter of opinion, not matter of
> faith; what I reason out according to me, not what I believe according to God;
> as children set forth their essays to be instructed, not to instruct; in a lay
> manner, not clerical, but always very religious. (I: 56, 234)

Montaigne's writing is therefore not confessional. It does not place itself in the eye of God. The *Essays* are not written in the hope of any conversion or sudden reversal. They are not apocalyptic. If anything, they rely upon a general endurance in nature, the body and history, which, more than any notion of a par-ticular public, gives the *Essays* their chance of universal appeal. Moreover, Mon-taigne's conviction in choosing the very title, *Essays*, is that he has discovered a method of writing which is a permanent contribution to human knowledge, and not just to our knowledge of Montaigne.

As a method of writing, the essay is a basic tool for the production of a corpo-real phenomenology.[3] As such, it is not quite as separate from the method of the natural sciences as Friedrich claims, any more than Bacon's *Essays* are unrelated to his theory of scientific method.[4] Thus Montaigne's style is not characterised by any distinctive form, so much as a method of self-inquiry ruled by the movement of life. His disclaimers about this are part of Montaigne's experience of being shaped in the course of creating a method of joining himself to himself, while remaining within the current of daily living. Hence the *Essays* are continuously reworked, just as life is reflected upon, and from time to time resolved towards its proper end. What is involved here is not correction but a continuous reaffirma-tion of the accumulation of living, thinking and feeling – like Molly's yes:

> Yes when I put the rose in my hair like the Andalusian girls used or shall I wear
> a red yes and how he kissed me under the Moorish wall and I thought well as
> him as another and then I asked him with my eyes to ask again yes and then he
> asked me would I yes to say yes my mountain flower and first I put my arms

around him yes and drew him down to me so he could feel my breasts all perfume yes and his heart was going like mad and yes I said yes I will yes.[5]

So Montaigne opened up his life to the *Essays*, writing them into his flesh and
bones, sinking them into every corner of his life. He thereby found a language
that is visceral and vital, spreading out upon the page, tensed and calm, poised
and effervescent. At their very best, the *Essays* seize life itself, balancing it in a
moment of leisure where the activity of reading and writing vibrates in harmony
with all of life and nature. Thus the writer confronts the waiting page like any
other clearing which he enters as a question, searching for the opportunity to
develop his own bodily capacities of movement and sensation. The writer's fingers move over the page, into the words, cutting a furrow whose fruit lies ahead,
blossoming into the sentence and the paragraph, from page to page. Writing is a
dance, a transformation of the body, lifting and moving ahead of itself, yet tired,
tiring, and forever trying to hide its necessary pauses. Writing is music, chasing
its own rhythms, shaping the body's strength into word after word upon which
there supervenes the sounding sense of a line coming into and after being. Therefore writing, like the dance, or like music, requires a regime, a bodily art of concentration and dispersal; a continuous poise and ever ready rhythm. Writing is a
bodily assumption of the virtual sense of the waiting page, and a necessary fall
into meaning. The page, then, is at the writer's fingertips and really not a space
in any co-ordinate sense, or a material upon which he writes; it is an unfolding of
time's body and the necessity of thought's speech waiting upon the same assumption in the reader's sensible, sounding body. Thus, in writing and reading we
fulfil the body's capacity for subtlety, lifting its weight, displacing it into the
ubiquity of thought. At the same time, the page produces the paradox of thought's
diaspora to the very extent that it concentrates a writer or reader upon himself,
bent upon the page and rapt in the pleasures and pains of writing and reading.
The art of writing does not raise the writer above his body into some spiritual
realm half traced upon the page. The writer's fingers and the page are a working
ensemble, an alternation of intelligible space and spatialised intelligence that permits Montaigne to speak of the consubstantiality between himself and his book.
We rightly speak of the body of literature.

Indeed, no book lies waiting for its reader without beckoning us; its presence
is irresistible, and we are as much in its pages as they are in us, even before we
actually pick it up and begin to read. Moreover, the book faces us like the body of
another mind that will be revealed to us in the moment we open the page and
begin to read with its voice. The book sweeps us up in its peculiarly promiscuous
embrace, dissolving the distance between the reader and the author by lending
everything it has to have them dwell together in its pages. A book cannot be left

71

alone. It waits on the shelf, in the library or on the table – like a friend. Like Montaigne, the reader is aware of neglecting, mishandling, being careless with, forgetting, losing and damaging his books. He misses them, loves them, is angered and frustrated by them. It is misery to have to sell one's books, a crime for them to be banned or destroyed. Reading, therefore, never alienates us. Rather, it is the very practice in which we can be assured that other minds and feelings can inhabit us as surely as any thought or emotion of our own. In reading, I can be here and elsewhere, myself and another. The exchange of lives which reading and writing together accomplish means that biography is not so much a literary genre as an instrument of literary intersubjectivity:

> Reading, then, is the act in which the subjective principle which I call 'I,' is modified in such a way that I no longer have the right, strictly speaking, to consider it as my 'I.' I am on loan to another, and this other thinks, feels, suffers, and acts within me. The phenomenon appears in its most obvious and even naivest form in the sort of spell brought about by certain cheap kinds of reading, such as thrillers, of which I say, 'It gripped me.' Now it is important to note that this possession of myself by another takes place not only on the level of objective thought, that is with regard to images, sensations, ideas which reading affords me, but also on the very level of my subjectivity.[6]

Montaigne had to write; his life became nothing apart from his literary life. In making his life consubstantial with his book, Montaigne secured his writing as an aristocratic gesture and not an alienated labour. That is to say, he discovered writing as a bodily pleasure, like the pleasure of reading, and he found in each a mutual joy. He thereby opened a field of reading and writing in anyone who later encounters the *Essays* as an influence in his own literary life and its necessary rearrangements. The writer and the reader, then, incorporate the will not to die, and it is from this will that there is a living literature embodied in their mutual essaying. Thus Montaigne becomes conscious of his authority as the *Essays* grow, from book to hook, taking their own time, exploring their own path, convincing him that they are, after all, his own property. That is to say, the essays strengthen his resources as a writer, enabling him to find his life in a fundamental surrender to the tide of writing. Montaigne is also the first reader of the *Essays*. We need to understand what this involves, since authors can hardly be said to read their own work in the same sense as any other reader. If that were the case, then the author would either be involved in a hopeless attempt to pre-empt the public versions of his work, or else have defined his writing as an instrument of home-made literature – an even more curious literary narcissism. But the writer, any more than the reader, cannot break the spell of reading. What the writer reads in the practice of his craft is one of the possible readings that inhabit his text as an already anonymous literary production which constrains him from the first moment it is under way. Thus, the writer is as obliged as any other reader to review continuously and even rehandle the words that he is trying to shape to a discourse whose pattern lies simultaneously ahead and in tow of the words that fulfil it. The writer reads his own work in order to feel where he is in the grip of language, how he has picked his way so far, and what his options are as a consequence. In this, he experiences a certain foreclosure, the unavailability of certain turns horizontal to his path and the need to compromise, we hope, within the ethical limits of his need to continue writing:

> the writer can never read his own work. It is, for him, strictly inaccessible, a secret which he does not wish to confront. The impossibility of self-reading coincides with the discovery that, from now on, there is no longer any room for any added creation in the space opened up by the work and that, consequently, the only possibility is that of forever writing the same work over again. . . . The particular loneliness of the writer . . . stems from the fact that, in the work, he belongs to what always precedes the work.[7]

The writer reads his own work in order to resume work, to continue living and writing, not to confront the source of his writing, for that never arises. Thus Montaigne confesses that his essays grow longer and take their own time. This is not because he has grown careless of their form and merely indulges in writing at what he fears is the reader's expense. Rather, he considers that the internal labyrinths of the essays now exhibit in a strong way what is sought through their collection. They thereby show the writer's sense of the strength of his beginnings, inasmuch as they carry him and the reader into the *Essays* without the anxiety of order and continuity. In reading his own work, Montaigne therefore practises his craft as a writer and not his lay interests as a reader, which he interprets elsewhere. Yet there is a certain relation between Montaigne's first reading of the *Essays* and his reading of other authors. In each case, Montaigne is concerned with that moment of condensation, or temporal thickening, which is the certainty of literary achievement. In these moments, literature distils what time dispenses, and draws together a life that is otherwise without its own icon. Nevertheless, Montaigne remains an essayist precisely because he knew that literature has no resource outside of time[8] and the irreconcilable movement of our sensory life. The writer's eyes, hands and ears are together instruments of speech whose animation literature only suspends retrospectively through the writer's devotion to life's temporary celebration. The essayist, in particular, knows that writing is a temporal instrument gauged to capture the reader and the writer in the stress of living, without seeking to subordinate their lives to the text *sub specie aeternitatis*. Essaying, or the movement from essay to essay, as well as within an essay, itself repeats the differentiation of lived temporality in which we never achieve a self-identity. In the same way, reading also repeats the movement of life and its essential excess. For no two readings are ever alike. And in every reacting there is a struggle between what the text requires of the reader's life and the reader's own rights of appropriation, whereby he expands his world and goes on living that life to which reading has become as necessary as writing in the author's life:

> If I read this sentence, this story or this word with pleasure, it is because they were written in pleasure (such pleasure does not contradict the writer's complaints). But the opposite? Does writing in pleasure guarantee – guarantee me, the writer – my reader's pleasure? Not at all. I must seek out this reader (must 'cruise' him) *without knowing where he is*. A site of bliss is then created. It is not the reader's 'person' that is necessary to me, it is this site: the possibility of a dialectics of desire, of an *unpredictability* of bliss: the bets are not placed, there can still be a game.[9]

Writing is an uncertain bodily odyssey. Its specific danger is that the author will be bewitched by the song of language and not wish to come home. The writer wishes to cross a certain gap of meaning. Once he hears the song of language, he is tempted to believe in the sheer power of expression to leap across his desire for meaning. If he succumbs to this song, the writer will be tempted to think of his own senses as arid lands. Unless he can stop his ears against the siren song, he risks losing all ordinary sense without being sure of gaining any other. In view of these risks, the writer will prudently speak of his enterprise as avoiding any goal. Thus Montaigne speaks of the *Essays* as a pastime. They continuously alter course, proceed haphazardly, turning their anxiety into a pleasant distraction. At the same time, the *Essays* are a happy combination of seriousness and free play, capable of any encounter this side of things, steering clear of all linguistic excesses, other than the need to write. The *Essays* tell only of their author. That is to say, they 'relate' Montaigne and everything that comes within the landscape revealed to self-inquiry. At the same time, the space opened up by the *Essays* never stretches out so as to lose Montaigne; it is more like the moving shadow east by his deliberate journeying. Above all, there is in the *Essays* the discovery of the structuring of lived time through writing. This makes it possible to grasp certainties here and there that launch the essays upon one another. The yield here is double. In the first place, the surrender to essaying convinces Montaigne of his literary vocation, that is to say, of his ability to bring about a constant metamorphosis of himself and his surroundings. Secondly, he can thereby be assured of his grasp of literature as the lived collection of time and space in the movement towards the œuvre or life-event that began with his decision to write down his scattered thoughts. It is therefore anvoidable that the *Essays* contain their own reflection upon the impressive revelation of this first literary moment. This is, of course, no abstract reflection. Rather, as Montaigne observed, it is necessarily fed by anything and everything, and by the least promising of things, so long as it is coupled with the question of self-inquiry. Perhaps, too, once the *Essays* are identified with Montaigne's own life, he cannot avoid letting them wander, as he loved to do in his travels. For otherwise he should have to bring them to that same end which inhabits all life. This is not to say that Montaigne shrinks from death: only that he refuses deliberately to put writing, any more than life itself, under the sign of death. Rather, he commits himself to writing – and it is wrong to speak as though he devoted himself like Narcissus to the *Essays* for they required of him a lively negligence, or a creative infidelity from which both could live, well out of the reach of any dead ceremony of literature. At the same time, we must recognise that the need to write cannot be simply subjectivised . For art asks nothing of the writer at the same time it requires everything of him, supporting and abandoning him like his life's energy. Writing, then, is like living itself, half joy and half pain. In a certain respect, writing is even an unhappy affair, since it traps the writer in the lies of literature and the vanity of its inventions. On the other hand, literature offers the writer a space in which to overcome his natural inabilities, provided he has the strength of his calling. What distinguishes Montaigne from Rousseau in this regard is that Montaigne is less subjective in his bodily experience of literary alienation. This is because he never dreams of setting himself outside the company of classical writers, even when he is aware of the innovation of his *Essays*. Montaigne's solitude is a place reserved in the republic of letters – he is not an exile waiting for the literary renovation of society and human nature. By the same token, Montaigne has none of Rousseau's enthusiasm for the reinvention of a language and society adequate to the certainty of the joy in Rousseau's relation to Jean-Jacques. The *Essays*, therefore, have not to plead their sincerity in a world threatening to carry off their author's very shadow. In this, Montaigne is kinder to his readers than is Rousseau. He requires of them a liberty and an innocence available to them without exceptional self-alienation, provided they are open towards their own essential follies.

Writing opens up a sheer spume of words, an incessant cry, demanding, cajoling, pleading for someone but no one in particular to pay attention. And yet this incarnate need can never be so inchoate as to be unable to organise itself, to disport itself, to somehow attract a reader. The writer is therefore never insane, yet more neurotic than healthy. The writer is driven to please: the proof of this is that he writes. This means that he is not overwhelmed by the need to please but neither is he whole enough (healthy) not to need to write and to be read. Thus in Montaigne's *Essays* there are sudden bursts of the writer's pleasure in words which bubble up on their own, in the sheer visceral play of word piling upon word, sweeping the reader into a whirlpool of delight, breaking completely with the restraints and publicity of narrative style:

> What of the hands? We beg, we promise, call, dismiss, threaten, pray, entreat, deny, refuse, question, admire, count, confess, repent, fear, blush, doubt, instruct, command, incite, encourage, swear, testify, accuse, condemn, absolve, insult, despise, defy, vex, flatter, applaud, bless, humiliate, mock, reconcile, commend, exalt, entertain, rejoice, complain, grieve, mope, despair, wonder, exclaim, are silent, and what not, with a variation and multiplication that vie with the tongue. With the head: we invite, send away, avow, disavow, give the lie, welcome, honor, venerate, disdain, demand, show out, cheer, lament, caress, scold, submit, brave, exhort, menace, assure, inquire. What of the eyebrows? What of the shoulders? There is no movement that does not speak both a language intelligible without instruction, and a public language; which means, seeing the variety and particular use of other languages, that this one must rather be judged the one proper to human nature. I omit what necessity teaches privately and promptly to those who need it, and the finger alphabets, and the grammars in gestures, and the sciences which are practiced and only by gestures, and the nations which Pliny says have no other language. (II: 12, 332)

Such passages alternate, like the body's own rhythms, with others that one does not read. One leafs through the *Essays* with the same alternations of boredom and pleasure as Montaigne himself describes in his own reading. Why should the *Essays* be read any more attentively than the great literature which Montaigne himself treated so impiously, yet religiously? This is an impossible demand, it arises from the failure to distinguish the quite (different demands of the *texte de plaisir*, which is integrated with its culture and yields a comfortable reading, and the *texte de jouissance*, which challenges all the reader's presumptions, misvalues and tastes and his whole relation to language. The reader cannot hope to combine both experiences, demanding pleasure to confirm his identity and at the same time seeking joy, which requires that he risk it. Thus, as Montaigne sees, there cannot be any official approval of books; only a rivalry of pleasures, censored by the state or the Church. Such censure might unite those who seek pleasure in reading. But all this is quite apart from the joyful company of books.

The *Essays* stand, waiting for a reader, seemingly without defence, lacking in organisation, and open to anything the reader night make of them. Yet is that possible? Montaigne is no more foolish as a writer than as a man. For anyone who takes him in one sense, he knows there are others who will make of him something else. Reading, therefore, is like the rest of our public activities. It requires of us a certain capacity that needs to be independent enough that, however tempted, the author cannot shape it.[10] Indeed, he could only lose by making slav-ish readers, since what the author needs is readers who are capable of breaking with their own habits in order to appreciate how it is the author himself engaged in the same struggle. In this sense, the book, or any work of art, is an offering, inviting communion between the author and those who take his work upon themselves as readers, viewers and listeners, thereby embodying once again as incarnate thought. Therefore it is with our bodies that we acquire the enjoyment of reading and writing. Not the body of the physician or the grammarian's corpus, but the body as expression: The pleasure of the text is that moment when my body pursues its own ideas – for my body does not have the same idea I do.[11] The idea of the pleasure of texts is likely to seem scandalous to most readers. After all, since they have a right to pleasure, just as they have eyes, how is it possible that this pleasure escapes or is wasted upon them? Worse still, the idea is lost upon critics who cannot conceive of pleasure as anything but simple . It therefore fails both the adherents of rigour and the purveyors of platitudes:

> The pleasure of the text is not necessarily of a triumphant, heroic, muscular type. No need to throw out one's chest. My pleasure can very well take the form of a drift. *Drifting* occurs whenever I do *not respect the whole,* and whenever by dint of seeming driven about by language's illusions, seductions and intimida-tions, like a cork on the waves, I remain motionless, pivoting on the *intractable* bliss that binds me to the text (to the world). Drifting occurs whenever social language, the sociolect, fails *me* (as we say: *my* courage *fails me).* Thus another name for drifting would be: *the Intractable* – or perhaps even: Stupidity.[12]

So often we see Montaigne launch an essay only in order to launch himself upon it, floating pleasurably towards himself by destroying the totality of an ordered argument pronounced in the titles of the essay. The sense of an essay is allowed to emerge sensual, individuating its author (not personalising; hence the *Essays* are not strictly autobiographical) and the reader whose senses are open and suf-fused by the text which from time to time goes to his head like wine. These open-ings are simultaneously breaks with custom and tradition and dispose the reader to the recollection of his very own senses and intellect:

> Whenever I attempt to 'analyze' a text which has given me pleasure, it is not my 'subjectivity' I encounter but my 'individuality,' the given which makes my body separate from other bodies and appropriates its suffering or its pleasure: it is my body of bliss I encounter. And this body of bliss is also *my historical sub-ject;* for it is at the conclusion of a very complex process of biographical, his-torical, sociological, neurotic elements (education, social class, childhood configuration, etc.) that I control the contradictory interplay of (cultural)

pleasure and (non–cultural) bliss, and that I write myself as a subject at present out of place, arriving too soon or too late (this too designating neither regret, fault, nor bad luck, but mere calling for a *non-site*): anachronic subject, adrift.[13]

The life of the *Essays* lies in the joy of writing and the pleasure of reading – if by the latter is meant not honouring the dead letter of the text. But Montaigne could hardly have wished for his own book a fate that he never for a moment conceded to other books. As a reader, he treated all texts as essentially vulnerable to his own need to write, a need as imperative as any other in his body and for that very reason dependent upon the family of literary texts. Indeed, no humanist thinker would have thought his literary life possible in any other way. Thus Montaigne can speak of the *Essays* as his children, and if we attribute any efficacy to the pedagogical essays, as we ought to do, Montaigne's family of the mind is large, and happily would include ourselves as readers, provided we expend the effort that turns mere literary skill into those fortunate moments where its ordinary pleasures are troubled with its extraordinary joys.

So far, we have tried to show how writing and reading may properly be regarded as a bodily conduct. Since reading and writing, in so far as any author is concerned, are inseparable activities, we need to consider writing as a bodily art, aimed at and experiencing the same corporeal integration and suffused pleasure as reading. In this sense, the author, whether reading or writing, is a kind of physician, a body probing another body. Indeed, in all of the arts there is an underlying corporeal hermeneutic that is presupposed by criticism and to which it must he attuned:

> For the relationship established on this level (i.e., of sympathetic understanding) between author and critic is not a relationship between pure minds. It is rather between incarnate beings, and the particularities of their physical existence constitute not obstacles to understanding, but rather a complex of supplementary signs, a veritable language which must be deciphered and which enhances mutual comprehension. Thus for Starobinski, as much physician as critic, *there is a reading of bodies which is likened to the reading of* minds. It is not of the sonic nature, nor does it bring the intelligence to bear on the same area of human knowledge. But for the critic who practices it, this criticism provides for a reciprocating exchange between different types of learning which have, perhaps, different degrees of transparency.[14]

Thus Starobinski reads Montaigne quite differently from Barrière – who considers Montaigne's literary vocation an illness[15] – because Starobinski is sensitive to the movement of thought's body which is the active principle of Montaigne's writing and the real source of what others speak of as his baroque style:

'Every movement reveals us.' Whoever wants to discover Montaigne should take his advice and start by considering his movement. To read any page of the *Essays* is to engage, once we are in contact with its prodigiously active language, in a whole series of mental gestures which transmits to our bodies a feeling of suppleness and energy. What is most intimate about Montaigne reveals itself through this corporeal vitality which is so shamelessly communicative.[16]

Like other critics, Starobinski starts from Montaigne's confession of a sense of lack within himself. But he grasps immediately that this lack is transformed into a vigorous assertion of the joyful activity of writing. Sensing no stable point within himself, or in any man, Montaigne responds with a powerful confrontation of the world and himself, a process of vigorous self-inquiry, sure of its strength only in its continued exercise – yet none the less sure. It is only at first sight that the world and those around us look so solid while we ourselves feel so empty. Montaigne's self is charged with the energy he generates in rejecting the world's apparent solidity and in exposing the essential distraction of others round him. That is not to say that Montaigne responded with a sense of vertigo to the lack he felt in himself. Moreover, in turning inwards against the world, he did not sink into an abyss of self-analysis. Rather, he developed a method of continuous sallies against the world, against the actions and opinions of others through which, on each occasion, he grasped something more of himself. It is never his practice, however, to look into himself as into a mirror and to hold up what he sees there in order to discredit his fellow men. The strength of his judgement lies not in its capacity for aggrandisement, which is always compatible with emptiness, but in his persistent exploration of the uncertainty of his knowledge and judgement once he tests them against his experience:

> Now I find my opinions infinitely bold and constant in condemning my inadequacy. In truth, this too is a subject on which I exercise my judgment as much as on any other. The world always looks straight ahead; as for me, I turn my gaze inward, I fix it there and keep it busy. Everyone looks in front of him; as for me, I look inside of me; I have no business but with myself. Others always go elsewhere, if they stop to think about it; they always go forward:
>> No man tries to descend into himself;
>
> Persius
>
> as for me, I Roll about in myself. (II: 17, 499)

As Starobinski observes, we can see in this passage a double movement whereby Montaigne shifts from a purely visual response to the world's bustle, holding it *sub specie aeternitatis*, and then relinquishing his visual grasp in order to open up the movement of his whole body and soul, which simultaneously generates self study and is in turn shaped and pleasurably intensified by it. This is the source of the bodily joy of reading and writing and it pervades every aspect of Montaigne's prose. When he speaks of 'rolling about in himself', it is not with any connotation of listless and nerveless inactivity, hut a kind of animal play between the soul and the body, each in delight of the other. It is within this pleasurable fold of the mind and the senses that there opens up the space of reading and writing, as well as for conversation, the arts and crafts. For in these activities, our senses learn and are not dumb instruments (as in sheer, alienated labour). Sensory experience is shared by the artist s whole body and mind in such a way that intelligence and pleasure are inextricably suffused This is marvellously illustrated in Montaigne's aesthetic grasp of the mixture of visceral and intellectual delight[17] in a poem of Lucretius, describing Mars' forceful embrace of Venus, or the inextrricable relation between force and tenderness:

> [The Latin poets] needed no sharp and subtle play on words: their language is as full and copious with a natural and constant vigor. They are all epigram, not only the tail but the head, stomach, and feet. There is nothing forced, nothing dragging: the whole thing moves at the same pace. *Their whole contexture is manly; they are not concerned with pretty little flowers* [Seneca] . This is not a soft and merely inoffensive eloquence; it is sinewy and solid, and does not so much please as fill and ravish; and it ravishes the strongest minds most. (III: 5, 665)

Montaigne admired all speech that has not lost its roots in the body. In this regard, he was as much a connoisseur of the language of the streets as of the Latin poets:

> The speech I love is simple, natural speech, the same on paper as in the mouth: a speech succulent and sinewy, brief and compressed, not so much dainty and well combed as vehement and brusque:
>
> > The speech that strikes the mind will have the most taste.
>
> > (Epitaph of Lucan)
>
> rather difficult than boring, remote from affectation, irregular, disconnected and bold: each bit making a body in itself; not pedantic, not monkish, not lawyer-like, but rather soldierly. . . . (I: 26, 127)

Naturally, Montaigne's own prose is exemplary of what he admired in literary style. The critics have generally appealed to the canons of baroque art in their commentary upon Montaigne's language.[18] But it is necessary to tie Montaigne's literary style to his phenomenological observation of the corporeal conduct of reading and writing. Otherwise, we are merely glossing these practices with the borrowed metaphors of painting and architecture[19] It is the continuous interaction of intellect and feeling and, above all, the conviction that the bodily and emotional frame of thought provides a transitive and intersubjective basis of understanding, which is the driving force of the baroque style. Unless a writer can convey the process of his thought's conception, he is unlikely to have it take hold in another person in the same way he experienced it himself. Here Montaigne harks back to the Stoic criterion of truth and its doctrine of clearness, which results in preference for we may call 'palpable' or energetic style:

> The true mind-picture is a stirring of the soul, which reveals both what is taking place in the soul and the object which has caused this . . . The distinctive note of a true mind-picture is its 'clearness' (*enargeia*) . . . To this clearness the mind cannot but bow.[20]

This leads to a prose style in which there is an emphasis upon the way a thought comes to mind, impacting in loosely related distinct moments that nevertheless belong together over their course. The writing practices that compose this style are known as the 'curt period', and the 'loose period'.[21] They are marked by a characteristic brevity achieved by, as it were, coming to the point of the idea from the very beginning. There follows a second member which continues the imaginative truth of the first idea. The two are asymmetric and not linked by ordinary syntactic connectives. The movement in their style is not towards a logical accumulation; it achieves rather an imaginative intensification of the energy of thought turned to writing. At the same time, this writing seeks to turn back upon itself and to compact in order not to stray into abstraction thereby losing energy and perhaps losing its reader:

> For me, who ask only to become wiser, not more learned or eloquent, these logical and Aristotelian arrangements are not to the point: I want for good solid reasons to begin with the conclusion; I understand well enough what death and pleasure are; let him not waste his time anatomising them: I look for good solid reasons from the start, which will instruct me in how to sustain their attack. Neither grammatical subtleties nor an ingenious contexture of words and argumentations are any good for that: I want reasonings that drive their first attack into the stronghold of doubt: his languish around the plot. (II: 10, 301)[22]

The other side of this concentration of visceral force and movement displayed in Montaigne's language is the experience of its release, like a wave which carries away the body and at the same time suffuses all its senses. The two corporeal movements are interrelated, the alternation of each being horizontal to the other. so that Montaigne's sense of the age of time, broken by reverie, is incredibly heightened:

Life is a material and corporeal movement, an action which by its very essence is imperfect and irregular; I apply myself by serving it in its own way:

> We suffer each a self-made fate.
>
> Virgil (III): 9, 756

Moreover, as Starobinski remarks, it is necessary to distinguish the good and bad openings and closures between the mind and the body. There is a joyful plenitude in the interaction or the grasp of the knower and the known, between the writer and his language, which generates the pleasure of self-inquiry as a genuine mode of being-in-the-world. This is the highest point of metamorphosis between the self and the universal condition of man; it represents the ultimate goal of the *Essays*. But there is also a debilitating kind of fullness in which the mind is passively burdened with its bodily self, and invaded by objects that fill it without any vital response of its own, carrying it away from its own resolve, swimming in images, dreams and fantasies. The danger in this direction is that the self loses its identity, which is to say, its resolve to explore itself in the exploration of things and others in the world. We then become the slaves of things and machines which we use without being able to make use of ourselves. Our philosophical, scientific and literary culture dangerously fosters the separation of the mind from the body, making a problem and an argument of the connections that nevertheless remain in our experience. Of course, it is possible to question this tradition in terms of itself, to reject the divorce between our mind and body, and, rather, to cultivate their proper relation:

> The body has a great part in our being, it holds a high rank in it; so its structure and composition are well worth consideration. Those who want to split up our two principal parts and sequester them from each other are wrong. On the contrary, we must couple and join them together again . We must order the soul not to draw aside and entertain itself apart, not to scorn and abandon the body (nor can it do so except by some counterfeit monkey trick), but to rally the body, embrace it, cherish it, assist it, control it, advise it, set it right and bring it back when it goes astray; in short to marry it and be a husband to it, so that their actions may appear not different and contrary, but harmonious and uniform. (II: 17, 484–5)

Montaigne, then, could not separate in himself the 'supercelestial thoughts and subterranean conduct'. He saw no possibility of man even getting beyond himself. At the same time, he is not an idle subjectivist, sunk in fantasy or carried away by endless imaginary projects. Yet he knew himself to be among the most variable of spirits, most changeable in his moods, irresolute and without method in the discharge of his affairs. For all this, the *Essays* are not a series of vile confessions, even though they insist upon self-observation and inquiry. Rather, they 'rebound' from everything that oppresses the mind and the body, whether through the negation of positivity or an affirmation in place of negativity, ruled, of course, by Montaigne's experience with things and himself. The *Essays* do not play with dialectics: they are rooted in the carnal ambiguity of man's relation to himself, to his reason, his senses, his body and his language. In each case, man must avoid the pursuit of absolute distinctions, of complete certainty and clarity, since these belie his own mixed composition. In exchange for forgoing my transcendental flight or excess, there opens up to the essayist a mundane presence of the literary self to the embodied self, to which the essayist must faithfully apprentice himself. It is through writing that Montaigne comes to build up something like a model of himself in order to ground the otherwise wholly metaphorical enterprise of the self-portrait. It is only through writing that he can find a mirror yielding images of which the mirror itself is a compelling image, but quite inadequate to the body's own reflection.

The argument for conceiving reading and writing as bodily arts will not seem so strange if we revise our cognitivist assumptions governing the representational function of language itself.[23] Here we are not simply pointing to the physical basis of language as a series of sounds or verbal images, produced in accordance with the laws of association, or stimulus and response. On such theories, speech is not even at the level of conduct, and the speaker lacks a voice in his own talk. Indeed, in these terms there is no speech (*parole*); only language (*langue*), which at best animates puppets. But this is a condition that is actually experienced only under pathological conditions. Thus a patient who can readily say the word 'no' to the doctor, in order to express a denial in his present emotional experience, has trouble to find the word outside of such contexts. Other patients can assemble colours of the same shade only with great trouble, making all sorts of unaccountable errors, supposing we judge the activity according to their immediately prior associations. It is as though they were glued to the specific colour word but lacked entirely the category, say, blue, and thus have both to think and labour to furnish it, whereas ordinarily it involves a categorial operation and neither a concrete nor an idealist attitude. We do not name things after first recognising them; naming them *is* recognising them. That is why for a child naming a thing is knowing it, just as adults have to wait upon their own words to find out what they are thinking. This is, of course, true for the listener, though both he and the speaker experience this more when the speech is authentic, and not just chatter each has heard before. In reading and writing, we can for a good deal of the time rest upon conventional language for our understanding. But there also occur alterations of language, changes of conventional sense which oblige us to surrender to the flow of words, or to the new arrangements of sound and colour in music and art. Once this occurs, the reader/listener/viewer must surrender himself to a certain embodied style, or mode of being-in-the-world, until he has caught on to its existential meaning, that is to say, until he has altered his own vocabulary and sensibility enough to be able to express his experience – to mimic it, waiting awkwardly for a similar response, whereby he is assured of being a representative speaker:

> These considerations enable us to restore to the act of speaking its true *physiognomy* . . . The word and speech must somehow cease to be a way of designating things or thoughts and become the presence of that thought in the phenomenal world and, moreover, not its clothing but its token or its *body*. There must be as psychologists say, a 'linguistic concept' *(Sprachbegriffe)* or a word concept (*Wortbegriff*), a 'central inner experience, specifically verbal, thanks to which the sound, heard, uttered, read or written, becomes a linguistic poet.' The process of expression, when it is successful, does not merely leave for the reader and the writer himself a kind of reminder, it brings the meaning into existence as a thing at the very heart of the text, it brings it to life in an *organism of words,* establishing it in the writer or the reader as a new sense organ, opening a new field or a new dimension to our experience.[24]

Once we see speech and meaning as visceral events occurring between the reader/writer and the words, we are able to see that the body is essential to to the gesture of meaning and expression. We do not communicate with 'thoughts' or utterances from which we 'abstract' meaning, but with a speaking person, whose bodily gestures draw us into his world in order to complete their intention. We do not need to introspect in order to understand another person's anger. His anger is in his looks and in his words – rather, these are his anger and they flood me as much as him, inhabiting my body long before I clarify their sense within a definite cultural setting which is, so to speak, my second nature. This conception of language or gesture requires that we simultaneously revise our conception of the body. Language transfigures the body. Thus a woman becomes beautiful by being told that she is loved and another man's life may be ruined by an insult. This is only possible because our body acquires a surplus meaning beyond its biological bearing and an expressive significance that makes it the carrier of culture from the simplest level of perception and the highest levels of art and literary expression:

> What then does language express, if it does not express thoughts? It presents or rather it *is* the subject's taking up of a position in the world of his meanings. The term 'world' here is not a manner of speaking: it means that the 'mental' or cultural life borrows its structures from natural life and that the thinking subject must have its basis in the subject incarnate. The phonetic 'gesture'

brings about, both for the speaking subject and his hearers, a certain structural coordination of experience, a certain modulation of existence, exactly as a pattern of my bodily behavior endows the objects around me with a certain significance both for me and for others. The meaning of the gesture is not contained in it like some physical or physiological phenomenon. The meaning of the word is not contained in the word as a sound. But the human body is defined in terms of its property of appropriating, in an indefinite series of discontinuous acts, significant cores which transcend and transfigure its natural powers.... We must therefore recognize as an ultimate fact this open and indefinite power of giving significance – that is, of both apprehending and conveying a meaning by which man transcends himself towards a new form of behavior or words or other people, or towards his own thought through his body and his speech.[25]

Reading and writing, therefore, like talking and listening involve an intersensory capacity for communication, which arises not just from the expressive values of the worlds when joined with due respect for logic and syntax, but also from my bodily experience of the world, other persons and the language I inhabit. Ultimately, language, like culture, defeats any attempt to conceive it as a system capable of revealing the genesis of its own meaning. This is because we are the language we are talking about. That is to say, we are the material truth of language through our body, which is a natural language.[26] It is through our body that we can speak of the world, because the world, in turn, speaks to us through the body:

In my book the body lives in and moves through space and is the home of a full human personality. The words I write are adapted to express first one of its functions then another. In *Lestrygonians* the stomach dominates and the rhythm of the episode is that of the peristaltic movement. But the minds, the thoughts of the characters, I began. If they had no body they would have no mind, said Joyce. It's all one. Walking towards his lunch my hero, Leopold Bloom, thinks of his wife, and says to himself, 'Molly's legs are out of plumb.' At another time of day he might have expressed the same thought without any underthought of food. But I want the reader to understand always through suggestion rather than direct statement.[27]

We start by reading an author like Montaigne, leaning at first upon the common associations of his words, until, gradually, the words begin to flow in us, and to open us to an original sound, which is the voice of the *Essays*, borrowing from us a visceral understanding that until then we did not know was ours to offer. Yet it comes only from what we ourselves bring to the *Essays*, our knowledge of the language, of ourselves, and life's questions, which we share with

Montaigne. Once we have acquired the essayist's style of thinking, our lives interweave in a presence which is the anticipation of the whole of Montaigne's intention and its simultaneous recovery which continues our understanding of the *Essays*. Similarly, in talking and listening to one another, we make an accommodation through language and the body in which we grow old together. We encroach upon one another, borrowing from each other's time, words and looks that we are looking for in ourselves. In this way, our mind and self may be thought of as an institution which we inhabit with others in a system of presences, which includes Socrates or Montaigne just as much as our present friends:

> When I speak or understand, I experience that presence of others in myself or of myself in others which is the stumbling-block of the theory of intersubjectivity. I experience that presence of what is represented which is the stumbling-block of the theory of time, and I finally understand what is meant by Husserl's enigmatic statement, 'Transcendental subjectivity is intersubjectivity.' To the extent that what I say has meaning, I am a different 'other' for myself when I am speaking; and I understand, I no longer know who is speaking and who is listening.[28]

In the *Essays*, Montaigne discovered himself and others, in talking, listening, reading and writing. In writing he found that aesthetic distance between himself and the world through which he could speak about the world, and the world in turn could speak in him. His thoughts and purposes are embodied in gestures whose expression deliberately essays the structures of habit and spontaneity. Finally, expression, as we learn from the *Essays*, is always an act of self-improvisation in which we borrow from the world, from others, and from our own past efforts, towards a synthesis of authority and tradition, imitation and novelty.

CHAPTER 5

Reading and Temperament

Writers are readers. This is not because they have no thoughts of their own, but precisely because they seek a thought that is their own: or rather, thought that becomes their own through the conversation of minds to be found in reading. To be sure, Montaigne begins by leaning heavily on his predecessors. To the extent that this is so, he can hardly be said to have found his vocation as a writer. Yet there are few vocations that are truly born in a moment; though we indulge the practice of retrospectively finding their moment of inspiration. Or else, because of the madness of the inspired moment, we hide our creative sources in night, reducing them later to the routinised formulae of methodology, encouraging the daytime illusion of public and common access to art and science. Montaigne speaks casually of his decision to write. Having retired in order to settle his mind in the idleness of old age, and finding himself rather a thousand times further from himself due to the vagaries of his imagination, he decided to write them down in order to keep an inventory, rather like a household record which usually shames us with its proof of our extravagance and wastefulness (1: 8, 21). In this task it is natural that he should find the writings of historians and moral philosophers congenial; and he borrows heavily from their topics and examples. In fact, in the first two books of the *Essays*, as he says in a later comment that he inserts, he does little more than keep a register of deaths, out of fascination with how it is men conduct themselves in those last hours that await us all:

> And there is nothing that I investigate so eagerly as the death of men: what words, what look, what bearing they maintained at that time; nor is there a place in the histories that I note so attentively. This shows in the abundance of my illustrative examples; I have indeed a particular fondness for this subject.

> If I were a *maker of books*, I would make a *register*, with comments, of various deaths. He who would teach men to die would teach them to live. (I: 20, 62)

Montaigne begins to write under the sign of death. Had he remained under this sign, he might indeed have achieved little more than a registrar, the keeper of an inventory. But even in this observation, Montaigne remarks that he more easily assumes death as his sign when he is ill than when he is healthy. We have to wait for this rebellious thought to mature; with it there matures Montaigne, essayist and writer. Meantime, Montaigne cast himself into writing. For in essaying, as in reading, or in war, or in medicine, we cannot be sure of the outcome, and Fortune has as much to do with it as with the grace and beauty we attribute to poetry and the arts (I: 24, 93). Moreover, there remains the abiding problem that scholarship is not the same thing as wisdom which may be found in quite unlearned persons, without any aspiration to philosophy or literature. By the time of the essay 'Of Pedantry', not halfway through Book One, Montaigne sees that the problem for the writer and essayist is to avoid those habits that put to sleep a genuinely inquiring mind.[1] But this means that he is also treading the path of rejecting the Stoic separation of the mind and the body. For it is perfectly possible to starve the mind by stuffing it with knowledge it has no way of making its own. The mind's alliance with the body is essential to its life. The *Essays* begin to assume their incarnate character, and we are introduced to Montaigne's characteristically visceral prose:

> I know a man who, when I ask him what he knows, asks me for a book in order to point it out to me, and wouldn't dare tell me that he has an itchy backside unless he goes immediately and studies in his lexicon what is itchy and what is a backside. We take the opinions and the knowledge of others into our keeping and that is all. We must make them our own. We are just like a man who, needing fire, should go and fetch some at his neighbor's house, and, having found a fine big fire there, should stop there and warm himself, forgetting to carry any back home. What good does it do us to have our belly full of meat if it is not digested, if it is not transformed into us, if it does not make us bigger and stronger? (I: 25, 100–1)

Montaigne is the enemy of all forms of pedantry and of any education system based upon it. The purpose of knowledge is not to separate our souls from our bodies, or to set learned men above ignorant men. Life gives the lie to all these distinctions. Book learning is no substitute for common sense and no philosophy will stop a running nose. Proper learning consists in the harmonious integration of good intellectual, moral and physical judgement: 'Now we must not attach learning to the mind, we must incorporate it; we must not sprinkle but dye' (1:

25, 103). Thus we are to judge a man's writing and reading habits according to the judgement he exercises in them, and not by his ability to run through books or to fill the page with fine quotations. Properly speaking, reading and writing are corporeal arts, moral integrations of the mind and the body, of diligence, perseverance, intelligence and energy. For this reason, Montaigne can only evaluate his own literary practices in terms of visceral metaphors, whose purpose is not simply to disparage himself, but precisely to essay the corporeal conduct of reading and writing:

> As for the natural faculties that are in me, of which this book is the essay, I feel them bending under the load. My conceptions and my judgment move only by groping, staggering, stumbling and blundering; and when I have gone ahead as far as I can still, I am not at all satisfied: I can still see country ahead, but with a dim and clouded vision, so that I cannot clearly distinguish it. And when I undertake to speak indiscriminately of everything that comes to my fancy without using any but my own natural resources, if I happen, as I often do to come across in the good authors those same subjects I have attempted to treat – as in Plutarch I have just this very moment come across his discourse on the power of imagination – seeing myself so weak and puny, so heavy and sluggish, in comparison with those men, I hold myself in pity and disdain. (I: 26, 107)

Reading and writing are like athletic contests;[2] they involve a struggle with ourselves and others. One can only dismiss these bodily metaphors in respect of reading and writing through an idealist prejudice in view of which knowledge appears to he a wholly spiritual practice. Montaigne does not separate what our living shows us to be inseparable. Rather, he essays in himself the encroachments and overlaps of the mind and body in order to strengthen reading and writing as natural talents, that is, as exercises of sound judgement and sense. The very notion of metaphor, in fact, indicates a fundamental experience of transference of an overlap, such as we experience in speaking of feeling burdened, or lighthearted. Montaigne's visceral metaphors are no more metaphorical than the realist's metaphor of the senses receiving impressions like wax from a seal or the idealist's metaphor of the body as a prison for the soul. Philosophical writing cannot escape these metaphorical constructions, any more than the rest of our conversation:

> language never is its own meaning, and is therefore always symbolic or metaphorical, but when this fact is as yet undiscovered by the user of language we say that he is using it 'metaphorically,' and when he realizes that words are mere symbols and distinguishes what they are from what they mean, then by facing and accepting the metaphorical character of all language he has overcome it and is henceforth using language 'literally'.[3]

Therefore we cannot dismiss Montaigne's visceral prose as a merely stylistic affect. It has a definite phenomenological function of returning thought to the level of feeling and in turn of reflecting feeling to the level of thought, thereby essaying the consubstantial relations between our mind and our body, between our life and our speech. In reading and in writing we make ourselves the crossroads between our own lives and the life of someone else Plutarch, Seneca, Virgil. We need to collect ourselves for these engagements as much as when we present ourselves to live company and conversation. In the act of reading we place another person's voice in the centre of our lives, displacing our own consciousness to the background, in order to share meaning and to dislodge our immediate preoccupations. This displacement from the level of self-consciousness towards the intersubjective world of reading and writing is effected through a verbal *mimesis*[4] of the authors (we speak of the author as reader and writer) emotions, images and sensuous life, which is simultaneously metamorphosed into the reflective operation of language.[5] At this level, the author is faced with the option of choosing language and symbolism that retain the complicity of consciousness and embodiment – thus we speak of Montaigne's visceral prose or what he himself calls 'essays in flesh and bone' – or else the writer chooses a language that entirely dissociates thought and body.

These considerations may he developed somewhat further if we consider Pierre Barrière's schematisation of the *Essays* in terms of the temperamental or bodily themes of retirement, suicide and diversion.[6] Barrière's reading of Montaigne stands in sharp contrast to Starobinski's approach, which we considered in Chapter 4. Barrière tries to explain the reading and writing practices of the *Essays* in terms of Montaigne's bodily experience, but in order to fault these activities entirely rather than to find in embodiment their essential ground. He finds in the *Essays* only the activity of an unhealthy retiring mind, given to the substitute satisfactions of reading and writing a popular view of things, though hardly true of Montaigne. The obsession with self-observation begins, according to Barrière, with Montaigne's sense of lacking any other worldly achievement worthy of memorialising. Without either an illustrious political or military career behind him, Montaigne entered old age with nothing but himself to write about. Given this artificial disposition, the practice of the *Essays* could serve only to imprison him in his sickly self-observation:

> And if no one reads me, have I wasted my time, entertaining myself for so many hours with such useful and agreeable thoughts? In modeling this figure upon myself, I have had to fashion and compose myself so often to bring myself out, that the model itself has to some extent grown firm and taken shape. Painting myself for others, I have painted my inward self with colors clearer than my

original ones. I have no more made my book than my book has made me – a book consubstantial with its author, concerned with my own self, an integral part of may life; not concerned with some third hand, extraneous purpose, like all other books. (Have I wasted my time by taking stock of myself so continually, so carefully? For those who go over themselves only in their minds and occasionally in speech do not penetrate to essentials in their examination as does a man who makes that his study, his work, and his trade, who binds himself to keep an enduring account, with all his faith, with all his strength.) (II: 18, 504)

Barrière quotes this passage, apart from the last two sentences that I have put in brackets in order to prove his thesis that the *Essays* are the work of a feeble, inconstant soul in need of an external support. Here, and elsewhere, as we shall see, Barrière only introduces his temperamental hypothesis in order to subvert the plain sense of Montaigne's argument. Barrière pays no attention to Montaigne's discovery that retirement, so far from leaving him in peace, left him prey to all the wanderings of his imagination, so that he was less at home with himself than he had been in public life. Montaigne therefore resolved to bring order into his soul through the strenuous activity of writing down his experience something which, as he observes, is far more demanding than idle reflection or self-centred conversation. It is hardly an exercise for the languishing creature Barrière has in mind. Nor could he account for the kind of young man whom Montaigne hoped to foster through his educational theory. Young men are to be taught to wrestle with the best minds in order to exercise their own natural judgement. They are not to be stuffed with other people's ideas so that all they can do is spew them back completely undigested. That is how weak and passive minds are created by pedants:

> The bees plunder the flowers here and there, but afterward they make of them honey, which is all theirs; it is no longer thyme or marjoram. Even so with the pieces borrowed from others; he will transform and blend them to make a work that is all his own, to wit, his judgment. His education, work, and study aim only at forming this. (I: 26, 111)

Above all, Montaigne argued against the injuries of using knowledge to break a student's will, to make him cunning in the anticipation of defeat, or else servile and unopinionated in order to conform with the rest. That is why Montaigne recommends the study of history, in order that a student may learn to become a sound judge of men and thereby capable of entering into the give and take not only of his own society, but of the world, he insists that knowledge need not wear a sad face, that virtue is a pleasure rather than a pain to practice, and that anything a man knows well can be said simply enough that anyone can understand it:

> To return to my subject, there is nothing like arousing appetite and affection; otherwise all you make out of them is asses loaded with books. By dint of whipping, they are given their pocketful of learning for safekeeping; but if learning is to do us any good, we must not merely lodge it within us, we must espouse it. (I: 26, 131)

What is healthy in Montaigne is that he preserves his self-love even while showing us all the reasons why he might be unlovable – as Pascal and Rousseau jealously concluded. Fortunately, he started with a certain amount of self-love which, as he tells us, he owed in part to his father's moderate way of raising him and to his position in life. Yet he was not entirely a rentier in this. He had put himself to life's tests in war and politics often enough and had acquitted himself well enough in the eyes of his king and townsmen to be able to look upon himself without fear of returning sheer narcissism. Moreover, the self-portrait to be drawn in the *Essays* would require from him – as it did from Rembrandt – the patience and probity of the rest of his life:

> Death mingles and fuses with our life throughout. Decline anticipates death's hour and intrudes even into the course of our progress. I have portraits of myself at twenty-five and thirty-five; I compare them with the one of the present: how irrevocably it is no longer myself. How much further is my present picture from them than from that of my death! We abuse Nature too much by pestering her so far that she is constrained to leave us and abandon our guidance – our eyes, our teeth, our legs, and the rest - to the mercy of foreign assistance that we have begged, and to resign us to the hands of art, weary of following us. (II: 13, 846)

Despite this, Barrière considers that the *Essays* are the work of 'a wretched fellow devoured by fears and attached to material well being.' Montaigne sought his comfort everywhere, being hateful of violence and fanaticism and, above all, afraid of death. We are then treated to another of those incredible schematisations of the *Essays*, which we reproduce here, to show how critical language is collapsed and how it cannot possibly animate the reading or writing that would be exemplary of a critical essaying of Montaigne. The schema offered by Barrière, and which we translate, goes as follows:

Book I: Retreat – Montaigne abandons the world and retires to his château in the hope of finding peace there, free from all his worries, material and otherwise.

I (a) Commentaries and anecdotes about war:
Chs.5, 6, 7–9, 10, 11, 13, 15, 16, 17, 18.
(b) Moral reflections suggested by these commentaries:
Chs.4, 8, 12, 14 (interspersed between the commentaries).
II The intellectual attitude to be adopted in confronting events:
(a) Attitude towards death and pain: Chs.19, 20, 21.
(b) Political attitude (conservatism): Chs.23, 24. Justification of a life
devoted to study: Chs.25, 26.
(c) Attitude towards religion: Ch.27. Remembrance of La Boètie who
inspired the preceding development: Chs.28, 29).
(d) Series of reflections on religion, death, custom, representing the
arguments set out in (a), (b), (c), and resulting in the idea of the contradictory nature of human sentiments: Chs.30–8.
Justification of Montaigne's retreat: Chs.39–42. (Series of Chapters
that are isolated, or else difficult to explain, reading notes, etc.:
Chs.43–8,
III On the uncertainty of our judgment: Chs.49–55.
IV Conclusion: Of Prayers, Of Age: Chs.56, 57.

Book II: Suicide – Montaigne did not find the relief he was looking for in
retirement: he hardly sees any other solution but suicide, and yet that is repug-
nant to his temperament. The composition is less dogmatic than in Book I: in
the latter, Montaigne had exhausted the three or four great theoretical topics
that absorbed him. Henceforth, he follows theory with a practical study in a
sort of journal or memoir; in general the chapters follow from an association of
ideas or from immediate events; the unity is provided by the inquiry into suicide begun in chapters 3–6, 13, 29, 35, 37.

I Series of examinations of conscience.
(a) Conditions of judgment, the question of suicide Chs.1–6. Montaigne's attachment to his book which allows him to study himself
Ch.8.
(b) Science and faith: only faith can preserve us from fear of death and
pain Chs.10–14.
II (a) Justification of virtue as Montaigne sees it, a virtue without Stoic
effort, hence without need of suicide Chs.15–18.
(b) Political philosophy: can the Edict of Tolerance by improving the
situation dispense Montaigne from suicide Chs.9–24.
(c) Endurance in the face of death and torture and then of suicide
Chs.28–37.

Book III: Diversion – This book is written after Montaigne's return to active life. In travel and his mayoralty of Bordeaux he found the calm he had vainly sought in retreat which had left him too much up against himself.

I   Account of his existence during the years of his active life
Chs.1–3. Result of this interruption, diversion Chs.4–5.

II   Intellectual experiences during this period Chs.7–8.

III Travel as a source of diversion Ch.9.

IV   One should not create 'obstacles' for oneself Chs.10–12.

V   Conclusion: Of experience, which alone can teach us to live and to judge systems.[7]

The exaggeration and distortions in Barrière's account of the *Essays* are astounding. In place of the charming serenity and gentle persuasiveness of Montaigne's childhood and education, we are presented with a sickly, self-centred child, ministered to by teachers, servants and villagers. Although Barrière is aware that from these surroundings Montaigne acquired a generous and critical spirit, with a fine respect for common sense and plain talk, he never questions his overall schema for Book One. He considers that Montaigne's education did nothing but aggravate a sickly and fearful disposition, which in Book Two obsesses him with thoughts of suicide! Now it is quite true that Montaigne is concerned with death, as we have already observed. More precisely, and with some reminder of Camus,[8] he is concerned with the truth of philosophical suicide and in the first two books of the *Essays* he surely reads and writes in order to test this recommendation in terms of the historical record and his own bodily experience. So far from fearing death, Montaigne sought to accustom himself to its inevitability, like illness and old age, as we shall see in the following chapter. By this, of course, he did not mean to instil in himself either forgetfulness or a dumb passivity. Book Three is, surely, the greatest testament to Montaigne's resolute essaying of these experiences, and hardly anywhere has writing been so proportionate to them, as we have tried to show.

But even in the places (II: 16, 1–6) Barrière trusts for his thesis, Montaigne's attachment to life is evident, and he sees no point in worrying about death, or war, unless we first know how to enjoy life and repose (II: 3. 254–5). At times, Montaigne seems to settle for the complete unimportance, the essential nullity of death. At other times, he is taken by such noble deaths as those of Cato the Younger and of Socrates. In the end, Cato's death repels him because he finds Cato's single-mindedness fanatical, while considering the death of Socrates nearer to us upon observing his sensual delight in scratching himself when released from chains. Even in his own ease, when suffering dreadfully from the kidney stone,[9] Montaigne did not lie languishing in the fear of death. Just as he lacks any positive notion of the embodiment of reading and writing, Barrière also fails to understand Montaigne's reaction to that indescribable pain which has united all sufferers from the kidney stone into a veritable fraternity. Yet the anguish of the stone could not put Montaigne even 'half in love with easeful death', which we might surely have expected from Barrière's thesis. Rather, Montaigne clings to life and writes against the pain:

> I am at grips with the worst of all maladies, the most sudden, the most painful, the most mortal and the most irremediable. I have already experienced five or six very long and painful bouts of it. However, either I flatter myself or else there is even in this condition enough to bear up a man whose soul is unburdened of the fear of death and unburdened of the threats, sentences, and consequences which medicine dins into our ears. But the very impact of the pain has not such sharp and piercing bitterness as to drive a well-poised man to madness or to despair. I have at least this profit from the stone, that it will complete what I have still not been able to accomplish in myself and reconcile and familiarize me completely with death: for the more my illness oppresses and bothers me, the less will death be something for me to fear. I had already accomplished this: to *hold to life only by life alone*. My illness will undo ever this bond; and God grant that in the end, if its sharpness comes to surpass my powers, it may not throw me back to the other extreme, which is no less a vice, of loving and desiring to die.

> Fear not the final clay nor wish for it.
>
> Martial

> Those are two passions to fear, but one has its remedy much more ready than the other. (II: 37, 576)

If Montaigne's familiarity with pain could not separate him from life, the importunings of philosophy were even less likely to go far with him. Montaigne enjoyed life. Indeed, he considered it a positive duty to appreciate the pleasures of bodily and sensuous life, and not to disdain them in the vain ambition of setting ourselves above our incarnate being. We cannot get outside of ourselves, whatever the tricks of philosophy; and philosophers are wrong not to see that we must cry out in pain, without this necessarily meaning that we are cowards at heart, or weak in spirit. Of course, it would be fine if the soul could move the body as philosophers say it should, and as, indeed, it sometimes seems to do: 'Oh, why have I not the faculty of that dreamer in Cicero who, dreaming he was embracing a wench, found that he had discharged his stone in the sheets! Mine extraordinarily diswench me' (II: 37, 577). Barrière, at any rate, is not moved by such examples. He remains convinced that Montaigne is a monster of egoism – not from any narrowness of spirit, but from his fear of action and a profound incapacity to assume any responsibility. According to this thesis, Montaigne's education only exacerbated his 'lymphatic and imaginative temperament', driving him to conjure up fearful chimeras which exhausted him physically and morally. In fact, Barrière believes that Montaigne's approval of theatre, and his part in it, as a child is evidence of his lack of personality, a sign of a disarticulated mind. This is an astounding misconception of the therapeutic functions of the theatre itself and of its associated metaphors when applied to social life in respect of the problem of appearance and authenticity.[10]

Here it is useful, in view of other comparisons we have drawn between Montaigne and Petrarch, to consider some features of Petrarch's melancholy, or *accidia*, a spiritual disease which seems to have become a major trope of Western philosophical and literary consciousness; and is hardly to be understood as a matter of personal temperament in the way that Barrière would argue. Montaigne's moods belong to this long literary tradition, and to ignore this is a serious flaw in any argument on the relation between embodiment and literary experience.

Melancholy had for centuries been identified as an evil of the monastery, depriving the monk of his joy in life, to the point of disgust and despair. *Acedia*, as it was called, came to be identified with the Christian sin of negligence or spiritual sloth. Gregory the Great joined *acedia* to the wider notion of the sin of *tristitia*, the vice of not loving God's creation as it deserves. From the thirteenth century on, the spread of popular religious instruction led to a simplification of the categories of religious psychology and a standard schematisation of numerous faults under the capital, or deadly sins, among which numbered *acedia*. It denoted sorrow, weariness and spiritual negligence, from missing Sunday mass to despair at one's salvation. Petrarch's melancholy (*accidia*) is related to the deadly sins of *acedia* or *tristitia*, but also to the Stoic notion of *aegritudo*, the sorrow or distress that is one of the four principal passions of the soul. The characteristic symptoms of *accidia* – grief, tedium, disgust and hatred of life, joylessness and despair – are part of the deadly sin of *acedia*. But there is a major shift in Petrarch's observation of his own secret delight in his sufferings. Moreover, his suffering was not motivated so much by his sense of failure to integrate his religious life as by his struggle to integrate the purely personal divisions (*dissidio*) he discovered in himself as inseparable from the very sense of himself. And in this he is the precursor of Montaigne, who similarly eschews any theological versions of his own unhappy consciousness.

Montaigne struggled to hold the middle ground between intellectual ecstasy and its melancholic reversal. It is interesting in this regard, especially in view of Montaigne's own stand on Socrates, to consider Marsilio Ficino's analysis of

Socratic melancholy. Fucino attempted to reconcile the melancholy which Aristotle considered to characterise an intellectual genius such as Socrates with Plato's divine frenzy.[11] In Ficino's system the poet-philosopher can be alienated either up or down the scale of intellect, reason, opinion and nature. At the lowest level, the *furor poeticus* (an ascent) can be a *furor melancholicus* (a descent). At the highest level, the furor of love can draw the poet-philosopher up to beauty, or else it may cast him down from it. Only divine love can unify the soul. Ficino believed that the Socratic melancholy involved only bodily alienation but not a separation from divine tranquillity.[12] Montaigne, as we know, cared nothing for the Platonist side of Socrates, and only considered him an ideal person to the extent that he could see the ordinary side of Socrates unsublimated by his wisdom, it should be observed that Montaigne's view of Socrates owes very little to Plato, whose influence he largely avoided. In addition to Plutarch's *Moralia*,[13] Xenophon's *Memorabilia* is the source for Montaigne's interpretation of the Socratic 'know thyself'. In Plato's *Phaedrus* the Delphic injunctionn is taken to mean that we ought not to concern ourselves with matters beyond us while we remain ignorant about ourselves. In Xenophon, the saying is interpreted to emphasise the intrinsic uselessness of knowledge except as an awareness of one's limitations in order better to live by them.[14] This view might at times encourage despondency or melancholy, but on the whole it seems to have represented a healthy stance well turned towards life.

Montaigne shared Petrarch's desire to join fine philosophy with eloquence. Neither wished to see wisdom incapable of moving men or men moved merely by empty speech. Eloquence cannot be satisfied with mere elegance; it must also work in the service of moral education:

> How much eloquence can accomplish in the shaping of human life is known both from reading in many authors and from the experience of everyday life. How great is the number of those we recognize in our own day, to whom even examples of virtue were of no help, who have been aroused and turned suddenly from a most wicked manner of life to a perfectly ordered one simply by the sound of others' voices.[15]

Of course, both Petrarch and Montaigne were averse to rhetoric out of place. Yet this did not mean that they despised rhetoric, so much as they were opposed to its scholastic abuse, especially by physicians, whose proper business was the cure of bodies rather than souls. Here, too, a misunderstandling needs to be avoided. They did not deny the psychosomatic unity of man. Rather, they insisted that moral philosophy can only integrate man's reason with his will to moral action provided it is in alliance with the virtues of an embodied eloquence. Whereas Petrarch was worried by Augustinian reservations upon the finitude of human speech in respect of sublime considerations which properly remove us to silence, Montaigne struggled with the public and private needs of honest speech. They both relied upon such a variety of literary sources that it is easy work to assemble the contradictions in their work.[16] But this is a superficial effect that arises within the field of a more persistent search in which the use of rhetorical principles obliged each author to exemplify the contradictions that inhabit our lives to pose the problem of consistency. Petrarch observed in himself a multiplicity of lives, just as Montaigne recorded the mutability of man's passions and his own moods:

> Let those who are called *physici* enquire with what contrary humors the body boils and is disturbed. But let each man ask only himself about the diverse and adverse influences by which the soul struggles with itself, and let each one respond how it is partly carried hither, partly thither by such varying and reversible impulses of the mind: never whole never one, differing with itself, pulling itself to pieces.

The same method suggested the study of historical examples of the constant struggle to achieve virtue. In these examples, Petrarch and Montaigne were agreed that the path to true self-knowledge is to be found in men who have acted with a consciousness of their mortality. Perhaps Petrarch struggled more than Montaigne with the reconciliation of the pagan and Christian sources of this *cogitatio mortis*. In Petrarch this struggle arises from the temptation to set the ideal Christian life above man's ordinary condition, to which at times the lowly ambitions of rhetoric seemed more appropriate. But in this Petrarch is equally close to Montaigne, although he does not start from the same sense of divine conflict as Petrarch. Neither could accept the stringency of the Stoic ideal of perfect consistency. They therefore settled for a love of virtue in the midst of life's distractions, and among other goods, those of the body, of friends, and above all, of literature.

Barrière considers that his hypothesis regarding Montaigne's lymphatic nature justifies a comparison between Montaigne and Rousseau. He writes as follows:

> Perhaps it would not be arbitrary at his point to draw a comparison between Montaigne and Rousseau. The abnormal upbringing that each of them had as a child made them incapable of living in the real world. The difference is that in one case, this initial vice turned into a mocking and disturbed scenticism; in the other case, it turned into a shrill indignation. But in both cases we have the same torment and the same indecision. Both of them created an existence for themselves beyond their actual condition, dreaming what they were unable to live: one writes the *Essais*, the other *Nouvelle Héloïse* and the *Confessions*. This analogy was vaguely perceived in the eighteenth century by those who

were equally infatuated by Montaigne and Rousseau. One can say that in this period their influence, if not equal, was at least on the same order in the formation of Romanticism. Both of them taught we should follow the capricious drives of an undisciplined personality and that we should withdraw our sensibility from the control of intelligence and reason.[17]

Although we cannot examine this comparison between Montaigne Rousseau in any detail, it surely comes to mind, though perhaps not in the way that Barrière introduces it. It is necessary a take the argument in two stages; it is offered both as a theory of reading and a theory of writing. Since our own argument is that reading and writing are bodily conducts, we must deal with Barrière view that reading and writing are essentially the activities of sickly persons, such as Montaigne and Rousseau. Barrière asks why Montaigne read, and proposes to base his answer upon Montaigne's own indications (he prefers to draw from essays 1, 26, 'Of the Education of Children', and III, 3, 'Of Three Kinds of Association', rather than the more obvious essay II, 10, 'Of Books'. Montaigne, then, read in order to take from others what he had not the inclination to produce for himself. But reading excited his mind with the pleasure of the finds that a reader can make that are not necessarily there in so many words, but which the author leaves there for an alert reader. The pleasure of these exchanges between a reader and the text is like the pleasure of such discoveries in travel or in conversation. But Barrière believes, despite Montaigne's deliberate insistence upon the active, sensuous and physical experience of reading, that Montaigne's taste for books derived only from the need to avoid the pain of being overwhelmed by his sickly imagination. Montaigne read as a substitute for the pleasurable company of ladies and good conversation. But he never, according to Barrière, developed any 'dialectical method' in his reading. He remained essentially a passive, imitative reader for whom even the solitary pleasure of books eventually paled:

> Finally, just as he was a solitary figure against his will, Montaigne was a reader: a book worm despite himself, without making standpoint of his own. It is clear that these spiritual memoirs of his cut a frail figure against the military memoirs of his contemporaries. It is always Montaigne Quixote who dreams of action while Montaigne Pancha shuts himself up in books.[18]

Here, as elsewhere, Barrière cites the essay 'Of the Three Kinds of Association'. But he does so in a fashion contrary to anything one would ordinarily read into it, even when one is agreed upon explicating the corporeal infrastructure of Montaigne's thought. Montaigne opens with the observation that it is unhealthy to attach ourselves to a single humour, or to persist in a single track until we are incapable of change. It is for this reason that we compared his experience of melancholy with that of Petrarch. It is alien to the variety that life requires if we allow ourselves to sink into a mere existence that we drag out like slaves. Montaigne admired most a man capable of doing many things so well that one could easily believe he was solely a specialist in any of the activities in which one happened to find him engaged. But there are few such men. Most men are either jack of all trades and master of none, or else narrow-minded and deformed specialists. In studying, reading and writing we must struggle to avoid these extremities. We have little chance of doing so, however, unless we know ourselves well. We must therefore be aware of our particular strengths and weaknesses:

> Life is an uneven, irregular, and multiform movement. We are not friends to ourselves, and still less masters, we are slaves, if we follow ourselves incessantly, and are so caught in our inclinations that we cannot depart from them or twist them about. I say this now because I cannot easily shake off the importunity of my soul, which cannot ordinarily apply itself unless it becomes wrapped up in a thing, or be employed unless with tension and with its whole being. However trivial a subject you give it, it is prone to enlarge and stretch it to the point where it must work on it with all its strength. For that reason its idleness is a painful occupation for me, and bad for my health. Most minds need foreign matter to arouse and exercise their them: mine needs it rather to settle down and *rest – the vices of idleness must be shaken off by occupation* (Seneca); for its principal and most laborious study is studying itself. (Ill: 3, 621)

Now this is the passage upon which Barrière bases so much of his argument for Montaigne's passive and essentially distracted approach to reading. Yet what Montaigne is saying is that, like anyone else, he can leaf through books, allowing his mind to wander or, worse still, to be filled with another person's thought. At other times, he has nothing but a practical interest in what he reads, and turns from book to book to find an author who has a special knowledge in the things that interest him at the moment. He is even tempted merely to collect books, lining the walls with them, but not cultivating his mind with them. Having confessed so much, he nevertheless insists that all such practices are painful to his essential disposition, which is to get to the bottom of things – not to stuff himself with learning, but to enjoy the pleasures of exercising his judgement and taste, having chosen the hardest of all studies in choosing self-study. For this has nothing to do with day-dreaming and could not possibly be undertaken by anyone sunk in melancholic reveries:

> Meditation is a powerful and full study for anyone who knows how to examine and exercise himself vigorously: I would rather fashion my mind then furnish it. There is no occupation that is either weaker or stronger, according to the

mind involved, than entertaining one's own thoughts. The greatest minds make in their profession, *to whom living is thinking* (Cicero). (III: 3. 621–2)

Here Montaigne's reflections are in accordance with the experience of all great thought. It is a common misunderstanding that the mind operates in some fashion different from the body.[19] But, in fact, even the active life of the body is inseparable from intelligence which itself is not excercised simply by closing one's eyes. It is false to our experience to separate entirely our mind and body. The theorists of disembodied mind oblige us to discount our moods and humours, which as often as not foster our intelligence and are essential to its life. It is because our lived experience once comes to us in a constant metamorphosis of mind and feeling that we are obliged to pace our work. We begin by getting ready for the start, often with a struggle, or else we jump in, in either case looking for that point where we strike our pace, finding it pleasurable, calling forth our very best efforts until we begin to tire and seek release from it. Within this overall structure, we have all sorts of bodily habits and practices whereby we attune ourselves and organise our materials, so that in the mutual transformation of each there results 'our work' in reading, in writing, or in any other occupation. It is only because we are obsessed with purely logical versions of scientific method that we fail to observe the necessary bodily exchanges involved with intellectual effort. We speak of them as 'breaks' as though they were outside of the work, necessities, or even as illicit pleasures that compromise the intelligence. Montaigne saw things more clearly. There is a healthy regime of the mind no less than of the body and, in fact, the two are inseparable. An inquiring mind will be just as active as a healthy body in the pursuit of its interests. Thus Montaigne found it necessary to build his library not simply to hold books, but to accommodate the needs of incarnate inquiry, allowing him to pace around in the course of his work: 'Every place of retirement requires a place to walk. My thoughts fall asleep if I make them sit down. My mind will not budge unless my legs move it. Those who study without a book are all in the same boat' (III: 3, 619).

So far from being distracted in his use of books, Montaigne insists that the pleasure of reading is not to be achieved unless we exercise ourselves towards a healthy integration of our spiritual and physical well being. Thus we cannot passively suck off books, swallowing their contents undigested. In this way we abuse both the text and ourself. Thus, in the essay 'Of Books' – which Barrière ignores – we have to understand Montaigne's remarks about his own reading habits as critical only of those who use books to stuff themselves with borrowed learning. His own reading practices are ruled by the need to find occasions that spark his capacity for judgement in human affairs.[20] After first leaning on the text, once he sees an opening into his own experience, he is under way, reading and writing interchangeably, shaping himself and the *Essays*. Then he is quite unafraid to evaluate the historians, poets and philosophers he so dearly loves, and, in doing so, to revise and deepen the opinions he holds of them. This is because Montaigne understands that all writing calls for a reader who must know what it is he wishes to become through his reading. It is a fiction of the manipulative arts that we can use things without being used by them. The artist, and, indeed, any experienced craftsman, knows better. We fashion ourselves in the use we make of things; our instruments borrow – from our lives and so we rightly return to them again and again, reworking and revising them in the light of our lives. Thus a reader cannot be a sheer skimmer. Rather, he will never read the same book twice, though in any rereading he will turn here rather than there for the places where he and the text can take hold.

For these ideas Montaigne is beholden to Seneca, as is well known.[21] His borrowings are extensive yet subtly transformed in response to Seneca's very teaching on the use of books. The sum of this advice is that books are the soul's food, if only we know how to take from them. If we read without attention, then books go through us like an undigested meal. On the other hand, we should soon find ourselves clogged by trying to absorb everything from books. We must know how to pick them over and to chew upon what interests in them until we have made it our own, to serve our own living. Montaigne does not hide his dependence on books. He can be quite hard on himself in this regard. But that is precisely why we need to keep such self-criticism in the larger framework of his educational views on the development of independent reading habits. We must not overlook his own practices as he grew more confident as a reader/writer of the *Essays*.

Thus he came to see that culture is lively in us in so far as we make it our own, not ornamentally, or in order to impress others, but by using it is as an ingrained resource for the practice of self-observation and discovery.[22] Clearly, the *Essays* are not a dull copybook of the sayings of ancient authors. By the standards of their day, and even more so today, they are a brilliant achievement of considered knowledge, bend upon making itself available in the most humane and reasonable fashion.[23] The *Essays* introduce us to a company of minds, to an art of conversation that is sociable and plain, imposing no hierarchy of principle, requiring no hierarchy of concepts. At the same time, the *Essays* are not easily read. We must learn their company in order to delight in it. Montaigne requires one who is already a lively reader in the literature through which he makes his own way. Otherwise it is not possible to measure the extent of the course of Montaigne's sallies in turning a classical author this or that way in the course of taking his own thought on the wing. Ideally, Montaigne's readers must rival him in judgement and taste. Unless we do this, the *Essays* will look like one of those dead weights from the past to which we feel an obligation but no affection. This is the passive view of tradition and culture in which so many of us are schooled. Irritated by it, we nevertheless have nothing to put in its place, except thin fabrication of vicarious experience that we consider more relevant to us because it is attuned to the emptiness in living. Such culture is, in fact, all the more authoritarian (and in a positive symbiosis with subjectivism) than authority of tradition which, properly understood, is the authority we find in ourselves as speakers, writers, readers and thinkers related to a community of minds in which we are resolved to have a voice.[24] In this sense, the man of tradition (not the traditionalist, who may be very up to date) is not the slave of the past, unable to *face* the present or the future. He is not defeated by the achievements of all those who have gone before him; nor is he jealous of them and soon destructive of what he praises.

Montaigne loved books and his library from where he could see the world and return to it all the better for the retreat they offered. Certainly, he never used books to leave the world. He was fidgety for that, and saw to it that his library was large enough to walk up and down to ease the swings of boredom and excitement that he recognised in himself.[25] Montaigne used books. He was in search of something. To the passive reader this is perhaps a little shocking. To the artist it is easily recognised, though perhaps not in public – where passive culture is the rule. Montaigne read books with the same purpose as he wrote each of his essays in order – to find their author. He summarises this practice as the basic principle of all sound education which, if observed, would destroy the hierarchical and passive relation between the teacher and student, the reader and writer.[26] Our schools would become fields of flowers in which each of us works mad dances like the bee to make honey of his own:

> For if he embraces Xenophon and Plato's opinions by his own reasoning they
> will no longer be his. He who follows another follows nothing; indeed he seeks
> nothing. *We are not under a king; let each one claim his own freedom* [Seneca]. Let
> him know that he knows at least. He must imbibe their ways of thinking, not
> learn their precepts. And let him boldly forget, if he wants, where he got them,
> but let him know how to make them his own. Truth and reason are common to
> everyone, and no more belong to the man who first spoke them than to the man
> who says them later. It is no more according to Plato than according to me,
> since he and I understand and see it in the same way. The bees plunder the
> flowers here and there, but afterward they make of them honey, which is all
> theirs; it is no longer thyme or marjoram. Even so with the pieces borrowed
> from others, he will transform and blend them to make a work that is all his
> own, to wit, his judgement. His education, work, and study aim only at forming this. (I: 26, III)

Of course, this recommendation is dependent upon historical changes which we identify with the Renaissance. About this time, we recognise a secularisation of the text and the world – the book of nature – as a field for individual discovery. At the same time, there occurred the discovery of the relative autonomy of the state, society, economy and the individual. With the multiplication of fields of conduct which resulted, there arose questions of integration, control and authenticity as problems of mundane reasoning and practice. In response to these developments Montaigne turned essayist, embarking upon himself, with a few books and his pen. This departure determined the economy of his use of Stoicism, modified by the poetry of Virgil and Horace, as well as his use of scepticism, or the habit of risking daily sallies and explorations of terrain of which the explorer cannot otherwise be sure. Montaigne's ideal essayist is, of course, Socrates who, no farther away than in the market place and in the company of those he found there, could explore himself and open up others to the same self-inquiry, the same courage in the face of the hardest of all trials, namely, daily life otherwise unglorified.

Montaigne wrote that he loved life more than he loved books. Yet he withdrew from life in order to write his love of life into a book. But this paradox is not anything over which we should stumble. For we are not to judge life by the things that are only possible through life. And so consistency and inconsistency do not rule life, as they might rule one's thought or speech in those very books of scholastic argument which Montaigne could never prefer to the tide of living. Montaigne wrote in order to pay tribute to life; and this he could do only by lending himself to the bottom life of thought and speech, apprenticing himself to the essay of their profuse shapings. Of course, he had no sense of life as an abstract standard for man's thoughts and passions, or as a fixed rule of conduct and speech. Indeed, it is this very notion that he rejected in the dryness of those books in which men's conduct is judged apart from the embodied complexity and contrariety of their situations. Montaigne scorned books only inasmuch as they revealed their own author's refusal to essay life from within the flux of living, believing, struggling and dying. Above all, he mistrusted words because of their capacity for giving a fix to things, beliefs and relationships that they do not possess in men's lives. At the same time, Montaigne knew that his mistrust of language could not be preserved outside of language. Thus his project of keeping language true to things involved him in keeping language true to itself, and this he could only do by giving himself up to writing.

The *Essays* are therefore the only book Montaigne could write. He turned to them day by day because, day by day, they assumed the shape of his life, as he himself grew more and more to know himself. Montaigne is nothing apart from the *Essays* because his exploration of life made writing essential to his living, and not a trade or pastime. Montaigne is the author of the single book that contains his life. Yet the *Essays* are not in any strict sense autobiographical or confessional explorations.[27] For these are ready-made exercises unavailable to a man who does not avail himself of divine certainty or secure custom without having tried them in himself. Montaigne is therefore hard on books and language, and severe with religion, authority and custom. But his harshness is not inspired by any facile scepticism or closed refusal. It is in ourselves that we must test things, and so we must be sure that we keep alive custom, authority and belief and do not merely set those things against themselves in empty contradictions spun from mere words. Neither trust nor mistrust are of themselves practical courses of action. Each acquires its sense through the other, and it is the very business of living that living that teaches us not to keep them apart. Montaigne tested everything he read, or heard or saw against himself for the sake of what it would tell him about his own nature. And the more he learned of himself, the more he enriched his understanding of the world that fed the *Essays*.

CHAPTER 6

The Paradox of Communication: Reading the *Essays* Otherwise

In two very challenging articles[1] Anthony Wilden has presented a reading of the *Essays* in which their literary project is analysed in terms of Montaigne's nostalgia for the lost plenitude of La Boétie's friendship. We propose now to set out Wilden's complex use of Marxist (Lukács) and Freudian (Lacan) interpretation and then critically to evaluate his arguments regarding Montaigne's concept of self and social relationships.[2] Wilden's approach to the *Essays* depends upon the strategy of locating Montaigne in a particular socio-economic context – substantifying him as an ideologist of bourgeois individualism. The force of this practice derives for Wilden from its authority in Marx, and in particular in Lukács' *The Theory of the Novel*.[3] It matters very little to Wilden that Montaigne himself is a student of the tendency of men to judge things according to their own measure, thereby absolutising customs, beliefs and practices that have only a municipal rather than universal force. It seems equally unimportant to him that Montaigne's times are those of the Religious Wars and the emergence of a central state in France – phenomena that at best describe certain elements of mercantile capitalism less favourable to a Catholic country gentleman than to the rising commercial and urban bourgeoisie allied with Protestantism, according to Max Weber's classical hypothesis.[4] Wilden, in any case, presents his argument on several other fronts. Thus, he is just as slipshod with Montaigne's place in the history of ideas as he is with Montaigne's location with respect to the rise of capitalism.[5] He speaks of the *Essays* as containing a concept of the self as 'a substantial, Cartesian-like rock of stability,' generated by the conflict between the desire for certitude and solidity and the experience of doubt and fluidity. He is aware that this interpretation involves what we might call an anticipatory reading of Montaigne. That is to say, Wilden knows that Montaigne is pre-Cartesian but he considers this observation a sufficient relaxation from his violence in rendering Montaigne's thought 'otherwise'. So far from joining any procession towards Cartesianism, apart from a general endorsement of clear-headedness over obfuscation, Montaigne would never have endorsed Cartesian dualism, as we have seen; and, of course, everything in the method of the *Essays* is opposed to the constructive analytic of the *Meditations* as a model of inquiry into man's knowledge of himself. Montaigne is surely the opponent of Cartesian 'mathematical' knowledge as a paradigm for inquiry in human affairs, supposing we indulge such anticipatory polemics. The only model of constructive reasoning that Montaigne had before him was Aristotle and it is the scholastic abuses of abstractive reasoning that he opposed. We should not forget Montaigne's general legal historicism. It is not possible to project his criticism of scholastic reasoning into a critique of the rationalisation of social relationships that characterise industrial society, unless one has a Marxist licence for reading history backwards and forwards.

But there is yet another argument employed to force Montaigne into the camp of bourgeois individualism. Wilden sees in the successive layering of the *Essays* a progression towards a substantialist theory of self achieved from the methodological standpoint of a transcendental ego, with the gratuitous exception that Montaigne's *Essays* are not caught in the solipsism of Sartre's *Being and Nothingness*. But any such comparison makes nonsense of Montaigne's discovery of himself as an 'unpremeditated and accidental philosopher' who found himself nowhere else than in the ordinary engagements of family, friendship, reading, writing and conversation. Nothing could be more remote from transcendental concerns than Montaigne's observation of his own beliefs and essay of his bodily experiences and his inability ever to step outside of the stream of everyday life, even towards death.

Wilden wants it both ways. It is the merit of the *Essays* to have exposed the errors of the belief in a substantive self while nevertheless continuing to hold on to such a belief. It would entirely miss the point, he says, to try to establish what is meant by the construct 'self' in Montaigne, or in any other author for that matter![6] We are asked to concede, then, that it would be unprofitable to inquire whether Montaigne really did subscribe to any philosophical or theological position amounting to a doctrine of the essential or natural self, discoverable either by means of a transcendental phenomenology or through the more conventional practices of spiritual and moral abnegation. The answer would, of course, be so overwhelmingly in the negative that one can only wonder at the errant practice in such a suggestion. But to avoid such a showdown, we need to 'translate' the textual resources for essaying the antinomies of self-dispersion and self-knowledge, or of public and private life, into the terms of Marxist psychology. The *Essays* are, then, merely a meta-construction upon the conflict between a 'normally fantasised past and a fantasised future.' Here the twin fantasies that generate the *Essays* are once again reconstructed by means of an anticipatory history which represents Montaigne as a man divided between the medieval fiction of *communitas* and a Pascalian self-alienation from God. Wilden's interpretative practice is again arbitrary, and it is so not only with respect to Montaigne but equally with respect to its own Marxist sources. Wilden needs to make Montaigne a medievalist in order to alienate him from Cartesian and Newtonian science, a Jansenist in order to express Montaigne's projected horror it the moral silence in the Cartesian universe. But it is clear upon any reading of the *Essays* that Montaigne is not a medievalist. Montaigne's interest is in ethical anthropology. He did not look to Nature for human nature.[7] He accepted the Socratic distinction between scientific knowledge and moral wisdom and thereafter took as his companions only those such as the poets and historians. Plutarch and Seneca, who were aids in the study of the art of living. Beyond this, Montaigne's conscience is quite free of Pascalian doubts, since he was completely willing to settle his end in faith. Montaigne is perhaps the least alienated of any writer one can think of from Augustine to Rousseau, while in no way inferior to them as a practitioner of self-study. Finally, we hardly need to locate Montaigne within the experience of the break between feudal society and mercantile capitalism (we should avoid the gross distinction between feudalism and capitalism) in order to account for his practice of disowning the masks that we adopt in society. It is doubtful that Montaigne would have espoused an alienated sociology derived from the notions of social role and the division of social labour.[8] Moreover, such a construction is the most problematic conclusion of Marx's own reflection upon these phenomena of social organisation and exchange. It is, in fact, here that, in Wilden's own terms, Marxism seeks a wholly imaginary reduction of social difference and social equality through a utopian identification of the desire of each with the desires of all.

But this is where we begin to read Montaigne himself. For, surely, we may be attracted as much to friendship, to family or to conversation as to communism as a mediation of the paradox of human differences and similarities. We owe to Lionel Trilling some careful reflection upon the problem of sincerity and authenticity, or the ethical dilemmas that arise once we come to pose for ourselves the question of the congruence between avowal and actual feeling:

> If sincerity is the avoidance of being false to any man through being true to one's own self, we can see that this state of personal existence is not to be attained without the most arduous effort. And yet at a certain point in history certain men and classes of men conceived that the making of this effort was of supreme importance in the moral life, and the value they attached to the

enterprise of sincerity become a salient, perhaps a definitive, characteristic of Western culture for some four hundred years.[9]

We cannot expect a single solution to this question. Polonius urged Laertes to be true to himself so that he might not be false to others. But this advice is oriented towards a conception of the public self as an end which Montaigne, for example, would not have set above the goal of a wholly private self, capable, to be sure, of lending oneself to public and familial duties, but always reserved for oneself. Moreover, things are complicated, inasmuch as sincerity is also required of us socially, and, like so many of the faces that we put on for society, it may bespeak nothing deeper. We therefore need to preserve the ultimate distinction between the self and society – especially in view of the increasing capacity of society to define and purvey so many moral qualities that formerly were thought to be the reserve of individuals and their private spiritual practices. Trilling suggests, therefore, that we employ for this purpose the concept of 'authenticity' in order to suggest 'a more strenuous moral experience than "sincerity" does, a more exigent conception of the self and what being true to it consists in, and a less acceptant and genial view of the social circumstances of life'.[10]

Montaigne certainly had enough of the sixteenth-century experience of dissimulation, feigning and pretence. Indeed, he made a study of it, like so much else around him. However, from the outset he was more deeply concerned with what underlies all forms of social and political bad faith, namely, the ability to deceive oneself. The most troublesome issue in the practice of self-inquiry lies in the status of its author's claims to truth and sincerity. Montaigne could not avoid this issue, although he hardly seems to have tormented himself with it as did Rousseau. Some general historical features of the problem of speaking the truth in the face of society are relevant here. What is involved is the emergence of the historical preconditions for the development of the interior space that we call privacy, and without which we cannot imagine the modern self with its introspective and autobiographical preoccupations.[11] The self needs distance upon society. It may need the sufficiency of a comfortable estate such as Montaigne enjoyed; or independence of the king and the court, for example, because of an attachment to the higher power of God's word, as in the Protestant practice of conscience. Or else the self may claim the divine protection of a Shakespearean fool.

Montaigne lived at an earlier phase of the developments that were eventually to blossom into bourgeois individualism than did Rousseau, and this cannot he overlooked in any comparison of how each perceived the question of authenticity in self-observation. Nor is Montaigne tossed between the extremes of social alienation and social adoration, as in Diderot's *Neveu de Rameau*, where criticism and flattery are absolutely inextricable.[12] Unlike Hegel, Montaigne could never have appreciated Rameau's alienation as an essential trope in the world historical development of the spirit. Montaigne worked too close to home for that. While he was sure enough of the departure contained in the *Essays*, he had no inclination to underwrite their significance in terms of any elaborate theory of the history of consciousness. Here he differs also from Rousseau whose claims for the *Confessions* are based upon a more prophetic grasp of the extreme alienative tendency of society. To understand these differences, we need to recall some of the main institutional developments that separate Montaigne and Rousseau. Broadly speaking, these events consist in the articulation of the spheres of the state, society, economy and the individual as distinct forms of life for which men would have to find new principles of conduct amid organisation. These changes raised severe communicative disorders. Thus Montaigne detested the power of politics to foster false speech. By the same token he did not try to preserve speech by restricting it to elevated topics. Rather, he believed that the goodness of speech – like the goodness of men's company – is preserved only in simple talk. He was critical of professional jargon, whether used in religion, architecture, poetry or politics. This criticism needs to be understood. After all, there are many humble trades whose languages are quite strange to one another, let alone to outsiders. The wine-maker and the wheelwright may find one another as hard to follow as any lawyer or theologian. Yet it may be said that tradesmen generally suit their talk to their work, whereas lawyers and theologians are more likely to suit their work to their talk, often forgetting what in the world they are doing. Montaigne saw that language is a fundamental human institution of which we are obliged to make ethical use. The power of language to work both good and evil among men is, of course, a commonplace of rhetoric, law, philosophy, poetry and religion. It was never so clear as in the civil and religious struggles that surrounded Montaigne. A man's speech, his word and good name, were at stake at every minute in the theological disputes, diplomatic missions and town politics of his day. On every side, there were risks in open and frank speech, advantages in distortion and falsehood. In such circumstances, we are not to suppose that Montaigne's love of simple speech was nothing but a yearning for naive spontaneity. Not at all.

Montaigne considered discussion as necessary for the exercise of the mind as any exercise of the body, and both were required in his ideal of the free man. The inability of the tyrant to compete for himself either in sport or in conversation deprives him of an art essential to his humanity. Moreover, discussion offers a model of communicative order that is essential to the proper conduct of society. Here Montaigne appeals to the conversational exchanges between shepherds and craftsmen, proportioned to their subject-matter and not mere exercises of learned subtlety and force:

> I will argue peaceably a whole day if the debate is conducted with order. It is
> not so much strength and subtlety that I ask for as order: the order that we see
> everyday in the altercations of shepherds and shop boys, never among us. If
> they get off the track, it is by way of incivility, so indeed do we. But their tur-
> bulence and impatience never sidetrack them for their theme: their argument
> follows its course. (III: 8, 706)

Such a communicative order is only possible among men willing to regard one
another as equals and, above all, when all submit themselves to respect the rules
of conversation as an art that complements nature's spontaneity. Otherwise men
are lost in formlessness, aggravated by violence and deceit. It is not, of course,
easy to subject oneself to the discipline of equal conversation; but that is the
strength men need to acquire in a free society.[13] It is therefore in the interests of
the tyrant to monopolise talk so that those around him are weaker than himself,
and without any chance to strengthen their opinions. The tyrant weakens men's
ability to understand their own affairs, to be patient with one another's view-
points and to work carefully towards consensus. The greatest injury inflicted by
tyranny is that it distorts and withers man's capacity for thought and speech, just
as it breaks his body and weakens his senses.

In speech, as in everything else, we essay ourselves and our circumstance. Montaigne was not at the mercy of his own easy tongue. In speaking frankly, Montaigne found he could speak only in character, no differently from the way he rode
a horse, ate or made love: 'As for me, both my word and my honor are, like the
rest, parts of this common body' (III: 1, 604). It is against these considerations
that we must understand Montaigne's views on literary style in the narrow sense.
The *Essays* are not written for a coterie. They do not contain much that is factual,
historical or encyclopedic. They are not marshalled on their own behalf to
attempt any lengthy discourse or treatise. They do not require a reader willing
faithfully to master definitions and syllogisms without which he will be unable to
reach any conclusion. Montaigne is not anxious to make his reader's experience
strange or fantastic. He wishes to speak directly, much as Julius Caesar spoke to
his men in the field and in his accounts of his campaigns. A general has no profit
in speaking to his men the way a lawyer or theologian speaks, in other words,
where it is almost impossible to grasp from the words and terminology the ultimately simple human relations that underlie such talk. The loss in scholastic
abstractions is that they can be mastered without thought and that men can then
build up fantastic constructions through which they separate the mind from the
body, masters from slaves, life from death, while in reality nothing matches these
distinctions. This is nowhere clearer than in religious controversy, where the
sense of a simple word, like *hoc* in the phrase *hoc est enim corpus meum*, may be so

hotly disputed that men are willing to murder, torture and pillage over it. Thus language is able to bewitch us to the point that we make the evident peace of bodily well-being and human community dependent upon a string of words, and are willing to sacrifice lives and whole countries in the name of the merest symbol. By the same token, Montaigne loved language and trusted himself to it as a politician and a writer, he tells us how often he risked his life and possessions on his own frank and open speech.

Language, like any other human facility, turns upon itself for good and evil. Rhetorical language will easily cheapen words like 'cruelty', 'tyranny' and 'treason', to the point where they circulate like small coin. Where men are brutalised by religious and political controversy, language becomes inflated in a vain struggle to recall the lost orders of reason and compassion. Montaigne manages to tie these experiences to the observation of some common family practises which make it clear that we cannot simply expostulate upon the evil of our times or upon some cosmic imperfection in accounting for cruelty and tyranny. To adopt such rhetoric may sound well. But it does so at the expense of our self-understanding. Thus Montaigne prefers to remind us that from our earliest years we begin to act towards animals and children in ways that foster the cruelty which as adults we later inflict upon each other in the name of all sorts of symbolic ideals:

> I find that our greatest vices take shape from our tenderest childhood, and that our most important training is in the hands of nurses. It is a pastime for mothers to see a child wring the neck of a chicken or amuse itself by hurting a dog or a cat; and there are fathers stupid enough to take it as a good omen of a martial soul when they see a son unjustly striking a peasant or a lackey who is not defending himself, and as a charming prank when they see him trick his playmate by a bit of malicious dishonesty and deceit. Nevertheless these are the true seeds and roots of cruelty, tyranny and treason; they sprout there, and afterward shoot up lustily, and flourish mightily in the hands of habit. (1: 23, 78)

Through the linguistic juxtapositions of 'pastime' and 'wringing the neck', 'amuse' and 'hurt', 'stupid' and 'good omen', Montaigne carefully mixes the elements of good and evil in men and women, while showing how cruelty is habitual with us, indeed, a family effort passed on from generation to generation. Mothers, fathers, dogs, cats, chickens and servants – not kings, queens, wars or sins – are the occasions of Montaigne's anthropological observations and thus his speech must accommodate his plain method by dwelling upon the domestic and familiar occasions of communicative self-understanding.

Wilden insists upon treating the communicative self–other relationship as a socio-economic phenomenon resolvable only through the desire for recognition alienated upon a collectivity whose creation provides the telos of Western history in accordance with the Marxist vision, in such a vision, class conflict and 'schizophrenia' are metaphors in a meta-communicative relationship between (primitive) communism lost and (future) communism regained. Self and other are merely the alternating figure and ground of a possessive individualism haunted by the remembrance of absolute dispossession as the future perfection of self and other:

> It is here, surely, that we can recognize a fundamental double bind both for us and for Montaigne: 'Know thyself' means on the one hand seek to isolate and examine the alienated, mediated, and inauthentic construct we call our self; on the other, it means that we cannot know ourselves 'authentically' unless we are in the world, unless we know others, for our self has no meaning and no existence except in its relation to Otherness. But in our mediation by the Imaginary Other, we lose ourselves in the objectifications of the socioeconomic discourse. Our cherished self turns out to be a thing, a piece of property, a commodity. 'Self' or 'other' become the two terms of a self-perpetuating oscillating series in a schizophrenic system of communication.[14]

Wilden's interpretation of the communicative paradox of self/other relationships, so far from lending any sense to Montaigne's *Essays*, in instead exemplary of that forceful expropriation of sense on behalf of an imaginary universalisation of meaning through which a Marxist revolution sublimates difference and equality. It is the essential violence of Wilden's revolutionary reading of the *Essays* that in our view makes him hostile to Montaigne's ideals of friendship and family. Consider Wilden's 'translation' of the friendship between Montaigne and La Boétie. In his terms, the image of La Boétie's friendship represents a meta-sexualisation of the plenitude of desire and loss which generates the *Essays* as a communicative relationship between Montaigne and the *Essays* themselves, as well as between Montaigne and his reader. Thus Montaigne's self-formation (*Bildung*) is dependent upon its necessary externalisation (*Entäusserung*) in the *Essays*, on one hand, and the communicative alienation of the self–other relationship in friendship on the other hand. The difference is that in the *Essays*, more than in friendship, Montaigne can experiment with the possibility of non-recognition by the reader as the Other of Montaigne's self-essay, while at the same time he gathers the certainty of his presence to himself and posterity through the *Essays* which have made him as much as he made them. But, as Wilden would have it, Montaigne only succeeds in making property of himself in the *Essays*. Thereby commodifying the communicative relationship between plenitude and loss, or self and friendship. This means that the subject of the *Essays* is not Montaigne but the social relationship of ownership and deprivation that regulates the discourse of bourgeois society:

It is in this sense that a particular individual, called Montaigne – who undoubtedly had all sorts of 'personal *problems*' - *IS SPOKEN BY* the socioeconomic discourse of his time, and by the discourse of the class with which he identifies himself (the landed aristocracy), than choose to view his relationship with La Boétie as a metaphor of the disintegration of a society, rather than simply as a symptom of some psychological problem or other. And we choose to view Montaigne's metacommunication about that relationship as a metacommunication about the Other who is speaking him, rather than simply as a personal 'analysis'.[15]

None the less, Wilden wishes to argue that in the *Essays* Montaigne succeeded in inventing an authentic, open-ended medium for the exploration of self formation. He likes to use cybernetic and computerised metaphors to describe this achievement as an immanent critique of an essentialist concept of human nature. This is a curious practice, since such metaphors are tied to a non-discursive rationality that is fundamentally antithetical to the form of reasoning exhibited in the *Essays*.[16] It is also another example of Wilden's forceful reading practices, specifically of his projective historicising, combined with metaphorical expropriations, which function to embed any reflection that positively rivals Marxism within an anachronistic schema of socialist development. This, however, is a practice essential to Wilden's conception of self-exploration. Thus he is able to speak of the Delphic injunction, 'Know thyself,' as a 'simple, normative possibility,' accepted as such by Montaigne and belied by the practice of the *Essays* which continually ruins any notion of transcendent interiority. He forces Montaigne into this 'modern' contradiction simply because his own method requires him to formulate modernity in conflict with tradition. It matters very little to him that the alleged dialectical tension produced in this manner is generated from binding two opposites by way of an inadequate conception of each comparative term. Modernity is just as compatible with a computerised homogeneity as it is with individual authenticity. Montaigne need not be set ahead of his times in order to account for his self-essaying, since he himself points very clearly to the long tradition of self-study from which he borrowed in order to make his own contribution. By the same token, Montaigne's refusal of any transcendent selfunderstanding does not project him into the hands of God, even though he was laid to rest in the arms of the Catholic Church.

Wilden's interpretation of the dialectic between self-formation (*Bildung*) and alienation (*Entfremdung*) is unfortunately dependent upon a false identification of the necessity of the externalisation of conduct or expression, which properly translates the notion of *Entäusserung* with the contingency that expression may fail us (*Entfremdung*), either in the sense that the worker's product is expropriated, or that our expressive, linguistic and artistic efforts are subject to communicative distortion and estrangement.[17] Wilden indulges in the common error of confusing the processes of externalisation (*Entäusserung*) which are, as Marx himself observed, a rational necessity for any embodied or sensory being, with the estrangement (*Entfremdung*) of these processes from man due to specific socio-economic relations.[18] If we identify *Entäusserung* with *Entfremdung* through our use of the single term 'alienation', we cut the ground from under any worldly process of counter-alienation or non-estrangement. Such a usage, by rejecting the externalization necessary to the human senses, completely spiritualises socialism and is in fact the very practice that Marx believed he had reason to criticise in Hegel. The dependency of the process of self-formation (*Bildung*) upon exchanges (*Entäusserung*) with the external environment of man and nature is the ground of slavery and emancipation. Wilden sees in this dependency only the absolute otherness of man and nature in a history where friendship, family and class are merely the sublimations or lost plenitudes of future socialist society. Prior to socialist society all communication is pathological. So much for the literary problem of *inventio* and *imitatio* which are found to be central to the ordinary working practice of writers and artists.[19] In the context of capitalism, the pursuit of self-knowledge or a devotion to friendship only involves us in the inauthentic possession of self as a commodity belonging indifferently to ourselves or to another. In such a world it is as impossible to be a friend as it is to befriend another.

We might also observe that the concept of *Bildung* cannot be simply faulted in Montaigne without specification of its literary tradition.[20] Until the eighteenth century, the terms *Bildung*, *imago* and portrait were synonymous. The original portrait, or *imago*, is the *imago dei*, the divine image, in which the pattern of man's self-formation is laid down for him. God is the supreme artist; man is at best an imitator. But there is also the classical tradition in which the art of living is man's self-imposed task, unaided by divine grace and achieved only through self-reliance. Montaigne's concept of *Bildung* is in this tradition, and in fact enormously advances its pedagogic basis, although that cannot be explored here (I: 26; II: 8, 37). The *Essays* are in some ways an anticipation of the *Bildungsroman*, or the apprentice novel of which Goethe's *Wilhelm Meisters Lehrjahre* is the prototype. Here the self is portrayed as the gradual product of the antagonism between the self and the world in a series of dramatic encounters. Thus Montaigne's own love of society and travel and his educational prescriptions are in this vein, although the *Essays* are far from being either heroic or autobiographic. But in so far as the *Essays* may be compared with the *Bildungsroman*, and therefore might allow for the role of a friend or tutor, they are thoroughly incompatible with the slave relationship Wilden attributes to Montaigne and La Boétie.

Wilden makes nothing of the underlying quest of the *Essays*, the journey into the self that is central to the *Bildungsprinzip*. The paradox of the Delphic oracle is that one cannot stay put in order to examine oneself. Self-study is not motionless yet it must avoid distraction. It needs the filters of pride and vanity without savouring every last bit of self. Self-study, at least in Montaigne, is irreverent yet loyal to the self it treats not as its property but as a trust, a patrimony to be used well, if not for the good of others. Montaigne, however, manages to avoid turning self-study into either a theodicy, a social romance or an autobiography in any strict narrative sense. Montaigne does not reconstruct his life. Yet he never presumes upon it. The *Essays* are remarkable for being under way without any premeditated start. Moreover, they continue along the path of self-inquiry without any resort to spiritual gradations, without setting heaven against earth or setting the soul against its body. The *Essays* are self-reliant. They do not resort to any union of the education of the World-Spirit, as in Hegel's *Phenomenology*, which is in many ways a philosophical *Bildungsroman*. Indeed, we might even regard *Capital* as a *Bildungsroman*, inasmuch as formally it consists of translating the Hegelian World-Spirit into a social conflict between the bourgeoisie and the proletariat in order to bring forth from history the new man.[21] But these are tropes far removed from Montaigne's usage. Nevertheless, they may be pointed out in order to make it clear that Wilden suppresses the literary tradition upon which his own critical stand is taken.

In yet another move, Wilden argues that the impossibility of Montaigne's quest for self-discovery within the friendship of La Boétie is rooted in the same failure as the pursuit of psychoanalysis as a substitute for socialism. The impossibility of transcendence outside of a socialist collectivity is revealed in the form of the analytic relationship in which the patient speaks, producing the emancipatory separation between 'I' and 'me' before an ideally silent analyst. In this relationship the patient enslaves himself to the analyst in order to emancipate his 'self' from the dependency of the othered 'me'. In this manner, he alienates his own creative power upon the analyst who remains silent because he refuses the collective alternative of an alliance with the patient in naming the institutional mediations of repressive otherness. Thus, according to this view, Montaigne oscillates between extravagant claims of self-mastery vis-à-vis his literary and philosophical sources and the opinions of the day, and importunate demands for recognition by the reader whom he seeks to captivate like a slave in willing surrender.[22]

It is essential to Wilden's reading of Montaigne to make of him a Hegelian 'unhappy consciousness' by separating what Montaigne 'thinks' from what he 'says'.[23] Thus, Montaigne's thought is essentialist, a nostalgic return to medieval essentialism and community. By contrast, Montaigne's speech is innovative and critically rational in its rejection of his own thought! In this manner, Wilden brings Montaigne into the world divided against himself, and is then able to make him hopelessly dependent upon La Boétie as the image of that lost plenitude everywhere rejected in the *Essays*. The price of modernity is degradation, i.e., separation from a lost ideal that is ever more transcendent through the awareness of its loss and the lack of any alternative praxis to literature and psychology:

> With the death of La Boétie, Montaigne is reduced to a relationship, not with an ideal person, but with an ideal period. His quest is for the *'ame de vieille marque'* to whom the *Essays* are addressed – a situation out of which or through which there is no evolution whatsoever, since Montaigne never stopped writing the *Essays:* *'Si mon ame pouvoit prendre pied, je ne m'essaierois pas, je me resoudrois'* (II.2 782b). La Boétie becomes 'La Boétie,' a fiction in turn metaphorically replaced by all that it stands for in Montaigne's personal lexicon: stability, being, judgment, plenitude. At the same time the real absence of a referent for 'La Boétie' creates in Montaigne's discourse all the things this absence stands for: flux, becoming, vanity, void. The goal of the *Essays* is both metonymically and metaphorically expressed in the words by which Montaigne characterizes La Boétie: *'un'ame pleine.'* And in all the passages where he describes the stability of his judgment, the stoicism of his attitude to life, the plenitude of his *'regard dedans,'* it is 'La Boétie' who speaks to Montaigne, rather than Montaigne to 'La Boétie.'[24]

How is Wilden able to produce a theory so contrary to Montaigne's relation to La Boétie, whereas other critics have considered this relation the communicative source of the *Essays*?[25] Wilden's argument is curiously overdetermined, to use a Freudian expression of which he is especially fond. Again, we are involved in a compensatory methodological move. That is to say, not content with having argued for Montaigne's political dependence by means of a Marxist foreshortening of history, Wilden needs, in terms of his reading of Hegel, to degrade Montaigne's relation to La Boétie into a master–slave relationship. He thereby joins Marx to Freud, in order to overcome an otherwise rival theory of identity that only a wounded Marxism can confront. In short, Wilden's method consists of compounding an historical trope, such as the master–slave dialectic, with a Freudian mechanism, namely, identification, in order once again to synthesise a bad identity between Montaigne's untimely deprivation of socialist consciousness and the plenitude of his literary friendship with La Boétie. As a man of his times, in other words, in so far as Wilden conceives of him as a bourgeois individualist, Montaigne experienced authentically the rupture between feudalism and capitalism as his own self-alienation. But in so far as Montaigne was only able to sublimate the historical loss of plenitude by means of losing his alienated identity in a labile identification with 'La Boétie,' eked out with all the metaphors of flux, wind and vanity, Montaigne laboured at the *Essays* only to erect a monument to the enslavement of friendship:

> *Se doubler* for Montaigne meant (in the past) unity and plenitude: what one might call his pre-reflexive *cognito*. A transformation was effected upon Montaigne by the assumption of the image of himself in La Boétie and it was a means to a rare and enviable friendship. But it bore the seeds of an unwelcome enslavement, an enslavement revealed only when the loss of the other irrevocably relegated him to the category of the Other and temporarily deprived Montaigne of the means to maintain the alienation which was so essential to his well-being. The whole problem of *identity* is involved. As René Girard has often pointed out, to have identity is *to be someone*, but it is also not to be *anybody else*. What is identical is not the same; to identify with someone is to assert one's own difference. For Montaigne, La Boétie effectively became interiorized as the immutable master, Montaigne became the mutable slave, and the relationship could only be sustained, the desire for reciprocal recognition worked out, by a transformation of the labor of the slave: or in other words by the symptomatic labor of the *Essays*.[26]

Wilden's method forces the coincidence of sociological and psychological truth in the interests of the power of Marxist hermeneutics; but at the expense of Montaigne's text. Yet Wilden is not entirely able to suppress Montaigne's independence of 'La Boétie.' Thus he is obliged to allow the *Essays* to speak, at least contradictorily, or by way of 'translating' the difference between the text and his own reading into a difference between Montaigne's independence and his fascination with dependency in the plenitude of an enslaved friendship. Clearly, he is unable to suppress the numerous testimonies of Montaigne's taste for self-preservation, for independent thought and speech and his hatred of subordination and deceit. He never considers for a moment that these are the traits that were attractive on either side to La Boétie and Montaigne. Having made of La Boétie nothing but the instrument of his own critical reading, he cannot raise any question about La Boétie's conception of friendship. But if La Boétie were nothing apart from the image of plenitude, he would have stood in no need of Montaigne, any more than Montaigne would have needed him had he possessed the capacity Wilden assigns him for 'imaginary' friendship. On Wilden's interpretation we have only a bad identity: La Boétie loving the slave in Montaigne; and Montaigne loving the master's enslavement to such slavery. Wilden makes nothing of La Boétie, the promising public servant and author of a treatise against tyranny (Le *Contr' Un*, as it came to be known), whose significance we have seen.[27] Are we to suppose that La Boétie tyrannised Montaigne in order to deny this relationship as the generative source of the *Discours de la servitude volontaire*? But we know that Montaigne was critical of La Boétie's personal Stoicism, as well as of his youthful writings. Wilden, like Butor, observes that Montaigne was tempted to make a portrait of La Boétie the centrepiece of the *Essays* rather than himself.[28] He sees in this the temptation of a slave, just as he regards the *Essays* generally as slave-labour. In fact, however, the *Essays* ever cease to address the very possibility of their self-proposed task. How is one to pursue by one's own means knowledge of a self that never stands still for inspection, of a self whose very nature seems given up to distraction? Gradually, Montaigne discovers the paradox of society, that in lending ourselves to custom, family, conversation and friendship we return ourselves to ourself. The 'loan' we make, however, is not underwritten by an easy scepticism or indifference; nor is it shielded by masks. It open and free, conscious of difference, mindful of the separations of pain, poverty and death, yet reserved and liberal:

> One can see in Montaigne's work the superstructural manifestation of a muta-tion whose roots are technical, social and economic. The *Essays* involve a series of choices if one is to interpret them in the light of the theory of ideology. . . . One can see in the *Essays* a crossroads of supporting ideologies: humanist, lin-guistic, national and conservative are on the side of power: a faith, a law, a king, a language. But the ideology of the self from which the classics would shy away, was to have a long bourgeois future. By their free expression of the self in search of a completely earthy pleasure, in a supple form that fuses genres and levels of language, the *Essays* appear ahead of their time. With Montaigne, we witness the promotion of individual liberty – together with its contradictions. It is there perhaps that the 'revolutionary' import of the message of the *Essays* is to be found.[29]

Wilden concludes with the argument that Montaigne could only continue as an essayist by disavowing the search for a plenitude that nevertheless remained the driving force of the *Essays*. The vanity of the *Essays* is not simply a device for embarking upon a dangerously self-conscious enterprise, as it might appear from the preface 'To the Reader'. It is a pervasive doubt struggling to become a literary resource rather than a philosopher's topic. The *Essays* are the expression of a double absence – the lack of a transcendent self in their author and the loss of a mirroring self in the friendship of La Boétie:

> What remains of Montaigne's dialectic with La Boétie and with the masters of antiquity is nevertheless our royal road to the essence of Montaigne. In talking to his Self, he is attempting to bridge the gap between conscious demand and unconscious desire, between the symbolic world of discourse and the imagi-nary world of *jouissance*, between a question which is an answer and an answer

which is a question. Only because this is an open-ended dialectic is it possible to read Montaigne and thus to escape the myth of the 'real' Montaigne.[30]

Wilden's interpretative method consists in (dis)locating Montaigne's literary origins in a point of departure defined vis-à-vis a subjective loss (the past plenitude of La Boétie's friendship) and the objective lack of a future of collective plenitude (socialism). The *Essays* are essentially a missing body, a literary corpse. But if this were true the *Essays* would either be haunted by memory or else a prey to hope. That neither is true of the *Essays* is due to Montaigne's nearly conversational presence to his readers whose attachment is surely not fostered by any promise of historical orientation or of spiritual salvation. Montaigne's point of departure is intimate, not because he chooses like Saint Augustine to converse with God, but because he holds his conversation to the conversation of mankind. The Essays presume upon friendship, neither as a sublimated resource, nor as alienated topic; but as a gift of time and a bond of place for anyone who, like ourselves, lives towards death. Montaigne's thought and speech are never separated from the experience of embodiment and mortality. The *Essays* are Montaigne's future, not because they so successfully recall his youthful friendship with La Boétie, but because they are the deliberate exercise of the last years of his life, an art of dying. The achievement of the *Essays* is to have avoided praise. They are not in service of philosophy, or of theology or of science. The *Essays* lean upon no remedy outside of themselves.

Wilden's interpretation of the *Essays* leaves no place for Montaigne's peculiar independence. Even in his interpretation of the essay 'Of Vanity' (III: 9) he persists in tying Montaigne's disavowal of his 'scribbling' (*cacoethes scribendi*) to a vain attempt to resurrect the wholesome image he once enjoyed in the eyes of La Boétie. There is so much that is false in this interpretation that it would be tiresome to correct it in every detail. His method relies upon relatively few passages from the *Essays* and he frequently bases his interpretation upon the passage (however, with suitable suppressions) that one might have taken to prove him wrong. Let us consider one such passage from the essay 'Of Vanity' in order to establish its particular sense and its place in the overall composition of the essay. It is necessary to do this because Wilden's method of compounding a Freudian (Lacan) and Marxist (Lukács) reading of the *Essays* is likely to overwhelm any reader with its brilliance and yet give no sense of what is lost in 'translation'. We need not provide a very painstaking analysis of the following passage[31] upon which Wilden has placed his theory of Montaigne's dependent identification with La Boétie. It can stand for itself. Instead we shall give a sense of its place in the whole essay and indicate how we might respect Montaigne's own view of his undertaking as an essayist mindful of death and the turmoil of his day:

121

> In true friendship, in which I am expert, I give myself to my friend more than I draw him to me. [I not only like doing him good better than having him do me good, but also would rather have him do good to himself than to me; he does me most good when he does himself good.] And if absence is pleasant or useful to him, it is much sweeter to me than his presence; and it is not really absence when we have means of communication. [In other days I made use and advantage of our separation.] We filled and extended our possession of life better by separating: he lived, he enjoyed, he saw for me, and I for him, as fully as if he had been there. One part of us remained idle when we were together; we were fused into one. Separation in space made the conjunction of our wills richer. This insatiable hunger for bodily presence betrays a certain weakness in the enjoyment of souls. (II: 9, 746–7)

Wilden interprets Montaigne's discovery of the absence essential to friendship as the important psychological truth that human love is not satisfied by real possession, which would defeat it. But then it is essential that neither the lover nor the loved one make objects of themselves to serve the other. In love and friendship it is precisely the independence of each in each that is the goal. Surely this, and not an abject identification with La Boétie, is what Montaigne expresses in his reflections on friendship. Friendship cannot grow from sheer self-love, any more than the *Essays* could have grown from unruly scribbling. At the same time the friend and essayist cannot offer solely what is loathsome in himself. The offer of friendship must be animated by a lively self-love. The difficulty lies, of course, in the implicit analogy between love of self and love for another as for oneself. It is a difficulty that exercised classical reflection on the nature of friendship as well as Christian teaching upon the care of our soul and love of our neighbour. Montaigne's view of friendship is classical, and in fact largely Aristotelian.[32] The good man, unlike the selfish man, only loves in himself those things that anyone else might love. But here again there is the difficulty that the friends of the good man are only those who love in him those things that he might truly love in himself, or else he risks being a slave to flattery:

> But since active loving is to treat the loved *qua* loved, and the friend is loved by the friend *qua* friend and not *qua* musician or doctor, the pleasure coming from him as being merely himself is the pleasure of friendship; for he loves the object as himself and not for being something else. So that if he does not rejoice in him for being good the primary friendship does not exist, nor should any of his qualities hinder more than his goodness gives pleasure.[33]

Thus the problem is to separate true friendship from any notion of utility, service and advantage.[34] Indeed, had Montaigne espoused anything like the bourgeois individualism Wilden attributes to him, he could never have held the classical doctrine of friendship. This is because the classical doctrine of friendship presupposes a notion of community that cannot be constructed from the premises of utilitarian association, we will see in a later chapter.[35] Capitalism makes friendship impossible, in the classical sense, as perhaps do both Christianity and communism. Montaigne's notion of friendship explicitly denies any end of friendship that might be the work of either of its partners rather than a mutual delight in living fully the life of each through friendship. On such a view, friendship is not dependent upon circumstance or calculation, but is rather a praxis espoused for itself without any consideration other than its own enjoyment.

If we now place Montaigne's remarks on friendship in the wider context of the essay 'Of Vanity,' we can understand how it is he understood any lasting arrangement between men. As Wilden observes, Montaigne begins by wondering whether his own 'scribbling' is not just part of the unruliness of the times. Indeed, this very essay seems to wander from topic to topic, unable to take a firm grasp upon its principal theme, as though its author were homeless and unable to construct anything to challenge the disorder and ruin around him. But, as with any essay of Montaigne, we must check an easy drift that carries us along unless we halt it with the exercise of our own judgement and self-knowledge. Did Montaigne encourage the disorders of the day by neglecting his own affairs for the idle habit of undisciplined writing? He is critical of his abilities as the manager of his estate. He likes to travel and to leave his household in the trust of others. Yet, amid the general ruin Montaigne's house stands untouched, and even a haven. Therefore it cannot be the case that good care requires our continuous presence – any more than it does in friendship:

> If we enjoy only what we touch, farewell to our crowns when they are in our coffers, and our children if they are off hunting. We want them nearer. In the garden – is that far? Half a day away? What about ten leagues is that far or near? If it is near, what about eleven, twelve, thirteen, and so on, step by step? . . . And let them boldly call philosophy to their aid, which someone might accuse – since it seems neither one end nor the other of the joint between too much and too little, long and short, light and heavy, near and far, since it cannot recognize either the beginning or the end of it – of being a very uncertain judge of the middle. (III: 9, 746)

By the same token, we cannot speak of Montaigne's travels as flights from home. For in travel he essays himself and marks his limits. Thus travelling is not to be compared with aimless wandering, any more than the thread of the *Essays* is drawn by a mere scribbler. But, most important, it gradually emerges that Montaigne's deepest attachment is not to a flighty self but a worldly self. The theme in 'Of Vanity' is Montaigne's worldliness, not as something stacked up to his own account, but as the resolution of the paradox of self-knowledge. For all his sad observations upon the religious wars, Montaigne nevertheless concludes that society has an incredible capacity for both self-injury and survival. Thus Rome is the symbol of world unity, despite every curiosity of practice and cruelty of division that have marked history. We have not to worry for such survival. Rather, it is sheer arrogance to imagine we have the key to human survival. It is an unsteady love of country, home and friend that seeks to protect them by imagining that we necessarily fail them if we are absent or thoughtless for a moment. We must serve them as we can. Perhaps, then, Montaigne's father will see that while his son did not protect his estate according to the strict practice of household economy, Montaigne the essayist never lost his estate even in the civil war. In any event, Montaigne can express the highest affection for France, and one of the most beautiful attachments to Paris, yet he is free to travel and to meet men without concern for nationality or creed. He confesses he cannot understand Socrates' fear of exile, for despite his love of home he took pride above all in his citizenship of Rome (III: 9, 743–4). Montaigne can return home to family and friends because he had never run away in the first place. He had made of himself a crossroad of the world and of home, of family and of self, and not a man easily blown from either side.

If Wilden were right, then the *Essays* would be nothing else than the folly of an unseasonable friendship that tore Montaigne away from the world and the business of living. Montaigne would have stayed in his tower, away from his family and quite removed from the world. But as it was, he was never more at home than in the world or on the road. He made of each day's journey a day proper to his own life, as well as to the *Essays*, so that he could even contemplate dying without feeling he had been cut off either from his destination or from any unfinished business of living.[36] Montaigne despised any attachment to life based upon the nostalgia of youth. He claimed for himself the rights of old age as fiercely as he proclaimed himself a world citizen:

> The longest of my plans has not a year in extent. Henceforth I think of nothing but making an end; I rid myself of all new hopes and enterprises: I take my last leave of every place I go away from, and dispossess myself every day of what I have: *For a long time I have had neither losses nor gains. I have more provisions for the road than I have road left* [Seneca]. (II: 29, 531–2)

Wilden makes of Montaigne a dependent creature, abandoned to his literary nostalgia of a lost plenitude. This reading of Montaigne expropriates the literary enterprise of the *Essays* in favour of Freudo–Marxist historicisation of the antinomy of self and society that has no place for friendship or mortality.[37] It depends upon dividing Montaigne's thought against his speech, as well as splitting his relationship with La Boétie into a silent and merely bespoken term of the *Essays*. Moreover, Wilden's method is unorthodox, even with regard to its own sources, and only more so in its use of Montaigne's text. Among the friends of Montaigne any reading of the *Essays* must be ruled by the very notion of self-essaying. In other words, as readers of Montaigne we must be careful to test any rule of composition that we impose upon the *Essays* against the presumption that their sense lies elsewhere than Montaigne was content to set it.

CHAPTER 7

Portrait of the Essayist Without Qualities

It is a commonplace of the interpretation surrounding the *Essays* that they are dominated by Montaigne's self-portrait. Such commentaries are generally developed without much attention to the intrinsic difficulties in the project of self-analysis.[1] It is therefore a welcome occasion to consider at length the issues that are raised by Butor's *Essay on the Essays*[2] where the imagery techniques and intentionality of the self-portrait are absolutely central but lack any adequate analytic use. In following Butor's argument, as we propose to do, we shall also have occasion to reconsider some of the major problems in any commentary upon the *Essays*, and to test further our sense of rival reading of Montaigne.

In view of the role it plays in Butor's interpretation, we must begin with some remarks upon the nature of self-inquiry as a literary and artistic enterprise.[3] We have to consider how we are to avoid the suspicion that the self which is proposed as the product of self-study is a fiction. In the first place, it is important to observe that the self-portrait and the autobiography are, after all, public institutions. They presuppose a cultural valuation of personal experience which authorises first-person speech. Moreover, the personal voice is assumed in relation to the viewer's reader's person. Montaigne's *Essays* differ from Saint Augustine's *Confessions*, or from those of Rousseau, in that they make no use of a divine interlocutor whose otherwise redundant omniscience is the rhetorical guarantee of their veracity. What Augustine required of God, Montaigne needed from the community of plain men. Moreover, Montaigne could not avail himself of the auspices of a profound revelation, or of any rupture between his previous life and life from the time he decided to write, although this is often a source of the autobiographer's claim to a sincere disposition. Instead, what we find in Montaigne is an appeal to a reader whose good sense is the sense of the community in which men are true to themselves. Hence Montaigne has not to insist, unlike Rousseau, upon the need to invent a language of sincerity. We have already remarked upon the significance of Montaigne's uneven style. If there is a difference here between Rousseau and Montaigne, it is rather that Montaigne may have thought he was the first to try to follow the unevenness of man's nature, but not to claim like Rousseau that he was the first man whose nature required unevenness, and thus a fundamental shift in language and society. He thought himself extraordinarily apt to hold himself in little regard (II: 17, 'Of Presumption').[4] But this meant that he neither overvalued nor undervalued himself. He was confident in his ability to observe his limits in everything that concerned his own thought and speech, as well as his appreciation of the intellectual and literary achievements of others:

> But to come to my own particular case, it would be very difficult, it seems to me, for anyone else to esteem himself less, or indeed for anyone else to esteem me less, than I esteem myself. I consider myself one of the common sort, except in that I consider myself so; guilty of the commoner and humbler faults, but not of faults disavowed or excused; and I value myself only for knowing my value. (II: 17, 481)

The self-portrait appears to be an exercise peculiar to Western civilisation, particularly during its critical moments. This is not to say that it depends upon a uniquely psychological experience. Rather, it derives from a huge displacement in the ratio between social and individual experience.[5] For most of human history, the individual has not set himself against the collectivity and the rhythms of its existence. No one thought of himself as the field of life's drama, neither at birth nor in death. Men, women and children entered the great liturgical cycle of society within which their highest moments were its collective representations.[6] These conditions do not predispose the individual to autobiographical inquiry. There has to be some break with the mythic representation of collective life; it needs some sense of the fraction of time, a loss of repetitions that creates the need for historical memory at the social level and autobiographical recollection on the individual level:

> The appearance of autobiography presupposes a new spiritual revolution: the artist and the model coincide, the historian takes himself as his object. That is to say, he considers himself a great person, worthy of man's memory, whereas he is in fact only a more or less obscure intellectual. Here there appears a new social space which inverts the ranks and reclassifies the values. Montaigne is a notable, of commercial origins; Rousseau, citizen of Geneva, is a sort of literary adventurer; all the same, both consider their destiny, despite its mediocrity

on the world's stage, as worthy of being offered in an exemplary way. Interest shifts from public history to private history: alongside the great men who bring about the official history of mankind, there are obscure men who give battle in the heartland of their spiritual life, conducting silent struggles whose ways and means, their triumphs and failures, also deserve a place in the universal memory.[7]

The landscape opened up by the self-portrait or autobiography in some ways repeats the opening of Europe to the New World. For the writer it resembles that endless opening which Rembrandt's Venetian mirror offered to him in the more than sixty self-portraits he made throughout his life.[8] Montaigne's *Essays* represent the same sort of carnal inquiry, the same incrustation and wearied accumulation of self-truth. Of course, there is the problem of self-flattery. But this is a problem in all spiritual inquiry. Moreover, its traps and disguises are well enough known not to take the artist by surprise, far less in one whose whole life is devoted to self-inquiry. Self-recollection is impossible without some organising legend, a personal myth. In the great artist such a legend is never a simple gloss upon his existence because it is never anything he can completely master. It is rather the underlying need in him, a centre of gravity which unites his life and his literary or artistic inquiry in such a fashion that each is the optic of the other.

Discussion of the nature of autobiographical inquiry and self-portrayal continues to centre upon the problem of the relative weights of fiction and history (*Dichtung and Wahrheit*). It seems best to avoid such global contrasts, and to approach the problem in terms of three levels of formal and mimetic values that can be found in a wide range of autobiography.[9] We shall then see what can be said of the *Essays* in terms of these relatively distinct but always overlapping levels. Hart suggests that we consider the following distinctions:

(i)   the mimetic question of the interplay of history and fiction;
(ii) the formal question of the tension between purposive form and experimental development;
(iii) the generic question of the autobiographer's changing idea of his purpose and of the reader he seeks.

With regard to the mimetic question, Montaigne, like Rousseau, claims that the *Essays* have no other purpose than to be true to their author's nature. This claim is made even though Montaigne was as clear as anyone about what it is in all men that makes it all but impossible to hold oneself steadily in the mirror, and to see there nothing but the truth of oneself. He who looks into himself will set off a thousand selves on the wings of imagination. As likely as not, what we call ourself is a borrowed thing. Even so, Montaigne held on to his enterprise because of a basic conviction that there is in each of us a bottom nature, so that our necessary borrowings owe as much to us as we to them:

> 'You are often playful: people will think you are in earnest when you are making believe.' 'Yes,' I say, 'but I correct the faults of inadvertence, not those of habit. Isn't this the way I speak everywhere? Don't I represent myself to the life? Enough, then, I have done what I wanted. *Everyone recognizes me in my book, and my book* in *me.*' (III: 5, 667)

Montaigne, of course, admits that he made some concessions to the difference between a naked portrait and what is compatible with public propriety. Nevertheless, the *Essays* keep pretty well to the bone, as any reader can see, while not torturing themselves with the spiritual scruples of a confession:

> In honor of the Huguenots, who condemn our private and auricular confession, I confess myself in public, religiously and purely. Saint Augustine, Origen, and Hippocrates have published the errors of their opinions: I, besides, those of my conduct. I am hungry to make myself known, and I care not to how many, provided it be truly. Or to put it better, I am hungry for nothing, but I have a mortal fear of being taken to be other than I am by those who come to know my name. (III: 5, 643)

No doubt this is because Montaigne wanted the ear of his reader more than that of his maker. Like any other reader, he was fascinated by the adventure that unfolds in the *Essays*.[10] Thus the mimetic and the formal questions overlap, as we can see from the comment stressed above. Montaigne knows very well that he started out writing rather impersonal essays, as though by looking into history he could literally abstract the truth of man whereby he might then conduct himself. 'And of my first essays, some smell a bit foreign' (III: 5, 667), he himself remarks. The difference is that over the years Montaigne had to come to terms with himself as a writer and reader, as well as with the problems of literary authority and tradition. Gradually, he came to understand that he was more involved in the experimental features than in the formal features of the *Essays*. Thus he is casual, negligent and nonchalant in respect of their shape; yet absolutely sure of himself as a working essayist at grips with self-inquiry:

> If a man is commonplace in conversation and rare in writing, that means that his capacity is in the place from which he borrows it, and not in himself. A learned man is not learned in all matters; but the capable man is capable in all matters, even in ignorance.
>
> In this case we go hand in hand at the same pace, my book and I. In other cases one may commend or blame the work apart from the workman; not so

here; he who touches the one, touches the other. He who judges it without knowing it will injure himself more than me; he who has known it will completely satisfy me. Happy beyond my deserts if I have just this share of public approval, that I make men of understanding feel that I was capable of profiting by knowledge, if I had any, and, that I deserved better assistance from my memory. (III: 2, 611–12)

Because of this experience in finding himself increasingly consubstantial with the *Essays*, and thereby becoming as much their source as anything else he could use to put into them, Montaigne already anticipates the overlap between the formal aim of the *Essays* and the hermeneutical competence they require of their reader. Montaigne's reader faces the same questions as the author of the *Essays*. He needs to know what it is he is trying to make of himself in reading. He seeks conversation, but he does not want to be cajoled and led on too easily. He wants to feel the author's need of him reading, without sensing any deliberate manipulations of the text, or any forceful apologetic:

Henry James wrote in his 'Preface' to *A Portrait of a Lady* that the house of fiction has many windows. Behind each window stands an artist looking out onto the same scene, each seeing it from a different angle. Hence the infinite varieties of art. The view through Montaigne's window is not a landscape but a portrait. And the reader of the *Essais* does not look out of the window onto a lovely scene, but into a strange double-faced mirror. If he is not alert, he may think he is looking through this window at someone else instead of through it with someone else. He needs to realize, too, that what he sees in the mirror is not the original, but a good copy. Only then can he gaze with the fullest of pleasure into the double-faced mirror which snows him two images simultaneously – Montaigne and his reader, the natural man artfully portrayed and the viewer himself.[11]

For similar reasons, when speaking of autobiographical literature, it is useful to distinguish between the 'form' and the 'functions' operative in the text, since it is possible for these to vary independently of one another while nevertheless remaining within a recognisable genre or institution of autobiographical writing. Thus writers in this genre will make different distributions of fiction and nonfiction, first- and third-person narration, of memoir, epistolary and apologetic modes. In view of these contingencies, which are certainly relevant to any serious consideration of the style and composition of the *Essays*, it has been suggested that we might identify certain constitutive rules for the practice of autobiography, provided we recognise that in any instance varying emphasis may be given to their consideration:

Rule 1.   An autobiographer undertakes a dual role. He is the source *of* the subject matter and the source for the structure to be found in his text:

   (a) The author claims individual responsibility for the creation and
arrangement of his text;

   (b) The individual who is exemplified in the organization of the text is
purported to share the identity of an individual to whom reference is
made via the subject matter of the text;

   (c) The existence of this individual, independent of the text itself, is
assumed to be susceptible to appropriate public verification procedures.

Rule 2.   Information and events reported in connection with the autobiographer are asserted to have been, to be, or to have potential for being the
case:

   (a) Under existing conventions, a claim is made for the truth-value of what
the autobiography reports – no matter how difficult the truth-value
might be to ascertain, whether the report treats of private experiences
or publicly observable occasions;

   (b) The audience is expected to accept those reports as true, and is free to
'check up' on them or attempt to discredit them.

Rule 3.   Whether or not what is reported can be discredited, whether or not it
can be reformulated in some more generally accepted way from another
point of view, the autobiographer purports to believe in what he is
saying.[12]

Butor's *Essay on the Essays* ignores the considerations we have raised so far.
Instead, Butor trades upon an entirely unexamined use of the idea of the self-
portrait and sacrifices Montaigne's concerns with the ratio between history and
fiction, as well as his reflections upon the experience of essaying, to a deliberately
fictive version of Montaigne's development of the three Books of essays. It is
striking that Butor's analysis draws upon continuously shifting topographical
metaphors contrived to keep pace with the evolution of Montaigne's self-portrait.
He begins with the fiction of Montaigne's isolated beginning, deprived of his
friend and shut up in his tower. Now it is true that the text of the *Essays* is over-
laid with continual revisions and additions. Of course, it is possible to date these
various states of the text, thereby producing a sense of their origin and of the
movement in Montaigne's thought. It is also possible to identify Montaigne's
sources, to count quotations, and from these facts to argue about the evolution of
his ideas. Butor begins by making it look as though these were considerations
that might seriously determine his own explorations. Instead, they merely suggest to him the need for a leap into origins – 'To discover this origin, let us dream
and phantasize [*revons donc et fantastiquons*]'.[13] Thus Butor fails to give to

Montaigne's essaying its proper due, preferring instead the critic's own fantastic method of beginning. But there is no literal start to the *Essays* unless we set Montaigne outside of his project, isolate him from La Boétie, and make his tower a symbol of alienation. In beginning the *Essays* Montaigne made a decision to shape his life, and not simply to organise the materials of writing:

> The translation of the word 'essay' as 'attempt,' which is the generally accepted one, only approximately gives the most important illusion to the literary model. For an essay is not the provisional or incidental expression of a conviction that might on a more favourable occasion be elevated to the status of truth or that might just as easily be recognized as error (of that kind are only the articles and features referred to as 'chips from their workshop,' with which learned persons favour us); an essay is the unique and unalterable form that a man's inner life assumes in a decisive thought. Nothing is more alien to it than that irresponsibility and semi-finishedness of mental images known as subjectivity; but neither are 'true" and 'false,' 'wise' and 'unwise,' terms that can be applied to such thoughts, which are nevertheless subject to laws that are no less strict than they appear to be delicate and ineffable. There have been quite a number of such essayists and masters of the floating life within, but there would be no point in naming them. Their domain lies between religion and knowledge, between example and doctrine, between *amor intellectualis* and poetry, they are saints with and without religion, and sometimes too they are simply men who have gone out on an adventure and lost their way.[14]

It is questionable, then, whether Montaigne's first essays are ever surpassed, any more than the first years of life cease to work upon a mature man. Indeed, the more certain the essayist becomes in his resolve to write, the more his beginnings are necessary revisionary ratios whereby he can measure his surer sense of things. This is especially true of Montaigne's literary sources. He tells us that he lived from them like a bee among the flowers. In other words, his sources are not visible in the *Essays* except where the *Essays* make them visibly Montaigne's own work of appreciation; and this makes it impossible to speak of his literary sources as though they underpin the *Essays*, providing supports where there would otherwise be collapse. We do not inspect the *Essays* in order to find their sources – rather we find their sources in what is original to the *Essays*. In short, it is because the *Essays* are composed that we speak of their elements which otherwise have no separate existence – despite the illusions of literary archeologists.

Butor sets Montaigne apart in order to have him begin the *Essays*. He speaks of his prodigious childhood and remarks upon the presumption behind Montaigne's ceremonial retirement in order to devote himself to the *Essays*. He implies that what obsessed Montaigne was a sense of failure and disappointment with a world that had not returned his own original promise. Alone in all the world, he had nothing to start with but the memory of La Boétie who had seen in him what he might have been. Hence there is an original ambivalence in the *Essays* regarding the self-portrait. If we are to believe Butor, Montaigne had made nothing of his own life to rival the heroic portraits that filled the history books he so loved – and had even less cause to prefer his own image to that of La Boétie as the centrepiece of the *Essays*. He is therefore tempted to make the *Essays* a literary monument to La Boétie. To realise this ambition, Montaigne proposes to set down with his tribute to their friendship (I, 28) La Boétie*'s Discours sur la servitude volontaire.*[15] Being forestalled by the Huguenot publication of that essay, Montaigne substitutes some youthful sonnets of La Boétie (I, 29) – and then strikes them out.

Although he notices that Montaigne's love of La Boétie never blinded his literary judgement upon the young man's political and poetic writings, Butor nevertheless considers that Montaigne held his own literary enterprise responsible to the demands of his lost friend. In particular, what Montaigne set himself to show was that his society had failed to see in La Boétie what in fact was the perfect image of a French gentleman. It follows that, by reflection, France would see in Montaigne everything she had lost in La Boétie.[16] By means of this hypothesis, Butor proceeds to find the organisational sense of the first Book of the *Essays*. Thus the very first twenty essays are seen to be concerned with military conduct, making predominant use of the historian brothers Du Bellay. Montaigne's purpose is to put to rout the notion that true bravery is necessarily a military virtue. Apart from the vicissitudes of fortune, it is evident, from the political climate of the day, that men take up arms from a spirit of voluntary servitude rather than from any genuine desire to maintain their independence. Here Montaigne trades upon La Boétie's *Discours* and, above all, he employs La Boétie's exemplary courage in the face of death as the most telling essay a man can make of his spiritual independence. Together, these events constitute Butor's more subtle argument, namely, that modern society is ill suited to receive the independent minds it really needs because it has not yet learned to accord more glory to the writer than to the servile soldier. In the light of this hypothesis, which we shall discuss in Chapter 9, we are able to read Montaigne's fascination with Greece and Rome, and with his contemporary Brazilian natives – that is to say, in terms of a search for settings in which the difference between military barbarism and genuine valour could be seen clearly. By implication, the two friends, La Boétie and Montaigne, reproduced themselves as heroes of the Graeco-Roman world, as much exiled from the civil barbarism of their own day as the Brazilian native in the port of Bordeaux. The result is a triptych which dominates Book One:

Thus at the center of the first book there is the portrait of three brothers in exile: La Boétie at the center, surrounded by two symmetrical figures, those of Montaigne and of the Cannibal. These three exiles form a chain joining the two happy and virtuous societies above the mire of contemporary France . . .[17]

But whereas this triple portrait might well have been finished with the inclusion of La Boétie's literary remains, its very manierist composition permitted it to accumulate endless oddities, always setting off the central piece, La Boétie, and his side companions, Montaigne and the Cannibal. Butor insists upon this arrangement even though, like Wilden's previous argument, it requires a literally absent centre. Neither the *Discours* nor the Sonnets figure in the actual text of the *Essays* as their organisational centre. Yet it is upon them that Butor fabricates his entire argument concerning the composition of Book One. This lack is nevertheless taken to constitute a displacement of the problem of centring the *Essays* somewhere between Books One and Two. Thus Butor resumes his task, refashioning his analysis in terms of newly imagined metaphors to guide him through the more extensive terrain of the *Essays*. The 'Apology for Raymond Sebond' is surely the dominating feature of Book Two of the *Essays*. Butor wishes to argue that it occupies a place similar to that of La Boétie's *Discours*, inasmuch as in both cases Montaigne wishes to show his loyalty to a person unfairly criticised or overlooked, and to show his love respectively for his friend and for his father. But the 'Apology' is a curious sort of defence. It so nearly subverts everything it stands for. Moreover, Montaigne is more directly responsible for its subversive effects, whereas it was the Huguenots who had forestalled him in a similar use of La Boétie's *Discours*. To cover his tracks, Montaigne could no longer compose the *Essays* around a central portrait. He was obliged, according to Butor, to disguise his purpose by turning the *Essays* into a labyrinth, an ornamental garden like those he so loved on his travels, where on a casual stroll one could admire things without too much questioning their purpose. Alternatively, should one stop to think, the figures serve more than to delight, and in fact form a defensive ring around an aggressive mind, unwilling to expose itself in a defenceless portrait.[18] Thus Montaigne increasingly hides behind his portrait, covers over his tracks, hiding his sources, complaining of a poor memory, and calling upon his reader's subtlety to track him down and find his meaning.

Having invented the idea that Chapters 28 and 29, namely, the essay on friendship and either the missing *Discours*, or else the Sonnets of La Boétie, are the centrepiece of Book One – which has 57 chapters – Butor must do the same for Book Two. In fact, he has to find a centre for Book Two that is also the centre for Books One and Two, in view of the problem of the missing centre for (the *Discours*) in Book One! The Apology is the candidate solution to the latter problem.[19] But, for

Book Two, Butor's literal notion of the centre requires that its location be found in Chapter 19, the essay on freedom of conscience. Having introduced the idea that the composition of Books One and Two is increasingly labyrinthine,[20] Butor then argues that Montaigne's real purpose is to defend himself against charges of religious subversion easily laid by any careful reader of the 'Apology'. Therefore Montaigne hides behind the substitute portrait of Julian the Apostate (II, 19) and even risks losing the *Essays* to the Vatican censors in order to test his defences. The strategy was so successful that he could return from Rome to find himself elected Mayor of Bordeaux even in his absence, and despite the *Essays*.

Here, as an alternative to Butor's proposal, it might be worthwhile, with due care, to compare Montaigne's experience with his self-portrait with the central experience of the *Bildungsroman*.[21] Montaigne's portrait (*Bild*) turns into the formative experience (*Bildung*) of a continuous essaying of himself, in which the exchanges between author and text replace any simple notion of a copy, image or example[22] grasped in a single moment. It is the tenacity with which he sticks to the task of essaying himself that produces Montaigne's development, not any device of arranging his materials so as to tell a story of self-lost and self-regained:

> As I was considering the way a painter I employ went about his work, I had a mind to imitate him. He chose the best spot, the middle of each wall, to put a picture labored over with all his skill, and the empty space all around he fills with grotesques which are fantastic paintings whose only charm lies in their variety and strangeness. And what are these things of mine, in truth, but grotesques and monstrous bodies, pieced together of divers members, without definite shape, having no order, sequence, or proportion other than accidental?
>
> A lovely woman tapers off into a fish
>   Horace
>
> I do indeed go along with my painter in this second point, but I fall short in the first and better part; for my ability does not go far enough for me to dare to undertake a rich, polished picture, formed according to art. (I: 28, 135)

Horace's saying, *ut pictura poesis*, fostered the Renaissance identification of the activity of poetry with that of painting probably more than he wished.[23] Aristotle said that painters as well as poets portrayed human nature in action. Horace in *Ars Poetica* (1–13) describes a painting of grotesque hybrids which he compares to a book whose images are taken from a sick man's dreams. He then defends the imaginative freedom of both poets and painters. In the famous simile, Horace's point is that great literature like great art will require broad sweeping strokes as well as fine detail, and that the one ought not to be judged in terms of the other since each contributes to the effects of composition. We need to keep this in mind when discussing the composition of the *Essays*, if we are not to lose sight of their shifting arrangements of things and sayings. It is clear, however, that Montaigne avoids the strokes of idealisation and universalisation in his own self-portrait.[24] He had little temptation to see the world in anything but its own colours. And to do so, he could agree with Aristotle's claim that the theme of painting is human beings in action, since here painting and essaying set themselves a similar task, namely, to portray the passions. To achieve this, it is essential to have a knowledge of how the human mind and imagination are expressively tied to the human body and its smallest activity.[25]

The quest for plenitude, revealed in the subordination of writing to speech, might also be argued to underlie the doctrine of *imitatio* in so far as it fails to question the ontological status of the model upon which it draws. Thus painting furnished the model for poetry (*ut pictura poesis*) because of the power of its images to reawaken the lived presence of objects. But here what is involved is rather the confirmation of the plenitude of the objects represented. Montaigne, of course, puts painting to the test of capturing the passage of things, and the result is essaying as a positive literary invention rather than a failed metaphysics of presence, as Derrida might argue.[26] Each of the essays repeats Montaigne's finding that the meaning of things is relative to a context of living that is built up, just as an essay itself builds up, permitting a rivalry of interpretations that is hardly haunted by any metaphysic of plenitude. The *Essays* rather risk the appearance of a rag and bone shop of history and biography than display any standard of metaphysical discourse.

Montaigne's incapacity to dramatise himself is not a failure of nerve but rather a discovery of the proper method of the *Essays*. History is full of stories made up along the lines of the hero's confrontation of the world, but very few historians bring home the life of the man. What the essayist must achieve is an exemplary self-education in which his book tests him as other men are tested by the events and fortunes of the world. Montaigne evaluates his own travels, conversations and the whirl of social and political life in just these terms. A man must throw himself into the world for his education, he cannot stuff the world into his head. That is the sickness of books and all pedagogy uniquely tied to them:

> This great world, which some multiply further as being only a species under one genus, is the mirror in which we must look at ourselves to recognize ourselves from the proper angle. In short, I want it to be the book of my student. (I: 26, 116)

In setting memory so low and judgement so high, as he often does, Montaigne wanted to make it clear that we cannot attend school sitting on a parrot's stool. He knew how much education can be the enemy of reason and how it can sicken the hunger for knowledge. Nothing is worse than knowledge without a proper self-consciousness and nothing emptier than consciousness without knowledge. Knowledge should nourish the student's imagination much as his food feeds his body. But then, in either case, he must be ready for action that will exercise his bodily and mental functions in crucial situations from which he can essay the man in himself. At the same time, not everything is possible by way of education. The child speaks long; he knows what he is saying. We owe much of what we will become to what our parents have already been: 'We awaken on a journey we have neither wished for nor led. Our very origins prevent us from being original'.[27] Here, then, is a considerable shift in the imagery of self-portrait. On the one hand, there is the image of looking into the self as into a mirror, into a place that is still, and removed from the world. On the other hand, there is the idea that, after all, the world of action is our mirror, and we shall discover our portrait only through how we manage to conduct ourselves within the storm. The goal of self-knowledge is transformed into a life's undertaking, shaping and shaped by this very purpose. Thus Montaigne's pedagogical essays are quite different from Rousseau's *Émile*, for example, in that he makes no assumptions about any innate goodness of man. Indeed, Montaigne would have rejected any maieutic of that kind as quite false to the mixed nature of man who would only be further corrupted by reliance upon any such technique.

As we know, Montaigne reworked Books One and Two with extensive additions, avoiding any major alterations and adding a third Book. How does Butor adapt his analysis to take account of the composition of the final text of the *Essays*? We have seen how the movement from Book One to Book Two obliges Butor to compound metaphors, turning the 'garden' of Montaigne's playful thoughts into a 'fortress', defending their subversiveness. By the same token, Montaigne's tower shifts its symbolic significance from that of a decor for the first idle pursuit of the *Essays* into a 'bastion' defending their author against the fate that had fallen to La Boétie's *Discours*. But the incessant accumulation of additions to Books One and Two finally spills over into Book Three, and the question arises as to whether we can retain the garden-fortress as an image of the whole of the *Essays*. Butor continues to try to hold things together by the centre, and we are offered the following numerological key to the *Essays*:

Book One:

	(29)	
18 chapters (19)	18 chapters (39)	18 chapters

Book Two:

	18 chapters (19)	18 chapters

Book Three:

6 chapters (7)   6 chapters

The rationale for this structure is that, once we displace the centre in each book of the *Essays*, we discover that they are composed to suit the arithmetical harmonies composed in so far as Book Three is two thirds the length of Book One, and one third the length of Book Two.[28] Given that the total number of chapters in the *Essays* is uneven, namely, 103, we arrive at a new centre for the *Essays*, that is, Chapter 54, 'Of Vain Subtleties.' This being so, it is perhaps worth noticing the closing remark in that essay, since it gives us an idea of what Montaigne would have thought of Butor's numerological subtlety unless we are to conclude that all is vanity in the game of interpretation:

> But I find again, as ordinarily happens after the mind has opened up a passage, that we have taken for a difficult exercise what is not so at all; and that after our inventiveness has been warmed up, it discovers an infinite number of similar examples. And so I shall add only this one: that if these essays are worthy of being judged, I think they might not be much liked by common and vulgar minds, or by singular and excellent ones; the former would not understand enough about them, the latter too much. But they might get by in the middle region. (I: 54 227)

Although at the expense of a further shift of metaphors, whereby the tower becomes an 'observatory'[29] rather than a 'garden-fortress', Butor offers the more reasonable interpretation that by the time of Book Three Montaigne has cut his ties with the feudal nobility. He is now prepared to argue for the virtues of an unrepentant essayist, none other than Michel de Montaigne. If there is a field of endeavour suited to a gentleman, it is writing. If Montaigne is to be remembered, to have any family, or to be at home anywhere in the world, it is as the author of the *Essays*. Reconciled to himself and to the world, Montaigne now contents himself with a humble self-portrait, the honest observation of how life attaches him to himself and to other men who, for all their differences, live and die in much the same way – whether a king, a peasant or a writer. Considered as a whole, the *Essays* are a series of portraits. As Butor sees it, each Book of the *Essays* is dominated by a single portrait. The first Book is dedicated to La Boétie's image. In the second Book, Montaigne has acquired the strength to substitute a self-portrait. But by the third Book, Butor argues that – from a passage erased in the Bordeaux Edition – the *Essays* are once again sketching a friend, one who in the future will love the *Essays*, as did Miss de Gournay.[30] The result is that the *Essays* are reduced to a series of portraits like those Montaigne admired in the galleries of the Vatican. But the *Essays* are actually neither a portrait – despite Butor's claims – nor an autobiography. A portrait would lack the movement that is proper to life; and yet every life somehow collects itself beyond the passage of time into essential gestures that are the ground of portraiture. The self-essayist is pulled between these two claims.[31] The portrait demands organisation and arrangement, while the press of life's events pushes him towards an inventory, or a diary, which can come to no summary statement. Between these options, the writer may seek to join the flow of his life with the intimacies of self-revelation. But however much he tries to limit himself to simple narration, or to impartial self-observation, he is obliged to interpret himself to himself, and thereby to others.

At the close of Book One, in the essay 'Of Age' (I: 57), Montaigne argues that we must be ready at any moment to count our lives full. This is in part because he believed that a man achieves nothing great after thirty. He had in mind the historical record, the examples of Alexander, Hannibal, Cato and Jesus, and his own experience of physical decline. The underlying idea is that most of us live long enough to fashion our basic character and ability, for which we are responsible, and then a bit longer; until by way of illness, accident and death, which further test us, our lives are over. In the first Book of the *Essays* Montaigne, although well into his life as a soldier and statesman, has yet to form himself as an essayist. He enters into essaying as an artless and private exercise, with at most some family interest. Yet, very soon he tests the historical, philosophical and literary sources upon which he at first leans against what he has himself seen, heard and felt in the small scenes of his own life, his family and estate, in politics and love; and always in reading and writing. Gradually Montaigne's standpoint emerges, without any systematic declaration, that the matter of living exceeds rational a priori formulation but rests instead upon a practical faith men find at hand in their bodies, families, customs and laws. All rational and dogmatic systems are false to the lived coexistence of sense and non-sense, vice and virtue out of which men make their lives and their communities. If we are to collect our self-study, we can do so only by trying to observe ourself at work, in our family, in the eyes of a friend and by listening to our own senses. But this is an art that, so far from raising us above ourselves, only ties us more closely to living. Thus, as the *Essays* themselves grow into a second book they are increasingly Montaigne's child, old enough to be of company and mutual exploration. And, indeed, by this time the *Essays* have expressed the elements of a beautifully open pedagogy through which any young person might truly flower, to face later the tests of plain living that will surely fall upon them. Thus Montaigne counselled that we live close to our children and handle them with love rather than fear. He thought it ridiculous that adults try to hide who they are from their children, while revealing themselves to the least stranger. Above all, he was opposed to any notion of property in children. He believed a parent sets his child on a course, and that the child is the one responsible for its merits. Thus he likened the *Essays* to a child of his, to whom he was both father and mother, with the difference that he was entirely responsible for his offspring:

> To this child, such as it is, what I give I give purely and irrevocably, as one gives to the child of one's body. The little good I have done for it is no longer at my disposal. It may know a good many things that I no longer know and hold from me what I have not retained and what, just like a stranger, I should have to borrow from it if I came to need it. If I am wiser than it, it is richer than I. (II: 8, 293)

Is Montaigne, then, both father and mother of the *Essays*? Or, are the *Essays* father and he the mother? This is not Montaigne's view of origins. Either way, with respect to the child a bias is introduced with the assumption of ownership and control. But we know from the essay 'Of Idleness' (III: 13) that Montaigne considered that marriage and family demand the cultivation of husband and wife who together must educate their children to grow out of their patriarchal dependence. What mediates these relationships is friendship which is impossible without an equal commitment to teaching and learning. Here, as elsewhere, Montaigne cautions against rigidity, recommending rather that we acquire an openness to reversibility grounded in the practice of weighted comparison. This is the pedagogical ethic which Montaigne elaborated in the course of writing the *Essays* and to which they owe their own exemplary status. Indeed, in this sense it is Montaigne himself who is the child of the *Essays*. Yet, no more than a child should repeat its parents, Montaigne, too, never repeats himself. Nor do I think Montaigne ever lamented the lack of such dutiful readers – especially not in the name of friendship and less still of 'failed' piety.[32] Montaigne so obviously embraced the practice of difference and context as an essayist, it is a wonder that Rousseau rather than Montaigne provided Derrida's departure for the critical practice of writing and dissemination.[33] But then books have their fates!

Montaigne was a family man. The longest of all the essays, The 'Apology for Raymond Sebond', he undertook out of devotion to his father. It was a heavy enterprise that threatened at times to break the back of the *Essays*. But, of course, the 'Apology' is both a work of devotion and the most subversive of all Montaigne's essays; and never very far from his own self-exploration, even when it seems to be caught up in the most dogmatic issues. It is in the 'Apology' that we see Montaigne take his stand; not a quivering, indecisive scepticism, but the firmness of a man capable of weighing things for himself, of knowing when to set sail and when to cling to the shore or head for port. 'It is a municipal law that you allege; you do not know what the universal law is' (II: 12, 389). Montaigne's strength lies in not overestimating himself. Thus there is no central self-portrait in the *Essays*: and the maturity that is reached in Book Two is not a height from which Montaigne can only fail.[34] By the end of the *Essays*, Montaigne has placed everything in the balance, including the essayist himself, since he knows he must soon die. The last essays of Book Three must stand as one of the most sober and considered affirmations of our incarnation anywhere in literature. In these moments Montaigne is neither above nor below himself. He is not tempted to bemoan this vale of tears, nor to gladly separate himself from the pains of the body, with the illnesses, old age and other evils it inflicts upon us. Nor is he glad to be removed from the struggles of his day, or from the new forms of politics and religion that had caused so much suffering and trouble in his lifetime. There are no regrets – no sourness. In such an hour, the greatest of the artist's temptations is to turn his back upon his work, cast it into universal condemnation as no better than any other of life's frivolous gestures, and worthless in the face of death. Instead, Montaigne takes his stand, beautifully unrepentant. From where, then, does he derive his strength? As we have seen, he avoids any idealisation of himself or of his art. He is immune to patriotic or religious flights. Yet he is not a lonely figure, locked in his tower and long dead to the world before his hour. Montaigne is able to die because he was able to live. Moreover, he is able to contemplate the balance of things without that remorse which often undermines old age, if not anyone dying, because he had long ago practised at the court of conscience:

> It is a rare life that remains well ordered even in private. Any man can play his part in the side show and represent a worthy man on the boards; but to be disciplined within, in his own bosom, where all is permissible, where all is concealed – that's the point. The next step to that is to be so in our own house, in our ordinary actions, for which we need render account to no one, where nothing is studied or artificial. And therefore Bias, depicting an excellent state of family life, says it is one in which the master is the same within, by his own volition, as he is outside for fear of the law and of what people will say. Men have seemed miraculous to the world, in whom their wives and valets have never seen anything even worth noticing. Few men have been admired by their own households. (III: 2, 613–14)

Montaigne had no need of confession, no fancy of an altered life. This is because he had found a way of placing himself under the hardest eye of all. Here we encounter the central paradox of the *Essays*. It is Montaigne's discovery that the freedom of privacy requires a stricter court than any to be found in society. Montaigne's strength in the hour of death is given to him without confession because he had discovered the paradox of family life as the ultimate court of conscience. The rude justice of family life weeds out all immodest claims and postures among its members, exposing and ridiculing them until they are with-drawn, or at least wounded. Therefore Montaigne was particularly careful to avoid any exaggeration in the composition of his last days. He had no intention of throwing into the scale at the last moment any claim for the philosophical worth of the *Essays*, beyond their worth as a testament to embodied thought. And, by the same token, he managed to avoid upsetting the scale of his life by adding to its average wisdom any excess of last words, beyond these by which we remember him:

> In my opinion it is living happily, not, as Antisthenes said, dying happily, that constitutes human felicity. I have made no effort to attach, monstrously, the tail of a philosopher to the head and body of a dissipated man; or that this sickly remainder of my life should disavow and belie its fairest, longest, and most complete part. If I had to live over again, I would live as I have lived. I have neither tears for the past nor fears for the future. And unless I am fooling myself, it has gone about the same way within me as without. It is one of the chief obligations I have to my fortune that my bodily state has run its course with each thing in due season. I have seen the grass, the flower, and the fruit; now I see the dryness – happily, since it is naturally. I bear the ills I have much more easily because they are properly timed, and also because they make me remember more pleasantly the long felicity of my past life.
>
> Likewise my wisdom may well have been of the same proportions in one age as in the other; but it was much more potent and graceful when green, gay, and natural, than it is now, being broken down, peevish, and labored. Therefore I renounce these casual and painful reformations. (III: 2, 619–20)

We never learn from Butor what were the working problems posed for Montaigne in the construction of a literary self-portrait. Butor sacrifices these concerns to his own imaginary reconstruction of Montaigne's motives, and of his psychological and political strategies that allegedly determine the composition of the *Essays*. Thus, it is necessary for us to correct Butor's thesis with some final remarks on the nature of the bodily inquiry that constitutes self-portrayal. In this regard, it is interesting to pursue the attempt to retrieve self-reflection through the mirror image by recalling Rembrandt's experience with self-portraits.[35] It is as though Rembrandt and Montaigne were embarked upon the same self-essay, each discovering a bodily resolution of its ultimate paradox. In each case, the problem of identity initiates a quest for the self that can ride the waves of time, that can survive its own follies and irrelevant accumulations, and in some way stand above the crowd that it resembles in every other aspect. Above all, there is to be no solution to the continual unfolding of this paradox of identity in difference by means of any simple self-exaltation, nor any divine elevation. The self-portrait is to be a daily task, a lifelong endeavour that discovers its own morality in the patience and endurance of its practised observation. Just as Montaigne never left off the *Essays* once he had begun, so Rembrandt never finished with his self-portraits – from year to year they accumulated, to more than a hundred in his lifetime. They stand as a continuous exploration of the bodily experience of time, of the accumulation of things, of the body's ability to suffer illusion, to wear on towards death while returning its question through the very look that animates the self-portrait. Rembrandt painted his self-portrait at every age, in all sorts of costumes and conditions of life, and always without any idealisation. He stands among the things that the Dutch bourgeoisie gave their lives to accumulate. Indeed, the portraits are one more beloved thing, representative of the solid illusion of accumulation.

In the same vein, Montaigne could portray himself without apology, or with none other than that of a gentleman engaged in the making of the world whose surroundings offered him a daily and ordinary reflection of his achievements. This is the faith of bourgeois materialism, more honest for not dressing itself up in antique settings. The *Essays* and, for example, the two portraits of Rembrandt from 1629,[36] reflect a solid marriage of the spirit and the flesh, of sensualism and intellect, while never losing the ultimate mystery of their union, or the subtle interplay of appearance and reality that is the texture of the human body. At the same time, Rembrandt is consumed with the illusion of solidity achieved from canvas to canvas, from one thing to another, in one mood after another, and from person to person to person. When we consider the portraits of the *Philosophers*,[37] how are we to decide the underlying question? Is it that Rembrandt is everywhere in search of himself or has he discovered that the self is a fiction hiding the reality of dispersal in things, moments and other persons? I think that Rembrandt, like Montaigne, may have discovered that the self-portrait can only recover the alienation of the self's appearance to others by means of setting up its own bodily theatre through which there is a continuous subversion of the idea that others are free to make of us. What is revealed in the postures that inhabit the self-portraits, is that we can meet every man in ourselves provided we have a place to receive him that is more honest than our minds.

In the *Oriental Prince* (1631) we have a striking example of Rembrandt's creation of the body's truths, mastering the spirit without its illusions, insisting upon the essential metamorphosis of living. Metamorphosis of thought and being, of spirit and flesh, of self and others – as in a mirror, as in a body. Or we might speak of Rembrandt's discovery of interpicturality, of the movement from portrait to portrait that parallels Montaigne's discovery of the intertextuality of essaying. In both cases, there is a profundity of borrowings, copies and plagiarism that are shocking to the originality of the substantial self, but absolutely true to the world's metamorphosis, and to the daily debts of our living. The self-essayist discovers that the self is not the foundation of the world's values. The world has no author, unless it be God. The self therefore can only consist of a daily improvisation. That is the radical ethic of the self-portrait. It is therefore disconcerting to critics who require for their trade a substantial self to be found without involving them in any self-dispossession of the truths they manipulate on behalf of literature and art.

Having discovered the impossibility of any definitive revelation, the artist and essayist have nevertheless to avoid the traps of narcissism and relativism, of wilful contradiction and ultimate self-defeat. Therefore we see in the self-portraits of Rembrandt, as in the *Essays* of Montaigne, the gradual dominance of the author's look, mocking, suspicious, candid, proud, humble and caught in the farce. But with all the strength of natural inquisitiveness and self-scrutiny, these portraits throw back the pain of living, of ageing and dying. In both cases there is a progressive deepening of the expressive potentials of the baroque, away from theatrical dispersion, towards the inner concentration of the soul's body. Thus in the portrait of 1648, *Rembrandt Drawing Himself by the Window*,[38] we have, as in Montaigne's comments upon his own activity as a writer, a subversion of the myth of representation by means of a reflection endlessly reflected upon, unless gathered religiously in each of us. We are face to face with the mystery of creative work, with its virtuosity to affect us long after its author has left his hand upon it.[39] Because of its illusionism, painting was considered exemplary of the very vanity it was employed to portray. The Dutch and Flemish paintings of rich clients surrounded by the objects they had given their lives to accumulate were, indeed, known as vanitates. The portrait is therefore yet another moral paradox since it arrests a moment of truth in the flux of life, rejecting illusions by means of illusion:

> For every painted still life has the *vanitas* motif 'built in' as it were, for those who want to look for it. The pleasures it stimulates are not real, they are mere illusion. Try and grasp the luscious fruit or the tempting beaker and you will hit against a hard cold panel. The more cunning the illusion the more impressive, in a way, is the sermon on semblance and reality.[40]

It would be wrong, of course, to suggest that Montaigne could approach the literary task of self-portrayal with anything like the ready-found techniques of *trompe-l'œil* worked out by painters. In addition to the moral paradox suggested by these methods, their very success in capturing the still life is antithetical to the temporal inquiry that animates self-essaying. All the same, Montaigne could not entirely ignore the genre of still life for its attention to 'things without honour', to the commonplace objects of our daily living and its insistence upon the artistic worth of essentially unheroic enterprises. But the mirror especially concerned him, as it has always bothered painters troubled by its rival power of exact representation. In the *Essays* Montaigne toyed with the mirror image of the self-portrait. But he knew that the movement of life required of writing an accumulating reflection that could not be achieved through a still model, however corrected. The problem here is more akin to Jan van Eyck's self-referential mirror in the Arnolfini portrait.[41] It is also worth noticing that Montaigne's artistic interest in faithful description was not inimical to the experimental optical science of its day, and that in this respect Montaigrie's concerns were part of a tradition of clarity that well precedes Descartes and is perhaps continuous with the Epicurean materialism that Montaigne also favoured.[42] In fact, the development of perspective also played into the seemingly opposite construction of mixed forms, or grotesques, to which Montaigne likened his portrait. As a lover of Ovid, and one continuously absorbed in the relativity of human affairs, Montaigne would have appreciated how Holbein exploited the principles of projection in plane geometry to make the point of relativity. Thus, in the portrait of the ambassadors (a role well known to Montaigne), the skull in the picture can only be focused through letting go of the four-square ambassadors – a reminder that in their presence not everything that is going on can be perceived.

What the artist explored in the relativity of perspective, Montaigne had to explore in essaying the changeable self, the centreless person, the nobody struggling to be somebody and hence everybody.[43] Here the problem is that where a man is his own mirror, a false man will never see himself. Where is the essayist to find a way of reading himself out of the contexts of self-deception? Where in such a world is the substance of things to be grasped? Once the reflective turn to self-knowledge is taken, the mirror image[44] becomes an essential reference point, at the same time that the beholder becomes doubly responsible for what he or she finds there. In the mirror we have substance for the moment, concentrated in a gaze that seems to send back our bodily presence in all its intensity and hold upon the world. Why should the artist not accord himself the sitting he has provided for others in order to complete the presence implicit in their recorded lives? Therefore the artist and the writer are drawn to the self-portrait. That is to say, they are drawn irresistibly towards the limits of self-creation. Nor is this sheer narcissism, since it is surely rooted in the Christian doctrine of man's free will and self-determination, as well as in Socratic practice and the innumerable Renaissance arts of self-making reflected in Castiglione's *Courtier*. Every art engages in 'the play within the play', wherein the artist hopes to capture the conscience of the artist. Thus Montaigne placed himself in the balance of the *Essays*, and began that constant shifting of words to match the living oscillation of his thoughts and moods.

Those who consider Montaigne's self-portrait see in it the kind of narcissism that leads them to the easy conclusion that Montaigne preferred the *Essays* to his family. Yet we wish to claim that the *Essays* are the work of a family philosopher. Nor do we underestimate Montaigne's friendship with La Boétie as a source of the *Essays*. We are also aware that it is generally thought that Montaigne considered friendship the highest human relationship and that he did not consider it a possibility between men and women, at least once married. This need not be questioned. There is no doubt, however, that Montaigne held the family in high regard. He speaks with respect of his wife and, of course, of his own father. His pedagogical essays make it clear how important he cared for them. We have also remarked on Montaigne's view that the family is the first court of conscience, having a healthy contempt for exaggerated individual postures. It is in this light that we must consider Montaigne's comparison of the *Essays* to the mind's child. There would be no force in this remark had Montaigne no love for children in the first place. Therefore his intention was to find in the way men love and cherish their children – whom they nevertheless educate to be independent of them – the deepest analogy for the way he felt for the *Essays*. If he had intended to dote upon the *Essays*, as some dote on pets in preference to children, they would neither have served his friendship for La Boétie nor have attracted others with a similar but independent love of the *Essays*.

We have entered an old-fashioned plea for the *Essays*. To regard them as the work of a family man is surely to pass up more exciting prospects, particularly in view of contemporary encroachments of sexuality and textuality. I should therefore try to show why I find such readings excessive. I do so at least for the *Essays* which, in view of what else I have claimed for them as carnal inquiry, may seem to invite a Freudian reading. We need, then, to consider an extremely clever reading of Montaigne's 'On Some Verses of Virgil' (III: 5) proposed by Terence Cave.[45] The essay is strewn with Latin quotations, as though such prudery might conceal its sexual concerns. Montaigne observes that poetry reproduces an indefinable mood that is more amorous than love itself. Venus is not so beautiful all naked, alive and panting, as she is here in Virgil:

> Dixerat, et niveis hinc atque hinc diva lacertis
> Cunctantem amplexu molli fovet. Ille repente
> accepit solitam flammam, notusque medullas
> Intravit calor, et labefacta per ossa cucurrit.
> Non secus atque olim tonitru cum rupta corusco
> Ignea nima micans percurrit limine nimbos
> ....Ea verba loquutus,
> Optatos dedit amplexus, placidumque petivit
> Conjugis infusus gremio per membra saporem[46]

But this is innuendo that hardly works since the treatment of sex is explicit, can be read without the Latin quotations and is in any case not sexual in tone; being part of a larger consideration of the relationship between sex or love outside of marriage and love inside marriage. The exoticism of Latin was hardly for Montaigne what it might be for today's readers of sexual manuals. Moreover, Montaigne's feeling for Latin (his first tongue) is precisely for what it reveals rather than conceals. The language of Lucretius is praised for its power of putting ideas into flesh and bone, for embodying thought in the way ordinary people prefer it without having to separate soul and body in the pursuit of abstract ideas they never truly grasp. It is along these lines, in fact, that Montaigne begins the essay on Virgil's verses, which, by the way, occupy only half a page (III: 5, 645), in an almost forty-seven page essay; and are, in any case, compared with a rival passage from Lucretius (III: 5, 664) upon which most of the discussion turns.[47]

What Virgil says of Venus and Vulcan, Lucretius had said more appropriately of a stolen enjoyment between her and Mars:

> belli fera moenera Mavors
> Armipotens regit, in gremium qui saepe tuum se
> Rejicit, aeterno devinctus vulnere amoris:
> Pascit amore avidos inhians in te, Dea, visus,
> Eque tuo pendet resupini spiritus ore:
> Hunc tua, diva, tuo recubantem corpore sancto
> Circumfusa super, suavelis ex ore loquelas
> Funde[48]

The vigour of the Latin language and of Montaigne's own Gascon are then praised by him precisely because they resist the separation of mind and body that theologians and philosophers urge upon us. The *Essays* employ similarly vigorous language and in this particular essay Montaigne is concerned to resist the temptation to let either spiritualism or bodily decay dominate one's old age. 'On Some Verses of Virgil' is therefore concerned with what is properly due to the seasons of youth and old age, supposing we do not overwhelm either with an unhealthy subordination of the body to the mind in the education of youth or to a sickly separation of the two as the proper mark of old age. This is the framework within which Montaigne considers the nature of love among men and women. By the same token, it provides the context for Montaigne's own reflections on the whole question of public – and not merely sexual – self-revelation in the *Essays*, Cave, however, is of the opinion that Montaigne employs the verses of Lucretius in order to identify textuality and sexuality:

This primary intertextual process, by which a fragment of Latin verse is reconstituted in French prose, begins with a rewriting of privileged words: *'Quand je rumine ce "rejicit, pascit, inhians, nolli, fovet, medullas, labefacta, pendet, percurrit," et cette noble "circumfusa", mère du gentil "infusus". . . .'* Subsequently, the value attributed to such words is developed through the metaphor of the text as a living organism. Heralded by the connotation of 'digestion' implicit in the word 'rumine', this metaphor writes itself out as a *topos* of rhetorical theory. But its development in specifically textual terms appears as the unfolding, within the Montaignian text, of the theme of the Lucretian passage; a description of sexual activity is displaced to become a figure of the relationship between a text and its reader – hence the connotations of erection, penetration, and fertilization, and the possibility of a play on words in the phrase 'les plaines conceptions'.[49]

Cave's interpretation of Montaigne's text involves, then, a double identification of literary topic and literary resource which sexualises the reader–writer relationship as well as the writer–text relation. It can then be argued that Montaigne feared losing his reader's attention unless he could primp his language with Latin and Gascon in order to invigorate an abstract and overcivilised tongue. In the same vein, he larded his text with quotations from others, risking his identity in order to save it from fears of literary impotence. Above all, his plunderings from Plutarch represent nothing but that coquettish half-concealment that spices love in those who fear its consummation. The art of quotation is employed as literary deferment; Montaigne was no more in a hurry to come to his theme in 'On Some Verses of Virgil' than any other lover – although Virgil's Venus and Lucretius' Mars seem to be more precipitate.

But this is sheer proliferation. Let us remind ourselves of the essay. Montaigne is concerned with the seasons of love. As with any other topic the essayist treats, he must speak of it in terms of his own experience. Montaigne is neither a sexual prude nor a sexual extrovert; he is the body's essayist. As an essayist, his method requires that, having thrown everything into the pot in order to stir up settled opinion, he then begins to draw some distinctions. This is the real exercise for both writer and reader. Nothing is more curious than our conceptions of love and sex unless we try to order them at least with respect to what is due to our condition inside and outside of marriage. The conventions of love are quite different from those of marriage. Virgil's Venus is more beautiful in his love poetry than in life but only so long as she keeps to her own side of love's border:

What I find worth considering here is that he portrays her as a little too passionate for a marital Venus. In this sober contract the appetites are not so wonton; they are dull and more blunted. Love hates people to be attached to each other except by himself, and takes a laggard part in relations that are set up and maintained under another title, as marriage is. Connections and means have, with reason, as much weight in it as graces and beauty, or more. We do not marry for ourselves, whatever we say; we marry just as much for our posterity, for our family. The practice and benefit of marriage concerns our race very far beyond us. Therefore I like this fashion of arranging it rather by a third hand than by our own, and by the sense of others rather than by our own. How opposite is all this to the conventions of love! And so it is a kind of incest to employ in this venerable and sacred alliance the efforts and extravagances of amorous license, as it seems to me I have said elsewhere. (III: 5, 645–6)

In short, Montaigne was no more likely to confuse textuality and sexuality than he was to confuse sex in love and sex in marriage. Montaigne no more played Don Juan to the *Essays* than to his wife; and for the same reason. He could tell the difference! He knew what each required of him and what it was proper of himself to ask of them. And he knew this because he knew what he could require of himself according to time and place and to the seasons of his life. As a young man he was given to love and not the *Essays* which he would no more exchange for the feeble exploits of old age than of his sporting youth. For the rest, Montaigne saw very well that men and women have their own sexuality about which they are enormously ambivalent. In particular, he questioned the double bind of chastity and eroticism in which men seem to confine women. Yet men and women are alike in being able to distinguish the relative goods and evils of promiscuous and married love; neither being tempted by the one when they want the other. Why, then, do our literary critics not accord them their ordinary intelligence in these matters? Only jealousy and envy disturb it and that is where so many of the incredible tales of love come to us. Even so, what we can learn from them is not that sex is the world's master but that we must try to keep sex and marriage within conventions proper to each; and not talk as though there were no such boundary. With this in mind, Montaigne reveals that he finds sex a natural release which like other body releases reminds the soul of its earthly companion. It also reminds us of our common humanity. It is curious that we are more likely to vilify the act whereby we enter life than the one in which we leave it. Perhaps, then, we do best to cultivate love to make of it an art, for which Montaigne so admired the Italians who were courtly in this respect even with prostitutes. In this, he observes they were right because a woman's will cannot be bought with her body; and without it sex is abhorrent:

I say likewise that we love a body without soul or sentiment, when we love a body without its consent and desire. Not all enjoyments are alike. A thousand causes other than good will may win us this concession from the ladies. It is not sufficient evidence of affection; there may be treachery in it as elsewhere; sometimes they go to it with only one buttock:

> As cool as if preparing frankincense and wine . . .
> You'd think her absent or of marble.
>
> Martial (III: 5, 673)

Women and men do not differ much more in their sexual lives than in the rest of their attitudes, although in the heat of passion we may mistake them and ourselves. Montaigne, on looking back, feels that his sexual exploits were in some ways enhanced and in others foiled by his basic disposition. He was not able to take pleasure without being able to give it. But this means, he could not love without being loved by one free and equal to love him. For this same reason, although he can muse upon how love might lighten his later years, even add a blush to his pale cheeks, he knows his body cannot respond in return. It is for this reason that Montaigne concludes that love is the business of the very young; well before marriage and hardly inside of it:

> A good marriage, if such there be, rejects the company and conditions of love. It tries to reproduce those of friendship. It is a sweet association in life, full of constancy, trust, and an infinite number of useful and solid services and mutual obligations. No woman who savors the taste of it.
>
> Whom the nuptial torch with welcome light has joined
> Catullus
>
> would want to have the place of a mistress or paramour to her husband. If she is lodged in his affection as a wife, she is lodged there much more honorably and securely. When he dances ardent and eager attention elsewhere, still let anyone ask him then on whom he would rather have some shame fall, on his wife or his mistress; whose misfortune would afflict him more; for whom he wishes more honor. These questions admit of no doubt in a sound marriage. (III: 5, 647)

With this in mind, we can be even more positive in rejecting the sexualisation of the *Essays*. Just as Montaigne would not seduce his wife, or his friend La Boétie, he would not seduce his reader. He tells us that war and hunting are equally good *topoi* for the metaphors that keep literature alive. He likens the reader and the writer to tennis players. Now in every case what is involved is an exercise in which the whole body is, as it were, the point of balance for each move incorporating what the game itself requires of the matched partners. Where everything is one sided, there is no game; and it is the game, whether in love, hunting, fencing or literature, that offers its own enjoyment. Montaigne no more seeks to caponise his reader than he himself cared for writers who tried that very move; above all, he did not intend the *Essays* to overstep the bounds of unrepentant modesty. And if, not to leave things too much on the side of reverence in speaking of love, he quotes as do churchmen in order to compensate his lack of poetry:

> May I die if your crack is more than a faint line
> Beza

> A friendly tool contents and treats her well
> Saint-Gelais (III: 5, 678)

he does so to show that he tolerates nature's way in this; neither more nor less.

Though sick and ageing, Montaigne was at the height of his literary powers in the last essays. Yet Cave trades upon Wilden's thesis to argue that Montaigne could still devalue the *Essays* in exchange for the lost plenitude of youthful sex:

the values intrinsic to sex (and thus to 'natural' life itself) are seen as diametrically opposed to the values which the *Essais* exploit and indeed rely on. In particular, this devaluation appears to affect the notion of *experience* and its correlate *essai* (since both are germane to *exercitation*): that is to say, it undermines the whole generative process which the book porports to celebrate. If *exercitation* is synonymous with *usage*, the *ordre* of the book (as of life itself) functions as the emptying out of an original plenitude. To put it another way, the *Essais*, by attempting to recover what was already lost before the writing began, proliferate at the expense of life. The hand that writes them is a '*main phtinopore*', simultaneously ripening and ravaging.[50]

The Cave–Wilden thesis is excessive. Montaigne portrayed himself whole, without regret, without nostalgia. He did not subordinate his life to any schema: and certainly not the *Essays*:

I expose myself entire: my portrait is a cadaver on which the veins, the muscles, and the tendons appear at a glance, each part in its place. One part of what I am was produced by a cough, another by a pallor or a palpitation of the heart – in any case dubiously. It is not my deeds I write down; it is myself, it is my essence. (II: 7, 274).

There are no ghosts and no skeletons in the *Essays*. There is Montaigne, his friend La Boétie and his family. The winds that howl around them are largely the winds of literary criticism.

CHAPTER 8

On Public and Private Life

The *Essays* oblige us continually to refer not only to the problem of their origin – but to the generative place of their common places (*topoi*). We must, then, essay the division between Montaigne's public and private life. Here, and elsewhere, we encounter readings of Montaigne's conscience as a writer and politician which go to the very heart of the *Essays*.[1] For this reason, we need to be careful in their exercise.

The problem we shall now focus upon is Montaigne's treatment of the relation between the public and private conscience of a man of politics.[2] Montaigne was a courtier in the time of the civil religious wars of sixteenth-century France, Mayor of Bordeaux and a profound essayist of man's inner estate. Thus, although it is conventional to remark upon Montaigne's retirement and to notice his own disparagement of the *Essays*, we are in fact dealing with a man whose active life was spent in politics at a time when the conflict between the state and religion, interwoven with deadly quarrels, the massacre of Saint Barthélemy, and individual assassinations, could cost a man his life and property for just a word or thought out of season. A first direction is to contrast Montaigne with Machiavelli, since political theorists can be counted upon to share an interest in Machiavelli and, presumably, in what might relate to him:

> Whereas Machiavelli assessed political activity positively and rejoiced in the vigor and glory peculiar to the exercise of political *virtù*, Montaigne denied that a life lived according to these principles was ultimately satisfying or praiseworthy for a man of judgment.[3]

Now, two remarks are in order here. In the first place, this sort of judgement is over influenced by a consideration of Montaigne's later years. It does not sufficiently weigh Montaigne's evaluation of what is an activity fitting to a young man – it is unquestionably war and politics – and what is fitting to an older man, whose body is as little suited to making war as it is to making love! Here, again, Montaigne's interests are in line with the Renaissance conviction that war must be the principal subject of historical analysis once history deals with *res gestae*.[4] War is particularly deserving of careful study because it is the field in which time forces of contingency (fortuna) and human character interact – with lessons for us all, but especially for young princes and noblemen. Philippe de Commines and Guicciardini, Montaigne's favourite historians, exemplified these practices respectively in the *Mémoires* and the *Storia d'Italia*. History is viewed as the study of the events shaped by character and fortune, requiring of participants and historiographers alike sound sense and moral judgement. Historical characters are mixtures of good and evil, intelligence and stupidity, and therefore complex individual actors whose portraits are not based upon fixed types. It can be shown that Montaigne does not disparage political life any more than Machiavelli.[5] Rather, he continued in his retirement and old age during which he was still engaged as Mayor of Bordeaux, and in long diplomatic missions – to reflect upon the problematic of political conscience. Secondly, it is worthwhile to explore in a little detail just what Montaigne did say with respect to Machiavellian considerations. Finally, we need to consider Montaigne's relationship to his friend La Boétie as the author of a political pamphlet, the *Discourse on Voluntary Servitude*. Here we must take up the classical problem of the relation between friendship and democracy in order to outline an implicit critique of political domination that may be found in the work of Montaigne and La Boétie. The whole of our argument might then be taken as an expansion of R.A. Sayce's extremely judicious assessment of Montaigne's political posture:

> We are thus faced with a Montaigne who is at once deeply conservative and radically liberal, even revolutionary, above all subversive. His conservatism, however, is pragmatic only. It is based entirely on the premise that all change runs the risk of producing a worse state of affairs than the present one, however bad it may be. In a sense, the worse it is shown to be, the stronger the argument. He is thus led to question all established values, to reveal the injustices, absurdities and hollowness of all venerated institutions, religious, political and social. He remains a conservative but his conservative position is revealed by a circuitous route which takes in all the potentially revolutionary themes which were eventually to find expression in action as well as thought. If we consider Montaigne in himself, especially from the point of view of temperament and personality, we shall no doubt stress his conservative side; if with the advantage of hindsight, we consider his influence and the later history of

his subversive ideas, we shall find that it is the revolutionary side which is uppermost.[6]

I Montaigne on the *Vita Activa*

Montaigne's later reflections upon political life cannot be separated from his own practice as a young man who committed himself heartily to military and political matters. In this, he stood close to his friend La Boétie, whose *Discourse on Voluntary Servitude* we must examine, and, of course, he simply met the conventional standard for a member of the *noblesse d'épée*. Moreover, he insisted upon these practices as the necessary elements of a young nobleman's education. We shall consider these aspects of Montaigne's thought as a necessary prelude to any closer comparison between his and Machiavelli's passion for political life. Montaigne has sometimes incurred the laughter of critics who believe that he aspired to a station, the *noblesse d'épée*, beyond his commercial origins and its normal reward in the *noblesse de robe*, But this overlooks Montaigne's distinguished career as a man of arms, the key position of Bordeaux in the Hundred Years' War between England and France, as well as Montaigne's importance in the Parlement of Bordeaux, and at the courts of the King of France, Charles IX, and Henri de Bourbon, King of Navarre. The conferral upon him in 1571 of the Order of Saint Michael involved the kind of public examination of his character and abilities of which Montaigne delighted – a test that he continued to set himself daily in the *Essays*.

Whatever we may think of it today, Montaigne loved the life of the gentleman-warrior, not the professional soldier and not the illiterate. Such a warrior needs to he well born, not in the sense of noble birth, but in that he is endowed with sufficient talent to resist dependence in the exercise of his mental and physical ability. More precisely, such a man needs to be in his youth open to the sort of pedagogical exercises that Montaigne insisted upon in the *Essays*:

To the examples may properly be fitted all the most profitable lessons of philosophy, by which human actions must be measured as their rule, lie will be told:

What you may justly wish: the use and ends of hard-earned coin; our debt to country and to friends; What heaven has ordered us to be, and where our stand, amid humanity, is fixed by high command; What we now are, what destiny for us is planned

Persius

155

what it is to know and not to know, and what must be the aim of study; what are valor, temperance and justice; what the difference is between ambition and avarice, servitude and submission, license and liberty; by what signs we may recognise true and solid contentment; how much we should fear death, pain and shame;

> What hardships to avoid, what to endure, and how;
>
> Virgil

what springs move us, amid the cause of such different impulses in us. For it seems to me that the first lessons in which we should steep his mind must be those that regulate his behavior and his sense, that will teach him to know *himself* and *to die well* and live well. *Among the liberal arts, let us begin with the art that liberates us.* (I: 26, 117)

The prototype of such a man was La Boétie, in whose company one could freely develop the capacity for sound judgement upon matters of life and state, as well as upon the fortunes of war. Here, as in philosophy or medicine, Montaigne is the enemy of professionalism. He did not believe that men are helped by the view that human affairs can be managed so that men will not have to respond capably to the inevitable intervention of Fortune. It is in this sense that Montaigne admires Alcibiades. Moreover, we ought not to imagine that Montaigne is simply engaging in the literary vice of vicarious imagination. Montaigne was quite familiar with war and his references to it, as we have just seen, are first hand. Today, we find it hard to think of the writer as a warrior. War has, of course, fascinated many writers but generally they are enamoured either of the heroes or the antiheroes of war. Their own life-style, at least as it is romantically conceived is otherwise antithetical to the organisation, blind obedience and overall insanity of professional militarism. But we need to recall that many men have gone into battle, and conducted themselves with bravery and honour, without any love of either war or the military life. Prior to the days of modern warfare, and its bureaucratisation of anonymous killing, men like Socrates, Marcus Aurelius and Montaigne all found themselves in battle. We must be careful to avoid any anachronistic distaste or disparagement of their deeds. In particular, we have not to imagine that their military exploits are referred to from any doubts about the manliness of their philosophical and literary pursuits. This is much more a problem of our own time, where the specialisation of the professions prevents us from crossing the lines. The general obsession with violence in modern society is in fact a testament to the uneasiness men feel in ordinarily not knowing how they will conduct themselves in the face of pain and death. In all previous centuries, and still in wide parts of the world today, men, women and even children are hardly in need of vicarious experience of suffering. Indeed, what Montaigne was equally conscious of is the ability of ordinary people to meet pain and death without elaborate provision, and untutored in the ways of the courtier.

Montaigne was, of course, attached to the Renaissance pursuit of glory (*gloria*) and virtue (*virtus*). The effort to combine this in a lasting monument represented a complex political ideal and not just a personal ambition.[7] Indeed, the achievement of this ideal was threatened by nothing so much as the temptation of personal ambition, an easy surrender to the crowd or the wickedness of a prince. Thus Montaigne's essay 'On Glory' is harsh upon its deceptions, for nothing turns so much upon fortune as a reputation, and nothing is less trustworthy than the occasions on which it is accorded. In fact, Montaigne's essay 'On Glory' is antiheroic in spirit.[8] He observes that war is full of chance. More than half of it unnoticed, the work of thousands of unnamed persons. What we call military honour is an arbitrary social practice of selecting a few deeds by a very few persons, whereas if the truth were known these might easily have been excelled by others:

> An infinity of fine actions must be lost without a witness before one appears to advantage. A man is not always at the top of a breach or at the head of an army, in sight of his general, as on a stage. He is taken by surprise between the hedge and the ditch; he must tempt fortune against a hen roost; he must root out four paltry musketeers from a barn; he must go out alone from his company and do a job alone, as the need presents itself. And if you watch carefully, you will find by experience that the least brilliant occasions happen to be the most dangerous; and that in wars that have taken place in our times, more good men have been lost on trivial and unimportant occasions and in fighting over some shack in worthy and honorable places. (II: 16, 471–2)

Such remarks represent the best of Montaigne's inimitable combination of experience and reflection. He is not revolted by war. He merely speaks from his experience as one necessarily engaged in it, and who tries to remain clear about its real nature. Here, as elsewhere, he joins philosophical reflection to the details of lived experience, without however going so far as to totally separate the values of the inner life from the public life:

> We must go to war out of duty, and expect this reward, which cannot fail for all noble nations, however hidden they be, and even for virtuous thoughts: the contentment that a well-regulated conscience receives in itself from welldoing. We must be valiant for ourselves and for the advantage we derive from having our courage firmly grounded and secure against the results of fortune. (II: 16, 472)

Whereas Castiglione insisted upon making his Courtier the sum of virtue, Montaigne advised that his gentleman-warrior not set himself above the common level – not from any democratic restraint but simply because the historical record shows that it is hard to excel, and less likely the more we presume upon our chances. Moreover, life at court and on the battlefield will require of him conduct that is far from ideal; he will need to be flexible and not opinionated.

Montaigne had, of course, to disengage himself from his military profession, if only because of age. It must be remembered that in Montaigne's day a man was considerably aged at forty years. Montaigne is extremely sensible of what is becoming to a man in the various seasons of his life. He is quite disinclined to try the foolishness of a bluster and debauchery that he might earlier have enjoyed without ruining himself. The *Essays* accommodate finely to Montaigne's experience of illness and old age – and that really the only proper meaning of their 'evolution' – *pace* Villey and others. Moreover, this is a major part of what we need to understand by Montaigne's 'retirement'. As a young man of social position, he threw himself into his duties as a soldier and statesman. Whether due to fortune, good sense or bravery, he survived a busy and dangerous life which still left him in his later years with considerable political risks and arduous journeys to undertake to a troublesome country.[9] In addition, he took upon himself the new enterprise of self-study, testing and essaying himself in life's great struggle with illness and death. Here it is generally noticed that Montaigne's attitude towards the problem of death changes somewhat, as though he was now familiar with what as a young man, in full health and vigour, he could only imagine. The difference is, as we have seen, that his own body became the tutor in place of the books and philosophical exhortation he had to rely upon in his youth.

II Montaigne's Anti-Machiavel

So far, we have tried to show from the way Montaigne embraced his military obligations that we can hardly base his differences with Machiavelli on any exaggerated distaste for political life. Such an argument relies too heavily upon a separation between the statesman and the warrior. In practice, Montaigne and men of his standing regarded military service truly chosen on behalf of their country as the highest of obligations:

> There is no occupation so pleasant as the military one, an occupation both noble in execution (for the strongest, most generous, and proudest of all virtues is valor) and noble in its cause: there is no more just and universal service than the protection of the peace and greatness of your country. (III: 13, 841)

This remained a conviction of Montaigne until the end of his life. But he knew, of course, that political life is often more complex, and in many ways more dangerous, because more treacherous, than the fortunes of war. Therefore, we must now try to evaluate Montaigne's conception of the virtues peculiar to the political realm, and then see how he struggled to reconcile them with the demands of private conscience and individual integrity which he laid upon himself and those under his guidance.[10] Here we shall compare Montaigne's views directly with what he has to say of Machiavelli. We can then raise the larger issue of the pre-political grounds of political action which is where the differences between Montaigne and Machiavelli are most acute. Yet, precisely because it is Montaigne who is more attuned to the sociological grounds of politics, we are again obliged to modify the claim that his love of privacy involved any lesser care for the political realm. For Montaigne did not impose upon political life standards that he could not find in other aspects of man's life and social relations. Had he done so, he would only have divided himself against himself. No one knew better than Montaigne the difficulty of establishing any firm standard among human beings whose capacity for inequality defies imagination:

> Plutarch says somewhere that he does not find so much difference between one animal and another as he does between one man and another. He is talking about the capacity of the soul and the inward qualities. In truth, I find Epaminondas, as I imagine him, so remote from some men I know – I mean men capable of common sense – that I would willingly outdo Plutarch and say that there is more distance from a given man to a given man than from a given man to a given animal:
>
>
>
> How far one man excels another!
> Terence
>
>
>
> and that there are many degrees in minds as there are fathoms from here to heaven, and as innumerable. (I: 42, 189)

The historical record shows such an anthropological diversity that it can be wondered how it is that society is possible at all. Men have evaluated every aspect of human conduct in such different ways that all that can be expected is a purely local order, the force of custom, habit, law and religion. Indeed, no sooner does the basis of these attachments become subject to speculation, than these attachments become as volatile as any other upon which men have exercised their reason and opinion. Witness the cruelty of the wars of religion, in particular over the bodily presence of Christ in the sacrament of communion. In view of all the terrible bodily mutilations that men have made a part of religion (II: 12, 388), including Christ's own passion and crucifixion, there might well be some merit in the Protestant argument for a purely abstract conception of God, quite free from magical images. Yet while rejecting any other image of God, Montaigne believes that there are necessary arguments for those corporeal images through which man represents God to himself. The first argument is a conservative one, in the purely political sense, and the second is an argument from Montaigne's fundamental anthropology:

> Pythagoras adumbrated truth more closely in judging that the knowledge of this first cause, being of beings, must be undefined, unprescribed, undeclared: that it was nothing else but the utmost effort of our imagination toward perfection, each man amplifying the idea of it according to his capacity. But if Numa undertook to make the piety of his people conform to this plan, to attach it to a purely intellectual religion, without any predetermined object or material admixture, he undertook something unusable, The human spirit cannot keep floating in this infinity of formless ideas; they must be compiled for it into a definite picture after its own pattern.
>
> The divine majesty has thus let itself be somewhat circumscribed within the corporeal limits on our behalf; his supernatural and heavenly sacraments show signs of our earthly condition; his worship is expressed by perceptible, rituals and words; for it is man that believes and prays. (II: 12, 381)

Society holds together best when we remember our bodily limits. To this end, the imagery of the body politic[11] no less than that of the body of Christ is a saving reminder. There is no limit to argument, and no length to which men will not go on behalf of abstract principles. The civil war that surrounded Montaigne was a testament to the way language bewitches men. Thus civil order is best served through rituals that give bodily and sensory shape to the concerns of men and society so that they are not diminished through abstraction and interminable controversy:

> The senses act as the proper and primary judges for us, and they perceive things only by their external accidents: thus it is no wonder that in all the functions that serve the welfare of society there is always such a universal admixture of ceremony and outward show that the best rind most effective part of a government consists in these externals. It is still man we are dealing with, and it is a wonder how physical [*merveilleusement corporelle*] his nature is. (III: 8, 710)

However, Montaigne did not record the differences in men's customs, beliefs and opinions merely to fall back upon an exhausted attachment to his own ways. It is rather that he essayed the weight of custom and habit upon us, the attachments of birth, family and village, in order to awaken man's critical faculty, while not exciting reason to limits it cannot exceed so long as we remain prudent men who avoid the more preposterous claims of universality. Montaigne, any more than Socrates, was not friendly to the blindness of opinion, to the weakness of habit, to the injustice of law or to the immorality of religion.[12] But he chose not to oppose them on the grounds of either the perfectability of man or of the state. He preferred rather a common patience, capable of improvement, but always fearful of self-destruction through excess of reason:

> These considerations, however, do not deter a man understanding from following the common style. On the contrary, it seems to me that all peculiar and out-of-the way fashions come rather from folly and ambitious affectation than from true reason, and that the wise man should withdraw his soul within, out of the crowd, and keep it in freedom and power to judge things freely; but as for externals, he should wholly follow the accepted fashion and forms. (I: 23, 86)

To this point, Montaigne's distinction between public and private values seems to suggest that true reason cannot prevail over the general role of external appearances, and so the wise man must accept public defeat and reserve his freedom to himself. Rather, what Montaigne is saying is that the wise man would only aggravate public folly if he thought his reason were strong enough to make his views a truly public standard. True wisdom requires that we recognise that public and social life is all encompassing; that it is not just a result of intellectual activities. Public life requires everything of us, and we are more likely to be of good service the less we put ourselves above society:

> Society in general can do without our thoughts; but the rest – our actions, our work, our fortunes, and our very life – we must lend and abandon to its service and to the common opinions just as the great and good Socrates refused to save this life by disobedience to the magistrate, even to a very unjust and very iniquitous magistrate. For it is the rule of rules, and the universal law of laws, that each man should observe those of the place he is in:
>
> > It is a fine thing to obey your country's laws.
> > Crispin (I: 23, 86)

Here Montaigne's sociological insight is the basis of what many treat as his political conservatism. It is the ground of his difference with ideologists of all sorts, but in particular with the Protestant reformers; although Luther and the Calvinists were much more authoritarian than anything Montaigne had in mind.[13] Montaigne himself had done as much as anyone to weaken the claims of religious rationalism in his 'Apology for Raymond Sebond' (II: 12), so it is not a matter of his uncritical reliance upon religious authority.[14] It is rather that he believed that society best rests upon an authority that is not open to changes of fashion and opinion, since the political realm is not a means to self-interest but is the very matrix from which all human interests take enduring shape.[15] Montaigne could be critical of the legal injustice, inequality and cruelty which prevailed in his day. His 'Apology for Raymond Sebond' is perhaps the most subversive testament to religious faith we have. Yet he did not believe that society, however improvable, is properly the object of any science of politics or political counsel. It is his practised suspicion of this particular claim that separates him from Machiavelli. Moreover, this suspicion represents, as will be seen in the next section of our argument, a fundamentally pluralist ethic, rather than mere political scepticism.

Of course, Montaigne confronted similar political and social conditions in France as Guicciardini and Machiavelli in Italy. Politics was a matter of the clash of multiple principalities and shifting hierarchies. Europe was opening onto America, thereby turning a mirror upon its own nature. Experience was not a matter of the hard lessons of increasingly autonomous fields of action, thought and judgement. Subtlety and supreme tact, tuned to the niceties and novelties of the situation, and unencumbered by unwieldy abstractions and generalisations, became the necessary political and social virtues. Around the courts, and in diplomatic relations these virtues of tact, dissimulation and interested service made political life particularly dangerous for those engaged in it, as well as a prize for those who were successful. The variability of human passions, the sudden alterability of man's condition, the infinite variety of man's circumstances, beliefs and actions, schooled men of the day in a hard empiricism. But the important question is to try to evaluate the difference in the overall moral relativism which this political empiricism inspired in men like Machiavelli and Montaigne. Are the two men divided, the one a thoroughgoing pessimist, and the other an optimist, provided he can draw the line between public and private life to suit himself? Montaigne could insist vehemently upon the values of decency, fidelity, honour and sincerity. He abominated lies. But did he weaken these claims by relegating them to his private life, accepting a radical break between morals and politics, whereas Machiavelli simply dispensed with such a weak division, accepting the wholly political animal?

The classical discussion of the rupture between morals and politics, to which men in the sixteenth century often addressed themselves, occurs in Cicero's *De officiis* (II, 19 33): *Pervertunt homines ea, quae sunt fundamenta naturae, cum utilitatem ab honestate seiungunt.* Here Cicero raises the problems of reconciling morals (*honestum*) and practice (*utile*) terms used by Guicciardini, Machiavelli and Montaigne. Whereas Cicero attempts to preserve their unity, later writers started from the disjunction of morals and expediency. For example, Cicero allows that while it is morally inadmissible (*turpis*) to kill a parent, nevertheless where the parent is a tyrant it may be allowable (*honestas*) from the standpoint of political practice (*utilitas*). Thus, although the moral standpoint is preserved, it is relativised without being subordinated to particular political functions. Of course, the path is a slippery one. How does one know when a ruler has come to the state of tyranny that would justify regicide, let alone patricide? Such questions are easily answered by anyone with political motives, and in Machiavelli's view the underlying ethical problem is wholly subsumed in political practice (*Discorsi*, III, 9 and 15). Montaigne differs with Machiavelli on this. He believes that the Machiavellian position, while perhaps effective in the short run, undermines itself through its own long-run repercussions:

> Those who, in our time, in establishing the duties of a prince, have considered only the good of his affairs, and have preferred that to caring for his fidelity and conscience, would have something to say to a prince whose affairs Fortune had so arranged that he could establish them once and for all by a single breach and betrayal of his word. But that is not the way it goes. You often fall into the same sort of bargain again; you make more than one peace, more than one treaty, in your life. The gain that lures them to the first breach of faith – and almost always there is gain in it, as in all other wicked deeds: sacrilege, murder, rebellion, treachery are always undertaken for some profit – this first gain brings after it endless losses, casting this prince out of all relations and means of negotiation in consequence of this breach of faith. (II: 17, 492)

Thus, Montaigne did not have his eyes closed to the facts of political life. He was quite able to see the role of intrigue, bargains and treachery of all sorts, as practised around him at times in the name of the state and sometimes in the name of religion. What he questioned is whether these practices could be rationalised as the definitive features of a distinctly political realm, thereby finding an exercise they were denied in moral life. For Montaigne was quite capable, apart from such an admission, of recognising a realm of practical political conduct in which men might well be obliged to undertake deeds that lacked any immediate congruency with their moral values. In his essay on 'The Useful and the Honorable' (III: 1) he considers the historical record in order to bring to bear the political experience of others and himself upon an otherwise abstract ordering of morals and politics. The political passions are as mixed as any other motives of human conduct. It is as though good and bad are not only inseparable in us but are even relative to one another, so that although we try to place virtue above vice, each seems in us always to have some tinge of the other: 'Our structure, both in public and private, is full of imperfection' (III: 1, 599).

In fact, Montaigne suspects that any attempt to alter these ratios in any fundamental way – beyond what is occasionally achieved by exceptional men – would
be a hazardous undertaking. It seems as though men's vices have as natural a place
in the moral economy as poisons that may be used with medical benefit. What is
important is to know one's own capacities; a man who is constitutionally incapable of the treachery and cruelty of politics should avoid getting himself into
such undertakings. Political life consists of a sufficiently varied business that we
must know to which of its offices we are best suited so that overall the public life
of society is served. Montaigne believed that it is quite possible to steer between
hostile parties provided one realises that extreme commitments generally go
beyond any real grounds we have for them. Yet he saw, too, that this is a counsel
that is fitted to some levels of political action more than others, where generally
extremist positions are demanded:

> This whole procedure of mine is just a bit dissonant from our ways. It would
> not be fit to produce great results or to endure. Innocence itself could neither
> negotiate among us without dissimulation nor bargain without lying. And so
> public occupations are by no means my quarry; what my profession requires, I
> perform in the most private manner I can. (III: 1, 603)

It should be noticed that Montaigne and Machiavelli admired the same military captains[16] – Alexander the Great, Alcibiades and Caesar, for example – but
whereas Machiavelli was interested solely in their political efficacy, Montaigne
was also concerned with their qualities as men. Montaigne is interested in the
workings of courage, confidence , intelligence and will-power. For all his admiration of Caesar, he did not give him pride of place among his heroes of antiquity.
Machiavelli, too, ranks Caesar third after the founders of religion and states. Only
Socrates commands all of Montaigne's admiration. In general, both preferred
men of action. Whereas Machiavelli counselled his Prince to trust the political
efficacy of his deeds rather than their intrinsic morality, Montaigne looked to politics as a field for the revelation of character. By the same token, what each understood by virtue was the republican values of courage and decisiveness in action –
not anything Christian.

Montaigne always speaks as a man who knows the strain of political life and we
must not forget that he is not simply reflecting upon the historical record in
abstraction from his own experience, the divisions in his very family the constant
threat to his life and property that faced him every day in the treacherous quarrels of France's civil-religious wars. He knew very well that deception was a
requirement of political life. What he insisted upon is that the politician make
every effort to judge whether he is indeed serving the public utility and not some
selfish motive of his own.

In politics, as in life generally, Montaigne stands for a certain antiheroism, for the value of survival as an ultimate good. Perhaps we are better able to appreciate this today, having seen how problematic are the results of modern progress, ideological politics and revolutions. Of course, such reflections immediately raise the charge of political conservatism, if not purism, and we need to look at Montaigne's position in this light. The problem is that we can easily marshal texts from the *Essays* that display Montaigne's critical ability to undermine the presumptive sanctity of law, custom, habit and opinion of every kind. Yet when he is faced with evaluating the social changes in his own day Montaigne comes down on the side of the status quo. Montaigne seems, then, to be a liberal in thought and a conservative in practice.[17] He himself says he was disgusted by the mischievous and cruel changes inspired by religious reform and he hardly seems to have considered the Protestant claims of individual conscience as the proper ground of religious authority.[18] His reasons for that are clear enough in the 'Apology for Raymond Sebond'. Moreover, it must be remembered that the Lutherans and Calvinists themselves did not think that their religious views entitled anyone to question the existing grounds of social and political authority. In this there is no difference between them and Montaigne, except that Montaigne considered they could not have it both ways: religious novelty and social stability.[19] He considered the Catholics of the League just as bad as the Protestants inasmuch as their response to the Protestant challenge involved further brutalisation of the political order. In the two essays, 'Of Coaches' (III, 6) and 'Of Cannibals' (I, 31), he is absolutely scathing on the barbarism of Christian colonialism.[20] Everywhere, Montaigne rejected human dogmatism as so evidently false to the historical and anthropological variety contained – and presumably consonant with the human condition:

> I do not share that common error of judging another by myself. I easily believe that another man may have qualities different from mine. Because I feel myself tied down to one form, I do not oblige everyone to espouse it, as all others do. I believe in and conceive a thousand contrary ways of life; and in contrast with the common run of men. I more easily admit difference than resemblance between us. I am as ready as you please to acquit man from sharing my conditions and principles. I consider him simply in himself, without relation to others; I mould him to his own model. (I: 37, 169)

There can be few more moving statements of the liberal credo than this. Most rational men would like to believe that they could uphold it. In practice, they will betray it in matters as simple as the prejudices of food, dress and sex, let alone over questions of scientific method, literary interpretation, religious belief and political ideology. Part of the problem is that intellectuals benefit from the knowledge of comparative culture, acquired in the calm of the study, but are far less tolerant when tested in the real world of action, bargaining and compromise. In some ways, Montaigne is unusual in that he seems to have been consistently more tolerant in practice than he was in theory. We shall return to this problem in the light of what we shall have to say later, regarding the classical ideal of friendship and its place in the political thought of La Boétie and Montaigne.

Just as Montaigne seems not to have given any consistent thought to the institutionalization of religious tolerance, he seems also not to have considered the problem of the right to revolution.[21] In part, this is because he rejected the notion that any single idea could be found that, in the first place, could not with equal reason he opposed, and secondly, which would not in fact encounter a group of men with contrary beliefs who would then have to be suppressed or destroyed. Who is to say that the results will be better rather than worse?

> Nothing presses a state hard except innovation; change alone lends shape to injustice and tyranny. When some part is dislocated, we can prop it up: we can fight against letting the alteration and corruption natural to all things carry us too far from our beginnings and principles. But to undertake to recast so great a mass, to change the foundations of so great a structure, that is a job for those who wipe out a picture in order to clean it, who want to reform defects of detail by universal confusion and cure illness by death, *who desire not so much to change as to overthrow everything* [Cicero]. The world is ill fitted to cure itself; it is so impatient of its affliction that it aims only at getting rid of it, without considering the cost. We see by a thousand examples that it usually cures itself to its own disadvantage. Riddance from a present evil is not cure unless there is an all-round improvement in condition. (III: 9, 731)

What is particularly important in this passage is Montaigne's rejection of political Platonism. The body politic, like our own body, is a complex unity; we can learn from its illnesses as such as from its health and we can prosper from its vices no less than from its virtues. We never live only in health and in virtue. Montaigne is repulsed by this ambition wherever he encounters it. Thus the *Essays* themselves are a portrait that grows by continuous accumulation – nothing is erased, he is quite unrepentant of their contradictions and weaknesses, because of the conviction that these are true to life and also because to try to avoid them deprives the reader of his freedom and judgement in dealing with the *Essays* according to his own ability and interests.

Montaigne rationalises political vice in quite a different fashion from Machiavelli, We have seen that Montaigne was a practical military man and a political realist.[22] The problem is that he seems to shrink from embracing any notion of political reform on the sceptical ground that it is impossible to formulate the welfare implications of any major social change. This is embarrassing since we are interested in Montaigne's *Essays* as part of the accumulating insight into the human condition that over the centuries has radically altered man's relation to society, the state and religion. We have to choose either to detect a failure of nerve in Montaigne or else to try to understand his reservations on their own terms. At bottom, Montaigne believed that all things have a complex form that is not of their own deliberate making, even though men must work to discover this form in themselves, their states and even their animals. Thus mastery in this matter is really a life art rather than the achievement of any a priori science of ethics, politics or economics. This does not mean that we are exempt from formulating projects for ourselves. It is simply the recognition that, due to the influence of factors in ourselves and others, and to the multiplying effects of their conjuncture, once we are launched into any enterprise we have to divide the results between fortune and ourselves. The same is true of political affairs. The law cannot be very far above the local customs and habits of a given society; and only the worst of horrors can result from such wholesale enterprises as the colonisation and Christianisation of allegedly simple societies. By the same token, Montaigne schooled himself against any final pessimism over events that were beyond his control and which made it look as though the world was surely headed for ruin. Human societies, like the human body, have a way of surviving and mending that is peculiar to them, even when wracked by civil war:

> In time, I see from our example that human society holds and is knit together at any cost whatever. Whatever position you set men in, they pile up and arrange themselves by moving and crowding together, just put in a bag without order, find of themselves a way to unite and to fall into place together, often better than they could have been arranged by art. King Philip collected the most wicked and incorrigible men he could find, and settled them all in a city he had built for them, which bore their name. I judge from their very vices they set up a political system among themselves and a workable and regular society. (III: 9, 730)

Even so, it may be said, Montaigne still avoids any of the revolutionary conclusions that can be drawn from the metaphor of the state as a body. For, after all, the image of the body politic can be used not only to justify the ordination of a hierarchical society – as in Plato's *Republic*, Book II. It can also be used to diagnose the excesses, illnesses and deprivations in the body politic – as in the fable of the plebeian secession from Rome related by Livy.[23] It is then that the body politic may be seen to stand in need of radical surgery, or of a purge that will restore its health and normal functioning.

Political revolutions also spring up from a disproportionate increase in any part of the State. For as a body is made up of many members, and every body ought to grow in proportion, that symmetry may be preserved; but loses its nature if the foot be four cubits long and the rest of the body two spans; and, should the abnormal increase be one of quality as well as of quantity, may even take the form of another animal; even so a state has many parts, of which some one may often grow imperceptibly; for example, the number of poor in democracies and constitutional states.[24]

But then we were embroiled in the philosophical problem of what we understand by a 'normal' or 'healthy' state, and whether there exists any science or art that is in charge of these questions.[25] Montaigne could not accept any analogy between politics and medicine because he had no faith in medicine's ability to deal with the complexity of man's bodily condition. Thus, whereas other political theorists in the sixteenth century[26] could use the metaphor of the body politic to locate its ills in tyranny and hereditary monarchy, with recommendations of regicide and the rule of talent, Montaigne had less faith in such diagnosis and seems to have trusted more the natural healing capacity of the body politic. Machiavelli, Bodin and Montaigne, to name only a few, were all agreed that a mixed constitution, such as that of Louis XII, was the most likely to preserve the body politic against excesses.

So far, then, we have tried to show that Montaigne's standards of private conscience did not prevent him from an active commitment to political life. If it is difficult to decide whether Montaigne is a political conservative or a liberal, this is not because he was caught up on a sceptical seesaw. He had a conception of the world's body in which the order of human life, as well as the life of the state, is more complexly interrelated than we are able to grasp from our place within it. Montaigne is a pro-ideological thinker and what we can learn from him concerns the grounds of political action as experienced by a soldier and politician caught in the transition to the modern state. Here too, however, there may be something to gain if we turn to a final consideration of the problem of voluntary servitude, at least as it looked before the days of fraternal revolution.

III Friendship and Tyranny

Montaigne has rendered proverbial his friendship as a young man with La Boétie.[27] Yet he seems to have had difficulty with La Boétie's political pamphlet, *Le Discours de la servitude volontaire*. It fell into the hands of the Huguenots who published it posthumously, as the *Contr'Un*, ahead of Montaigne's plan to include it in his *Essays*. Montaigne was obliged to dissociate himself from the

Discours as a youthful work, quite incompatible with his own loyalism or that of La Boétie. Recently, however, the *Discours*[28] has again been published as a prescient attack on statism, and here we have the opportunity to deepen Montaigne's reflections upon the relationship between society and the state. In particular, it offers us a chance to consider the classical problem of friendship and politics as a prelude to the problem of servitude in modern state democracies.

Although Montaigne regarded the *Discours* as a youthful work, today we can see that it raises a serious question regarding the foundations of political order and our chances of setting a limit to state power. When we look a little more closely, we find Montaigne nearer to La Boétie in his views on the state and the sociological basis of its mass power. We begin with a passage from La Boétie in order to convey the unusual tone of the *Discours*:

> He who dominates you so much has only two eyes, only two hands, and a single body; he has nothing else more than the least man in the countless number of your villages, except the advantage you accord him of destroying you. From where does he get all the eyes to spy on you unless you give them to him; how does he have so many hands to beat you unless he gets them from you? Where does he get the feet to crowd your cities unless they are yours? How does he have any power at all over you except through you? How could he dare to run over you if he did not have your cooperation? What could he do to you if you did not welcome the thief who robs you, if you were not the accomplice of the murderer who kills you, and traitors to yourselves?
>
> You sow your fruits so that he can enjoy them; you furnish and fill your homes so that he can pillage them; you raise your daughters to satisfy his pleasure, you raise your children so that the best he has in store for them is to take off to his wars to lead them into butchery, to make them the agents of his covetousness, to make them the executors of his vengeance. You break yourselves with pain so that he can wallow in his delights and stuff himself with vile and filthy pleasures: you weaken yourselves in order to make him stronger and tougher, keeping you on short bridle. From so many indignities that not even the animals could suffer, or else would not stand them at all, you can deliver yourselves if you try to, not by trying to get free of them, but simply by wanting to do so. Resolve yourselves to serve no longer, and then you will be free; I do not ask that you push him or overthrow him, but simply that you do not support him any longer, and then you will see him like a great colossus deprived of his base, fall down and break of his own weight.[29]

La Boétie's thought is striking for the extended use it makes of image of the body politic. What we have here is an early anticipation of Leviathan, grounded in a sociology of the authoritarian basis of the state. The puzzle is to understand how men are enslaved, given the disparity in power between the king and his people.[30] Without any resort to the fiction of a pro-political state, La Boétie mounts a straightforward thesis in political sociology: it is impossible for the state to be omnipotent unless men willingly make themselves the agents and objects of its domination. Power can hardly stem from the differences between men, for these are far less extreme in nature than we find them in society. Political rule is founded upon the original obedience that men acquire in the family, supported by a false idea of religious duty and strength against challenge by techniques of isolation, corruption and silence which divide the strength of the people in favour of the tyrant.

La Boétie and Montaigne were equally opposed to the very idea of domination. Where one man rules, no one is truly a man. Thus Montaigne tells us he obeyed without liking obedience and could command without liking to command. He could commend himself unconditionally to a master, yet he was capable of changing leaders, and of steering between them if he got the chance. Is this merely evidence of Montaigne's political schizophrenia, or does it represent a more basic political philosophy? Lacking any explicit attack upon kings and tyrants, Montaigne nevertheless makes it very clear that their position among men is a human failing in which rulers are as much to be pitied as the ruled; for both of them deprive each other of their basic humanity:

> But above all Hiero emphasizes the fact that he finds himself deprived of all mutual friendship and society, wherein consists the sweetest and most perfect fruit of human life. For what testimony of affection and good will can I extract from a man who, willy-nilly, owes me everything he can do? (1: 42, 195)

It is the ideal of friendship which provides the basis for the critique of domination in *Le Discours de la servitude volontaire* and it is this ideal exemplified in the friendship of La Boétie and Montaigne which made them the enemies of tyranny and democracy alike.[31] Unless we understand something of the classical theory of friendship, we shall be forced to set up Montaigne's opposition to political life in terms of a false antithesis between the values of public and private conscience. The basis of Montaigne's hostility to political domination is the classical ideal of friendship in politics. It is important to stress this connection because Montaigne's friendship with La Boétie has often been treated as a simple autobiographical incident producing in him, after the early loss of La Boétie, an even greater retirement from social and political affairs. A more serious argument is that of Wilden,[32] who maintains that Montaigne's *Essays* are the substitute metacommunication of a bourgeois individualist, a lament for the loss of a feudal friendship whose plenitude could only be fully restored in a truly communist society. If, however, we evaluate Montaigne's friendship with La Boétie in less

Freudian and Marxist terms than Wilden, referring it instead to the classical institution of friendship in politics, we certainly find in it a critical ideal of the communicative basis of political order,[33] although it is as unfriendly to democracy as it is to the tyranny of the absolute monarch. It would extend the present argument too much to lay out all of the considerations involved, nevertheless we shall now give some idea of the role of friendship in politics and try to relate some features of the account to a final evaluation of La Boétie's *Discours*.

To begin, we must be aware that in classical antiquity friendship (*hetaireia*) was an institution of practical politics and not simply an ideal by which politics were judged.[34] It represented a union of young men of the same age cohort and social standing who shared their education and military, legal and political activities. The *hetaireia* were the basic organisational units for the achievement of a political career, for the pursuit of law, philosophy and love:

> And I say that a lover who is detected in doing any dishonourable act, or submitting through cowardice when any dishonour is done to him by another, will be more pained at being detected by his beloved than at being seen by his father, or by his companions, or by anyone else. The beloved too, when he is found in any disgraceful situation, has the same feeling about his lover. And if there were only some way of contriving that a state or an army should be made up of lovers and their loves, they would be the very best governors of their own city, abstaining from all dishonour, and emulating one another in honour . . .[35]

It served to inspire standards of loyalty and bravery among equals whose sense of aristocracy made them the enemies alike of tyrants and mobs. Because the *hetaireia* were organisational elements in the Greek party system, which was extremely conspiratorial, they were often identified with quarrelsomeness, and even Plato thought that this was due to the enmities their erotic activities so easily inspired. After the democracy of Cleisthenes in 508 BC, the *hetaireia* certainly played a considerable role in the popular assemblies and the courts, as well as in briberies and assassinations. Indeed, they inspired a commercial variant of their own activities, known as the sycophants.[36] The *hetaireia* represented the oldest principle in the Greek moral code, helping one's friends and harming one's enemies.[37] We must, however, keep in mind an essential change in the relationship between justice and equality that occurred in the shift of influence from the aristocracy to the democracy. This shift also involved a philosophical redefinition of friendship in an attempt to integrate theory and political practice. The tensions involved may help us understand a continuing ambivalence in the political thought of Montaigne and La Boétie. Montaigne recalls the 'salutary love'[38] of the friends Harmodius and Aristogeiton, who in a conspiracy slew the tyrant Hippias' brother Hipparchus and conferred equality (*isonomia*) on the people (*demos*).

They thereby initiated a continuing problem for democracy, namely, the tendency for the conspiratorial equality of friends (*hetaireia*) to unbalance the equality of the demos. In turn, the state now found itself subject to conflicts due to the friendships and privileges that still obtain in a democracy:

> But equality does not seem to take the same form in acts of justice and in friendship; for in acts of justice what is equal in the primary sense is that which is in proportion to merit, while quantitative equality is secondary, but in friendship quantitative equality is primary and proportion to merit secondary.[39]

It therefore became necessary to work out a new theory of justice and citizenship without the limits of the friendship allegiances of either aristocrats or democrats. Aristotle's theory of friendship is the expression of this need. The transition was prepared by Plato, who replaced the old code of justice as helping one's friends and undermining one's enemies with the idea of justice as a harmony and proportion between the soul and the state. In practice, politics lagged behind philosophy and justice was never extended to anything but a privileged citizenry in colonialist and slave-based democracies. Moreover, the debate renewed itself once men had to reflect upon the conflict between republican (aristocratic) and imperialist contexts of virtue, justice and liberality.

This debate carried over into the Renaissance, and *Le Discours de la servitude volontaire*, as well as Montaigne's remarks on princes and friendship, is part of that continuous political tradition. This is evident from reflections on Roman politics in Machiavelli, the *Discours* and the *Essays*.[40] How often does Montaigne strike a pose like that of Cicero's friend Atticus, who was a pacific friend and host to politicians while remaining indifferent to their passions. It is essential, all the same, to treat Montaigne's reflections on friendship as more than a concern with his private distraction.[41] Montaigne was no solipsist, he discovered himself in his life with others, in his family, his estate and political relations, no less than in books and the conversation of minds' past. His friendship with La Boétie was not a simple intimacy. It represented to him an Aristotelian ideal[42] of independence and union by which all social and political relations stood to be tested:

> There is nothing to which nature seems to have inclined us more than to society. And Aristotle says that good legislators have had more care for friendship than for justice. Now the ultimate point in the perfection of society is this. For in general, all associations that are forged and nourished by pleasure and profit, by public or private needs, are the less beautiful and noble, and the less friendships, in so far as they mix into friendship another cause and object and reward their friendship itself. Nor do the four ancient types –

natural, social, hospitable, erotic – come up to real friendship, either separately or together. (I: 28, 136)

The very worst condition of man is to be alone. It is less than human. The worst polity is that in which a single man dominates. Indeed, such a man is as much to be pitied as the society that elevates him. Plato advised the tyrant of Sicily that only a city whose ruler has friends can be ruled justly. The ruler must therefore become a just man in order to have loyal friends with whom he can maintain a just polity.[43] The love that holds between the just man and his friends is a love of wisdom which preserves harmony (*homonoia*) in the state as in the souls of himself and his friends. In his essay 'Of the Disadvantage of Greatness' (III: 7), Montaigne reveals his thoughts on the condition of the almighty man, deprived of friendship and the thrust and parry of intellectual exchange. Such a role would test the powers of any man. It is a sickly position, thoroughly inimical to the maturity of those around him, and at bottom an infantile disorder. The king can never know the true worth of his own thoughts, or the value of his deeds, any more than of those who surround him. All are mesmerised by kingship – something that never could happen in a society of friends:

It is a pity to have so much power that everything gives way to you. Your fortune repels society and companionship too far from you; it plants you too far apart. That ease and slack facility of making everything bow beneath you is the enemy of every kind of pleasure. That is sliding not walking; sleeping, not living. Imagine man accompanied by omnipotence: he is sunk, he must ask you for hindrance and resistance, as an alms; his being and his welfare are in indigence. (III: 7, 701–2)

Here again the devitalisation of the body politic furnishes the critique of Leviathan, without any explicitly revolutionary or democratic appeal. Leviathan prevails where the ideal of friendship is not there to leaven politics. The necessary other (*alter*) between individuals cannot be either the state or the citizen who is simply the state's creature. At first sight, La Boétie's response to statism is undeveloped; it rests upon a voluntarist declaration of liberty, which can hardly counter his own anthropological discovery of the grounds of voluntary submission to domination. Yet, gradually the *Discours* rises to its theme; namely, that in friendship there is a module of society, integrity and justice that is the sole means of excluding tyranny.[44] It is in friendship that the refusal to serve is strengthened, that the charms of the tyrant are weakened and the very principle of domination questioned in every political regime. It is between friends that the question of the human origins of servitude can be raised outside of the service it offers to princes and rulers. However, there is also a danger, as Claude Lefort points out,[45] that

La Boétie's discourse, through its own charm, simply replaces the tyrant's powers of persuasion with a new siren call of liberty that will bind the people even more tightly. So long as the people figure as the interlocutor in a mere meta-communication upon liberty, the pamphleteer risks usurping the tyrant's role towards them. It is perhaps this risk that turns Montaigne away from this pamphlet as a youthful work, a thing too easily the prey of ideologists. Yet La Boétie also believed, like Montaigne, that it is books that make men free, provided they come into the hands of a company of men who can withstand the allurements of tyranny rooted in the desire of each of us to identify with dominion. The friends are those who are truly craftsmen of themselves and who through their own labour acquire a freedom of control that is independent of domination and servitude. Such a society cannot be directed by a single ruler, since it can only be reproduced where men are related to each other as friends. Since the principle of domination is entirely incompatible with the equality of friends, La Boétie leaves it for his readers, and those who read Montaigne's *Essays*, to conclude that it is yet another dream to expect rulers to implement a truly liberal democracy.

It is tempting to conclude that the *Essays* are anti-authoritarian in a purely private way. All we can do is to aim at being an authority upon ourselves, recognising it as hard enough. But Montaigne does lay claim to be of help even to others. His remarks in this connection are extremely subtle and they require our attention because they bear in an interesting way upon the kind of political role he saw for the essayist. Princes, kings and other officers of society are required on its behalf to be authorities. In this, despite appearances, they are peculiarly disadvantaged. They are expected to be above the ordinary in wisdom and justice and much of the panoply of their office serves to remind them of this difference. Yet they are men like any other man, and are surrounded by subjects and followers more likely to foster what is base and stupid in their rulers and themselves, rather than to try the difficult and dangerous path of educating their prince. In the first place, it takes a lot to presume to the office of educator and, secondly, it requires a very strong prince to be able to withstand the things he needs to be told by his counsellor, without vengeance. Very few persons could fulfil these conditions. Certainly, a teacher who could only play the schoolmaster, pronouncing abstract lessons, would achieve nothing. Rather, what is needed is a constant presence to the prince's ordinary behaviour, his moods, statements and dealings with other persons. Nothing is served by direct confrontation, regardless of occasion, simply because one is assured of being in the right. To have the necessary independence and ability to talk on the prince's level as well as with a variety of men under the prince, it would be best for the counsellor to be a man of middle rank. He must also be a man alone so as to avoid an undesirable spread of confidences a man whose virtue is pre-eminently the fidelity of silence. Such a man is Montaigne:

I should have had enough fidelity, judgment and independence for that. It would be a nameless office; otherwise it would lose its effect and its grace. And it is a part that cannot be played indiscriminately by all. For truth itself does not have privilege to be employed at any time and in any way; its use, noble as it is, has its circumscriptions and limits. It often happens, as the world goes, that people blurt it out into a prince's ear not only fruitlessly, but harmfully, and even unjustly. And no one will make me believe that a righteous remonstrance cannot be applied wrongfully, and that the interest of the substance must not often yield to the interest of the form. (III: 13, 825–6)

La Boétie took the difficult path of trying to reveal the forces that underlie the paradox of voluntary servitude. At first sight, *Le Discours de la servitude volontaire* is merely a political pamphlet of a liberal and democratic persuasion. But this is to miss the critical question that the *Discours* raises within democratic theory itself, namely, how is it that there are societies which are internally suited to domination by the state, and not utterly hostile to such a fate? Those who believe in democracy must consider this question even more seriously than those who are cynical Machiavellians. It is this question that obliges us to rescue the *Discours* from the vagaries of its history as a pamphlet. La Boétie is not simply concerned to denounce the ways of political and religious tyranny, leaving the assumption that men are otherwise more determined to seek freedom than servitude. This is the reading that simply places the *Discours* in the pantheon of democratic, revolutionary thought. But then the pantheon of the Left is no better than the pantheon of the Right. Both are concerned to avoid the ambiguity in the classical texts from which they derive their respective traditions.

It is equally wrong to compare the *Discours* with such contemporary works of political theory as the *Francogallia*, or the *Vindiciae contra tyrannos*, or with the aims of any political pamphleteer. The *Discours* is, however, part of the humanist 'anti-Machiavellian' literature which sought to instruct princes in the hatred of tyranny, and was largely inspired by Erasmus's *Institutio principis christiani*. The *Discours* approaches the institution of the prince from two sides, as it were. Thus La Boétie recreates the tyrant's institution, hoping thereby to open his eyes to the good prince, to the practice of religion and letters and to the fear of historical judgement. At the same time, La Boétie seems to recognise that the institution of the good prince cannot succeed without the institution of the people. There is a similar cord in Montaigne. The argument is that the prince cannot become anything but a tyrant unless he is surrounded by friends and a populace unafraid to provide him with a true sounding of himself. Thus friends and people are essential to the institution of the good prince as, in turn, he is to them, and each should avoid the corruption of the other.[46]

The *Discours* asks why it is men work at their own servitude with even more effort than they strive for freedom. The existence of political movements is part of that question, not a series of solutions. In short, then, La Boétie raises the question that underlies all wild politics, namely, how is it that men have chosen to live in statist societies? This question constitutes the subtle bond between La Boétie and Montaigne, and it separates the two friends from the society of their day, as much as the cannibals whose astonishment at the violence and servitude of the Christian state Montaigne recorded – echoing the double loss of his friend and pre-statist society.

La Boétie died young and Montaigne did not become a revolutionary. Two kinds of freedom. La Boétie was not a domesticated democrat. He was too worried by the servitude inherent in any political system. Montaigne held to himself at a time when the forces of the state and religion made it hardest for a man not to lose his freedom in choosing sides. Both men were inhabited by a question that owed nothing in its allegiances to divine law, natural reason or the philosophical system of the day. Neither of them, of course, was anything but deliberately ignorant in retaining for themselves a question they seemed to introduce into their society with the same inquisitiveness as a visiting savage. How could two such civilised men as La Boétie and Montaigne have preserved their freedom to rethink the political, social and private life of man? It is the novelty of the problematic that La Boétie and Montaigne envisaged that allows us to speak of them as first men. Perhaps what they saw beyond the innate conservatism of the peasants they loved, was that the encroachments of the state represented, apart from the will of princes and monarchs, the emergence of an absolutely politicised society, capable of reshaping language, thought and personality. Montaigne lived long enough to see that the problem of modern man is how to live on terms with the state production of society, without limits of traditional religion, law and immorality. There is, in short, a definite anti-Machiavellianism in the problematic of the *Contr'un*, as the *Discours* was also called, and as we hope to have shown Montaigne's dispersed comments on the communicative problems of princes and monarchs who destroy friends.

CHAPTER 9

Civilisation, Literacy and Barbarism

The *Essays* require a lively reader. They have certainly challenged many a critic, and it is to the continuing rivalry over a pair of essays that we now turn, namely, the essay 'Of Coaches' (III: 6) which must also be read with the essay 'Of Cannibals' (I: 31). We begin with a plain account of the essay 'Of Coaches' avoiding as nearly as possible any elaborate gloss upon its construction. We shall then come to grips with some contemporary readings of the essay. Our purpose is not to be purely polemical. Rather, we are interested in the natural rivalry that is provoked by any adequate concern with differences in our practices of reading and writing. We do not intend simply to proliferate critical readings of Montaigne. Thus, to conclude, we shall set the essays on coaches and cannibals within Montaigne's broader problematic of the internal relativism of literacy and civilisational barbarism:

> It is the inattentive reader who loses my subject, not I. Some word about it will always be found off in a corner, which will not fail to be sufficient, though it takes little room.
>
> I want the matter to make its own divisions. It shows well enough where it changes, where it concludes, where it begins, where it resumes, without my interlacing it with words, with links and seams introduced for the benefit of weak or headless ears, and without writing glosses on myself. Who is there who would rather not be read than be read sleepily or in passing?
>
> *Nothing is so useful that it can be of value when taken on the run* [Seneca]. If to take up books were to take them in, and if to see them were to consider them, and to run through them were to grasp them, I should be wrong to make myself out quite as ignorant as I say I am. (III: 9, 761)

What Montaigne makes very clear to us in this passage is that we cannot separate the writer's practices from those of the reader. The writer is always the first reader of what he writes. This is so, obviously, not with the same detachment as any other reader, although even a public reading is horizontally present to the writer's constant referencing back and forth to his sources, and to himself as a source both of what he has written and is writing. It is in the light of these interchangeable practices of reading and writing that we must approach the whole question of the unity and form of the *Essays*, as of any text. If we ignore the author's own writing and reading practices – an incredible procedure in the light of Montaigne's specific references to them – we make ourselves omnipotent critics. The measure of such ambition, however, is not to be decided by those professional literary and critical practices which merely make books and articles that exempt themselves from self-essay. Moreover, these practices expropriate the meaning of the text in favour of contrived reconstructions whose merit is minimal, even at the level of critical reading (unless, of course, one is wholly surrendered to a version of scientific procedure as elementary analysis). To think of bringing back to one's reading of the *Essays* any of the schemas from Sayle or from Buffum and Etiemble, to be considered shortly, requires a prior emptying of the reader's mind that is quite inconceivable. Perhaps what is involved is nothing but a prejudice of poor but legal literary critics who believe that their efforts produce the best results on a tabula rasa – usually their own creation, and hardly the state of intelligent students of literature on whom they impose. In view of these destructive literary practices, perhaps one can be sympathetic towards the resort to organic and artistic metaphors of wholeness and movement, even while rejecting them as borrowed conventions that only result in further glosses upon the nature of the *Essays* – and that, in any case, never seriously rival Montaigne's own appraisals.

Are we to suppose that a writer like Montaigne goes about his business without any sense of the practices whereby he works from page to page, paragraphing, referencing, illustrating, chaptering and the like? Are we to suppose that he does not deliberately work upon the words, does not choose his adjectives and adverbs; does not consciously carve out his metaphors and periods the way an artist chooses forms and colours, light and shade? Can we imagine anything else than that a writer works with words upon a page the way a sculptor works in stone or wood and metal? Socrates thought that even philosophy could not be practised . . . and Montaigne thought the same with regard to writing:

> Socrates makes his soul move with a natural and common motion. So says a peasant so says a woman. His mouth is full of nothing but carters, joiners, cobblers, and masons. His inductions and simil(e)s draw from the commonest and best known actions of men; everyone understands him. (III: 12, 793)

Every artist understands that in working upon his chosen materials of stone, or colour or words, he is working upon himself. Indeed, there is no other way to engage in self-expression, given that we are embodied, intersensory beings, and not pure minds – for whom the problem of expression would hardly arise. Because we do not have a divine grasp of things in all their immediacy, we draw upon our living for our learning. That is to say, we must build up the institutions of language, art and science in historical accomplishments to which we relate ourselves generally as inhabitants of tradition and culture. In turn, we renew these institutions in the history of our own lives, in our education and, if it is given to us, through our own creative contributions. No one is more sensitive to these considerations than Montaigne. That is why we know so much from him directly about his use of books, conversation, language and poetry and, of course, about his views on education.

The reader Montaigne seeks for the *Essays* can only be a self-conscious accomplice. Ideally, Montaigne's reader would he what Lowry Nelson calls an 'optimum reader',[1] one simultaneously aware of the shift between his real self and his fictional self, confirmed by the self-commentary of the *Essays*. Essaying is especially exemplary of what we have called the literary covenant between the writer and the reader, and between the writer and those readers who are primarily literary critics. The method of essaying consists not so much in the accumulation of statements about the world, nor in an affirmation of the reader's beliefs it is neither poor science nor bad rhetoric but in the exploration of the form of an argument proposed as a topic or title. As we have seen commentators often remark on the way Montaigne treats the relation between topic and content in his essays.[2] They know very well that Montaigne disdained syllogistic and scholastic arguments. But they are as much tempted to give psychological explanations for this – admittedly abetted by Montaigne as to give good reasons for it. In essaying his topic, allowing it to begin where it will, and by force of examples to shift his own viewpoint, Montaigne draws the reader into his own experience of reading the essays. Thus the reader cannot hope to be ahead of an essay in virtue of its title, or the apparent certainty of its initial observations; nor can he be sure of any conclusion. But this very experience, shared both by the author and the reader, is precisely the proper institution of the republic of science, in the sense that a common experience is questioned, the reader is aroused and begins to follow the author's struggle an experience quite different from 'following' his logic or sophistical (purely persuasive) rhetoric. The exercise, then, consists in the acquisition of the habits of an open and inquiring mind, unafraid of its own experiences and aware that genuine knowledge is always relative to one's character, morally speaking – and not in a subjective or psychological sense. Thus, so many features of the *Essays* that critics deal with as indications of Montaigne's mind – the break with discursive forms, leaps in sentences and paragraphs, and ambiguity – are in fact to be understood as qualities that Montaigne required of any reader's mind – including his own. The stylistic features of the *Essays* that are glossed with the categories of art and painting are properly features or practices of writing in search of an uncomplacent reading. This being the proper end of the *Essays*, rather than the compilation and ordering of facts, they are best understood as consummatory, self-satisfying or 'self-consuming artefacts'[3] whose end is achieved in the occurrence of a lively reading.

It is important not to make the surprises, contradictions and paradoxes that are constitutive of Montaigne's style a matter of his own peculiarity. We can only do this by overlooking the institution of negligence[4] – the coupled claims of irresponsibility, spontaneity and consubstantiality – in which Montaigne was as perfectly versed as Castiglione's ideal Courtier:

> to practice in all things a certain *sprezzatura* (nonchalance), so as to conceal all art and make whatever is done or said appear to be without effort and almost without any thought about it. And I believe much grace comes of this: because everyone knows the difficulty of things that are rare and well done; wherefore facility in such things causes the greatest wonder; whereas, on the other hand, to labor and, as we say, drag forth by the hair of the head, shows an extreme want of grace, and causes everything, no matter how great it may be, to be held in little account.[5]

This will explain, too, Montaigne's hostility to pedantry and his insistence that books, like conversation, be guided by and contribute to the liveliness and pleasure of social life. His objections to scholastic classifications and schedules are directed against their lack of give and take in which men exercise themselves wholly and not just their tongues. On the side of the reader, Montaigne's digressions, his sudden shifts of ground and his side-spins require of him an activity that is equal to the author's liveliness, and return him to the pleasures of intelligent reading:

> the imitation of speech, because of its facility may be quickly picked up by a whole people; the imitation of judgment and invention does not come so fast. Most readers, because they have found a similar robe, think very wrongly that they have hold of a similar body. Strength and sinews are not to be borrowed; the attire and the cloak may be borrowed. Most of the people who frequent me speak like the *Essays*; but I don't know whether they think like them. (I: 26, 127–8)

Essaying, therefore, is not strictly a method of writing, in the sense that it can be used to prevent the reader/writer from obscuring an unprejudiced report of the facts of the world. It is a decisional or therapeutic practice, which attunes the mind to its incapacities in order to bring it to the recognition of its object as its own creation. To the extent that this is achieved in any of the *Essays*, writing and reading are experienced as articulations of the lived, embodied self. Moreover, essaying requires an exchange of lives, in that the reader must dwell in the temporal flow of the writer's discovery of his thought. There is nothing in the prose of the *Essays* that helps Montaigne to preserve an atemporal or disembodied stance. So far from enslaving the reader, the uneven movement of the *Essays* solicits only his freedom and incarnation. From the preface 'To the Reader', it is clear that the *Essays* are in search of the reader as an accomplice. There can be no doubt, in view of Montaigne's practices of addressing his reader, of turning literary and philosophical observation upon his own experiences of pleasure, pain, illness and old age, in which any man can follow him, that Montaigne solicits the reader's use of his own life. At the same time, he is sufficiently self-critical, and almost destructive in his confidences regarding his own reading and writing habits, that the reader must be wary in following too easily lest he be repulsed all the more carelessly.

With these observations in mind, we shall now proceed to look more closely at some of the interpretative and analytic practices with which contemporary critics have tackled the essays on coaches and cannibals.

The essay 'Of Coaches' (III: 6) opens with the observation that it is extremely difficult to ascertain the principal cause of anything; although we cannot refrain from doing so. This practice, however, merely results in piling up causes for such things as sneezing, seasickness and the like. Frequently, our own experience fails to bear out particular theories; and we are better advised to trust to what we find in fact to be the case. Thus, although Plutarch, who is a discerning judge of things, attributes seasickness to fear, Montaigne finds that, while he himself is not afraid of the sea, he nevertheless gets seasick; and the same is true of pigs, who are scarcely intelligent enough to be apprehensive. Indeed, the notion of fear itself is hardly clear enough for us to attribute to it the unequivocal cause of something supposedly less well understood. There are marvelous examples of men able to conquer fear, and so it is not necessarily the cause of anything like the behaviour we otherwise attribute to its supposed presence. In fact, where we expect fear and its results, we may find nothing of the sort – only coolness in the face of danger. Montaigne, however, does not claim to be capable of the latter kind of control in his own behaviour. So far as he can determine, his seasickness is similar to his discomfort in a coach or a litter. The slow, uneven motion of these conveyances upsets his head and stomach, but he is not upset so long as the movement is uniform. Generally, Montaigne prefers to ride horseback.

Coaches themselves have such a variety of uses, as can be seen from the historical record, that here, again, if we try to explain a thing in terms of its function, we should only record the local custom; but not find a universal explanation. Coaches have been used to carry all sorts of things in war and peace and have been drawn by everything from oxen to ostriches. If this seems strange, it is surely just as strange for a monarch to use coaches in order to display his wealth at home. One might understand it abroad. Otherwise it is like dressing up at home rather than letting one's house, kitchen and servants speak for one's status. A young man may well indulge himself in dress, as did Montaigne, but this is because a young man lacks other avenues of expression. In a monarch it is hardly fitting. A monarch should adorn his city, not himself, and leave to his nation ports, fortifications, schools, hospitals, roads and streets. This is because a king ought not to pretend to liberality, since he generally only gives to the people what he has either taken or received from them:

> Liberality itself is not in its proper light in the hands of a sovereign; private people have more right to exercise it. For, to be precise about it, a king has nothing that is properly his own; he owes his very self to others. (III: 6, 688–9)

It is therefore quite mistaken of the tutors to young princes to teach them that their special virtue is liberality. This involves a misconception of the end of the highest office – which is to serve others, and not itself. It is only too easy to learn to be lavish with what is not yours in the first place. The royal virtue is not liberality, but justice; or rather, since kings seem to have identified themselves with liberality, it is justice in regard of liberality. It is the tyrant who distributes largesse regardless of merit, feeding the dependence of the people through the insatiability of their wants. All the same, one can hardly withhold admiration for such incredible displays as that put on by the Emperor Probus.

Even from the vanities of kings, we are obliged to concede how difficult it is to find any determining cause for human behaviour. Thus, in speaking of man we can hardly go straight to the point; all we can do is tell of this and that, drawing tentative conclusions, and trying always to improve our judgement. What we know in our own day is only a small part of what remains to be known of either the past or the future. Our knowledge is really only the greater part of our ignorance; almost anything with which we astonish ourselves is commonplace elsewhere in history or in nature:

> There is nothing unique and rare as regards nature, but there certainly is as regards our knowledge, which is a miserable foundation for our rules and which is apt to represent to us a very false picture of things. (III: 6, 693)

We cannot judge the rest of the world on the basis of events in our society. Consider how often men have thought the world was at an end, just because events in their own times seemed to them overwhelming. This would be a temptation in the present religious wars. It is, however, more likely that one society rises as another begins to decline, or that a decadent society destroys this cycle. Witness the Spanish Conquest of the New World. Fifty years ago, it knew nothing of letters, weights, measures, clothes, wheat or vines. But without any natural superiority we have conquered this world in order to give it the civilised arts. It is very clear from the magnificence of the city of Cuzco and of cities in Mexico that their king and his people were splendidly intelligent, industrious and law-abiding. We conquered them with our arms and trickery; we did not outmatch them in virtue. We might have added to the best in them the best of Greek and Roman virtues. But we set our values upon trade and commerce. We destroyed these people and their cities and in every way debased them through our contact. Thus, again, we see that apart from specific contexts, it is impossible to say what the outcome will be of the possession of particular human virtues and vices.

At this point (III: 6, 696) Montaigne is reminded of his essay. 'On Cannibals' (I: 31) and the account of Brazil he had from a traveller who had spent ten or twelve years there. Moritaigne was inclined to accept the man's story on the grounds of his simple and crude nature which, although it may have limited his curiosity, nevertheless preserved him from larding his account with interpretations that are too clever by far: 'We need a man either very honest, or so simple that he has not the stuff to build up false inventions and give them plausibility; and wedded to no theory' (I: 31, 152). The problem of adequate ethnography touched upon here is inseparable from the wider problematic entailed in the relativity of civilisation and barbarism.[6] Since ethnography is generally the practice of civilised peoples, constructing accounts of what they take to be barbarism, the value of such knowledge, like so much else that we know and believe, is questionable. Thus the Brazilians can only be considered barbarians if we mean that they are artless with respect to such civilised practices as literature, accounting, slavery, poverty, litigation, lying and treachery:

> I think there is nothing barbarous and savage in that nation, from what I have been told, except that each man calls barbarism whatever is not his own practice; for indeed it seems we have no other test of truth and reason than the example and pattern of the opinions and customs of the country we live in. There is always the perfect religion, the perfect government, the perfect and accomplished manner in all things. (I: 31, 152)

It is not that the Brazilians are entirely without blame. They are, after all, cannibals. The problem is that, in remarking this failure, Montaigne's contemporaries could not draw the lesson regarding the barbarity of their own civil war,[7] and, despite their other virtues, persist in dismissing the Brazilians' claims to serious civilised attention for the unserious reason that they do not wear breeches!

> I am not sorry that we notice the barbarous horror of such acts, but I am heartily sorry that, judging their faults rightly, we should be so blind to our own. I think there is more barbarity in eating a man alive than in eating him dead; and in tearing by tortures and the rack a body still full of feeling, in roasting a man bit by bit, in having him bitten and mangled by dogs and swine (as we have not only read but seen with fresh memory, not among ancient enemies, but among neighbors and fellow citizens, and what is worse, on the pretext of piety and religion), than in roasting and eating him after he is dead. (I: 31, 155)

After this mention of the essay 'Of Cannibals', Montaigne's reflections upon coaches resume with the most moving account of the dreadful deaths inflicted upon the kings of Peru and Mexico. These events are related by the Spaniards themselves as a testimony to their zeal in spreading the Christian faith to barbarians. But Montaigne returns to his topic, inasmuch as it pertains to pomp and magnificence and their proper place in the rule of kings, and notes that the public works, especially the roads but by the king of Peru, far surpassed anything in the classical world. Now on the day he died such a terrible death, the king of Peru was borne on the shoulders of his men in a golden chair, rather than a coach. And for every man the Spaniards killed, in order to take the king alive, others rushed to his place. Thousands were slaughtered in this way, until in the end a Spanish horseman pulled the king down. Thus this great king died in a conflict symbolised by the man in a golden chair overwhelmed by a horseman in armour.

Montaigne's essay 'Of Coaches' is woven with consummate artistry. It is only through sheer superficiality that the reader loses his way with the topic. We need only supply the middle ground of contextuality to relate Montaigne's topic with his mode of presentation. Coaches are part of the pomp that is evidence of the greatness of kings. Put what is the proper virtue of kings? We should distinguish lavishness, which costs the king nothing, and corrupts his people, from his proper duty of serving the people, rather than himself, by building lasting public works. It is difficult to make these distinctions because we generally presume upon the practices of our own customs and institutions. Consider how Christian kings have brutally slaughtered the kings of Mexico and Peru, even though these kings were truly magnanimous in the public sense and their people completely uncorrupt. The apparent superiority of Christian civilisation over these barbarians is portrayed in the final episode of the essay in which the Peruvian king is carried in a golden chair by his devoted men who are slaughtered in thousands;

until finally a Spaniard on horseback topples him. Thus the possibility of a marvelous marriage of the best in civilised and barbarian culture was lost in the clash represented by these two modes of transportation. But we must not abstract these vehicles from their cultural context in order to indulge our practice of assigning relative superiority or inferiority to either one. On balance, we ought perhaps to prefer the culture which is least brutal as a minimal solution to the problem of relativity in human affairs.

So much for our summary of the essay on coaches. We turn now to a reading by Etiemble, whose purpose is to challenge a widespread argument on the lack of unity or composition in the *Essays*, and, at the same time, to reveal the true political meaning of the essay Of Coaches.[8] Etiemble begins by objecting to the practice, which held at the beginning of this century, whereby any interpreter of Montaigne's *Essays* considered it methodologically appropriate to begin by deconstructing each essay into separable, analytic themes, despite the pain (and pleasure) with which Montaigne had so deliberately composed the various essays. He sets aside the justifications that such commentators as Villey, Saint-Beuve and Gide have offered in defence of this procedure, by citing Montaigne's inability to manage any sustained theme, his poor memory and generally dilatory habits. Though Etiemble does not explicitly say so, such commentary rests upon an analytic bias in favour of elementary reduction eked out with a psycho-logistic appeal to a corresponding working method as the source of the text requiring commentary. Such a procedure, of course, neglects to consider how it is that any of the essays present in the first place a totality or composite structure whose meaning is as much relied upon as it is in any sense derived from the commentator's analytic procedures. Worse still, these reductionist schemas merely recompose the essays into essentially abstract and wholly contrived themes. Etiemble is particularly critical of the reductive schemas employed by E. Wittkower, and by R.A. Sayce, whose method we shall consider in more detail further on. Wittkower's schematisation of the form of the *Essays*, while rejecting the conventional view that they are the work of a writer incapable of organisation, nevertheless simply proceeds to organise the *Essays* in terms of the barest of philosophical schemas. Thus, according to Wittkower, the plan of the essay on coaches is made up as follows: Philosophical Problems – Traditional Examples – Philosophical Problems – Traditional Examples – Self-Characterisation – Traditional Examples – Philosophical Problems – Historical Examples – and so forth.[9] In terms of this forced schema, Wittkower is obliged to treat Montaigne's remarks on seasickness as a philosophical problem, when in fact it is merely an example of the philosophical problem of causation, even on her own terms. But, of course, this problem is not what gives the essay 'Of Coaches' its underlying unity. How, then, do we read this essay without forcing upon it such unworkable abstract schemas, grabbed from the philosopher's toolbox and employed only with minimal skill and even less respect for the text?

Etiemble proceeds by setting aside all such literary glosses as those of Villey, Sayce and Friedrich regarding the features of 'baroque' and 'free association' in the *Essays*:

> I don't see any baroquism or any associationism. I do see a determined mind, lucid and courageous, with strongly and finely woven thoughts. I see two great symmetrical parts, of strictly equal length, framed by a sinuous entry into dangerous materials and by a piquant *conclusio verborum*. Like all the great essays I have studied, Of Coaches proves to me that Montaigne composed in accordance with the only idea of beauty I consider valid, namely, that which Henri Focillon in his *La Vie des Formes* calls classical.[10]

We can more easily accept Etiemble's dismissal of Montaigne's alleged passion for disorder than we can lend credence to his own mode of argument. At first sight, it looks as though we are being introduced to a reading of the essay on coaches that is ruled solely by strictly textual exegesis. In fact, what we have is a textual gloss. The unity of Montaigne's thought is found by Etiemble in a constructive/analytic metaphor of the balance of two equal sections, of eight pages or so, carved out of the text by the device of an appeal to the typography of the Sacy edition of the *Essays* with parallel texts of 1588 and 1595. The two parts, then, are (i) pages 978–85 and (ii) 985–92 in the Sacy edition. Apart from not holding for other editions of the *Essays*, and certainly not for the pagination of English editions, Etiemble's metaphor of balanced parts of seven pages each, framed by an introduction and conclusion, pays no attention to the disproportionate length of the introduction (three and two-thirds pages) vis-à-vis the balanced sections or of the conclusion (over two pages). We leave aside problems raised by the varying weight of interpolations within any of these divisions, although, of course, they make it impossible to subject the *Essays* to purely spatial metaphors that ignore their temporal life or, more importantly, their mythological foundations.[11]

Even if we disregard Etiemble's spatial metaphors as nothing but a mere textual play (compare Butor's method discussed earlier), can we nevertheless attribute to them any discovery of sense? Etiemble affects a close reading of the 'connecting words' in the first part, as he discerns it, which provides for the following summary:

> 'Our kings' are wrong to try to prove themselves through 'excessive expenses':
> a) 'The outlay would seem to me much more royal as well as more useful, just and durable, if it were spent on ports, harbors, fortifications and walls, on

sumptuous buildings, hospitals, colleges, and the improvement of streets and roads';

b) Besides, the spectators are entertained 'at their own expense' because 'a king has nothing that is properly his own';

c) Therefore princes should not be taught prodigality but 'justice';

d) Besides, the more a prince wastes money, 'the poorer he makes himself in friends';

e) The Roman emperors at least had the excuse of continuing a tradition of private extravagance and of producing beautiful spectacles; they are nonetheless wrong to waste public funds.

Thus Etiemble concludes that the sense of the first part of the essay is a critique of the internal economic policy of Henri III and his failure to engage in sound public investments. To maintain this position he needs, however, to separate Montaigne's discussion of the proper, virtue of kings from his opening reflections upon the difficulty of assigning unequivocal causes, purposes or functions to anything at all, especially in human affairs. To the extent that we explain things in this way, it is only by relying upon the context of local usage. What we thus take to be certain, so far from being general, is limited in time and space, so that we can hardly imagine how things were earlier or are elsewhere. Moreover, these considerations are continued after the discussion of the proper virtue of kings in a page or so, which Etiemble treats – although they are also counted in his first part as a 'subtle transition' to the second part, where Montaigne describes the conduct of the kings of Peru and Mexico. He then proceeds to find the sense of the second part of the essay to be distributed through the following three arguments:

I. 'As for boldness and courage, as for firmness, constancy' . . . these people were worth more than us;

a) we possess horses and firearms; they do not;

b) they died 'for the defense of their gods and of their liberty';

c) we did not know how to 'polish' and 'clear away' what was barbarous in them; On the contrary:
   – the Spaniards overwhelmed them by treason; even our religion is a deception in the new world;
   – here are three examples to prove it: the horrible torture of the king of Peru; of the king of Mexico; of 460 Indians.

II. 'As for the fact that the revenue from this, even in the hands of a thrifty and prudent prince, corresponds so little to the expectation . . .'; even if our princes were not at all prodigal, their pillages would yield little fruit, since the Indians, instead of using gold, piled it up for the glory of their kings and gods. 'Imagine it if our kings thus accumulated all the gold they could find for many centuries and kept it idle.' Unfortunately, they *cut it up small* and change its form.

III. 'As for pomp and magnificence, whereby I entered upon this subject . . .' The kings of Mexico and Peru built incomparably 'useful' roads for the passage of travelers and armies with 'fine palaces furnished with provisions' at the end of each day's journey.

From this abstract of the second part of the essay, Etiemble concludes that Montaigne's purpose was to connect the critique of the king's internal policies in the first part of the essay with a critique of his wasteful and destructive colonial policies, since both were based upon an ignorance of the relation between money and investment processes.[12] Montaigne is not simply castigating the cruelty of the Spanish Conquest and its evangelical methods. He is the first critic of French colonialism. If no one was able to see this from 1870 to 1940, and therefore could only approach the essay 'Of Coaches' in terms of stylistic considerations, speaking of its baroquism or associationism, it is not because previous critics were less astute than Etiemble. The key to the essay is given to Etiemble, he says, simply because he happens to have lived during a period of French decolonisation.

Etiemble's conclusion is quite spurious. A simple précis of Montaigne's argument shows only that he was critical of any prince's monetary excesses and critical of Spanish, not French, colonialism. Perhaps Etiemble considers these distinctions to be swallowed up by a general European responsibility for the Conquest, regardless, say, of the divisions between Catholics and Protestants. But this requires a Marxist preference for class analysis that is surely false to Montaigne's grasp of his own social standing.[13] Apart from Etiemble's excessive conclusion, we may also object to the way his abstract of the second part of the essay ignores Montaigne's reflections upon the problem of the internal relation between civilisation and barbarism. Because he overlooks this problematic, Etiemble is able to indulge his own free-floating conclusion at the expense of Montaigne's final portrayal of the confrontation between the cultures of the old and the new world. Finally, it is in keeping with Etiemble's economistic reduction of the essay that he misses altogether Montaigne's concern with moderation in politics, and above all in religion. Once again, this is evidence of Etiemble's anachronistic gloss upon the actual themes of the essay 'Of Coaches'.

As we have remarked earlier, Etiemble is extremely critical of Sayce's interpretation of the essay 'Of Coaches'. In fact, he virtually ridicules Sayce's method of analysis.[14] Given our own quarrel with Etiemble, it seems preferable to consider Sayce's interpretation on its own merits. Sayce, unlike Etiemble, does not consider Montaigne a classical stylist, but as an essentially baroque artist. Admittedly by the end of his argument Sayce qualifies Montaigne as a transitional figure, anticipating seventeenth-century French classicism. The notion of the baroque is borrowed from Wölfflin's 'Kunstgeschichtliche Grundbegriffe' and connotes the preference for (i) the malerisch over the linear, (ii) depth over flatness, (iii) open form over closed form, (iv) unity based upon multiplicity over a single visioned unity, (v) clarity over relative absence of clarity.[15] Sayce is aware of the difficulties in these notions. He nevertheless feels that the form and methodology of the *Essays* can be illuminated by the analogy with the practices of baroque painting. But we should not overlook the substantive question underlying the search for a method.[16] Montaigne is concerned with a self-portrait pursued in depth, struggling with temporal diffusion, appearance and reality, threatened continuously by a regressive play within the play of self-portrayal:

> Nothing is more suited to the Baroque than a profound sentiment of mobility and metamorphosis in man and the world; but the anxiety of death closes man in upon himself, forces him back onto his own being, and brings him to a halt in the baroque movement towards the outside, towards his public self; and it distracts him from projecting himself into a figure detached enough to serve him as a mask or game.[17]

Sayce proposes to demonstrate that 'each mature essay has its own unity, as well as the unity it derives from the whole work'. He chooses for this purpose to analyse the plan of the essay on coaches. He does so as follows, the page numbers being taken from the Plélade edition to show the essay's proportions. The 'associating or linking words' are italicised and 'coaches' is capitalised by Sayce:

876	Authors multiply *causes*
	causes of blessing *sneezes*
	causes of seasickness – fear
877	Not *fear* in my case
	Fear overcome by great men
878	Absence of *fear* in me due to insensibility not strength
	for I cannot stand for long COACH, litter or boat
878(c)	I would give the history of COACHES in war (if I had a better memory)
879(c)	Examples of COACHES in war
	Early French *kings* traveled in *ox-carts*
879–83	Roman emperors drawn in COACHES by strange beasts Monarchs should not indulge in vain *expense* (developed)
883–5	*Yet* Roman *emperors* did well to give great displays (described at length) remarkable for *ingenuity*, not merely *expense*

885	*Ingenuity* of ancients compared with us
886	We have made little progress, our *knowledge* of history is very limited
	And our *knowledge* of the *world*
	We have just found another *world*
886–94	Attack on Spanish cruelties in *New World*
894	*Retombons à nos COACHES*
	COACHES in *New World* (or rather their absence)[18]

Sayce is aware of the gross simplification and deformation inherent in this method of reducing the text. Yet he believes it to be justified on the ground that it shows how Montaigne moved from one subject to another, hopping freely on the association of word to word and not in accordance with any strict logic.[19] Etiemble finds Sayce's method foolhardy. But he has no arguments against it, and no method that is better.[20] In fact, apart from Etiemble's Marxisant conclusion, the two methods are similar. Both reduce the themes of the essay 'Of Coaches' to royal magnificence and the Spanish Conquest. Neither gives sufficient attention to the broader problematic of the internal relation between civilisation and its alter, barbarism, What is more, as critics Etiemble and Sayce both indulge in reading practices that are absolutely destructive of any reader's intelligence. Surely, no reader requires that an essay be literally abstracted in order to be able to grasp its sense? Our ordinary reading involves the constant production and silent revision of such schemas through which the sense of the text is continuously revised or revisioned in that growth of intelligent friendship which Montaigne knew the *Essays* would encourage. Nevertheless, even while they are deplored, such schemas continue in use, if only for permanent subversion. Thus, Gutwirth proposed to capture the sense and movement of the essay on coaches through the central metaphor of the *wheel!*[21] While preferring Etiemble to Sayce, and not ignoring his playfulness, Gutwirth believes, as we do, that Etiemble's political thesis loses sight of Montaigne's coaches. But what he means is that Etiemble's schema is inadequate because it flattens the movement in the essay! To be adequate, an interpretation of coaches must be based upon a dynamic model, to capture the theme of the rise and fall of civilisations and to exemplify the internal dynamics of the essay's composition:

Thus a tripartite relation shapes the deep structure (of thought now, and not of language any more) of the essay's body – a relation that is defined with respect to a common centre: the idea of ostentation. Turning around this centre, as though they were attached to the rim of a wheel by their three separate spokes, ancient Rome, the sovereigns of Europe, the kings of Mexico and Peru, pursue each other without ever catching up – like the dancers on Keats's urn – with the trace of their contradictions in time, in space and in the invariant but distinct profusion of their magnificence.[22]

In Gutwirth's view, support for this dynamic interpretation is suggested by Traeger's summary of the content of the essay 'Of Coaches', provided we adopt its enumeration to reproduce the rising and falling movement that composes its elements. Traeger's account, somewhat abbreviated, reduces the essay to the following elements:

1. Curious explanations of phenomena whose truth escapes us. Examples, etc.
2. Ancient ostentation: coaches. Splendour out of place, abusive liberality. Limits of human knowledge.
3. Discovery of the new world. We have hastened its decadence, etc.

    Conclusion:
a. return to causes: Mexican views on the end of the world
b. return to the theme of ostentation: the straight road of Peru
c. return to coaches: capture of the king of Peru.[23]

Gutwirth then proposes to substitute for Traeger's schema one of his own which would be composed of a progression in five movements, followed by a recapitulation in two movements (marked weak and strong). The composition and dynamics of 'Of Coaches' then becomes:

First movement: Seasickness

Like so many of Montaigne's openings, this is a weak movement. By the same token its descending motion exemplifies Montaigne's fear of falling, whether from his coach, or horse. He is similarly terrified of sneezing since it throws the head high and then low!

Second movement: Magnificence

Recovering from the bumps and jostling of the coaches, Montagne's mind now spins with their magnificence and the rising uncertainty over whether it can ever be matched.

Third movement: Our world has just discovered another

A half-turn since the New World reveals the bumptiousness (excuse my pun) of our own.

Fourth movement: Why did not such a noble conquest fall to Alexander . . .
It might have been: The saddest words of tongue or pen!

Here in Montaigne's dream we reach the height of the essay and one of the most lyrical expressions of the broken marriage between the ancient and new world that might truly have ennobled its European offspring.

Fifth movement: Regression

It was not to be.
    Conclusion:

As for pomp . . .

Turning from the useless extravagance of the Roman emperors, we again contemplate the straight, munificent roads of the New World. And with a last turn of the wheel, the essay descends . . .

Let us fall back to our coaches

Everything in this world passes away – on wheels or not! From this transcendent standpoint, the essay 'Of Coaches' is not about coaches but their *absence* – and the memorable ruin of the New World:

> Between the theme of coaches and the indigenous civilisation of the two Americas there exists the profound relation that the *WHEEL*, without which coaches, progress and technological advances in the art of war are all inconceivable, was not invented in these latitudes. Thus the remarkable thing about these famous coaches is that *they do not* exist. The prodigy of the road cut right into the Cordillera range of the Andes . . . lies just as much in that its splendour is a kind of grandiose uselessness. At least in appearance, because the human miracle that Montaigne reserves for his epilogue – those bearers who calmly take each other's place at the shaft of the sedan in the heat of the battle not only portrays the Indians' courage, but in a general way their endurance, whereby the messenger's and bearers plough the famous road like a train second to nothing our own transports. Through an original synthesis of human genius and the worth of men, this civilisation which our own knew no better than to crush, without either equalling or knowing anything of it, had succeeded in reconciling natural vigour and the splendour of artifice; it had domesticated the unflattenable road and the unharnessed velocity of the human biped.[24]

We do not wish to be misunderstood in rejecting such metaphorical plays upon the essay as Gutwirth's missing wheel. It would offend everything we have said earlier about Montaigne's literary pleasure in reading and writing, as well as his own playful practices within many of the essays.[25] Indeed, we need find no shock in Montaigne's reflections on friendship, books and women, provided we see in them an essential literary play reflecting the separations of mankind and our inability ever to do more than essay our lost plenitudes. By the same token, this need not encourage desperate literary juggling, or heedless deconstruction that generally achieves little beyond enslaving its readers and initiators to the authority of style.

What Gutwirth misses in the essay on coaches by trusting to their absence, he nevertheless catches better in returning to the basic question of civilisation raised by the essay.[26] To this we now turn. The essayist risks nudity, that is, he challenges the assumption that men are truly human only through the subordination of nature to culture, to language, religion and clothing. In daring to speak of himself and to expose his faults to public view, Montaigne questioned the taboo upon self-display quite as much as in his explicit observations upon his sexual experience. But in the essayist there is a subtle shifting between the terms of the artifices nevertheless imposed upon 'nudity' and the personal quest involved in the 'naked' truth. Here we find it useful to follow Berger's distinction: 'To be naked is to be oneself. To be nude is to be seen naked by others and yet not recognized for oneself.'[27]

Montaigne is concerned neither with shock value nor with self-humiliation. In either case, the essayist would simply abuse his reader were he to encourage him to see the writer as an object of scorn in whom the reader could not see himself. The risk in nakedness is encountered for the sake of the confidence and wholeness which supervenes when it is properly essayed and shared. Nudity, then, may be seen as a failure in nakedness, an objectification of the other, or of ourself as other, through withholding the potentially shared wholesomeness of nudity. Thus civilised peoples are able to hold alien cultures at a distance through the contrast between dress and nakedness. Similarly, Montaigne would argue, men reduce women to the level of nature, identifying them with a nude, if not unsatiable, sexuality. However, in doing so they are merely separating themselves from themselves in a vain attempt to separate what is good in themselves from what is evil in themselves: 'Why does this seem hard to believe? Between my way of dressing and that of a peasant of my region I find more distance than there is between his way and that of a man dressed only in his skin' (I: 36, 167). Thus we separate our minds from our senses, our words from their meaning, and our hearts from our intentions as much as we separate ourselves from one another – and all in the name of culture. What we find strange in the encounter with naked cultures is nothing but the mirror of our daily differences in dress, food, religion and speech:

> These people are wild, just as we call wild the fruits that nature has produced by herself and in her normal course; whereas really it is those that we have changed artificially and led astray from the common order, that we should rather call wild. (I: 31. 152)

We find the same principles operating in the essay 'Of Cannibals'.[28] At first sight, the reader is likely to trade upon the distance between himself and the exotic practices reported in the essay. Whatever the physical distance between France and the New World, or between antiquity and Montaigne's own day, the stories that reach from either source are beset by the hermeneutical distance that separates reason and barbarism – or so it would seem, on first hearing. Of all the wonders in the world, surely the most difficult to comprehend is cannibalism. While we can imagine ourselves in all sorts of exploits beyond our ordinary experience, a sympathetic understanding of cannibalism seems to risk us in a loss of identity; or in a degradation of our very reason and humanity. Yet, no sooner has Montaigne pitched his topic than in the opening paragraph he begins the slide into essaying the very resource of self-distance required by an exotic reading of the essay. Thus he reports that while it was the practice of the Greeks to regard the Romans as barbarians, it was clear to them when encountering the Roman military organisation that in this respect, at least they seemed to share reason. Now if the Greeks had to admit the viability of Roman institutions, it is just as likely that we shall have to concede the same for institutions in the New World, which is otherwise beyond the pale of European authority. Therefore, if we are to gain any access to the practices of the New World, we are more likely to learn something from a man unencumbered by our own standards of reason. From what we have been told by Montaigne's simple informant, there is nothing barbarous about the Brazilians; unless in our eyes living in harmony with natural simplicity renders them wild savages.

Thus Montaigne obliges the reader to divest himself of his own authority, and like Montaigne's simple informant to allow himself to see without cultural bias an underlying humanity and reasonableness in the behaviour of the Brazilians with whom the reader is now tempted to identify. But this would be an easy conversion, whereas Montaigne still has harder things in mind for the reader. After all, the Brazilians are cannibals. The reader's encounter with this practice piles upon him in a single paragraph of the whole essay. The Brazilians eat their prisoners. They do not do this for nourishment, like the Scythians, but out of revenge. The proof of this is that when they saw how cruelly the Portuguese treated their prisoners they gave up cannibalism in favour of their method, 'which was to bury them up to the waist, shoot the rest of their body full of arrows, and afterward hang them'. The reader is now pushed to the point where he must bite upon the truth that we are far stranger to ourselves than any aliens we put at a distance from us. The essay, then, involves the reader in an exotic journey in which the truly distant point is the very ground upon which he believed himself to stand. The essay tests the reader's prejudices. But it does so by steering clear of purely ideological consent to abstract principles of humanity and universalism.

The reader must see how easily such principles are put to rout and confusion –
expressed, of course, by the conventional reader finding the essay itself unclear,
contradictory and confused. Such a reader requires of the essayist a clear demon-
stration, a cogent proof, deliberately composed. Montaigne's essays reject such
conventions. From the outset, he embroils his authorities in such a fashion that
the reader will find him a necessary companion rather than a wilful opponent of
all around him. Together, then, there begins that mutual essay which is the
strength of Montaigne's writing as well as the defence of our own reading. It has
been argued that Montaigne is deliberately unclear as to whether he believed the
Indians to be more virtuous than their conquerors because of the passivity (an
anathema to Montaigne's (Graeco-Roman culture) with which they met death at
the hands of the Spaniards.[29] This argument, however, completely misses
Montaigne's emphasis upon the effect of cultural frameworks in assigning a victory to the Spaniards they might not have gained otherwise. Moreover, Montaigne does not contradict himself in wishing for a marriage between classical and
Indian cultures, since he distinguishes between the ancient world of Europe and
sixteenth-century Spanish colonialism. Hence he is not comparing the childlike
nature of the Indians with the maturity of the ancients. He is contrasting the barbarity of sixteenth-century Europe with the civilisation of the New World –
thereby essaying the relativism of civilisation and barbarism.

Montaigne relativises civilisation and barbarism not only to jeopardise the distinction between Christianity and paganism but also question the rationalist distinction between nature and artifice.[30] Although the natural is not identical with
the good, and may well be evil, it is Montaigne's view that natural evils are less
barbarous than the artificial evil of Christian colonialism. He means, therefore, to
bring the reader to see that barbarism consists in his own unexamined artifices
that separate him further from himself than he imagines the distance between
nature and society to be. Thus Montaigne uses the cannibals to the same end as
his admired Tacitus used his German tribes in order to expose the vices of Roman
civilisation, and this is still a common literary device:

> Tacitus, Montaigne, and Lévi-Strauss are linked by the 'fictive' uses they make
> of the concepts of 'barbarism', 'wildness', and 'savagery'. In their works they
> telegraph their awareness that the antitheses they have set up between a 'nat-
> ural' humanity on the one side and an 'artificial' humanity on the other are not
> to be taken literally, but used only as the conceptual limits necessary for gain-
> ing critical focus on the conditions of our own civilized existence. By joining
> them in acting as if we believed mankind could be so radically differentiated,
> put into two mutually exclusive classes, the 'natural' and the 'artificial', we are
> drawn, by the dialectic of thought itself, toward the center of our own complex

existence as member's of civilized communities. By playing with the extremes, we are forced to the mean; by torturing one concept with its antithesis, we are cloven to closer attention to our own perceptions; by manipulating the fictions of artificiality and naturalness, we gradually approximate a truth about a world that is as complex and changing as our possible ways of comprehending that world.[31]

The barbarian is nothing but the bad conscience of civilised man – a reminder of the distance between the masque of society and our bottom nature. In society we may be above ourselves, it is true; but we may also sink to levels of depravity, cruelty and honesty that defile us beyond relief. It is then that we are tempted to think of our innocence as a state before society, before adulthood – or as a lost paradise to be regained in the new world, if at all. Thus philosophers and moralists have railed against power, luxury and sensuality as corruptions of man's original nature. Others, explorers, anthropologists and tourists, have hoped to find in the world the blessed isles that the philosophers and prophets have placed nowhere, or else at the end of the world. But, of course, Montaigne is not in pursuit of any lost innocence. He can leave that to Rousseau and the French Revolution. No men live outside of society and, however simple, they are all tied to culture. Montaigne's interest in the essays on coaches and cannibals lies in the degree to which we are able to sustain the transparency of culture, to hold out a reserve while nevertheless meeting our commitments. The Romans, Mexicans and Peruvians all built wonderful civilisations and yet they managed to produce men whose characters are models of virtue even today. This is the achievement that occupies Montaigne. How shall a man of his own day act so that he, too, might be remembered in that illustrious line of portraits between ancient and modern tunes? It is in this light that we may also understand Montaigne's pedagogical essays. They challenge the law of custom with the liberty of a well-educated man. It is the man of liberal education who represents the synthesis of nature and society that Montaigne knew could not be found either in prehistory or as the fanciful construction of philosophical utopias. Such a man is made nowhere else than in society; and a society of such men would realise the deepest ambition of the friendship that united Montaigne and La Boétie.

To the civilised man there is something naive about our nature that is revealed wherever it is without clothing, or masks or deliberate speech. Cultured man is therefore as fascinated with the naked body as he is with clear and unadorned speech. In each case, he is tempted by the fiction of a scenic truth – the first man, the garden of Eden or Plato's first city. In order to believe in this fiction, however, civilised man must invent it, while disclaiming in it any distortion or deception that would contaminate it like the rest of his culture. Thus Montaigne says of the cannibals:

> These nations, then, seem to me barbarous in this sense, that they have been fashioned very little by the human mind, and are still very close to their original naturalness. The laws of nature still rule them, very little corrupted by ours ... I am sorry that Lycurgus and Plato did not know of them: for it seems to me that what we actually see in these nations surpasses not only all the pictures in which poets have idealized the golden age and all their inventions in imagining a happy state of man, but also the conceptions and very desire of philosophy. (I: 31, 153)

In portraying the first men as men like ourselves, Montaigne faced the same problems he encountered in his own self-portrait. How is one to domesticate the civilised arts of invention whereby man has mastered almost everything but the mystery of his own self? In other words, there arises for rational cultures the problem of alien cultures, whether in the discovery of non-rational societies or in the persistence of those non-rational capacities of civilised man himself. Montaigne's contribution to cross-cultural anthropology and to psychoanalysis (essaying), if you will, is to correct the imputation of absolute human differences with a narrative that historicises and contextualises the variety of human conduct as never anything above or below humankind.[32] It is for the same reason that Montaigne loved travel. For by displacing himself into foreign lands, with new customs, different food and drink, as well as other ways among the ladies, priests and courtiers, he could discover in a bodily way the range of difference and identity that ties mankind. Such detours are as necessary to self-knowledge as the *Essays* he composed when at home:

> That *Des Coches* harks back to *Des Cannibales* (Montaigne travels to the new world for the second time) is a case in point: the essayist meditates upon the tangle of the known and the unknown, as the one and the other are displaced and translated into one another through travel and time. The travel is not purely geographic, historical or anthropological. It does not simply represent a passage from one point over to the next, from one coast across the ocean. It signifies *a transfer from the travelled to the traveller; from the object through to the subject, through the body of the subject;* the interpretative matrix (the interpretant) of *Des Coches* being Montaigne's stomach as it cannot quite be held *à pied, à cheval* or *en voiture*. The passage about *'nous venons de découvrir un nouveau monde'* [III: 6, 693] is thus clearly linked, not only, and naturally, to the fact of travel (the distance covered, the contact established with the new inhabitants), but also to the actual bodily transformations in him who wants to experience the

discovery. The traveler must be changed: he must become, so to speak, that which he set about to find as alien. And *Des Coches* is thus properly the vehicle which makes possible the coverage of the distance between one point and another, between the self and the other.[33]

The reason that the *Essays* are not properly described as autobiography, except in our earlier remarks, is that each of the essays employs its topic as the occasion for moving self-certainty off-centre, into a maze of possibilities and variations that make it impossible to return to the initial pronouncement with the self unchanged. It is here that Montaigne's anecdotes function to turn the self outward towards its other. Thus after our first disgust with cannibalism, for example, we come to see how men hunger for meaning to the point that they are everywhere capable of hunting and killing one another in the pursuit of a collective truth.

The ultimate distance that each essay carries the essayist is the distance Montaigne covers with respect to other writers, poets and philosophers, to other lives, however illustrious. It is in this distance that he comes to himself as a writer and because of the necessity of that vocation Montaigne cannot begin with his life as the provision of an autobiography. Montaigne's reading serves to show him his differences with other writers, differences of opinion, style and sheer poetry. At the same time, these differences are the way to his own convictions as a writer, reader, thinker, stylist, who can be absolutely sure of himself as an essayist. The ultimate difference in the *Essays* resides in the body that gives Montaigne's writing its absolute particularity, its sure grip upon its other, namely, upon the reader who finds himself addressed irresistibly, and who must therefore consider his own self-essay. To the extent this is achieved, there is a mutual encroachment of the reader and the writer upon one another, At the start, the topic of any essay functions as a pretext or a departure in which the reader and the writer can divide identity and difference without necessarily bringing home any integration of self and other. Unless the essay succeeds in bringing each to redefine himself through the seemingly alien experience it assembles, there is a failure of literary authority. It is in this sense that we can further appreciate the writer's preoccupation with death. We are never so distant from others as when we hear of their death, more so even than when we hear stories of the strange ways in which men have encountered death. Thus the essay on cannibals is an occasion to reflect upon how we are all consumed by death, but also upon how we consume ourselves in vanities of every kind, so that life feeds upon life, thereby furnishing death with its own image. The writer, too, consumes himself, like every other temporal creature, including his reader. The *Essays* mark the place where once lived Montaigne – not as a mask but as a memorial whose literary authority remains alive so long as it still compels its readers; as indeed it does.

So the *Essays* are not simply the product of Montaigne's inner turmoil brought to order in the privacy of the study where he had hit upon the technique of the essay. Montaigne's 'retreat' never closes the window upon the political and religious strife to which the *Essays* are no less addressed. This should be evident from Montaigne's espousal of La Boétie, 'The Apology' and the essays on the New World Conquests, let alone his constant meditations on the history of power and violence which we have analysed throughout this book. Still, a recent work by David Quint[34] nicely puts the ethical posture of the *Essays* as one of *trust* and *accommodation* rather than fear and domination. The *Essays* are therefore a major contribution to the civilising process: The brunt of so many of the essays is to expose the zero-sum results of hyper individualism, of autarchic struggle to the death which perpetuates a state of nature unknown to 'barbarians' but to which Europe was beginning to be accustomed and even rationalized in the works of Machiavelli and later Hobbes. It is not from squeamishness that Montaigne decries cruelty. It is to show that it leads to no political viable outcome. But, as Quint argues, when Montaigne calls for political clemency, for the virtue of mercy, it is to introduce a dialogue that is grounded in the discovery of the *principle of tolerance* in religious and political matters. Montaigne, therefore, is constantly critical of the excesses of humanist individualism, in particular of its aggression towards others, women and children who lack the will-to-power. The paradox of autarchy is that it produces *slavery even in the master*.[35] Thus Montaigne shifts the virtues and glory of war and politics into the quest for literary strength exercised in the encounter of opinion and judgement. In the midst of civil war, the *Essays* construct a technology of generosity and mutual recognition in all our relationships. In this Montaigne is the forerunner of later work in deliberative democracy and cultural violence by Rawls[36] and Habermas.[37] Thus Montaigne kept an open house and an open mind at a time when his country was torn apart – leaving a lucky testament to survival.

CHAPTER 10

On Living and Dying as We Do

It is only in the life of a human being that the question about the meaning of being human can be asked. This is not to say that each of us asks this question. Rather, it is more likely that we dwell in the midst of the answer that others have given to this question without much imagining that there will ever come a time when we shall have to ask for ourselves what it means to be human in order to go on living, or to bring our lives to a close. Of course, in a daily way we provide for our lives to be sufficient. We trust to family, to community and religion or to our own selfishness, prejudices and ideologies in order to defend ourselves from the ultimate question underlying the gift of this life, its brief trust and certain loss.

What we are, we are for others and yet the question of who we are remains for ourselves. We cannot borrow ourselves from others; or not entirely. Nor can we keep ourselves to ourselves without what others bring to us of ourselves. This is the riddle of our public and private lives.[1] It never ceased to occupy Montaigne. We cannot come to the end of ourselves and we cannot keep that distance upon ourselves that others likewise observe towards us. We must, however, observe their standpoint in order to make ourselves known to those around us. At the same time we must withhold that source within us from which we launch our life, its dreams and its freedom. We never possess ourselves, yet we need to call ourselves our own. Despite the abiding difference between who we are and what we are, we must nevertheless seek self-knowledge and place ourselves in the trust of others. For we cannot suspend our living in the mystery that a man we are to ourself and that others are to us.

We might seek who we are in that infinite difference between ourselves and God, of which the lack in ourselves is the merest though most positive, reverberation. For we are earthborn and borrow briefly its seasons on our way to death:

But what do I love when I love my God? Not material beauty or beauty of a temporal order; not the brilliance of earthly light, so welcome to our eyes; not the sweet melody of harmony and song; not the fragrance of flowers, perfumes, and spices, not manna or honey; not limbs such as the body delights to embrace. It is not these that I love when I love my God. And yet, when I love him, it is true that I love a light of a certain kind, a voice, a perfume, a food, an embrace; but they are of the kind that I love in my inner self, when my soul is bathed in light that is not bound by space: when it listens to sound that never dies away: when it breathes fragrance that is not borne away on the wind: when it tastes food that is never consumed by the eating; when it clings to an embrace from which it is not severed by fulfillment of desire. This is what I love when I love my God.

But what is my God? I put my question to the earth. It answered, 'I am not God', and all things on earth declared the same. I asked the sea and the chasms of the deep and the living things that creep in them, but they answered, 'We are not your God. Seek what is above us.' I spoke to the winds that blow, and the whole air and all that lives in it replied, 'Anaximenes is wrong. I am not God.' I asked the sky, the sun, the moon, and the stars, but they told me, 'Neither are we the God whom you seek.' I spoke to all the things that are about me, all that can be admitted by the door of the senses, and I said, 'Since you are not my God, tell me about him. Tell me something of my God.' Clear and loud they answered, 'God is he who made us.' I asked these questions simply by gazing at these things, and their beauty was all the answer they gave.

Then I turned to myself and asked, 'Who are You?' 'A man', I replied. But it is clear that I have both body and soul, the one the outer, the other the inner part of me. Which of these two ought I to have asked to help me find my God? With my bodily powers I had already tried to find him in earth and sky, as far as the sight of my eyes could reach, like an envoy sent upon a search. But my inner self is the better of the two, for it was to the inner part of me that my bodily senses brought their messages. They delivered to their arbiter and judge the replies which they carried back from the sky and the earth and replies that they contain, those replies which stated 'We are not God' and 'God is he who made us.' The inner part of man knows these things through the agency of the outer part. I, the inner man, know these things; I, the soul, know them through the senses of my body. I asked the whole mass of the universe about my God, and it replied, 'I am not God. God is he who made me!' (Saint Augustine).[2]

Here we shall explore with Montaigne the essay of human embodiment. In this exploration Montaigne is a friendly guide, careful of the concerns that others have expressed for their lives, while testing their practices in himself as he finds himself in the person of the essayist. Montaigne seeks the particulars of embodied living that tie us to the general condition of mankind. Yet Montaigne is neither a philosopher, nor a theologian; and is quite outside of any school. Like Socrates, Montaigne begins with no received version of our incarnation. He requires of us that we essay the problem of living in a manner that is faithful only to the diversity of life's moods and historical patterns, trusting to no centre but what we truly find in ourselves. Thus any exploration that is guided by Montaigne is simultaneously an essay in sharing our humanity with one who, like Socrates, was never more himself than in the company of others, but who shaped his own life by never leaving hold of the question it offered him.

Thus we take upon our own humanity as an experiment. We need to place ourselves in a natural light, to show ourselves neither more nor less than we are. In this, vanity and self-abasement are equal traps.[3] For we can always exceed ourselves in fortune, or in misery, and in either one never come upon our selves, though we may well surpass others whom we call to witness our masques. The problem, then, is to find some measure between endless self-questioning and the answers upon which we build our lives and self-assurance. No man can withhold himself from others, or from himself, in order to make his life an open question without any underlying form. To do so, he would have to be blind to the repetitions and encroachments of embodied living from which none of us is separable, and from which each of us draws an original bearing and habit. At the same time, we cannot surrender ourselves to the circumstances of our birth and family; nor can we remain slaves to custom and fashion. We owe something to ourselves, as well as to our land; something to conscience, as well as to the law. How, then, are we to keep alive the meaning of the question we are, while remaining wise enough to live as others do, holding ourselves neither above them nor beneath them?

We encounter our own living only through the way others live. It is in their families, in their villages and in their customs that we behold our own. Here too, however, the meaning of our lives is no more settled by the findings of anthropology than it is by the facts of anatomy and biology. For the knowledge we accumulate through the comparison of men's beliefs and bodily practices serves only to deepen the inquiry concerning the possibility of the universal ideal of humanity that might be entertained by all men whatever the circumstances of their living.[4] Ethical anthropology is therefore not an idle accumulation of the differences between men. Rather, it informs itself of these differences in order to avoid embracing an abstract unity of mankind. But to do this, an ethical anthropologist must essay the differences he finds between men, just as he must abide with the differences he finds in himself over the course of his life's journey.

The meaning of our humanity cannot be raised as a question that puts us outside of the practices of those around us living today, or in earliest times, in our own country or in far-off places.[5] The pursuit of this question leads us to ourselves only through other people. We have no certain mark upon ourselves given to us in our animal nature. We can count less upon our instincts than upon our habitat and the sublime accommodations of our language and culture:

> I do not want to forget this, that I never rebel so much against France as not to regard Paris with a friendly eye; she has had my heart since childhood. And it has happened to me in this as happens with excellent things: the more other beautiful cities I have seen since, the more the beauty of Paris has power over me and wins my affection. I love her for herself, and more in her own essence than overloaded with foreign pomp. I love her tenderly even to her warts and her spots. I am a Frenchman only by this great city: great in population, great in the felicity of her situation, but above all great and uncomparable in variety and diversity of the good things of life; the glory of France, and one of the noblest ornaments of the world. (III: 9, 743)

At first sight, self-love would seem to be the easiest of all attachments. After all, how is it possible that we should not value our most, at least among living creatures? However we might belittle ourself before God, having nevertheless been made in the image of God, we are surely lord of the rest of creation. Since God has made all people in his image, and placed us so far above other creatures in the hierarchy of creation, the value that we have for one another ought to go without saying. Rather, humanism is at best a prayer of thanksgiving and not an argument essential to the human condition. On the lips of a Christian, humanism, then, would sound like Pico della Mirandola's exaltation upon the dignity of man:

> It is truly divine possession of all these natures at the same time flowing into one, so that it pleases us to exclaim with Hermes, 'A great miracle, O Asclepius, is man.' The human condition can especially be glorified for this reason, through which it happens that no created substance disdains to serve him. To him the earth and the elements, to him the animals arc ready for service, for him the heavens fight, for him the angelic minds procure safety and goodness, if indeed it is true as Paul wrote that all ministering spirits are sent in ministry on account of those who are destined to heirs of salvation. No wonder that he is loved by all in whom all recognize something of their own, indeed their whole selves and all their possessions.[6]

However inspirational the Christian hierarchy of being might be for humanist meditation, it is not at all tempting to Montaigne. It represents a form of excess upon our incarnation that Montaigne wished to avoid. Moreover, it is easily jeopardised by an equally Christian practice of meditation upon the emptiness of man in contrast with the plenitude of his divine maker.[7] Montaigne himself had inscribed upon the ceiling of his study these reminders of man's vanity:

> Holy Writ declares those of us wretches who think well of ourselves: 'Dust and ashes,' it says to them, 'what has thou to glory in?' And elsewhere: 'God has made man like the shadow, of which who shall judge when, with the passing of the light, it shall have vanished away.' In truth we are nothing. (II: 12, 368)

It is Montaigne's opinion that nothing in human reason permits us to ground our reasoning outside of itself, or to reason upon things outside of man's own experience. The task of a humanist, as understood by Montaigne, is to work in the middle ground between the excesses of Christian optimism and despair. The ground of this humanism is its learned ignorance,[8] that is to say, Socratic ignorance, which knows itself, tests itself and is thus never a complete ignorance:

> The wisest man that ever was, when they asked him what he knew, answered that he knew this much, that he knew nothing. He was verifying what they say, that the greatest part of what we know is the least of those parts that we do not know: that is to say that the very thing we think we know is a part, and a very small part, of our ignorance. (II: 12, 370)

The problem of the nature of the best life for humankind, of the right pursuit of honour, wisdom or pleasure, with corresponding relations between the parts of the soul, body and society, has remained a concern since classical times.[9] Montaigne's views on the false contrast between the life of pleasure and the life of reason and his preference for a mixed life remind us of the argument in the *Philebus*. In this regard, Aristotle's *Eudemian Ethics* is surely another source of Montaigne's preference for a life of mixed virtues.[10] Three forms of life are distinguished, each governed by thought, virtue and pleasure, though some men seek to couple or even combine all of these ends. Although Aristotle probably relies upon the *Philebus* in going beyond Plato's *Republic*, he surpasses Plato in attributing a distinctive virtue to political life, and in making problematic rather than clear the choice between a life of ambition and a life devoted to philosophy. Certainly this, too, is in the direction of Montaigne's own thought and experience. The same is true of the desire expressed by Aristotle and Diogenes Laertius that the wise man will marry, have children and engage in politics, alternating between action and contemplation; a life of pure contemplation belongs only to God. Indeed, the limits of human knowledge suggest the vanity of a man's claim to lead the contemplative life. Hence he is more likely to be achieving some good proportionate to his capacities in a life of politics and action. Montaigne would also have found a similar argument in Cicero's *De officiis* (I, XLIII) where, again, man's social duties are considered to conform better with his nature than the excesses of contemplation. Moreover, try as they may, philosophers and lawyers never succeed in fitting the variety of human practice and circumstance within the limits of their laws and definitions. Indeed, their attempts to do so merely multiply interpretation so that there is no end to its perplexities. We can no more come to the bottom of things than Aesop's dogs could drink up the sea.

Montaigne makes a great deal of the Socratic distinction between external knowledge of things and persons and internal knowledge of the self. Although the self is as vain as any other thing in the world, it is possible to achieve a kind of composition in respect of it that is impossible in the endless flux and variability of things revealed to us by history, geography and anthropology. By self-knowledge Montaigne has in mind a status whereby one acts necessarily or 'naturally' in accordance with knowledge that has been internalised, like food, and is therefore disposed towards action, Montaigne, like Socrates, speaks of this knowledge as ignorance because it does not seek any possessive accumulation of facts and principles, according to the stereotype of knowledge. In reality, of course, it leads to the possession of one's self via this first dispossession of things.[11] Montaigne's manner of expressing this reversal is always to bring home the lessons of self-knowledge by restoring the incarnate grounds it at first seems to transcend:

> The nice inscription with which the Athenians honored the entry of Pompey into their city is in accord with my meaning.
>
> > You are as much a god as you will own
> > That you are nothing but a man alone.
> > Amyot's Plutarch
>
> It is an absolute perfection and virtually divine to know how to enjoy our being rightfully. We seek other conditions because we do not fully understand the use of our own and go outside of ourselves because we do not know what it is like inside. Yet there is no use our mounting on stilts, for on stilts we must still walk on our own legs. And on the loftiest throne in the world we are still sitting only on our own rump. (III: 13, 857)

It is essential that we do not separate Montaigne's reliance upon the doctrine of learned ignorance from his reflections upon the limitations of the human mind in relation to our bodily estate. Montaigne's humanism is essentially tied to our condition as living beings in whom reason and the senses are inseparable and thereby impose a limit to the excesses of philosophy and Christianity alike. Thus it is impossible to confine Montaigne's thought within the forced alternatives of the Sceptics, Stoics and Epicureans, or between Christian hope and despair.[12] In every case, the excesses in these positions are betrayed by the living tie between our minds and our bodies that makes our life the ultimate ground of goodness.[13] It is possible for us to suspend belief in the finest of philosophical arguments; yet Socrates himself could not resist the good in scratching himself once they released his chains. To be sure, there is nothing about the human body, considered in itself, that cannot be surpassed for strength, agility, vision, health and longevity in animals.[14] Indeed, there are many human qualities that are modelled upon those of animals to whom they are natural yet to man valued achievements. In fact, humans and animals have always had a certain fascination for each other, even to the point of love (II: 12, 347). Yet we are far below the animals in our willingness to maim and slaughter one another, and quite unlike them in the ingenuity we exercise in subjecting one another to pain. Although all people have the same bodies, and are subject to the same bodily necessities of birth, hunger, sex, pleasure, pain and death, just as their souls are cast in the same divine mould, they are nevertheless engaged in infinitely varied adaptations to their circumstances, which create among men differences of reason and sensation far beyond the differences between men and animals.

In the face of the fantastic variation between men and women, kings and cobblers, Frenchmen and Italians, Catholics and Protestants, Stoics and Sceptics, not to mention every variation in custom and belief regarding dress, food, virtue and vice, the humanist is hard pressed to remind us of ourself. No creature in the world is as capable as we are of creating distinctions between ourself and our fellows. Above all, our ability to separate ourself from ourself, to engage in cruel and deadly controversies, and generally to submit our fellows to our whims, is abetted by the belief that the soul or reason is somehow higher than the body. Thus we have subjected our own bodies, as well as the bodies of others, to incredible fates in the pursuit of reasoned glories. In fact, we have so convinced ourselves that we are destined through these pursuits to achieve *'fanciful* goods, goods future and absent' – like reason, knowledge and honour that we have been content to assign to the animals 'essential, tangible, and *palpable goods*: peace, repose, security, innocence, and health' (II: 12, 357).

In this regard, Montaigne cites two stories and then proceeds to weigh them in a comment which I think contains the very fundament of his humanist convictions. In the first, he reports that even the Stoics dared to say that if Heraclitus and Pherecydes could have exchanged their wisdom for their health, in order to be rid of the dropsy in one case, and of lice in the other, they would have done well. They preferred, however, to set wisdom above health. But the Stoics have another story about Ulysses and Circe, in which they say that if Ulysses had been forced by Circe to choose between two potions, one to make a fool a wise man, the other a wise man a fool, he ought to have chosen the cup of folly rather than allow

207

her to change his human figure into that of a beast. They argued in this way because they believed that Wisdom herself preferred the figure of man to that of an ass. From this confession of the Stoics Montaigne concludes, in the strongest terms, that all things, even God, are proportionate to man, provided man accepts his properly mixed condition of embodied soul:

> What? So our philosophers abandon this great and divine wisdom for this corporeal and terrestrial veil? Then it is no longer by our reason, our intelligence, and our soul that we are superior to the beasts; it is by our beauty, our fair complexion, and the fine symmetry of our limbs, for which we should abandon our intelligence, our wisdom, and all the rest.
>
> Well I accept this naive, frank confession. Indeed, they knew that those qualities about which we make so much ado are but idle fancy. Even if the beasts, then, had all the virtue, knowledge, wisdom and capability of the Stoics, they would still be beasts. Nor would they for all that be comparable to a wretched, wicked, senseless man, In short, whatever is not as we are is worth nothing. And God himself, to make himself appreciated must resemble us . . . (II: 12. 358)

Everything in the human record shows that we are at once the poorest of creatures and yet the most given to excess. We cannot escape this carnal paradox so long as we continue to separate ourselves from ourselves in the service of philosophical and religious arguments about the relationship between life and death, or between the mind and the body. The excess of humans over one another is unparalleled. There is no practice among us that is not contradicted by the practice of others. What creature – other than us – can treat life as death, poverty as wealth, pleasure as pain? What other creature can be so divided over the meaning given to food, dress, housing, wealth, health, illness, power, weakness? How is it possible that, however a man or woman conceives of himself or herself, or whatever it is they think right or wrong, will be found by some other men and women to be constituted in quite a different fashion, so that there is more difference – that is to say, an absolute excess – between men than there is between men and animals? How can the human condition be so at odds with itself, while at the same time nothing that obtains of us can be truly said to be alien to us? It is on this anthropological question, and its incarnations, rather than upon any epistemological or theological question, that the *Essays* dwell. Moreover, they never abandon this visceral inquiry, so that it is quite useless to try to find in Montaigne any trope of philosophical development whereby he came to terms with the anthropological question. Like Socrates, Montaigne had no other interest than ourselves. Every topic of the *Essays* serves only to further his study of human nature. In the search he overlooks nothing, and therefore anything can serve his purpose, giving to the *Essays* an incredible variety of topics and discourse.

History, philosophy, poetry and theology, education, war, food, dress, love, friendship and death are only a few of the themes to which Montaigne addresses himself in his search for our kind.

At first sight it is possible to see in the variety of the *Essays* nothing but that busy indolence in Montaigne which allowed him to pick here and there, without anywhere achieving any depth or certainty in his inquiry. The result of many years of work in this way offers us a rich pastime, but deserves to be read only by a similarly nonchalant reader, happy to while away his time in the labyrinth of the *Essays*. Indeed, much of what Montaigne himself says about the method of their composition, his use of books, his generally poor memory and disinterested specialised knowledge favours the conclusion that the *Essays* are hardly a professional anthropological treatise.[15] From what he tells us of himself. Montaigne lacked the stamina for any serious moral treatise:

> As for the natural faculties that are in me, of which this book is the essay, I feel them bending under the load. My conceptions and my judgment move only by groping, staggering, stumbling and blundering; and when I have gone ahead as far as I can, still I am not at all satisfied: I can still see the country beyond, so that I cannot clearly distinguish it. And when I undertake to speak indiscriminately of everything that comes to my fancy without using any but my own natural resources, if I happen, as I often do, to come across in the good authors those same subjects I have attempted to treat – as in Plutarch I have just come across his discourse on the power of the imagination – seeing myself so weak and puny, so heavy and sluggish, in comparison with those men, I hold myself in pity and disdain. (I: 26, 107)

Yet, even in such a confession we see the strength of Montaigne's anthropological method. Just as he sets himself aside as a thinker of any importance, even diminishing his contribution as an author, so he fills the *Essays* with observations upon the ambitions of men, only in order to marginalise their significance. But, then, it is from this very margin of intimate self-observation that he is able to reaffirm the abiding achievements of some great men and women of history, as well as the ordinary accomplishments of those like himself who have learned how to live with a limited ignorance. Thus Montaigne is not content to indulge the tropes of Christian humility, disparaging the puffed up attempts of man to raise himself in the world. Of course, he is critical of reason and custom, of vanity and glory – nothing human escapes his watchful eye. But there is no transcendental standpoint, no divine alienation underlying Montaigne's carnal observations. This is because Montaigne's anthropology is ruled by the ethical limits of self-essaying. The *Essays*, therefore, are not content to record human ignorance or to humiliate man in God's favour. Montaigne is resolutely on the side of human beings and truly human ignorance attaches him more to us than do those flights of fantasy and excesses of reason whereby we hope to find ourselves on the side of the gods. To anyone who exclaims, 'O what a vile and abject thing is man if he does not raise himself above humanity!' Montaigne makes the following reply:

> That is a good statement and a useful desire, but equally absurd. For to make the handful bigger than the hand, the armful bigger than the arm, and to hope to straddle more than the reach of our legs, is impossible and unnatural. Nor can man raise himself above himself and humanity; for he can see only with his own eyes, and seize only with his own grasp. (II: 12, 457)

Here, as elsewhere, we see Montaigne's anthropological method tied resolutely to the human frame, to the body's reach, and to the lessons of its plain living. The *Essays* explore, from beginning to end the human, reversibility of truth and falsity, pleasure and pain, virtue and vice. Above all, they never stray far from the contemplation of the central Delphic paradox of the command of self-knowledge laid upon the one creature in this world most given to self-ignorance, fantasy and aberration. It is possible to argue that Montaigne loved paradox for its intellectual and aesthetic properties. But this would be as true of him as of any other good mind in his day. Rather, Montaigne was attached to the use of paradox because it displays the embodied tension of living, which cannot proceed without an intelligent and sensible capacity for dwelling within the limits of relationships that resist fantasies of omnipotence. Thus we may learn in and from the course of living, but we will never learn to live nor learn to die. This is not an irrationalist argument. We could hardly understand the *Essays* if we were tempted by such a reaction. Montaigne's paradoxes are distributed between life and reason. The thinker who abstracts from the limits of embodiment is no better than a dreamer.

So much of the *Essays* turn upon the paradoxical relationships between Life and Death, or between Knowledge and Ignorance, that we cannot avoid a closer examination of Montaigne's use of these themes. For many people, philosophy and religion are recognisable as commitments to reflection upon the paradox that Life is Death, and the reversed truth that Death is Life, or that Knowledge is Ignorance, and only Ignorance is Knowledge. The religious paradox arises from the acceptance of a life after death. In the Platonic tradition, the philosophical paradox turns upon a mind–body dualism that denies the status of knowledge to the senses on the ground that they are merely the instruments of opinion. The mind, inasmuch as it separates itself from the senses, whether in this life or the next – and here philosophy and religion overlap – is capable of true contemplation of the eternal ideas of Truth, Justice and Beauty. Montaigne, of course, was quite familiar with the classical and Christian tradition of reflection upon the double paradox of Life and Death, Reason and Ignorance and their permutations.

Thus the Christian may prefer to remain ignorant in this life, at least from the standpoint of philosophical knowledge, in order to know God in the next life. Indeed, a philosopher like Socrates will prefer ignorance as a mark even of the philosophical life rather than pursue the vanities of (scientific) Reason. At bottom, however, both the believer and the philosopher are caught in the paradox of ignorance, namely, how it is they know that they cannot know truly either God or the eternal ideas. This problem is more pervasive than the problem of that professional pride in scholars and medical men which Montaigne was at pains to ridicule. It is a question of where it is we stand once we refuse the disembodied excesses of philosophy and religion. And, of course, the religious and civil war that surrounded him made Montaigne a man sick of such excesses. Thus his attachment to the use of paradox cannot be understood as merely another instance of the general passion for argument and contradiction. Montaigne's use of paradox is ruled by the ethical purpose of subjecting us to a sense of bodily limit and tolerance. It is intended to restore the community of thought and speech by making it clear that there is no principle from which reason can be reduced to a monologue.

The *Essays*, as Montaigne himself tells us, are 'essays in flesh and bone'. They are, then, concerned from the very opening with the study of our incarnate being, that is, with our embodied reason whereby we seek to shape our moods and passions – and, above all, the fear of pain, poverty and death. What Montaigne read of the history of war, human suffering, and cruelty, he measured against the reflections of philosophers and poets, with a careful eye for their sense of the mixture of virtue and vice, pleasure and pain, as well as reason and ignorance that characterises human society because we are incarnate creatures, and never above this universal condition. Thus, Edward, Prince of Wales, could be moved to pity by the resistance of three brave men, but not by the heartbreaking cry of mercy from the women and children of Guyenne. Montaigne never tired of reflection upon how variably men and women allow their passions to move their minds, or how curiously their minds have claimed to control their bodies and emotions. In the early *Essays*, he seems to have found a thread through the labyrinth in the nearly universal concern that men show to survive the death of their bodies. Yet, even in this practice, it seems that, from the way men treat bodily relics, they believe that the body and its glorious deed on earth have some power to emanate its effects from beyond the grave. Thus Edward I ordered his son to boil the flesh from the dead king's body and take the remains with him to his wars against the Scots, for he had noticed the English always won the battles at which he lent his presence. And from the trouble men take to provide for their own funerals, it seems that they expect to avoid disappointments and neglect that they could only fear as incarnate persons.

Generally, the concern men, women and even children have shown to preserve their honour, at any bodily cost, reveals that they have disvalued their lives because of a sense of shame that could only influence them on the supposition that they continue to be embodied beings after death. At all events, we do not easily accept the philosopher's injunction to separate our bodies from our souls as much as we can for the sake of the eternal joy of our empty souls, since we seem to imagine our risen state to be like an embodied community, where shame, glory, justice and punishment have their way. It is for some such reason that we have attached so much importance to our comportment in the hour of death, judging that these last earthly moments will count in winning for us a glorious reputation after the grave, at least among the living, if not in the company of the dead.[16] And it seems as though even the company of the dead is thought to be sensible to such concerns.

To say of death that it is nothing, merely opens up further paradoxy familiar to any Renaissance reader.[17] The idea of the void, of infinity, is far from being a comforting thought to beings used to living under the eye of God, or under the watchful concern of their family and fellows. Montaigne tries to assuage the existential horror in our anticipation of our own annihilation:

Death is to be feared less than nothing, if there is anything less than nothing:

> For us far less a thing must death be thought
> If ought there be that can be less than nought
> > Lucretius

It does not concern you dead or alive; alive, because you are; dead, because you are no more. (I: 20, 66)

Montaigne is free from any Pascalian anxieties about the physical void, because he did not believe in our capacity for anything beyond a limited reflection and rather trusted the divine plenitude. But Pascal despised Montaigne's provincial man for his ability to shut out the anxious void which Pascal had discovered beyond any moral conceit to be a fact of the universe:

For, after all, what is man in nature? A nothing compared to the infinite, a whole compared to the nothing, a middle point between all and nothing, infinitely remote from an understanding of the extremes; the end of things and their principles are unattainably hidden from him in impenetrable secrecy.

Equally incapable of seeing the nothingness from which he emerges and the infinity in which he is engulfed.[18]

Hugo Friedrich has commented upon Montaigne's nihilating method in the Apology and it might well remind us of Pascal's method.[19] But Montaigne's method has nothing to do with any numbers game – 'nothing' and 'infinite' are actually not numbers – nor is his world view accommodating to moral gamblers. And, as we shall see, Montaigne's hold upon the body politic gives his thought a quite different existential tendency from that of Pascal.[20]

We cannot practise our death, although many men have tried to do just this. We can, however, come near to it, as in sleep or a near fatal accident such as Montaigne himself experienced. After a fall from his horse, he describes (II: 6) how he clung to life, half-conscious and yet in a sweet and peaceful state in which the line between life and death seemed easily crossed. His pain only set in once he had regained consciousness. If we could lend ourselves to Nature we might meet death in this way. But so long as we are conscious beings, our principled confrontations with death are likely to be painful and deprive us of a peaceful union with our end. Thus Montaigne came close to experiencing death without the benefit of philosophy or religion. He recognises that there have been attempts to inculcate a certain lucidity in the face of death; and many examples of it, too (III: 4). But Montaigne believes that in every case such conduct is only possible because of an attachment to an afterlife, or to the prosperity of our children and good name. We should rather try to get our minds off the determination to die, or off any other great enterprise that will constrain the ordinary mixture of ability and incompetence in us: 'I saw death nonchalantly when I saw it universally, as the end of life. I dominate it in the mass; in detail it harasses me' (III: 4, 636).

A man is a fool not to think of death; and it is only fools who don't. Like the Egyptians, who in the middle of a feast would bring in a man's skeleton to remind themselves of death, Montaigne says he, too, never lost any occasion to reflect upon the passing of his own life. He made a practice of studying the deaths of others and tried to hold himself ready at any moment to leave hold of life. Indeed, he speaks of the *Essays* as probably having turned into a registry of deaths, had he chosen to write a book (I: 20, 62). Even in the early essay, 'That to Philosophize is to learn to Die' (I: 20), Montaigne notices that he is much more able to accept the philosophical shibboleth when he is in poor rather than in good health. Once the body ceases to be pleasurable in its functions, it is easier to believe the philosopher's claim that it is our soul rather than our body which is the highest good. Moreover, we are shortsighted not to see that we shall die just as we were born, as part of an ever recurring cycle of nature, in which the time allotted to us is never too short or too long, since such discriminations are infinitesimal from the perspective of nature:

Shall I change for you this beautiful contexture of things? Death is the condition of your creation, it is a part of you; you are fleeing from your own selves.

This being of yours that you enjoy is equally divided between death and life.
The first day of your birth leads you toward death as toward life:

> The hour which gave us life led to its end.
>
> Seneca (I: 20, 65)

In this vein, Montaigne finds in death a perfect justice. What can there be to complain of in something we have yet to experience? The value of our life is not judged by its length but by the use we make of living; and this is an art that can be found in all men since, large or small, we are all faced with the business of living and dying. Once we put ourselves in this common perspective, we shall diminish our fear of death, live our lives as best we can, with as much enjoyment as we are suited to, and always open to the end. We may hope to make our death our own, so to speak. But to do so, we ought not to leave things to the final act. We should rather prepare all our lives by not mounting a stage but by cultivating our gardens until the last: 'I want a man to act and to prolong the functions of life as long as he can: and I want death to find me planting my cabbages, but careless of death, and still more of my unfinished garden' (I: 20, 62).

It may be said that Montaigne has made the argument too easy. 'Half in love with easeful death,' does he not play down the justifiable fear that men have of dying – often in agony, their bodies wracked by disease, pain, torture and war? It is easy enough, perhaps, to dispense with the fear of death, if it can be argued that, after all, death is nothing we can know of and so there is literally nothing to be afraid of: 'It is not death, but dying, that I fear' (Epicharmus). But Montaigne considers that what we fear is the anticipation of death and this we can learn to deal with from the cultural perspective the *Essays* introduce. It is, after all, obvious that men's attitudes to bodily pain, even to the point of death, are as variable as any other opinion they hold. We cannot say that men are afraid of dying; and they need not be afraid of death. Montaigne is not satisfied, however, to resolve the problem of death and dying upon an easy distinction. His method is rather to essay in himself and others the experience of age, illness, violence, cruelty, suicide and the local practices of dying in order to discover his own bond with the living and dying; but especially as a writer. This is a development in which he had gradually to liberate himself from his first copybook essays, weighed down by Stoic principles, if not Christian dogma. Thus, as a writer he needed to lift the burden of the dead past in order to find his own living response without clothing it in the borrowed dress of philosophy and religion. He had also to avoid the literary temptation to design for himself the scenario of his own last hours: and rather to live patiently towards them, recording carefully what he learned interchangeably from his body and his writing. He learned above all to listen to his body. We cannot overlook the importance of Montaigne's sensory approach to that preconceptual and visceral knowledge that is the underlying basis of the universal claim of nature, and of the *Essays*. The death of La Boétie, because of its very model nature, left Montaigne with the hard business of living a life which, due to circumstance and his own cautious and moderate nature, achieved no such climax. He was conscious of the harder task, in which he was united with the most ordinary of men, of having to acquire the strength to live each day as it comes. Of course, he did not mean by this that one must simply yield to the moment, or sail with the tide, any more than he thought of turning life into a search for the exquisite moment beside which all else is dross. He intended some even course. Thus he could not trust himself to philosophical speculations and historical examples of suicide. Men vary so much in what they can tolerate; and societies too. Moreover, our affairs are subject to sudden changes of improvement and we may too easily give up: 'There is much more fortitude in wearing out the chain that binds us than in breaking it, and more proof of strength in Regulus than in Cato' (II: 3, 253). Montaigne thought any philosophy excessive that went beyond the ordinary mixture of virtue and vice that we experience in our embodied selves. Thus he was repelled by Cato's endurance, and would even have felt less friendly towards Socrates had he to believe that the exercise of virtue found no resistance in him.[21] He places especial store by Socrates' pleasure in scratching himself once his chains came off. His reflections upon Cato and Socrates come to different valuations because of an underlying belief in the need to find moral examples that we can bring to the level of our own daily lives and that would not require of us an otherwise exceptional death.

The model of humanity which attracted Montaigne most was the life and death of Socrates. It is significant that we never speak of Socrates' life except in the light of his death. Socrates died under the laws of the city in which he was the most free and ordinary citizen. His freedom lay not in any superior position, politically or philosophically speaking, but in his patient apprenticeship to self-knowledge. Socrates recognised his need of the city and the conversation of ordinary men as the proper resource of self-inquiry. That Socrates was not welcome to his fellow citizens was not due to his neglect of civic duties. At the same time, Socrates was not ruled by the letter of the law. If Socrates knew his limits, it was not because they were given to him by religion and the state. It was rather because his own self-examination had taught him that the city and the laws were true to the limited nature of man, so long as they serve men in the everyday affairs and do not try to make men heroes in the name of abstractions. It is harder to live each day unknown than to die celebrated as a hero. It is even harder to live each day without alienating our undertaking in favour of priests and professional philosophers, let alone soothsayers of every kind who exploit the misery in ordinary lives.

Surely, then, it is merely a conceit to single out Socrates as one upon whom we can model our lives? Moreover, it would be pernicious, since Socrates was at pains to achieve nothing extraordinary in his life that might offer a reason for any cult around him. Above all, Socrates left us no teaching, at least, not directly. Socrates conducted his inquiries by means of a conversational art which depended upon the dialogical presence of others at the same time that it suspended the usages of ordinary discourse in favour of the very question of ethical use. These Socratic essays are known to us only through Plato's artful writing. Montaigne could not hope, especially in his own troubled times, to find such interlocutors as Socrates had enjoyed, however much he claims to have preferred speaking to writing.

Montaigne makes reference to Socrates from the very earliest essays of Book One. Indeed, the first extensive reference (I:11, 29–30) already shows how sane Montaigne can be, once he shifts inside his ostensible topic – 'Of Prognostications' – to self-observation. On this ground, he can compare his own experience of an inner voice of reason, moved more by intuition than logic, with that of Socrates. Here Socrates is not appealed to as an authority, but rather comes to mind from a similar quest into self-knowledge. Indeed, in reflecting upon the way ordinary people, without much benefit of philosophy, meet quite awful deaths with equanimity (I: 14, 34), he again thinks of Socrates, remarking that there is nothing to choose in his favour. Of course, it is because Socrates, too, ignored philosophy he faced death in his calm fashion – and even with good humour: 'To the man who told Socrates, 'The thirty tyrants have condemned you to death,' he replied: 'And nature, them' (I: 20, 64). Here we can see Montaigne's appreciation of Socrates already searching for that middle ground of constancy and plain speech that avoids the excesses of man's self-wrought vanity and misery. Thus, in contemplating the hold that custom and habit have upon us, despite our flights of fantasy and philosophy, Montaigne nevertheless weighs our local attachments on the scale of what we owe to human society, to which we cannot he indifferent: and here again the example of Socrates comes to mind:

> Society in general can do without our thoughts; but the rest – our actions, our work, our fortunes, and our very life – we must lend and abandon to its service and to the common opinions, just as the great and good Socrates refused to save his life by disobedience to the magistrate, even to a very unjust and very iniquitous magistrate. (I: 23, 86)

Of course, the knowledge that society can do without us is, as Socrates shows to the Hippias, the kind of knowledge that feeds upon divisions and competitiveness, which has no place in a well-ordered state (1: 25, 105–6). Such knowledge may give a man local importance, for it is not much different from the attachments and prejudices whereby men judge everything in the light of their own circumstance, imagining what they see and believe to hold good for everyone and anyone elsewhere in the world. What is remarkable in Socrates is that he could be loyal to his community without absolutising its values. Already in Book One, Montaigne admires Socrates as a citizen of the world because he understood the world to contain all differences without any possibility of a single dominant perspective:

> Wonderful brilliance may be gained for human judgment by getting to know men. We are all huddled and concentrated in ourselves, and our vision is reduced to the length of our nose. Socrates was asked where he was from. He replied not 'Athens' but 'the world.' He, whose imagination was fuller and more extensive, embraced the universe as his city, and distributed his knowledge, his company, and his affections to all mankind, unlike us who look only at what is underfoot. (I: 26, 116)

At the same time, when Athens was under the plague, Socrates never left it to save his skin and seems never to have been worse for it – something which Montaigne was quite unable to emulate under similar circumstances as Mayor of Bordeaux! And, again, it seems that Socrates and Montaigne were divided over the use of travel, but not so for as to prevent Montaigne's appreciation of Socrates' humour: 'Someone said to Socrates that a certain man had grown no better by his travels. "I should think not," he said, "he took himself along with him"' (I: 39, 176). Montaigne, of course, loved travel, because like Socrates he understood the difference between escapism and the kind of journey that employs its shifting circumstances as occasions for the practice of self-inquiry. Finally, if we consider the last of the principal references to Socrates in the first book only of the *Essays*, it is quite clear how in this instance, as in so many others, we cannot schematise Montaigne's development according to any simple trope of philosophical development. Montaigne's relation to Socrates is from the very beginning close but not servile. Certainly, there is no need to see in the cumulative references to Socrates the underlying ideal of the *Essays*. In the essay 'Of Solitude' Montaigne repeats Socrates' comment upon the activities best suited to one's state in life: the young should learn, grown men should practise doing good, and old men should retire from office (I: 39, 178). Montaigne straightaway modifies Socrates' advice in the light of his own more studied experience of the relation between man's embodied character or temperament and his beliefs and ideas. In Montaigne's view, there is no virtue in fighting our nature, and a great deal in trying to follow it, especially when it leads us away from the acts of an 'excessive virtue'. The more Montaigne relates to Socrates, not simply as the exponent of learned ignorance and the art of dialogical self-questioning, but as man subject to the bodily limits of birth, illness, death and marriage, the more Montaigne shapes Socrates in his own image.

Indeed, Montaigne twice came very close to rejecting the Socratic ideal of humanity, when he considered the possibility that in Socrates virtue experiences no internal opposition and that this assurance of victory really emptied Socrates' equanimity in the face of death (II: 11, 308). It is essential to Montaigne's view of Socrates that his bodily experience was similar to that of any other man and thus he places far more belief in Socrates' equanimity in the face of death upon noticing how Socrates could not resist scratching himself when released from chains. In this small detail, Socrates, unlike the noble Cato, provided for any man to identify with his otherwise matchless calm:

> And who that has a mind however little tinctured with true philosophy can be satisfied with imagining Socrates as merely free from fear and passion in the incident of his imprisonment, his fetters, and his condemnation? And who does not recognize in him not only firmness and constancy (that was his ordinary attitude), but also I know not what new contentment, and a blithe cheerfulness in his last words and actions.
>
> By that quiver of pleasure that he feels in scratching his leg after the irons were off, does he not betray a like sweetness and joy in his soul at being unfettered by past discomforts and prepared to enter into the knowledge of things to come? Cato will pardon me, if he please; his death is more tragic and tense, but this one is still, I know not how, more beautiful. (II: 11. 310)

Montaigne cannot admire Socrates as a paragon of virtue. It is essential to his admiration that Socrates display a tendency to vice (II: 11, 313), and an ultimate subjection to the limits of embodiment. Socrates would be of no significance to us had he not been a man like the rest of us, and of this his bodily experience is the ultimate testimony that we have of his truly human achievement:

> The saliva of a wretched mastiff, spilled on Socrates' hand, could shake all his wisdom and all his great and well regulated ideas, and annihilate them in such a way that no trace would remain of his former knowledge:
>
> > The power of the soul
> > Is troubled . . . and, asunder cleft,
> > Is all dispelled, by that same poison reft
> >   Lucretius
>
> And this venom would find no more resistance in this soul than in that of a child of four; a venom capable of making all philosophy, if it were incarnate, raving mad. (II: 12, 412)

Montaigne's references to Socrates are fairly evenly distributed throughout the three books of the *Essays*.[22] It cannot be denied that Montaigne had a profound respect for Socrates. Yet it is clear from the very beginning that what interests Montaigne is the evidence of Socrates' humanity, his humour and irritability, as much as anything in his teaching. Above all, Montaigne rejects any interpretation of Socrates that makes him a monster of reason and self-control, if only because virtue unmixed with vice would he a lesser virtue – or else unheard of among men and of no relevance to their affairs. Indeed, it does not tarnish his image of Socrates to consider that his equanimity in the face of death was due to his preference for death rather than see his mind collapse with old age (III: 2, 620). For the lesson he saw in Socrates and himself was that one must live in relation to one's capacities and circumstances – a thing harder to accomplish than the conquests of Alexander:

> Therefore retired lives, whatever people may say, accomplish duties as harsh and strenuous as other lives, or more so. And private persons, says Aristotle, render higher and more difficult service to virtue than those who are in authority. We prepare ourselves for eminent occasions more for glory than for conscience. The shortest way to attain glory would be to do for conscience what we do for glory. Amid Alexander's virtue seems to me to represent much less vigor in his theater than does that of Socrates in his lowly and obscure activity. I can easily imagine Socrates in Alexander's place; Alexander in that of Socrates, I cannot. If you ask the former what he knows how to do, he will answer 'Subdue the world'; if you ask the latter, he will say, 'lead the life of man in conformity with its natural condition;' a knowledge much more general, more weighty, and more legitimate. (III: 2, 614)

Man is quick to glory and the world is full of the marvels he has left as monuments to his own name, his family, state and religion. There is nothing so strange that it cannot be pressed into the service of man's glory. So long as men are mortal, we can expect them to continue in the pursuit of being remembered. What makes Socrates remarkable is that he knew there is no external mark of our success in self-understanding and nowhere else to look for it than within ourselves, on the very spot where all our flights of vainglory are fuelled. That Socrates could stay at home does not mean that he was afraid or tired of the world. It means that he had mastered the art of not straying from himself and the daily care of his soul. Thus Montaigne, too, could stay at home, attendant to the daily care of the *Essays*. But he confesses he could never bring himself to prefer death to exile, as Socrates did. Though he can admire him for it, he cannot love him for that decision (III: 9, 743). Still, he would have chosen with Socrates to drink the hemlock, rather than with Cato to have stabbed himself to death (III: 9, 752). Montaigne needs only an imperfect ideal – another man however exceptional, a friend but not a god – Socrates married and could not count. He spoke of nothing but carters, joiners, cobblers and masons, using words and similes from life that anyone can understand:

> There is nothing borrowed from art and the sciences; even the simplest can recognize in him their means and their strength; it is impossible to go back further and lower. He did a great favor to human nature by showing how much it can do by itself. (III: 12, 794)

It is in keeping with the Silenus figure that Montaigne should express some of his most profound reflections upon his painful experience with the kidney stone, a thing without honour,[23] except as we consider its occasions more carefully. As usual, Montaigne moves on several fronts. It might be good if medicine, like law and philosophy, were able to deliver on its promises. In practice, medicine has its own ills and we do well to hold on to the reasonable practices we can assemble for ourselves, whatever their contradictions, rather than suffer and die out of our ordinary ways, which is the ultimate nemesis of medical practice. Actually, there are these advantages in the kidney stone. In the first place, Montaigne finds it natural at his age for his body to begin to collapse and function less reliably. Indeed, the company of sufferers from his ailment is quite illustrious, from what we know of history. The stone has the decided advantage, in comparison with many illnesses, that it is an intermittent crisis, dreadfully painful at the time (or in presentiment), but manageable with experience, and afterwards heightening the pleasure of ordinary health as the sweetest gift of life. Thus out of the contortions of this awful malady, Montaigne achieves a serenity and harmony of nature that repeats the paradox of beauty and serenity hidden in ugliness and terror.

In the very last pages of the *Essays* Montaigne decidedly rejects that side of Socrates which had to do with his daemon. It is essential to the contemplation of the death of Socrates that his last words were those of an ordinary man speaking in his own voice and not the instrument of either the gods or their poetry – though he (and La Boétie) might have been better looking (III:12, 810) as befits the beauty of his soul! The death of Socrates remains a glorious example for us, not because his soul was immortal but for the very reason that he was mortal. Therefore Socrates lives only in those who have learned from him to live in themselves.

Montaigne is adamant that there can be no first principles of reasoning regarding man. Every line of thought and feeling is subject to the overlap of mind and body. What is difficult in man, as opposed to the animals, is that his nature is not given to him apart from his own efforts to find it out and to ascertain its limits. This is the humanist enterprise and the *Essays* are a fundamental innovation in its method of self-inquiry:

My behavior is natural; I have not called in the help of any teaching to build it. But feeble as it is, when the desire to tell it seized me, and when, to make it appear in public a little more decently, I set myself to support it with reasons and examples, it was a marvel to myself to find it, simply by chance, in conformity with so many philosophical examples and reasons. What rule my life belonged to, I did not learn until after it was completed and spent. A new figure: and unpremeditated and accidental philosopher! (II: 12, 409)

Thus, Montaigne is quite free of any constructive or principled inquiry into the nature of our incarnation because such an enterprise already presupposes what it pretends to be in search of with respect to reason. The humanist enterprise cannot be grounded transcendentally, any more than it can rest for very long upon an alienated and ironic comparison between types of men or the varieties of folly. The *Essays* are therefore a genuine methodological innovation, the discovery of an unpremeditated and accidental inquiry into the nature of a corporeal being, which is without any intrinsic nature apart from this very inquiry. In short, Montaigne discovers that the self is a form of writing, a bodily improvisation of nature and culture that not even Wisdom herself is willing to separate from man. Writing is the moving trace of our temporality, holding in being what comes to be through its withholding. Writing, like love, is an event within that fold of being created by a man bent upon himself in the evocation of his life, through which he sounds out the truth and goodness of his own sense and reason as exemplars of his kind. Writing is the unfinished creation of man because man is never ahead of himself, but always there at work upon himself, bodily proportioned to his abilities and circumstances, and strengthened by the traditions and community which previous writings continue to resound. Writing, then, resounds man's being. But not in the sense that it engages in any literal transcription; nor even that it saves the first sounds of speech. Writing/reading resounds humane being because it is an intersensory and bodily accumulation of man's experience that has always to be taken up in telling or listening, in pain and in pleasure.

Notes

Notes to Introduction

1 All passages from Montaigne are taken from *The Complete Works of Montaigne: Essays, Travel Journal, Letters*, newly translated by Donald M. Frame. Stanford: Stanford University Press, 1948.

2 J.M. Blanchard, 'Le Je(u) de Montaigne', *Neophilologus* (Summer, 1977): 347–55; Michel Beaujour, *Poetics of the Literary Sect – Portrait*, trans. Yara Milos. New York: New York University Press, 1991.

3 Jeffrey Mehlman, *Revolution and Repetition: Marx/Hugo, Balzac*. Berkeley: University of California Press, 1977.

4 Although he ignores the bodily grounds of reading and writing, their inseparability is also argued for in Pierre Macherey, *A Theory of Literary Production*, trans. by Geoffrey Wall. London: Routledge & Kegan Paul, 1978.

5 Harold Bloom, *The Anxiety of Influence, A Theory of Poetry*. New York: Oxford University Press, 1973; and Richard McKeon, 'Literary Criticism and the Concept of the Imitation in Antiquity'. *Modern Philology*, vol. XXXIV, no. 1 (August 1936): 1–35.

6 For a discussion of the problem of 'real' and 'fictional' transitive beginning, see Edward W. Said, *Beginnings, Intention and Method*. New York: Basic Books, 1975, Chap. 2, 'A Meditation on Beginnings'.

7 Erving Goffman, *Frame Analysis: An Essay on the Organization of Experience*. New York: Harper & Row, 1974, p.16. Cf. Cary Nelson, 'Reading Criticism' *PMLA*, 91, no. 5 (October 1976): 801–15.

8 Robert De Maria, Jr, 'The Ideal Reader: A Critical Fiction'. *PMLA*, vol. 93, no. 3 (May 1978): 463–74.

9 G.W.F. Hegel, *The Phenomenology of Mind*, translated, with an Introduction and Notes by J.B. Baillie. London: George Allan & Unwin, 1949, p.67; Jean Hyppolite, 'The Structure of Philosophical Language According to the "Preface" to Hegel's 'Phenomenology of the Mind", pp.157–85 in *The Languages of Criticism and the Sciences of Man: The Structuralist Controversy*, ed. Richard Macksey and Euginio Donato. Baltimore and London: Johns Hopkins University Press, 1970.

10 See the reflections on Hegel's Preface to the *Phenomenology*, by Jacques Derrida, 'Hors de livre, préfaces', pp. 9–67 in his *La Dissémination*. Paris: Éditions du Seuil, 1972.

11 Kurt H. Wolff, 'Beginning: In Hegel and Today', pp. 72–105 in *The Critical Spirit:*

Essays in Honor of Herbert Marcuse, ed. Kurt H. Wolff and Barrington Moore, Jr Boston: Beacon Press., 1967.

12   Chap. 6, 'The Paradox of Communication: Reading the *Essays* Otherwise'. See also our remarks on Terence Cave's reading of the essay, 'Of Some Verses of Virgil', Chapter 7.

13   Georg Luckács, 'On the Nature and Form of the Essay', pp.9–10 in *Soul and Form*, trans. Anna Bostock, Cambridge, MA, The MIT Press, 1974; cf. Lucien Goldmann, *Structures mentales et création culturelle*. Paris: Éditions Anthropos, 1970.

14   Jean-Paul Sartre, *What is Literature?*, trans. Wallace Fowlie. New York: Harper & Row, 1967, p.45; John O'Neill, 'Situation, Action and Language'. pp.81–95 in his *Sociology as a Skin Trade, Essays Towards a Reflexive Sociology*. New York: Harper & Row, 1972.

15   Dave Bleich, *Subjective Criticism*. Baltimore: Johns Hopkins University Press, 1978.

16   Rodolphe Gasché, 'The Scene of Writing: A Deferred Outset', pp.150–71, *Glyph 1*, Johns Hopkins Textual Studies, Baltimore: Johns Hopkins University Press, 1977.

17   Goffman, *op.cit.*, p.12.

18   Isabelle Mahieu, 'Fetishism and Beyond: Notes on Reading and Pleasure', *Cambridge Review*, vol. 95, no. 2219 (March 1974): 99–102.

19   Cf. Pierre Macherey, *op.cit.*, Chap. 12, 'Pact and Contract', pp.69–74.

20   The theme of mastery and slavery is fundamental to the discipline of culture. See Hegel, *op.cit.*, 'Spirit in Self-Estrangement – The Discipline of Culture, pp.507–610; and the discussion of this theme in Lionel Trilling, *Sincerity and Authenticity*. Cambridge, MA: Harvard University Press, 1974, Chap. 2, 'The Honest Soul and the Disintegrated Consciousness'.

21   *'On Literary Intention: Critical Essays*, selected and introduced by David Newton-De Molina. Edinburgh: Edinburgh University Press, 1976.

22   Chap. 3, 'Rival Readings'.

23   Geoffrey H. Hartman, *The Fate of Reading and Other Essays*. Chicago: University of Chicago Press, 1975, pp.10–11.

24   Plato, *Phaedrus*, 258 c–d, trans. B. Jowett, *The Dialogues of Plato*. Oxford: Clarendon Press, 1953, vol. III, p.166.

25   Chaim Perelman, 'La Méthode dialectique et le rôle d'interlocuteur dans le dialogue', *Revue de métaphysique et de morale*, vols 60–1 (1955–56): 26–31.

26   See, for example, the issues raised by the essays on coaches and on cannibals, Chap. 9, 'Civilisation, Literacy and Barbarism'.

27   Wolfgang Iser, 'Indeterminacy and the Reader's Response in Prose Fiction', pp. 1–45 in *Aspects of Narrative*, ed. J. Hillis Miller. New York: Columbia University Press, 1971; Rien Segers, 'Readers, Text, and Author: Some Implications of 'Rezeptionsaesthetik',' *Yearbook of Comparative and General Literature*, no. 24 (1975): 15–23.

28   'This process [the reader's work of creating the configurative meaning of the text] is steered by two main structural components within the text: first a repertoire of familiar literary patterns and recurrent literary themes: second techniques or strategies used to set the familiar against the unfamiliar, Wolfgang Iser, 'The Reading Process: A Phenomenological Approach', *New Literary History*, vol. III, no. 2 (Winter 1972): 293.

29   The literary cannot be reduced to a linguistic circuit – 'literary creation externalizes itself first as style and only secondarily as grammar or language. . . . It follows that in interpreting literature's stylistic phenomena we shall be well advised to pay more attention to the causes of literary creation, the sources of a particular imaginative act and their correlatives in the reader's part of the cycle, than with the consequences in language.' F.W. Bateson, 'Linguistics and Literary Criticism', pp.3–16 in *The Disciplines of Criticis: Essays in Literary Theory, Interpretation and History*, ed. Peter Demetz, Thomas Greene and Lowry Nelson, Jr New Haven: Yale University Press, 1968; and F.W. Bateson, *The Scholar-Critic: An Introduction to Literary Research*. London: Routledge & Kegan Paul, 1972, pp.101–10.

30   Roland Barthes, *The Pleasure of the Text*, trans. Richard Miller. New York: Hill & Wang, 1975.

31   John O'Neill, *Perception, Expression and History.* Evanston: Northwestern University Press, 1970; and O'Neill, *Making Sense Together: An Introduction to Wild Sociology.* New York: Harper & Row, 1974.

32   Maurice Merleau-Ponty, *Phenomenology, Language and Sociology, Selected Essays,* edited and with an Introduction by John O'Neill. London: Heinemann Educational, 1974, p.xxxvii.

33   On the nature of exemplarity, see Myron P. Gilmore, 'The Renaissance Conception of the Lessons of History', pp.73–101 in *Facets of the Renaissance*, ed. William H. Werkmeister. New York: Harper and Row, 1963; Timothy Hampton, *Writing from History: The Rhetoric of Exemplarity in Renaissance Literature.* Ithaca: Cornell University Press, 1990.

34   John O'Neill, 'The Literary Production of Natural and Social Science Inquiry', *Canadian Journal of Sociology*, vol. 6, no. 2 (Spring 1981): 105–20.

Notes to Chapter One

1   Robert Sayre, *Solitude in Society: A Sociological Study in French Literature.* Cambridge, MA: Harvard University Press, 1978, Chap. 2, 'L'Ancien Régime: Agreeable Wilderness, Pleasant Solitude'.

2   John O'Neill, 'Time's Body, Vico on the Love of Language and Institution', in *Giambattista Vico's Science of Humanity*, ed. Giorgio Tagliacozzo and Donald Phillip Verene. Baltimore: Johns Hopkins University Press.

3   F. Joukovsky, *Montaigne et le problème du temps.* Paris: A.G. Nizet, 1972.

4   'Reading Montaigne', pp.198–210 in *Signs*, trans. Richard C. McCleary. Evanston: Northwestern University Press, 1964; also 'Between Montaigne and Machiavelli', pp.65–89 in John O'Neill, *Perception, Expression and History: The Social Phenomenology of Maurice Merleau-Ponty.* Evanston: Northwestern University Press, 1970.

5   Merleau-Ponty, *op.cit.*, p.203.

6   Ibid., p.205.

7   Ibid., p.207.

8   Jean Starobinski, 'Montaigne: des morts exemplaires à la vie sans exemple', *Critique*, no. 258 (November 1968): 923–35.

9   Pierre Duvernois, 'L'Emportement de l'écriture', *Critique*, no. 302 (1972): 595–609.

10   See Chap. 4, 'Writing and Embodiment', and Chap. 7, 'Portrait of the Essayist Without Qualities'.

11   Imrie Buffum, *L'Influence du voyage de Montaigne sur les essais.* Princeton: Princeton University Press, 1946, and M.A. Screech, Medicine and Literature: Aspects of Rabelais and Montaigne (with a Glance at the Law), pp.156–69 in *French Renaissance Studies 1540–70; Humanism and the Encyclopaedia*, ed., Peter Sharrat, Edinburgh: University Press, 1976.

12   See Chap. 9, 'Civilisation, Literacy and Barbarism'.

13   See Chap. 6, 'The Paradox of Communication: Reading the *Essays* Otherwise'.

14   Phillip P. Hallie, *The Scar of Montaigne: An Essay in Personal Philosophy.* Middletown: Wesleyan University Press, 1966, Appendix A, 'Montaigne's and Descartes' Doctrines of Language'.

15   John O'Neill, 'Making Sense Together: An Introduction to Wild Sociology'. New York, Harper & Row, 1974.

16   John O'Neill, 'On Simmel's "Sociological Apriorities"', in *Phenomenological Sociology, Issues and Applications.* New York: John Wiley, 1973, especially pp.98–100, 'Knowledge, Truth and Falsehood in Human Relations'.

17   On this, see Julian H. Franklin, 'The Emergence of an Art of Reading History and The Challenge of Historical Pyrrhonism', in his *Jean Bodin and the Sixteenth Century*

Revolution in the Methodology of Law and History. New York: Columbia University Press, 1966, pp.83–8, 89–102; and Floyd Gray, 'Montaigne's Pyrrhonism', pp.119–36 in *O Un Amy! Essays on Montaigne in Honor of Donald M. Frame*, ed. Raymond C. La Charité. Lexington, KY.: French Forum, 1977.

18   Hannah Arendt, *The Human Condition.* Chicago: University of Chicago Press, 1958.

19   Edward L. Sturtz, S.J., 'The Defence of Pleasure in More's Utopia', *Studies in Philology*, vol. XLVI, no. 2 (April 1949): 99–112.

20   A.E. Malloch, 'The Techniques and Function of the Renaissance Paradox', *Studies in Philology*, vol. LIII (1956): 191–203.

21   Rosalie L. Colie, *Paradoxia Epidemica: The Renaissance Tradition of Paradox.* Princeton: Princeton University Press, 1966.

22   For a discussion of Montaigne's essay 'Of Names' (I: 46), see François Rigolot, *Poétique et onomastique: L'exemple de la Renaissance.* Geneva: Librarie Droz, 1977, pp.235–9.

23   Donald R. Kelley, 'Guillaume Budé and the First Historical School of Law', *American Historical Review*, no. LXII (1967): 807–34.

24   For the argument that Montaigne's technique of essaying carries with it an ethical and political innovation, see David Quint, *Montaigne and the Quality of Mercy: Ethical and Political Themes in the Essays.* Princeton: Princeton University Press, 1996.

25   Robert J. Clements, 'Critical Theory and Practice of the Pléiade', *Harvard Studies in Romance Languages*, vol. XVIII (1942); Antoinette Roubichou-Stretz, *La Vision de l'histoire dans L'œuvre de la Pléiade, thèmes et structure.* Paris: Librarie A.G. Nizet, 1973.

26   Hugo Friedrich, *Montaigne.* Paris: Gallimard, 1968, p.377. Friedrich considers the Pléiade to be linguistic nationalists. Donald Frame thinks it worth exploring Montaigne's relation to the Pléiade: see 'What Next in Montaigne Studies?': *French Review*, no. 36 (1962–3): 579.

27   E.N. Tigerstedt 'The Poet as Creator: Origins of a Metaphor', *Comparative Literature Studies*, no. 5 (1968): 455–88.

28   W.A.R. Kerr, 'The Pléiade and Platonism', *Modern Philology*, vol. 5 (1907–8): 1–15.

29   Felix Gilbert, *Machiavelli and Guicciardini: Politics and History in Sixteenth-Century Florence.* Princeton: Princeton University Press, 1966. Chap. 5, 'The Theory and Practice of History in the Fifteenth Century'.

30   Myron P. Gilmore, 'The Renaissance Conception of the Lessons of History'. pp.73–86 in *Facets of the Renaissance*, ed. William H. Werkmeister. Los Angeles: University of Southern California Press, 1959.

31   On the theme of literary glory in the Renaissance, to which Montaigne reacts, see Robert Griffin, *Coronation of the Poet: Joachim Du Bellay's Debt to the Trivium.* Berkeley: University of California Press, 1969. See also J.J. Supple, 'Montaigne's "De la Gloire": Structure and Method'. *French Studies*, vol. XXVII, no. 4 (October 1973): 385–94.

32   Horace, *Satires, Epistles and Ars Poetica*, trans. H. Rushton Fairclough. London: Heinemann, 1978, p.478.

33   Jurgen von Stackelberg, 'Das Bienengleichnis: ein Beitrag zur Geschichte der literarischen Imitatio', *Romanische Forschungen*, no. 68 (1956): 271–93.

34   Plato, *Ion*, 533d–534b, trans. by B. Jowett, *The Dialogues of Plato.* Oxford: Clarendon Press, 1953, vol. I, pp.107–8.

35   Seneca, *Ad Lucilium epistulae morales*, Epistle LXXXIV, 'On Gathering Ideas', trans. Richard M. Gummere. London: Heinemann, 1962, vol. II, p.277.

36   John O'Neill, 'Language and the Voice of Philosophy', pp.xi–xvi in Maurice Merleau-Ponty, *The Prose of the World*, trans. John O'Neill. Evanston: Northwestern University Press, 1973.

37   Robert F. Jones, 'On the Dialogic Impulse in the Genesis of Montaigne's *Essais*', *Renaissance Quarterly*, vol. XXX, no. 2 (Summer 1977): 172–80; and Cathleen M. Bauschatz, 'Montaigne's Conception of Reading in the Context of Renaissance Poetics and

Modern Criticism', pp.264–91 in *The Reader in the Text*, ed. Susan R. Suleiman and Inge Crosman, Princeton: Princeton University Press, 1980.

Notes to Chapter Two

1 There are a number of attempts to derive the best sense of the term *essais*, using philological and textual comparisons. See the *Bulletin de la Société des Amis de Montaigne*: Andreas Blinkenberg, 'Quel sens Montaingne a-t-il voulu donner au mot Essais dans le titre de son œuvre?' *Bulletin de la Société des Amis de Montaigne*, Fourth Series, nos., 28–32 (1963–4): 22–32; S. Hamel, 'Expérience–Essai: contribution à l'étude du vocabulaire de Montaigne', *op. cit.*, Third Series, nos. 11–12 (1959): 23–32.

2 Although she speaks of Montaigne's modesty, there is no fundamental analysis of its intentionally other than to refer it to rhetorical practice; see Margaret McGowan, *Montaigne's Deceits: The Art of Persuasion in the Essais*. London: University of London Press, 1974.

3 Petrarch, 'A Self-Portrait', pp.34–35 in Ernst Cassirer, *The Renaissance Philosophy of Man*. Chicago: University of Chicago Press, 1948.

4 Camille Aymonier, 'Montaigne à table', *Revue philomatique de Bordeaux et du Sud*, vol. V no. 37 (1934): 179–91; Mikhail Bakhtin, *Rabelais and his World*, trans. Helene Iswolsky. Cambridge, MA.: The MIT Press, 1968.

5 G. Mallory Masters, *Rabelaisian Dialectic and the Platonic-Hermetic Tradition*. Albany: State University of New York Press, 1969.

6 Rabelais, *Gargantua and Pantagruel*, trans. Jacques Le Clereq. New York: Modern Library, 1944, p.651. See also, Alfred G. Engstrom, 'A Few Comparisons and Contrasts on the Wordcraft of Rabelais and Joyce', pp.65–82 in *Renaissance and Other Studies in Honor of William Leon Wiley*, ed. George Bernard Daniel, Jr, Chapel Hill: University of North Carolina Press, 1968.

7 Rabelais, *op. cit.*, p.590.

8 William Hardy Alexander, 'Montaigne's Classical Bookshelf', *University of Toronto Quarterly*, no. X (1941): 78–86; Craig B. Brush, 'The Essayist is Learned: Montaigne's *Journal de voyage* and the *Essais*', *Romantic Review*, no. 62 (1971): 16–27; Lino Pertile, 'Paper and Ink: The Structure of Unpredictability', pp.190–218 in *O Un Amy! Essays on Montaigne in Honor of Donald M. Frame*, ed. Raymond C. La Charité. Lexington: French Forum, 1977.

9 Michel Charles, 'Sur une phrase de Montaigne', pp.289–97 in his *Rhétorique de la lecture*. Paris: Éditions du Seuil, 1977.

10 Gaston Bachelard, *The Poetics of Space*, trans. Maria Jolas. Boston: Beacon Press, 1969, p.xxii.

11 Quoted in Leo Bersani, *A Future for Astyanax: Character and Desire in Literature*. Boston: Little Brown, 1976, p.226.

12 Harold Bloom, *The Anxiety of Influence: A Theory of Poetry*. New York: Oxford University Press, 1973.

13 *Ibid.*, p.5; Harold Bloom, *A Map of Misreading*. New York: Oxford University Press, 1975.

14 Nancy S. Struever, *The Language of History in the Renaissance: Rhetoric and Historical Consciousness in Florentine Humanism*. Princeton: Princeton University Press, 1970, p.44.

15 John C. Lapp, 'Montaigne's 'negligence' and some lines from Virgil', *Romantic Review*, no. LXI (1970): 167–81.

16 Thomas Bergin, *Petrarch*. New York: Twayne, 1970, p.191.

17 Hans Baron, 'Petrarch: His Inner Struggles and the Humanistic Discovery of Man's Nature', pp.18–51 in *Florilegium Historiale: Essays Presented to Wallace K. Ferguson*, ed. J.G. Rowe and W.H. Stockdale. Toronto: University of Toronto Press, 1971; and Hugh M. Richmond, 'Personal Identity and Literary Personae: A Study in Historical

Psychology', *PMLA*, vol. 90, no. 2 (1975): 209–21.

18   Craig La Drière, 'Horace and the Theory of Imitation', *American Journal of Philology*, vol. LX (1939): 288–300. Of special importance is the question of translation of the classics into a lively and independent vernacular. On this see Glyn P. Norton, 'Translation Theory in Renaissance France: Étienne Dolet and the Rhetorical Tradition', *Renaissance and Reformation*, vol. X, no. 1 (1974): 1–13; and 'Translation Theory in Renaissance France: The Poetic Controversy', *Renaissance and Reformation*, vol. XI, no. 1 (1975): 30–44.

19   Charles Trinkhaus, *In Our Image and Likeness: Humanity and Divinity in Italian Humanist Thought*, in 2 vols, London: Constable, 1970. See vol. 1, p.326, note 11. In this he follows Saint Augustine's rejection of the Stoic view of human misery and his critique of the inability of the Ciceronian concept of virtue to deal with this experience. See Saint Augustine, *The City of God*, Book IX, Chap. 4: Book XIV, Chaps 8 and 9, and, of course, the *Confessions*.

20   Petrarch, *De ignorantia*, trans. Hans Nachod, in Cassirer, *op. cit.*, p.104.

21   Translated by Thomas Twyne, *Phisicke against Fortune, as well Prosperous, as Adverse*. London: Richard Watkyns, 1579.

22   For the remarkable similarity in the self-portraits of Petrarch and Montaigne, see Ernest Hatch Wilkins, *Life of Petrarch*. Chicago: University of Chicago Press, 1961, Chap. XXXVII, 'Portrait of Petrarch'.

23   Albert Cook, 'Comparisons: Dante, "Inferno", 1.80; Petrarch, Montaigne, Etc.', *Romantic Review*, vol. 12, no. 2 (April–June 1921): 185–6.

24   Seneca, *Ad Lucilium epistulae morales*, Epistle II, 'On Discursiveness in Reading', vol. I, pp.7–8.

25   This practice requires what Thomas M. Green calls a 'sub-reading' from the surface of the text to the fragments buried beneath it; see his 'Petrarch and the Humanist Hermeneutic'. pp.201–24 in *Italian Literature: Roots and Branches, Essays in Honor of Thomas Goddard Bergin*, ed. Glose Rimanelli and Kenneth John Atchity. New Haven: Yale University Press, 1976.

26   Petrarca, Francesco, *Sonnets and Songs*, trans. Anna Maria Armi. New York: Pantheon, 1946.

27   Marcel Tetel, 'Montaigne et Pétrarque: irrésolution et solitude', *Journal of Medieval and Renaissance Studies*, vol. 4, no. 2 (Autumn 1974): 203–20.

28   See Chap. 5, 'Reading and Temperament'.

29   Siegfried Wenzel, 'Petrarch's Accidia', *Studies in the Renaissance*, vol. 8 (1961): 46.

30   Rudolf Pfeiffer, *History of Classical Scholarship, from 1300 to 1850*. Oxford: Clarendon Press, 1976, pp.3–20.

31   Myron P. Gilmore, *Humanists and Jurists: Six Studies in the Renaissance*. Cambridge, MA.: Belknap Press, 1963, pp.7–18.

32   Petrarch, 'Four Dialogues for Scholars', from *De remediis utriusque fortunae*, ed. and newly translated into English by Conrad H. Rawski. Cleveland: Western Reserve University Press, 1967. I take Petrarch's literary joy to be a nice anticipation of Barthe's pleasure of the text.

33   Ernest Hatch Wilkins, *Petrarch's Correspondence*. Padua: Editrice Antenore, 1960, p.247.

34   Don Cameron Allen, 'The Degeneration of Man and Renaissance Pessimism', *Studies in Philology*, no. XXV (1938): 202–27.

35   Thomas Greene, 'The Flexibility of the Self in Renaissance Literature' in *The Disciplines of Criticism*, ed. Peter Demetz, Thomas Greene and Lowry Nelson, Jr, New Haven: Yale University Press, 1968, p.250.

36   See Chap. 8, 'On Public and Private Life'.

37   Saint Augustine, *Confessions*, trans. R.S. Pine-Coffin. Harmondsworth: Penguin Books, 1961, Book X, 16: 222–3. It would be interesting to compare the ending of the

Confessions with the Third Book of the *Essays*. On this see the essays by Eugene Vance, 'Augstine's *Confessions* and the Grammar of Selfhood', *Genre*, vol. 6 (1973): 1–28; and 'Le Moi comme langage: Saint Augustin et l'autobiographie', *Poétique*, vol. 14 (1973): 163–77; Neil M. Larkin, 'Montaigne's Last Words', *L'Esprit créateur*, vol. 15, no. 1 (Spring 1975): 21–38.

Notes to Chapter Three

1   Jean-Yves Pouilloux, *Lire les 'essais' de Montaigne*. Paris: François Maspero, 1970.
2   Jean-Yves Pouilloux, 'Deux discours de Montaigne: du manque d'espace à l'espace du manque', *Scolies*, Fasc. 3–4 (1973–4): 83–98.
3   For example, E. Lablénie, *Essai sur Montaigne*. Paris: Gallimard, 1968.
4   See Chap. 9, 'Civilisation, Literacy and Barbarism'.
5   See, for example, S. John Holyoake, 'How to Read Montaigne', *Kentucky Romance Quarterly*, vol. XIX, no. 3 (1972): 337–45.
6   Pouilloux, *Lire les 'essais'*, p.57.
7   See Chap. 6, 'The Paradox of Communication: Reading the *Essays* Otherwise'.
8   Floyd Gray, 'Montaigne's Friends', *French Studies*, vol. XV, no. 3 (July 1961): 203–12.
9   Horst Hutter, *Politics as Friendship: The Origins of Classical Notions of Politics in the Theory and Practice of Friendship*. Waterloo: Wilfrid Laurier University Press, 1978.
10   Pouilloux, *Lire les 'essais'*, pp.58–59. My translation.
11   See Chap. 7, 'Portrait of the Essayist Without Qualities'.
12   This, rather than any deliberate deception, is the function of titles and topics. I cannot, therefore, agree with Patrick Henry, 'Les Titres Façades, la censure et l'écriture défensive chez Montaigne', *Bulletin de la Société des Amis de Montaigne*, Fifth Series, no. 24 (October–December 1977): 11–28.
13   Pouilloux, *Lire les 'essais'*, p.117.
14   Pouilloux, *op. cit.*, p.118. My translation.
15   *The Living Thoughts of Montaigne*, presented by André Gide. London: Cassell, 1946, p.7. Compare Michel Guggenheim, 'Gide and Montaigne', *Yale French Studies*, no. 7, (1951): 107–14.
16   S. Dresden, 'La Précision paradoxale de Montaigne', *Neophilologus*, nos. 46–47 (1962–3): 269–77.
17   Erich Auerbach, *Mimesis: The Representation of Reality in Western Literature*. New York: Doubleday Anchor Books, 1953, 'L'Humaine Condition', pp.249–73.
18   Michel Charles, *Rhétorique de la lecture*. Paris: Éditions du Seuil, 1977, pp.24–25. My translation.
19   Richard L. Regosin, *The Matter of My Book: Montaigne's 'Essays' as the Book of the Self*. Berkeley: University of California Press, 1977, Part 1, 'The Secular Conversion'. Regosin's views have altered somewhat, see his *Montaigne's Unruly Brood: Textual Engendering and the Challenge to Paternal Authority*. Berkeley: University of California Press, 1996.
20   Regosin, *op. cit.*, p.23.
21   *Ibid.*, p.27.
22   For an analysis of the literary structure of Augustine's *Confessions* and the stages of conversion, see I.W.A. Jamieson, 'Augustine's Confessions: The Structure of Humility', *Augustiniana*, vol. 24 (1974): 234–46.
23   R.L. Colie, *Paradoxia Epidemica: The Renaissance Tradition of Paradox*. Princeton: Princeton University Press, 1966, p.377.
24   R.L. Colie, *op. cit.*, Part IV, Chapter 13, 1, 'Traditions of Paradox in Renaissance Verse–Epistemologies'. See also the argument between David Lewis Schafer, *The Political Philosophy of Montaigne*. Itachca: Cornell University Press, 1990 and John Christian Laursen, *The Politics of Scepticism in the Ancients: Montaigne, Hume and Kant*. Leiden: E.J. Brill, 1992.

25   Henry Cornelius Agrippa, *Three Books of Occult Philosophy*, cited in Colie, *op. cit.*, pp.400–1.

26   Rosalie L. Colie, *The Resources of Kind: Genre-Theory in the Renaissance*, ed. Barbara K. Lewalski. Berkeley: University of California Press, 1973, p.36.

27   For a writer to be conscious of the autonomy of language is a step away from confounding his creative use of it with the divine creation. Yet Regosin's view has also been adopted in respect of Rabelais's literary consciousness; see Pierre Goumarre, 'Rabelais: les possibilités de l'écriture, et celles de la nature', *Rivista di litterature moderne*, vol. 28 (December 1975): 245–51.

28   Regosin, *op. cit.*, p.151.

29   Regosin, *op. cit.*, p.174.

30   Phillis Gracey, *Montaigne et la poésie*. Paris: Les Presses Universitaires de France, 1935, Chap. VI, 'Montaigne et Horace', pp.91–105.

31   Regosin refers to the problems of Dürer's self-portraits, *op. cit.*, p.194.

32   Chap. 7, 'Portrait of the Essayist Without Qualities'.

33   Regosin, *op. cit.*, p.36.

34   Regosin, *op. cit.*, p.206, also argues like Glauser that Montaigne had no pre-literary self.

35   J.B. Jansen, *Sources vives de la Pensée de Montaigne: études sur les fondements psychologiques et biographiques des 'Essais'*. Copenhagen: Leven & Muskgaard, 1935, p.56.

36   Alfred Glauser, *Montaigne Paradoxal*. Paris: A.G. Nizet, 1972.

37   Glauser, *op. cit.*, p.19. My translation.

38   We treat the notion of literary illness as formulated by Barrère in Chap. 5, 'Reading and Temperament'.

39   Glauser, *op. cit.*, pp.152–56.

Notes to Chapter Four

1   Hugo Friedrich, *Montaigne*. Paris: Gallimard, 1968, Chapter VIII, 'La Conscience littéraire de Montaigne et la forme des Essais'.

2   Roland Barthes, 'To Write: An Intransitive Verb?', in *The Languages of Criticism and the Sciences of Man*, ed. Richard Macksey and Eugenio Donato. Baltimore: Johns Hopkins University Press, 1980, p.143.

3   John O'Neill, *Perception, Expression and History*. Evanston: Northwestern University Press, 1970, pp.36–45, 'Corporeality and Intersubjectivity'.

4   Neal W. Gilbert, *Renaissance Concepts of Method*. New York: Columbia University Press, 1963.

5   James Joyce, *Ulysses*. Harmondsworth: Penguin Books, 1968, p.704.

6   Georges Poulet, 'Criticism and the Experience of Interiority', in Macksey and Donato (eds.), *op. cit.*, pp.56–73.

7   Maurice Blanchot, *L'Espace littéraire*. Paris: Gallimard, 1955, p.14, quoted in Paul De Man, *Blindness and Insight, Essays in the Rhetoric of Contemporary Criticism*. New York: Oxford University Press, 1971, p.65.

8   Angel Medina, *Reflection, Time, and the Novel: Toward a Communicative Theory of the Novel*. London: Routledge & Kegan Paul, 1979.

9   Roland Barthes, *The Pleasure of the Text*, trans. Richard Miller. New York: Hill & Wang, 1975, p.4.

10   The writer needs readers who can create the writer. On this, see the study of *Moll Flanders, Clarissa*, and *Tom Jones* by John Preston, *The Created Self, The Reader's Role in Eighteenth Century Fiction*. New York: Barnes & Noble, 1970; especially the 'Coda: The Reader as Actor'.

11   Barthes, *The Pleasure of the Text*, p.17.

12   *Ibid.*, pp.18–19.

13   *Ibid.*, pp.62–3.

14   Georges Poulet, 'Phenomenology of Reading', *New Literary History*, no. 1 (1969–70): 64.

15   See Chap. 5, 'Reading and Temperament'.

16   Jean Starobinski, 'Montaigne en mouvement', *Nouvelle Revue française*, vol. 15 (1960): 16–22, 254–66. Starobinski's quotation is from *Essays*, I: 50, 219. Cf. R.A. Sayce, *The Essays of Montaigne, A Critical Exploration*. London: Weidenfeld & Nicolson, 1972, Chap. 6, 'Movement and Change'.

17   In this connection there is a nice essay starting from Montaigne's grasp of the difference, almost lost today, between sensual literature and literary sensuality: See Albert Thibaudet, 'Langage, littérature et sensualité', *Nouvelle Revue française*, no. 38, (1932): 716–26.

18   Montaigne's style can also be considered mannerist (Margot Recksieck, *Montaignes Verhältnis zu Klassik und Manierismus*. Bonn thesis, 1966), if we mean by that: 'reaction against the optimism of the early Renaissance, doubling of the personality, scepticism, narcissism, oblique and labyrinthine forms, paradox, word play' (Sayce, *op.cit.*, p.324). The problem with these labels is that they mix elements of form and substance, without any sense of the specific transformations between them needed to yield a theory of writing. See also 'The Concept of Baroque in Literary Scholarship', in René Wellek, *Concepts of Criticism*, ed. Stephen G. Nichols, Jr, New Haven: Yale University Press, 1963, pp.69–127. Much more to the point is the procedure of Mikhail Bakhtin, *Rabelais and his World*, trans. Helene Iswolsky. Cambridge, MA.: The MIT Press, 1968, Chap. 5, 'The Grotesque Image of the Body'.

19   See Chap. 7, 'Portrait of the Essayist Without Qualities'.

20   E.V. Arnold, *Roman Stoicism*. New York: Humanities Press, 1958, p.148, quoted in George Williamson, *The Senecan Amble, Study in Prose Form from Bacon to Collier*. Chicago: University of Chicago Press, 1966, p.140. Cf. Morris W. Croll, 'Attic Prose in the Seventeenth Century', *Studies in Philology*, vol. XVIII, no. 2 (April 1921):116–17; and the excellent discussion in Terence Cave, *The Cornucopian Text: Problems of Writing in the French Renaissance*. Oxford: Clarendon Press, 1979, Chap. 4, 'Improvisation and Inspiration'.

21   Morris W. Croll, 'The Baroque Style in Prose', in *Studies in English Philology: A Miscellany in Honor of Frederick Klaeber*, ed. Kemp Malone and Martin Brown Rudd. Minneapolis: University of Minnesota Press, 1929, pp.427–57.

22   Incidentally, here I have changed the punctuation of Frame's translation to fit at least with the Pléiade edition (p.393). The reason for this is that Frame's punctuation is not always faithful to the historical practices that relate thought and style. 'In brief we must measure the customs of the age of semicolons and colons by the customs of the age of commas and periods. The only possible punctuation of seventeenth-century prose is that which it used itself. We might sometimes reveal its grammar more clearly by re-punctuating it with commas or periods, but we should certainly destroy its rhetoric.' Croll, *The Baroque Style in Prose*, p.456.

23   Maurice Merleau-Ponty, *Phenomenology of Perception*, trans. Colin Smith. London: Routledge & Kegan Paul, 1962, Part One, Chap. 6, 'The Body as Expression, and Speech'.

24   Merleau-Ponty, *op.cit.*, p.182. My emphasis in last sentence.

25   Merleau-Ponty, *op. cit.*, pp.193–4.

26   This does not mean that there are not artificial languages independent of bodily ties. It means that language is the natural organ of embodied persons; artificial languages are, of course, added to this first language.

27   Frank Budgen, *James Joyce and the Making of Ulysses*. Bloomington: Indiana University Press, 1960, p.21.

28   Maurice Merleau-Ponty, *Signs*, trans. Richard C. McCleary, Evanston: Northwestern University Press, 1964, p.97.

Notes to Chapter Five

1   Georges Tronquart, 'Montaigne à la recherche des Essais', *Bulletin de la Société des Amis de Montaigne*, Third Series, nos. 11–12, 1959, pp.16–22.

2   For the identification of the metaphors of athletic contest and struggle with virtue and its development from the Greek games into the Christian spiritual life, see Colin Eisler, 'The Athlete of Virtue: The Iconography of Ascetisms', pp.82–97 in *De Artibus Opuscula XL: Essays in Honor of Erwin Panofsky*, ed. Millard Meiss. New York: University Press, 1961, vol. I.

3   R.G. Collingwood, *Speculum Mentis: On the Map of Knowledge*. Oxford: Clarendon Press, 1924, p.130.

4   Georges Poulet, 'Phenomenology of Reading', *New Literary History*, no. I (1969–70): 53–68.

5   Stanley E. Fish, 'Literature in the Reader: Affective Stylistics', *New Literary History*, vol. 2, no. 1 (Autumn 1970): 123–62; 'Interpreting the *Variorum*', *Critical Inquiry*, no. 2 (Spring 1976): 465–85.

6   Pierre Barrière, *La Vie intellectuelle en Périgord 1550–1800*. Bordeaux: Éditions Delmas, 1936.

7   Barrière, *op. cit.*, pp.107–8

8   Albert Camus, *The myth of Sisyphus, and Other Essays*, trans. Justin O'Brien. New York: Vintage Books, 1955.

9   For a wonderfully rhetorical description of the urinary tract, the formation of kidney stones and the fraternity of its sufferers and Montaigne's place among them, see Richard, 'Kidney Stone', *Esquire*, vol. 82 (August 1974): 100–1, 118–20.

10   C. E. Rathé, 'The Theatricality of Montaigne and the Problem of Self-Knowledge', pp.83–98 in *Historical and Literary Perspectives: Essays and Studies in Honor of Albert D. Menut*, ed. Sandoro Sticca. Lawrence, Kansas: Coronada Press, 1973.

11   Raymond Klibansky, Erwin Panofsky and Fritz Saxl, *Saturn and Melancholy: Studies in the History of Natural Philosophy, Religion and Art*. London: Thomas Nelson, 1964, pp.39–41. See also, Michael Screech, *Montaigne and Melancholy: The Wisdom of the 'Essais'*. London: Duckworth, 1983.

12   *Ibid.*, pp.254–74.

13   Robert Aulotte, *Amyot et Plutarque: la tradition des moralia au XVIe siècle*. Geneva: Librairie Droz, 1965.

14   Floyd Gray, 'Montaigne and the "Memorabilia"', *Studies in Philology*, vol. 58 (1961): 130–39.

15   Petrarch, *Familiariam rerum libri*, I. 9, 6, cited in Jerold E. Seigel, 'Ideals of Eloquence and Silence in Petrarch', *Journal of the History of Ideas*, vol. XXVI, no. 2, (April–June 1965): 149.

16   Klaus Heitmann, *Fortuna und Virtus: Eine Studie zu Petrarcas Lebensweisheit*. Cologne: Böhlau Verlag, 1958.

17   Barrière, *op. cit.*, p.iii.

18   Barrière, *op. cit.*, p.129.

19   Marjorie Grene, *Approaches to a Philosophical Biology*. New York: Basic Books, 1968.

20   S. John Holyoake, 'The Idea of *Jugement* in Montaigne', *Modern Language Review*, vol. LXIII, 1968, 340–51.

21   Pierre Villey, *Les Sources et l'évolution des Essais de Montaigne*. Paris: Librairie Hachette, 1908, vol. I, pp.214–17. Camilla Hill Hay, *Montaigne: lecteur et imitateur de Sénèque*. Poitiers: Société Française d'Imprimerie, 1938, juxtaposes texts from Seneca and Montaigne to show the extent of borrowing and subtle transformation: also, Carol E.

Clark, 'Seneca's Letters to Lucilius as a Source of Some of Montaigne's Imagery', *Bibliothèque d'Humanisme et Renaissance*, vol. 30 (1968): 249–66.

22   Hugo Friedrich, *Montaigne*. Paris: Gallimard, 1968, Chapter II, 'Tradition et Culture'.

23   *Ibid.*, note 14, pp.392–3, for an extensive comment on the practices of citation in classical and humanist writers with which Montaigne's own art should be compared.

24   Hans-Georg Gadamer, *Truth and Method*. New York: Seabury Press, 1975; John O'Neill, 'Can Phenomenology be Critical?' pp.200–16 in *Phenomenology and Sociology*, ed. Thomas Luckmann. Harmondsworth: Penguin Books, 1978.

25   Gilbert Mayer, 'Les Images dans Montaigne, d'aprés le chapitre de l'institution des enfants', pp.110–18 in *Mélanges de philologie et d'histoire littéraire offerts à Edmond Huguet*, 1940. Mayer makes a careful study of the visceral imagery of this essay but seems to ignore the honey metaphor.

26   John O'Neill, 'Le Langage et la décolonisation: Fanon et Freire', *Sociologie et Sociétés*, vol. 2 (November 1974): 53–65.

27   Here again Montaigne shows his independence of his favourite Plutarch, whereas so many others were absorbed by him; see Aulotte, *op.cit.*, and Alfred Owen Aldridge, 'International Influences upon Biography as a Literary Genre'. pp.927–81 *in Proceedings of the IV Congress of the International Comparative Literature Association*, ed. François Jost. The Hague: Mouton, 1966.

Notes to Chapter Six

1   Anthony Wilden, 'Par divers moyens on arrive à pareille fin: A Reading of Montaigne', *Modern Language Notes*, vol. 83 (1968): 577–97; 'Montaigne on the Paradoxes of Individualism: A Communication About Communication', pp.88–109 in Anthony Wilden, *System and Structure: Essays in Communication and Exchange*. London: Tavistock, 1972. Hereafter cited as MLN and SS, respectively.

2   Wilden's pioneer introduction of Lacan to English readers deserves every credit. For the contemporary state of the discussion see *Yale French Studies*, nos. 55–6 (1977) 'Literature and Psychoanalysis, The Question of Reading: Otherwise'.

3   Georg Lukács, *The Theory of the Novel: A Historico-philosophical Essay on the Forms of Great Epic Literature*, trans. Anna Bostock. Cambridge: MA.: The MIT Press, 1971. It would be another exercise to comment in detail upon Wilden's use of Lukács' theory of the novel. Cf. Lucien Goldmann, 'Introduction aux premiers écrits de Georges Lukács'. pp.156–190 in Georges Lukács, *La Théorie du roman*, trans. Jean Clairevoye. Geneva: Éditions Gonthier, 1963.

4   Max Weber, *The Protestant Ethic and the Spirit of Capitalism*, trans. Talcott Parsons, with a foreword by R.H. Tawney. New York: Scribner, 1958.

5   Horkheimer argues that Montaigne's scepticism placed him above Protestantism, while his social position enabled him to identify with the rise of French absolutism. See Max Horkheimer, 'Montaigne und die Funktion der Skepsis', *Zeitschrift für Sozialforschung*, vol. 1/2 (1938): 1–54. For a more careful analysis of the position of the sixteenth-century 'gentry', see George Huppert, *Les Bourgeois Gentilshommes: An Essay on the Definition of Elites in Renaissance France*. Chicago: University of Chicago Press, 1977, pp.166–77. See also note 15 below.

6   Alma B. Altizer, *Self and Symbolism in the Poetry of Michelangelo, John Donne, and Agrippa d'Aubigné*. The Hague: Nijhoff, 1973.

7   For the sense of this remark see Chap. 9, 'Civilisation, Literacy and Barbarism'.

8   John O'Neill, 'Self-Prescription and Social Machiavellianism'. pp.11–19 in his *Sociology as a Skin Trade*. New York: Harper & Row, 1972, pp.11–19.

9   Lionel Trilling, *Sincerity and Authenticity*. Cambridge, MA.: Harvard University Press, 1974, pp.5–6.

10 *Ibid.*, p.11.

11 See Chap. 7, 'Portrait of the Essayist Without Qualities'.

12 Carol Blum, *Diderot: The Virtue of a Philosopher*. New York: Viking Press, 1974.

13 See Chap. 8, 'On Public ad Private Life'. Also Timothy J. Reiss, 'Montaigne and the Subject of Polity', pp.115–49 in *Literary Theory/Renaissance Texts*, ed. Patricia Parker and David Quint. Baltimore: The Johns Hopkins University Press, 1986; Michael Archer, *Sovereignty and Intelligence: Spying and Court Culture in the English Renaissance*. Stanford: Stanford University Press, 1993.

14 SS, pp.107–8.

15 SS, p.90. We note, incidentally, Wilden's more accurate observation of Montaigne's class position. See note 5 above.

16 Compare the debate over the sources of social rationality between the systems theorist, Luhmann, and the Marxist critical theorist, Habermas, in Friedrich W. Sixel, 'The Problem of Sense: Habermas v. Luhmann', pp.184–204 in *On Critical Theory*, ed. John O'Neill. New York: Seabury Press, 1976.

17 John O'Neill, 'Hegel and Marx on History as Human History'. pp.xi–xx in Jean Hyppolite, *Studies on Marx and Hegel*, edited and translated by John O'Neill. New York: Basic Books, 1969.

18 John O'Neill, 'The Concept of Estrangement in the Early and Later Writings of Karl Marx', *Philosophy and Phenomenological Research*, no. XXV (September 1964): 69–84.

19 See Chapter 2, 'Literary Anxiety and the Romance of Books'.

20 François Jost, 'La Tradition du *Bildungsroman*, *Comparative Literature*, vol. XXI, no. 2 (Spring 1969): 97–115. The *Bildungsroman* might also be compared with the *picaro*, see Claudio Guillen, *Literature as System: Essays Towards the Theory of Literary History*. New Jersey: Princeton University Press, 1971, pp.81–2.

21 Ernst Bloch, *A Philosophy of the Future*, trans. John Cumming. New York: Herder & Herder, 1970, 'The Journey: Method and Motive', Chaps 7–10.

22 For remarks on Montaigne's cultivation of independent readers, see above, 'To the Reader'.

23 Goldmann, *op. cit.*, p.174.

24 MLN, p.588.

25 Maurice Riveline, *Montaigne et l'amitié*. Paris: Librairie Alcan, 1939.

26 MLN, pp.589–90.

27 Chap. 8, 'On Public and Private Life'.

28 Chap. 7, 'Portrait of the Essayist Without Qualities'.

29 André Berthiaume, 'Pour une approche idéologique des 'Essais' de Montaigne', *Renaissance and Reformation*, New Series vol. II, no. 1 (1978): 30–1.

30 MLN, p.597.

31 The sentences in brackets are suppressed in Wilden's quotation of this passage in MLN, pp.593–4.

32 Jean-Claude Fraisse, *Philia: la notion d'amitié dans la philosophie antique*. Paris: Libraire Philosophique, J. Vrin, 1974, Chap II, 'Aristote: amité conscience de soi et vie théoretique'. That Wilden's views confuse the Platonic and Aristotelian conceptions of friendship is noted by Barry Weller, 'The Rhetoric of Friendship in Montaigne's *Essais*', *New Literary History*, vol. IX no. 3 (Spring 1978): 503–23, especially pp.507–9.

33 Aristotle, *Ethica Eudemia*, Book VII, 2, 1237a, 40–45. See Chap. 8, 'On Public and Private Life'.

34 Albert D. Meunut, 'Montaigne and the Nicomachean Ethics', *Modern Philology*, vol. XXXI, no. 3 (February 1934): 225–42.

35 Chap 8, 'On Public and Private Life'.

36 Jean Starobinski, 'Distance et plénitude', *Mercure de France*, no. 348 (1963): 400–9.

37 John O'Neill, 'Critique and Remembrance', pp.1–11 in *On Critical Theory*, ed. John O'Neill. New York: Seabury Press, 1976.

Notes to Chapter Seven
1 Cf., for example, Marvin Lowenthal, *The Autobiography of Michel de Montaigne*. Boston: Houghton Mifflin, 1935; and Donald, M. Frame, *Montaigne, A Biography*. New York, Harcourt, Brace & World, 1965. Lowenthal speaks of his method as follows: 'I decided to invite him to collaborate with me. Aided by scissors, paste and patience, I have let him retell his life story' (*op. cit.*, p. xvii). Frame addresses his project in a preface of a single paragraph: 'I have tried to make this a scholarly and readable biography: scholarly in presenting the evidence on which my statements are based and in identifying conjecture wherever I have used it in the absence of fact; readable in making the scholarly apparatus unobtrusive. . . . When in doubt I have tried to err on the scholarly side; I hope I have not fallen between two stools, and that the nonspecialist may read this book with interest, the scholar with confidence' (*op. cit.*, p.v).
2 Michel Butor, *Essais sur les Essais*. Paris: Gallimard, 1968.
3 For a study of the impossibility of the speculative displacement of the self and writing, see Jeffrey Mehlman, *A Structural Study of Autobiography: Proust, Leiris, Sartre, Lévi-Strauss*. Ithaca, NY, Cornell University Press, 1974; Michel Beaujour, *Poetics of the Literary Self-Portrait*, trans. Yara Milos. New York: New York University Press, 1991.
4 Michel de Montaigne, *The Essays of Michel de Montaigne*, translated and edited by Jacob Zeitlin, New York, Alfred Knopf, 1935, vol. II, Chapter XVII, Notes, pp.564–70.
5 Georges Gusdorf, 'Conditions et limites de l'autiobiographie', pp.105–123 in *Formen der Selbstdarstellung*, ed. Günter Reichenkron and Erich Haase. Berlin: Dunker & Humbolt, 1956.
6 Émile Durkheim, *The Elementary Forms of the Religious Life*. London: Allen & Unwin, 1912.
7 Gusdorf, *op. cit.*, p.108; cf. Agnes Heller, *Renaissance Man*. London: Routledge & Kegan Paul, 1978, Part 3, Chapter 7, 'Individuality, Knowledge of Men, Self-knowledge, Autiobiography', pp.230–45.
8 Robert Genaille, *Rembrandt: Self-Portraits*. London: Methuen, 1963.
9 Francis R. Hart, 'Notes for an Anatomy of Modern Autobiography', *New Literary History*, no. I (1970): 485–511.
10 Ian J. Winter, *Montaigne's Self-Portrait, and its Influence in France, 1580–1630*. Lexington: French Forum, 1976.
11 Karen F. Wiley, 'Montaigne's Artful Praise of Artlessness, *Modern Language Studies*, vol. V, no. 2 (Autumn 1975): 83.
12 Elizabeth W. Bruss, *Autobiographical Acts, The Changing Situation of a Literary Genre*. Baltimore: Johns Hopkins University Press, 1976, pp.10–11; see also Philippe Lejeune, *Le Pacte autobiographique*. Paris: Éditions du Seuil, 1975.
13 *Ibid.*, p.23.
14 Robert Musil, *The Man Without Qualities*, trans. Eithne Wilkins and Ernst Kaiser. New York: Capricorn Books, 1965, vol. 1, p.301.
15 On this see Montaigne, *op. cit.*, vol. I, Chapter XVIII, Notes, pp.366–73.
16 *Ibid.*, p.45.
17 Butor, *op. cit.*, p.64. My translation.
18 Butor, *op. cit.*, pp.112–13.
19 Butor's attempt to establish a central essay for the first two Books is rejected, and his adoption of II: 19 considered 'to misread Montaigne badly' in the opinion of Donald M. Frame, *Montaigne's Essais: A Study*. Atlantic Highlands: Prentice-Hall, 1969, pp.74–7. See also Philip A. Wadsworth, 'Montaigne's Conclusion to Book II of his *Essais*' in

Renaissance and Other Studies in Honor of William Leon Wiley. Chapel Hill: University of North Carolina Press, 1968.

20   Here again Butor uses the metaphors of the garden and labyrinth as mere glosses upon otherwise quite complex literary structures. See John Vernon, *The Garden and the Map, Schizophrenia in Twentieth Century Literature and Culture.* Urbana: University of Illinois Press, 1973.

21   François Jost, 'La Tradition du Bildungsroman', *Comparative Literature*, vol. XXI, no. 2 (Spring 1969): 97–115; Jerome H. Buckley, 'Autobiography in the English *Bildungsroman*'. pp.93–104 in *The Interpretation of Narrative Theory and Practice*, ed. Morton W. Bloomfield. Cambridge, MA.: Harvard University Press, 1970. Agnes Heller also suggests the comparison between autobiography and the *Bildungsroman*, in her *Renaissance Man*, p.232.

22   J.Th. Welter, *L'Exemplum dans la littérature religieuse et didactique du Moyen Age.* Paris: Occitania, 1927. See also, Michel Charles, *Rhétorique de la Lecture.* Paris: Éditions du Seuil, 1977; Richard L. Regosin, 'Conceptions of the Text and the Generation(s) of Meaning: Montaigne's *Essais* and the Place(s) of the Reader', *Journal of Medieval and Renaissance Studies*, 15, No.1 (Spring 1985): 101–14.

23   Rensselaer W. Lee, 'Ut pictura poesis: The Humanistic Theory of a Painting', *Art Bulletin*, no. XXII (December 1940): 197–269; 'Ut pictura poesis', pp.3–27 in Mario Praz, *Mnemosyne, The Parallel between Literature and the Visual Arts.* New Jersey: Princeton University Press, 1970.

24   It has also been argued, somewhat exceptionally, that Montaigne is very careful in presenting the most self-flattering portrait he could possibly manage. See Pietro Toldo, 'L'Homme sage de Montaigne', pp.132–53 in *Mélanges offerts par ses amis et ses elèves è M. Gustave Lanson.* Paris: Librairie Hachette, 1922.

25   For an account of the connections between Elizabethan dramatic imagery and the psychology of emotions see H.K. Russell, 'Elizabethan Dramatic Poetry in The Light of Natural and Moral Philosophy', *Philological Quarterly*, vol. XII, no. 2 (April 1933): 187–93.

26   Jacques Derrida, *Of Grammatology*, trans. Gayatri Chakravorty Spivak. Baltimore: Johns Hopkins University Press, 1976. We have, in any case, examined Wilden's version of the same argument in Chapter 6.

27   Roger Judrin, *Montaigne et son œuvre.* Paris: Éditions Seghers, 1971, p.28.

28   Butor, *op. cit.*, pp.173–4. There are 57 chapters in Book One, 37 in Book Two and 13 chapters in Book Three.

29   *Ibid.*, p.187.

30   *Ibid.*, pp.214–16.

31   Jean Starobinski, *L'Œil vivant II, La Relation critique.* Paris: Gallimard, 1970, pp.83–98.

32   Catherine Bauschatz, 'Leur plus universelle qualité, c'est la diversité: Women as Ideal Readers in Montaigne's *Essais*', *Journal of Medieval and Renaissance Studies* 19 (1989): 83–101; Donna C. Stanton, 'Women as Object and Subject of Exchange: Marie de Gournay's *Le Proumenour* (1594)', *L'Esprit Createur*, Vol. XXIII, No 2 (1983): 9–25; 'Autobiography: The Case of Marie de Gournay's *Apologie pour celle qui escrit*', *French Literature Series*, Volume XII (1985): 18–31; Robert Cottrell, 'Gender Imprinting in Montaigne's *Essais*'. *L'Esprit Créateur*, Vol. XXX, No. 4 (1990): 85–96; Lawrence Kritzman, 'Montaigne's Fantastic Monsters and the Construction of Gender'. *Writing the Renaissaince: Essays in Sixteenth Century Literature in Honor of Floyd Gray*, ed. Raymond C. La Charité. Lexington: French Forum, 1992; Richard L. Regosin, *Montaigne's Unruly Brood: Textual Engendering and the Challenge to Paternal Authority.* Berkeley: University of California Press, 1996.

33   Jacques Derrida, *Of Grammatology, op. cit.*; *Writing and Difference*, trans. Alan Bass. Chicago: University of Chicago Press, 1974; *Dissemination*, trans. Barbara Johnson, Chicago: University of Chicago Press, 1981.

34   Nor do I think the *Essays* are the result of any male crisis, as is argued by S. de Sacy, 'Montaigne essaie ses facultés naturelles', *Mercure de France*, vol. 1, no VI (1952): 285–306.

35   Jean Paris, *Tel qu'en lui-même il se voit, 'Rembrandt'* Paris: Librairie Hachette, 1965, pp.97–121.

36   *Ibid.*, pp.100–1.

37   *Ibid.*, pp.236–7.

38   *Ibid.*, p.122.

39   Edward E. Lowinsky, *Secret Chromatic Art in the Netherlands Motet*. New York: Russell & Russell, 1946.

40   E.H. Gombrich, 'Tradition and Expression in Western Still Life'. p.104 in *Meditations on a Hobby Horse*. London: Phaidon, 1963.

41   Erwin Panofsky, *Early Netherlandish Paining, Its Origins and Character*. New York: Harper & Row, 1971.

42   James Ackerman, 'Science and Visual Art' in *Seventeenth Century Science and the Arts*. Princeton: Princeton University Press, 1962, pp.74–8.

43   Rosalie L. Colie, 'I am that I am: Problems of Self-Reference', *Paradoxia Epidemica, The Renaissance Tradition of Paradox*. Princeton: Princeton University Press, 1966, Part IV, Chap. 12.

44   Jacques Lacan, 'The Mirror-Phase', trans. Jean Roussel, *New Left Review*, no. 51 (1968): 71–7. For a historical study of the conventions of mirror imagery, see also Frederick Goldin, *The Mirror of Narcissus in the Courtly Love Lyric*. Ithaca: Cornell University Press, 1967; and Herbert Grabes, *Speculum, Mirror and Looking-glass*. Tübingen: Max Niemeyer Verlag, 1973.

45   Terence Cave, *The Cornucopian Text: Problems of Writing in the French Renaissance*. Oxford: Clarendon Press, 1979, Part II, Chap. 4, 'Montaigne'. But in view of my differences with Wilden (see Chap. 6) upon whom Cave seems to rely, however creatively, I find I should set in context any gross sexualisation of the corporeal conduct of reading and writing which I otherwise defend.

46   The goddess ceased to speak, and snowy arms outflung
    Around him faltering, soft fondling as she clung
    He quickly caught the wonted flame: the heat well-known
    Entered his marrow, ran through every trembling bone.
    Often a brilliant lightning flash, not otherwise.
    Split by a thunderclap, runs through the cloudy skies.
         . . . .
    Gave the embraces that she craved; then on her breast, He spoke,
    Outpoured at last, gave himself up to sleep and rest. (III: 5, 645).

47   In fact, Montaigne also makes considerable use of Martial's *Epigrammata*; on this see D. Coleman, 'Montaigne's "Sur des vers de Virgile": Taboo Subject, Taboo Author'. pp.135–40 in *Classical Influences on European Culture A.D. 1500–1700*, ed. R.R. Bolgar. Cambridge: Cambridge University Press, 1976.

48   He who rules the savage things
    Of war, the mighty Mars, oft on thy bosom flings
    Wide-mouthed, with greedy eyes thy person he devours,
    Head-back, his very soul upon they lips suspended:
    Take him in thy embrace, goddess, let him be blended
    With thy holy body as he lies; let sweet words pour
    Out of thy mouth. (III: 5, 664)

49   Cave, *op. cit.*, p.287.

50   Cave, *op. cit.*, p.295

Notes to Chapter Eight
1   See Chapters 6 and 9.
2   Manfred Kölsch, *Recht und Macht bei Montaigne, Ein Beitrag zur Erforschung der Grundlagen von Staat und Recht*. Berlin: Duncker & Humblot, 1974.
3   Nannerl O. Keohane, 'Montaigne's Individualism', *Political Theory*, vol. 5, no. 3 (August 1977): 363–90.
4   Myron P. Gilmore, *Humanists and Jurists. Six Studies in the Renaissance*. Cambridge: MA., Belknap Press, 1963, pp.45–7.
5   Sylvia G. Sanders, 'Montaigne et les idées politiques de Machiavel', *Bulletin de la Société des Amis de Montaigne*, Fifth Series, nos. 18–19 (April–September 1976): 85–98.
6   R.A. Sayce, *The Essays of Montaigne, A Critical Exploration*. London: Weidenfeld & Nicolson, 1972, p.259. My emphasis.
7   Octave Nadal, 'L'Éthique de la gloire au dix-septième siècle', *Mercure de France*, vol. 308 (1950): 22–34; Kristen B. Neuschel, *Word of Honor: Interpreting Noble Culture in Sixteenth-Century France*. Ithaca: Cornell University Press, 1989.
8   Abraham C. Keller, 'Anti-War Writing in France 1500–1600', *PMLA*, no. LXVII (1952): 240–50.
9   Frederic J. Baumgartner, *Radical Reactionaries: The Political Thought of the French Catholic League*. Geneva: Libraire Droz, 1975.
10   Michel de Montaigne, *The Essays of Michel de Montaigne*, translated and edited by Jacob Zeitlin. New York: Alfred Knopf, 1935, vol. 3, Chap. I, are a wonderful source of commentary that is not always given due recognition.
11   John O'Neill, 'On Body Politics', pp.251–67 in *Recent Sociology No. 4*: Family, Marriage and the Struggle of the Sexes, ed.Hans Peter Dreitzel. New York: Macmillan, 1972.
12   For Montaigne's views on law and custom, see F. Joukovsky, *Montaigne et le problème du temps*. Paris: A.G. Nizet, 1972, Chap. IV, 'Le Conservatisme'.
13   Eugene M. Decker, 'The Against One and the Political Thought of the Reformation', *Forum*, vol. 9, no. 2 (1971): 12–14.
14   We should not confuse Montaigne's notion of tolerance with later liberal conceptions. On this see, Marcel Françon, 'Montaigne et l'édit de janvier (1562)', *Bulletin de la Société des Amis de Montaigne*, Fifth Series, nos. 3–4 (July–December 1972):17–26.
15   Edward Williamson, 'On the Liberalizing of Montaigne: A Remonstrance', French *Review*, vol. XXIII (October 1949): 92–100.
16   Pierre J. Goumarre, 'Montaigne et Machiavel et les grands capitaines de l'antiquité', *Les Lettres romanes*, vol. XXVI, no. 1 (February 1973): 3–15.
17   Abraham C. Keller, 'Optimism in the Essays of Montaigne', *Studies in Philology*, vol. 54 (1957): 408–28.
18   There is a very complex relationship between the Thomistic and Augstinian streams of Catholicism, the Christian humanists and the Protestant notions of religious devotion. This is the background to Montaigne's refusal of any easy either/or in matters of religion and politics. See R. Guelley, 'L'Évolution des méthodes théologiques à Louvain d'Erasme à Jansénius', *Revue d'histoire ecclésiastique*, vol. 37 (1941): 31–141; V. Dedieu, 'Survivances et influences de l'apologétique traditionnelle dans les "Pensées",' *Revue d'histoire littéraire de la France* (1930): 481–513; (1931): 1–39.
19   For La Boétie's views on this question, see the discussion of his 'Mémoire sur l'édit de janvier' in M. Dréano', *La Religion de Montaigne*. Paris: A.G. Nizet (1969): 45–54.
20   For further discussion see Chapter 9, 'Civilisation, Literacy and Barbarism'.
21   Jean-Pierre Dhommeaux, 'Les Idées politiques de Montaigne', *Bulletin de la Société des Amis de Montaigne*, Fifth Series, no. 17 (January–March 1976): 5–30; Arletta Jovanna, *Le devoir de revolte: La noblesse française et la gestation de l'État moderne (1559–1661)*. Paris: Fayard, 1989.

22   He prefers established authority but does not advise that it seek to maintain itself at all costs. Such advice would only weaken society as much as the unforeseen troubles of change.

23   Titus Livius, *The History of Rome*, trans. George Baker. London: Jones, 1830, vol. 1 Book II, xxxii, p.64.

24   Artistotle, *Politica*, Book V, 3, 1302b34–1303a3, trans. Benjamin Jowett, *The Works of Aristotle*, ed. W.D. Ross Oxford: Clarendon Press, 1921, vol. X.

25   Carol E. Clark, 'Montaigne and the Imagery of Political Discourse in Sixteenth-Century France', *French Studies*, vol. XXIV, no. 4 (October 1970): 337–55.

26   P. Archambault, 'The Analogy of the Body in Renaissance Political Literature', *Bibliothèque d'Humanisme et Renaissance*, vol. XXIX, no. 1 (1967): 21–53.

27   Floyd Gray, 'Montaigne's Friends', *French Studies*, vol. XV, no. 3 (July 1961): 203–12. François Rigolot, 'Montaigne's Purloined Letters', pp.145–66 in *Montaigne: Essays in Reading*, ed. Gerard Defaux, *Yale French Studies*, 64 (1984).

28   Étienne de la Boétie, *Le Discours de la servitude volontaire, texte établi par P. Leonard, avec La Boétie et la question du politique*, textes de Lammenais, P. Leroux, A. Vermonel, G. Landauer, S. Weit et de Pierre Clastres et Claude Lefort. Paris: Payot, 1976; translated by Harry Kurz as *The Politics of Obedience: The Discourse of Voluntary Servitude*, Introduction by Murray N. Rothbard. New York: Free Life Editions, 1975. See the excellent review by Brian Singer, *Telos*, no. 43 (Spring 1980): 215–29.

29   La Boétie, *Le Discours de la servitude volontaire*, pp.116–17. My translation.

30   For an assessment of Machiavelli's views on republicanism and popular sovereignty, see Hans Baron, 'Machiavelli: The Republican Citizen and the Author of *The Prince*', *English Historical Review*, no. LXXVI (1961): 217–53; Walter Ullmann, *Medieval Political Thought*, Harmondsworth: Penguin Books, 1975, pp.200–14.

31   François Combres, *Essai sur les idées politiques de Montaigne et La Boétie*. Bordeaux: Librairie H. Duthu, 1882; Eric MacPhail, 'Friendship as a Political Ideal in Mntaigne's *Essais*', *Montaigne Studies* 1 (1989): 177–87.

32   Anthony Wilden, 'Montaigne on the Paradoxes of Individualism: A Communication about Communication', pp.88–109 in his *System and Structure: Essays in Communication and Exchange*. London: Tavistock, 1972. On this see Chap. 6, 'The Paradox of Communication: Reading the Essay Otherwise'.

33   John O'Neill, 'Language and the Legitimation Problem', *Sociology*, vol. 11, no. 2 (May 1977): 351–8.

34   R.F. Willetts, *Aristocratic Society in Ancient Crete*. London: Routledge & Kegan Paul, 1955.

35   Plato, *Symposium*, 178d–179a, trans. B. Jowett. *The Dialogues of Plato*. Oxford: Clarendon Press, 1953, vol. I, p.510.

36   John Oscar Lofberg, *Sycophancy in Athens*. Chicago: University of Chicago Press, 1917.

37   Lionel Pearson, *Popular Ethics in Ancient Greece*. Stanford: Stanford University Press, 1962, Chap. Five, 'Justice, Friendship and Loyalty'.

38   *Essays*: 28, 139.

39   Aristotle, *Ethica Nicomachea*, 1158b, 29–33, trans. W.D. Ross, *The Works of Aristotle*, vol. IX.

40   For the discovered importance of Tacitus in these reflections upon imperial domination see, Kenneth C. Schellhase, *Tacitus in Renaissance Political Thought*. Chicago: University of Chicago Press, 1976.

41   Seneca, *Ad serenum de tranquillitate animi*, VII, 36, *Moral Essays*, trans. John W. Basore. London: Heinemann, 1965, vol. II.

42   Aristotle, *Ethica Eudemia*, 1236a–b, 1237a, in W.D. Ross (ed.) *The Works of Aristotle*, vol. IX.

43   Herman L. Sinaiko, *Love, Knowledge and Discourse in Plato: Dialogue and Dialectic in Phaedrus, Republic, Parmenides*. Chicago: University of Chicago Press, 1965.

44   La Boétie, *Le Discours de la servitude volontaire*, p.160.

45   *Ibid.*, p.265.

46   Joseph Barrère, *L'Humanisme et la politique dans 'Le Discours de la servitude volontaire': étude sur les origines du texte et l'objet du discours d'Estienne de la Boétie*. Paris: Librairie Ancienne Edouard Champion, 1923, Chap. V, 'La Contribution politique des humanistes (Les Institutions des princes)', pp.209–42.

Notes to Chapter Nine

1   Lowry Nelson, Jr, 'The Fictive Reader and Literary Self-Reflexiveness', pp.173–91 in *The Disciplines of Criticism*, ed. Peter Demetz et al. New Haven: Yale University Press, 1968.

2   Hugo Friedrich, *Montaigne*. Paris: Gallimard, 1968, pp.358–64. It is not possible to deal with these problems simply by trying to refurbish a single term, as, for example, S. Dresden, 'Le Dilettantisme de Montaigne', *Bibliothèque d'Humanisme et Renaissance*, no. XV (1953): 45–56.

3   Stanley E. Fish, *Self-Consuming Artifacts, The Experience of Seventeenth-Century Literature*. Berkeley: University of California Press, 1972, pp.3–4.

4   John C. Lapp, *The Esthetics of Negligence: La Fontaine's Contes*. Cambridge: Cambridge University Press, 1971, pp.1–30.

5   Baldesar Castiglione, *The Book of the Courtier*, trans. Charles S. Singleton. New York: Anchor Books, 1959, p.43; and Eduardo Saccone, 'Grazia, Sprezzatura, and Affettazione in Castiglione's *Book of the Courtier*', pp.34–54, *Glyph 5*, Johns Hopkins Textual Studies. Baltimore: Johns Hopkins University Press, 1979.

6   For the extent of Montaigne's knowledge of the 'geography' of the New World, see Geoffrey Atkinson, *Les Nouveaux Horizons de la Renaissance Française*. Paris: Librairie Droz, 1935. It is argued – somewhat excessively, in my view – that Montaigne is merely playing upon the distinction between experience and fiction and has nothing else in mind in this essay than a 'comic boutade'. See Joseph R. De Lutri, 'Montaigne and the Noble Savage: A Shift in Perspective', *French Review*, vol. XIX, no. 2 (December 1975): 206–11, and Montaigne's 'Des Cannibales, Invention/Experience', *Bibliothèque d'Humanisme et Renaissance*, no. XXXVIII (1976): 77–82. A more reasonable argument is to be found in Bernard Weinberg, 'Montaigne's Readings for Des Cannibales', pp.261–79, *Renaissance and Other Studies in Honor of William Leon Wiley*, ed. George Bernard Daniel, Jr. Chapel Hill: University of North Carolina Press, 1968; and Marcel Bataillon, 'Montaigne et les conquérants de l'or', *Studi Francesi*, vol. III, no. 9 (1959): 353–67.

7   Guy Mermier, 'L'Essai "Des Cannibales" de Montaigne', *Bulletin de la Société des Amis de Montaigne*, nos 7–8 (July–December 1973): 27–38.

8   René Etiemble, 'Sens et structure dans un essai de Montaigne', *Cahiers de l'Association Internationale des Études Françaises*, vol. 14 (1962): 263–74.

9   Elly Witttkower, *Die Form der Essais von Montaigne*. Basle thesis, 1935.

10   Etiemble, *op. cit.*, pp.273–74. He considers these stylistic glosses to have been completely dismissed by Jasinski's plain reading of the 'internal composition' of the essays. Yet while criticising Jasinski's own expression of this unity, he fails to notice that Jasinski's reading of the essay grasps its sense – 'Which side is in the right? Which one is truly courageous?' – without any elaborate appeal to the contemporary colonial politics of France. Cf. René Jasinski, 'Sur la composition chez Montaigne', pp.257–67 in *Mélenages d'histoire littéraire offerts è Henri Chamard*. Paris: Librairie Nizet, 1951.

11   Daniel Martin, *L'Architecture des Essais de Montaigne: Mémoire Artificielle et Mythologie*. Paris: Librairie Nizet, 1992.

12   For Montaigne's views on monarchy, see Chap. 8, 'On Public and Private Life'.

13   For further analysis of Wilden's Marxist reading of the *Essays*, see Chap. 6, 'The Paradox of Communication: Reading the *Essays* Otherwise'.

14   Etiemble, op. cit., pp.266–7. Etiemble refers to R.A. Sayce, 'Baroque Elements in Montaigne', *French Studies*, vol. 8 (1954): 1–15. Sayce's use of baroque comparison is at least given more illustration from the history of painting by Imbrie Buffum who nevertheless applies Sayce's 'method' to the essay 'Of Vanity' (III: 9) with all the problems it entails. Moreover, even the appeal to specific examples of baroque painting fails, without actual illustration by means of reproduction, to be anything else but a gloss upon the baroque and not an analysis of the concept. Cf. Imrie Buffum, *Studies in the Baroque from Montaigne to Rotrou*. New Haven: Yale University Press, 1957, Chap. 1, 'The Baroque Categories as Exemplified by Montaigne'. On the problem of defining the Renaissance, see Erwin Panofsky, *Renaissance and Renascences in Western Art*. Stockholm: Almqvist & Wiksell, 1960.

15   Sayce, *op. cit.*, p.2. Buffum offers as illustration of Wölfflin's criteria for distinguishing Renaissance and baroque art the differences between a Dürer and a Rembrandt Death of the Virgin, a Titian and a Velazquez *Venus*. Cf. our own discussion in the preceding chapter.

16   See Chap. 7, 'Portrait of the Essayist Without Qualities'.

17   Jean Rousset, *La Littérature de l'âge baroque en France: Circé et Paon*. Paris, Librairie Jose Corti, 1953, p.237.

18   Sayce, *op. cit.*, pp.272–73.

19   Curiously enough, Sayce refers to Wittkower's thesis at this point. See his note 30. Sayce's argument, moreover, is repeated without any reference even to Etiemble (in an otherwise extensive bibliography) in his later *The Essays of Montaigne, A Critical Exploration*. London: Weidenfeld & Nicolson, 1972, pp.272–75.

20   Traeger also objects to Sayce's method of relying upon 'key words' for the sense of Montaigne's essays, as though their meaning were purely verbal rather than in Montaigne's mind. He rightly cautions against the use of paragraphing that is not to be found in Montaigne's deliberately run-on style: see Wolf Eberhard Traeger, *Aufbau und Gedankenführung in Montaignes Essays*. Heidelberg: Carl Winter Universität Verlag, 1961, pp.227–30; 133, n. 24.

21   Marcel Gutwirth, "Des Coches', ou la structuration d'une absence', *L'Esprit créateur*, vol. XV, nos 1–2, (Spring–Summer 1975): 8–20. The whole issue of movement in Montaigne's essays must be analysed philologically, as in an exemplary study by Jules Brody, 'De mesnager sa volonté (III; 10): lecture philologique d'un essai', pp.34–71 in *O un Amy! Essays on Montaigne in Honor of Donald M. Frame*, ed. Raymond C. La Charité. Lexington: French Forum, 1977.

22   Gutwirth, *op. cit.*, pp.12–13. Gutwirth points to his difference with Etiemble by insisting that the term 'ostentation' is used in a wider sense than the economic or material notion of luxury.

23   Traeger, *op. cit.*, pp.228–9.

24   Gutwirth, *op. cit.*, p.19. My translation.

25   Daniel A. Gajda, 'Play in Montaigne's "De trois commerces"', *Romance Notes*, vol. 16, no. 1 (Autumn 1974): 172–7.

26   Marcel Gutwirth, *Michel de Montaigne, ou le pari d'exemplarité*. Montréal: Les Presses de l'Université de Montréal, 1977, Chap. II, 'L'Homme vraiment-nu', pp.47–84.

27   John Berger, *Ways of Seeing*, London: British Broadcasting Corporation and Penguin Books, 1972, p.54. Berger nicely overturns Kenneth Clark's usage: 'The English language, with its elaborate generosity, distinguishes between the naked and the nude. To be naked is to be deprived of our clothes and the word implies some of the embarrassment which most of us feel in that condition. The word nude, on the other hand, carries, in educated usage, no uncomfortable overtone. The vague image it projects into the mind is not

241

of a huddled and defenceless body, but of a balanced, prosperous and confident body: the body reformed.' *The Nude: A Study of Ideal Art.* Harmondsworth: Penguin Books, 1960, p.1.

28   Steven Rendall, 'Dialectical Structure and Tactics in Montaigne's 'Of Cannibals',' *Pacific Coast Philology*, no. XII (1977): 56–63; Raymond Lebèque, 'Montaigne et le paradoxe des cannibales', pp.359–63 in *Studi di letteratura storia e filosofia in onore di Bruno Revel.* Florence: Leo S. Olschki Editore, 1965.

29   Dain A. Taffon, 'Ancients and Indians in Montaigne's 'Des Coches',' *Symposium* (Spring 1973): 76–90. Cf. Marcel Raymond, 'Montaigne devant les sauvages d'Amérique'. pp.13–37 in his *Être et dire, études,* Neuchâtel, Éditions de la Baconnière, 1970.

30   The essays on coaches and cannibals are, of course, as much concerned to essay the nature of our reasoning as the nature of their topics. See Caroline Locher, 'Primary and Secondary Themes in Montaigne's 'Des Cannibales' (I, 31)', *French Forum*, vol. I (1976): 119–26.

31   Hayden White, 'The Forms of Wildness: Archeology of an Idea', p. 33 in *The Wild Man Within, An Image in Western Thought from the Renaissance to Romanticism,* ed. Edward Dodley and Maximillian E. Novak. Pittsburgh: University of Pittsburgh Press, 1972.

32   Jean Marc Blanchard, 'Of Cannibalism and Autobiography', *MLN*, vol. 93, no. 4, (May 1978): 654–76.

33   *Ibid.,* p.666.

34   David Quint, *Montaigne and the Quality of Mercy: Ethical and Political Themes in the Essais.* Princeton: Princeton University Press, 1998, Chap. 3, 'The Culture that Cannot Pardon, and Quint's note (3) at page 158 for references to recent commentary on 'Of Cannibals'.

35   John O'Neill (ed) *Hegel's Dialectic of Desire and Recognition: Texts and Commentary.* Albany: State University of New York, 1996

36   John Rawls, *Political Liberalism.* New York: Columbia University Press, 1996.

37   Jürgen Habermas, *Between Facts and Norms: Contributions to a Discourse Theory of Law and Democracy.* Cambridge, MA.: The MIT Press, 1996.

Notes to Chapter Ten

1   See Chapter 8, 'On Public and Private Life'.

2   Saint Augustine, *Confessions,* trans. R.S. Pine-Coffin. Harmondsworth: Penguin Books, 1961, Book X, 6, 211–12.

3   F. Starowski, 'Une Source italienne des 'Essais de Montaigne: 'L'Examen Vanitatis Doctrinae Gentium' de François Pic de la Mirandole', *Bulletin italien,* vol. V, no. 4 (October–December 1905): 309–13.

4   Robert M. Ornstein, 'Donne, Montaigne and Natural Law', *JEGP*, no. LV (1956): 213–29.

5   See Chap 9, 'Civilisation, Literacy and Barbarism'.

6   Giovanni Pico della Mirandola, *De hominis dignitate, Heptaplus, De Ente et uno, e scritti vari,* ed. Eugenio Garin. Florence, 1942, pp.302–4.

7   These alterations – of humiliation and reconciliation – furnish the interpretative themes of Friedrich's *Montaigne.* Paris: Gallimard, 1968, Chaps III and IV. Cf. Marianne S. Meijer, 'Montaigne et la Bible', *Bulletin de la Société des Amis de Montaigne,* Fifth Series, no. 20 (October–December 1976): 23–57.

8   Ernest Marchand, 'Montaigne and the Cult of Ignorance', *Romantic Review*, vol. XXXVI, no. 4 (December 1945): 275–82.

9   Robert Joly, *Le Thème philosophique des genres de vie dans l'antiquité classique.* Brussels: Palais des Académies, 1956.

10   For a discussion of the textual source of the *Μέσός Βίος* in Arius Didymus, 'Résumé of the Moral Doctrines of Aristotle and other Peripatetics', see Joly, *op. cit.,*

Chapter VIII.

11   Frederick Kellerman, 'The *Essais* and Socrates', *Symposium*, vol. 10 (1956): 204–16. Julien-Eymard d'Angers, 'Le Stoicisme en France dans la première moitié du XVIIe siècle', *Études franciscaines*, New Series, vol. 2, no. 6 (August 1951):132–57; vol. 2, no. 8 (June 1952): 1–19.

12   Don Cameron Allen, 'The Rehabilitation of Epicurus and his Theory of Pleasure in the Early Renaissance', *Studies in Philology*, no. XLI (1944): 1–15.

13   *Ibid.*, 1–15.

14   The *Essays* are an important source of the paradox of theriophily, namely, the argument that wild animals and wild men are, in virtue of their naturalness, superior to man. Of course, Montaigne could draw upon Pliny, Seneca and Plutarch, as well as his contemporaries, Ortensio Landi, Giraldi, and Pièrre Boaystuau, for arguments upon the wisdom of beasts and savages; not to mention arguments upon the disadvantages of reason advanced by Agrippa and Nicholas of Cusa. Montaigne's ideas and their history are treated at length in George Boas, *The Happy Beast in French Thought of the Sevnteenth Century*. New York: Octagon Books, 1966.

15   N. van Wijngaarden, *Les Odyssées philosophiques en France entre 1616 et 1789*. Haarlem: Drukkerij Vijlbriet, 1932.

16   Nancy Lee Beaty, *The Craft of Dying: A Study in the Literary Tradition of the Ars Moriendi in England*. New Haven: Yale University Press, 1970; and Ian J. Winter, 'From Self-Concept to Self-Knowledge; Death and Nature in Montaigne's 'De la Phisionomie'.' pp.351–65 in *French Renaissance Studies in Honor of Isidore Silver*, ed. Frieda S. Brown, *Kentucky Romance Quarterly*, vol. XXI, Supplement no. 2 (1974): 351–65.

17   Rosalie L. Colie, *Paradoxia Epidemica: The Renaissance Tradition of Paradox*. Princeton: Princeton University Press, 1966, Part III, Chap. 7, 'Nothing is but what is not: Solutions to the Problem of Nothing'.

18   Pascal, *Pensées*, translated with an Introduction by A.J. Krailsheimer. Harmondsworth: Penguin, Books, 1966, no. 72, p.90.

19   See also Michel de Montaigne, *The Essays of Michel de Montaigne*, translated and edited by Jacob Zeitlin. New York: Alfred Knopf, 1935, vol. II, Chap. XII, Notes, pp.481–519.

20   Gregory Sims, 'Stoic Virtues/Stoic Vices: Montaigne's Pyrrhic Rhetoric', *Journal of Medieval and Renaissance Studies*, 23 (1993): 235–66.

21   Frederick Kellerman, 'Montaigne's Socrates', *Romantic Review*, vol. XLV, no. 3 (October 1954):170–7.

22   Elaine Limbrick, 'Montaigne and Socrates', *Renaissance and Reformation*, vol. IX, no. 2 (1973): 46–57.

23   A.S. Pease, 'Things Without Honor', *Classical Philology*, no. XXI (1926): 27–42.

Bibliography

Ackerman, James, 'Science and Visual Art', pp.74–78 in *Seventeenth Century Science and the Arts*. New Jersey: Princeton University Press, 1962.

Agrippa, Henry Cornelius, 'Three Books of Occult Philosophy', cited in R.L. Colie, *Paradoxia Epidemica: The Renaissance Tradition of Paradox*. Princeton: Princeton University Press, 1966.

Aldridge, Alfred Owen, 'International Influences upon Biography as a Literary Genre', pp.972–81. *Proceedings of the IV Congress of the International Comparative Literature Association*, ed. François Jost. The Hague: Mouton, 1966.

Alexander, William Hardy, 'Montaigne's Classical Bookshelf,' *University of Toronto Quarterly*, no. X (1941): 78–86.

Allen, Don Cameron, 'The Degeneration of Man and Renaissance Pessimism', *Studies in Philology*, no. XXV (1938): 202–27.

—— 'The Rehabilitation of Epicurus and his Theory of Pleasure in the Early Renaissance', *Studies in Philology*, no. XLI (1944): 1–15.

Altizer, Alma B., *Self and Symbolism in the Poetry of Michelangelo, John Donne, and Agrippa d'Aubigné*. The Hague: Nijhoff, 1973.

Angers, Julien-Eymard de, 'Le Stoicisme en France dans la première moitié du XVIIe siècle', *Études franciscaines*, New Series, vol. 2, no. 6 (August 1951):132–57; vol. 2, no. 8 (June 1952): 1–19.

Archambault, P., 'The Analogy of the "Body" in Renaissance Political Literature', *Bibliothèque d'Humanisme et Renaissance*, vol. XXIX, no. 1 (1967): 21–53.

Arendt, Hannah, *The Human Condition*. Chicago: University of Chicago Press, 1958.

Aristotle, 'Ethica Eudemia', trans. W.D. Ross, *The Works of Artistotle*, vol. IX.

—— 'Politica', trans. Benjamin Jowett, *The Works of Aristotle*, vol. X.

Arnold, E.V., *Roman Stoicism*. New York: Humanities Press, 1958.

Atkinson, Geoffrey, *Les Nouveaux Horizons de la Renaissance Française*. Paris: Librairie Droz, 1935.

Auerbach, Erich, *Mimesis: The Representation of Reality in Western Literature*, New

York: Doubleday Anchor Books, 1953.

Augustine, Saint, *The City of God.* London: J.M. Dent, 1945.

—— *Confessions*, trans. R.S. Pine-Coffin. Harmondsworth: Penguin Books, 1961.

Aulotte, Robert, *Amyot et Plutarque: la tradition des moralia au XVIe siècle.* Geneva: Librairie Droz, 1965.

Aymonier, Camille, 'Montaigne à table', *Revue philomatique de Bordeaux et du Sud*, vol. V, no. 37 (1934): 179–91.

Bachelard, Gaston, *The Poetics of Space*, trans. Maria Jolas. Boston: Beacon Press, 1969.

Bakhtin, Mikhail, *Rabelais and his World*, trans. Helene Iswolsky. Cambridge, MA.: The MIT Press, 1968.

Baron, Hans, Machiavelli, 'The Republican Citizen and the Author of *The Prince*,' *English Historical Review*, no. LXXVI (1961): 217–53.

Baron, Hans, Petrarch: 'His Inner Struggles and the Humanistic Discovery of Man's Nature', pp.18–51 in *Florilegium Historiale: Essays Presented to Wallace K. Ferguson*, ed. J.G. Rowe and W.H. Stockdale. Toronto: University of Toronto Press, 1971.

Barrère, Joseph, *L'Humanisme et la politique dans 'Le Discours de la servitude volontaire', Étude sur les origines du texte et l'objet du discours d'Estienne de la Boétie.* Paris: Librairie Ancienne Edouard Champion, 1923.

Barrière, Pierre, *La Vie intellectuelle en Périgord 1550–1800.* Bordeaux: Éditions Delmas, 1936.

Barthes, Roland, *The Pleasure of the Text*, trans. Richard Miller. New York: Hill & Wang, 1975.

—— 'To Write: An Intransitive Verb?' in *The Languages of Criticism and the Sciences of Man, The Structuralist Controversy*, ed. Richard Macksey and Eugenio Donato. Baltimore: Johns Hopkins University Press, 1970.

Bataillon, Marrel, 'Montaigne et les conquérants de l'or, *Studi Francesi*, vol. III, no. 9 (1959): 353–67.

Bateson, F.W., 'Linguistics and Literary Criticism', pp.3–16 in *The Disciplines of Criticism, Essays in Literary Theory, Interpretation and History*, ed. Peter Demetz, Thomas Greene and Lowry Nelson, Jr. New Haven: Yale University Press, 1968.

—— *The Scholar-Critic: An Introduction to Literary Research.* London: Routledge & Kegan Paul, 1972.

Baumgartner, Frederic J., *Radical Reactionaries: The Political Thought of the French Catholic League.* Geneva: Librairie Droz, 1975.

Bauschatz, Cathleen M., 'Montaigne's Conception of Reading in the Context of Renaissance Poetics and Modern Criticism', pp.264–91 in *The Reader in the Text*, ed. Susan R. Suleiman and Inge Crosman. Princeton: Princeton University Press, 1980; 'Leur plus universelle qualité, c'es la diversité: Women as Ideal Readers in Montaigne's *Essais*', *Journal of Medieval and Renaissance Studies*, 19 (1989): 83–101.

Beaty, Nancy Lee, *The Craft of Dying, A Study in the Literary Tradition of the Ars Moriendi in England.* New Haven: Yale University Press, 1970.

Beaujour, Michel, *Poetics of the Literary Self-Portrait*, trans. Yara Milos. New York: New York University Press.

Berger, John, *Ways of Seeing*. London: British Broadcasting Corporation and Penguin Books, 1972.

Bergin, Thomas, *Petrarch*. New York: Twayne, 1970.

Bersani, Leo, *A Future for Astyanax, Character and Desire in Literature*. Boston: Little, Brown, 1976.

Berthiaume, André, 'Pour une approche idéologique des *Essais* de Montaigne', *Renaissance and Reformation*, New Series, vol. II, no. 1 (1978): 23–32.

Blanchard, Jean Marc, 'Of Cannibalism and Autobiography', *MLN*, vol. 93, no. 4 (May 1978): 654–76.

—— 'Le Je(u) de Montaigne', *Neophilologus* (Summer 1977): 347–55.

Blanchot, Maurice, *L'Espace littéraire*. Paris: Gallimard, 1955.

Bleich, David, *Subjective Criticisim*. Baltimore: Johns Hopkins University Press, 1978.

Blinkenberg, Andreas, 'Quel sens Montaigne a-t-il voulu donner au mot Essais dans le titre de son œuvre?', *Bulletin de la Société des Amis de Montaigne*, Fourth Series, nos. 28–32 (1963–4): 22–32.

Bloch, Ernst, *A Philosophy of the Future*, trans. John Cumming. New York: Herder & Herder, 1970.

Bloom, Harold, *A Map of Misreading*, New York: Oxford University Press, 1975.

Blum, Carol, *Diderot: The Virtue of a Philosopher*. New York: Viking Press, 1974.

Boss, George, *The Happy Beast in French Thought of the Seventeenth Century*. New York: Octagon Books, 1966.

Bolgar, R.R. (ed.), *Classical Influences on European Culture AD 1500–1700*. Cambridge: Cambridge University Press, 1976.

Brody, Jules, 'De mesnager sa volonté (III: 10): lecture philologique d'un essai', pp.34–71 in *O Un Amy! Essays on Montaigne in Honor of Donald M. Frame*, edited by Raymond C. La Charité. Lexington: French Forum, 1977.

Brush, Craig B., 'The Essayist is Learned: Montaigne's 'Journal de voyage' and the *Essais*', *Romantic Review*, no. 62 (1971): 16–27.

Bruss, Elizabeth W., *Autobiographical Acts: The Changing Situation of a Literary Genre*. Baltimore: Johns Hopkins University Press, 1976.

Buckley, Jerome H., 'Autobiography in the English *Bildungsroman*', pp.93–104 in *The Interpretation of Narrative Theory and Practice*, ed. Morton W. Bloomfield, Cambridge, MA.: Harvard University Press, 1970.

Budgen, Frank, *James Joyce and the Making of Ulysses*. Bloomington: Indiana University Press, 1960.

Buffum, Imrie, *L'Influence du voyage de Montaigne sur les 'Essais'*. Princeton: Princeton University Press, 1946.

—— *Studies in the Baroque from Montaigne to Rotrou*. New Haven: Yale University Press, 1957.

Butor, Michel, *Essais sur les Essais*. Paris: Gallimard, 1968.

Camus, Albert, *The Myth of Sisyphus, and Other Essays*, trans. Justin O'Brien. New York: Vintage Books, 1955.

Cassirer, Ernst, *The Renaissance Philosophy of Man*. Chicago: University of Chicago Press, 1948.

Castiglione, Baldesar, *The Book of the Courtier*, trans. Charles S. Singleton. New York: Anchor Books, 1959.

Cave, Terence, *The Cornucopian Text: Problems of Writing in the French Renaissance*. Oxford: Clarendon Press, 1979.

Charles, Michel, *Rhétorique de la lecture*. Paris: Éditions du Seuil, 1977.

Clark, Carol E., 'Montaigne and the Imagery of Political Discourse in Sixteenth-Century France', *French Studies*, vol. XXIV, no. 4 (October 1970): 337–55.

—— 'Seneca's Letters to Lucilius as a Source of Some of Montaigne's Imagery', *Bibliothèque d'Humanisme et Renaissance*, vol. 30 (1968): 249–66.

Clark, Kenneth, *The Nude: A Study of Ideal Art*. Harmondsworth: Penguin Books, 1960.

Clements, Robert J., 'Critical Theory and Practice of the Pléiade', *Harvard Studies in Romance Languages*, vol. XVIII (1942).

Coleman, D., Montaigne's *'Sur des vers de Virgile:* Taboo Subject, Taboo Author', pp.135–40 in *Classical Influences on European Culture AD 1500–1700*, ed. R.R. Bolgar. Cambridge: Cambridge University Press, 1976.

Colie, Rosalie L., *The Resources of Kind: Genre-Theory in the Renaissance*, ed. Barbara K. Lewalski. Berkeley: University of California Press, 1973.

Collingwood, R.G., *Speculum Mentis: On the Map of Knowledge*. Oxford: Clarendon Press, 1924.

Combres, François, *Essais sur les idées politiques de Montaigne et La Boétie*. Bordeaux: Librairie H. Duthu, 1882.

Cook, Albert, 'Comparisons: Dante, *Inferno*, 1.80; Petrarch, Montaigne, Etc.', *Romantic Review*, vol. 12, no. 2 (April–June 1921): 185–6.

Cottrell, Robert, ' Gender Imprinting in Montaigne's *Essais,*' *L'esprit créateur*, Vol. XXX, No. 4 (1990): 85–96

Croll, Morris W., '"Attic Prose" in the Seventeenth Century', *Studies in Philology*, vol. XVIII, no. 2 (April 1921): 79–128.

—— 'The Baroque Style in Prose'. pp.427–57 in *Studies in English Philology: A Miscellany in Honor of Frederick Klaeber*, ed. Kemp Malone and Martin Brown Rudd. Minneapolis: University of Minnesota Press, 1929,

Decker, Eugene M., 'The Against One and the Political Thought of the Reformation', *Forum*, vol. 9, no. 2 (1971): 12–14.

Dedieu, V., 'Survivances et influences de l'apologétique traditionnelle dans les *Pensées*', *Revue d'histoire littéraire de la France* (1930): 481–513; (1931): 1–39.

De Lutri, Joseph R., 'Montaigne and the Nobel Savage: A Shift in Perspective', *French Review*, vol. XIX, no. 2 (December 1975): 206–11.

De Man, Paul, *Blindness and Insight, Essays in the Rhetoric of Contemporary Criticism*, New York: Oxford University Press, 1971.

De Maria, Robert, Jr, 'The Ideal Reader: A Critical Fiction', *PMLA*, vol. 93, no. 3 (May 1978): 463–74.

Demetz, Peter, Grene, Thomas, and Nelson, Lowry, Jr (eds), *The Disciplines of Criticism, Essays in Literary Theory, Intepretation and History*. New Haven: Yale University Press, 1968.

Derrida, Jacques, 'Hors livre préfaces', pp.9–67 in his *La Dissémination*. Paris: Éditions du Seuil, 1972.

—— *Of Grammatology*, trans. Gayatri Chakravorty Spivak. Baltimore: Johns Hopkins University Press, 1976.

—— *Writing and Difference*, trans. Alan Bass. Chicago: University of Chicago

Press, 1974.

—— *Dissemination*, trans. Barbara Johnson, Chicago: University of Chicago Press, 1981.

Dhommeaux, Jean-Pierre, 'Les Idées politiques de Montaigne', *Bulletin de la Société des Amis de Montaigne*, Fifth Series, no. 17 (January/March 1976): 5–30.

Dréano, M., *La Religion de Montaigne*. Paris; A.G. Nizet, 1969.

Dresden, S., 'Le Dilettantisme de Montaigne', *Bibliothèque d'Humanisme et Renaissance*, no. XV (1953): 45–56.

—— 'La Précision paradoxale de Montaigne', *Neophilologus*, nos. 46–7 (1962–3): 269–77.

Durkheim, Emile, *The Elementary Forms of the Religious Life*. London: Allen & Unwin, 1912.

Duvernois, Pierre, 'L'Emportement de l'écriture', *Critique*, no. 302 (1972): 595–609.

Eisler, Colin, *The Athelete of Virtue: The Iconography of Asceticism*, pp.82–97 in *De Artibus Opuscula XL, Essays in Honor of Erwin Panofsky*, ed. Millard Meiss. New York: New York University Press, 1961.

Engstrom, Alfred G., 'A Few Comparisons and Contrasts on the Wordcraft of Rabelais and Joyce', pp.65–82 in *Renaissance and Other Studies in Honor of William Leon Wiley*. Chapel Hill: University of North Carolina Press, 1968.

Etiemble, René, 'Sens et structure dans un essai de Montaigne', *Cahiers de l'Association Internationale des Études Françaises*, vol. 14 (1962): 263–74.

Fish, Stanley E., 'Interpreting the *Variorum*', *Critical Inquiry*, no. 2 (Spring 1976): 465–85.

—— 'Literature in the Reader: Affective Stylistics', *New Literary History*, vol. 2, no. 1 (Autumn 1970): 123–62.

—— *Self-Consuming Artifacts, The Experience of Seventeenth-Century Literature*. Berkeley: University of California Press, 1972.

Fraisse, Jean-Claude, *Philia, la notion d'amitié dans la philosophie antique*. Paris: Libraire Philosophique, J. Vrin, 1974.

Frame, Donald M., *Montaigne: A Biography*. New York: Harcourt, Brace & World, 1965.

—— *Montaigne's Essais: A Study*. Atlantic Highlands: Prentice-Hall, 1969.

—— 'What Next in Montaigne Studies?', *French Review*, no. 36 (1962–3).

Françon, Marcel, 'Montaigne et l'édit de janvier (1562)', *Bulletin de la Société des Amis de Montaigne*, Fifth Series, nos. 3–4 (July/December 1972): 17–26.

Franklin, Julian H., 'The Emergence of an Art of Reading History and the Challenge of Historical Pyrrhonism', pp.83–88, 89–102 in his *Jean Bodin and the Sixteenth Century Revolution in the Methodology of Law and History*. New York: Columbia University Press, 1966, pp.83–88, 89–102.

Friedrich, Hugo, *Montaigne*. Paris: Gallimard, 1968.

Gadamer, Hans-Georg, *Truth and Method*. New York: Seabury Press, 1975.

Gajda, Daniel A., 'Play in Montaigne's "De trois commerces"', *Romance Notes*, vol. 16, no. 1 (Autumn 1974): 172–77.

Gasché, Rodolphe, 'The Scene of Writing: A Deferred Outset'. pp.150–71 in *Glyph 1*, Johns Hopkins University Press, 1977.

Genaille, Robert, *Rembrandt: Self-Portraits*. London: Methuen, 1963.

Gide, André, *The Living Thoughts of Montaigne*. London: Cassell, 1946.

Gilbert, Felix, *Machiavelli and Guicciardini: Politics and History in Sixteenth-Century Florence*. Princeton: Princeton University Press, 1966.

Gilbert, Neal W., *Renaissance Concepts of Method*. New York: Columbia University Press, 1963.

Gilmore, Myron P., *Humanists and Jurists, Six Studies in the Renaissance*. Cambridge, MA.: Belknap Press, 1963.

—— 'The Renaissance Conception of the Lessons of History', *in Facets of the Renaissance*, ed. William H. Werkmeister. Los Angeles: University of Southern California Press, 1959.

Glauser, Alfred, *Montaigne Paradoxal*. Paris: A.G. Nizet, 1972.

Goffman, Erving, *Frame Analysis, An Essay on the Organization of Experience*. New York: Harper & Row, 1974.

Goldin, Frederick, *The Mirror of Narcissus in the Courtly Love Lyric*. Ithaca: Cornell University Press, 1967.

Goldmann, Lucien, 'Introduction aux premiers écrits de Georges Lukács', pp.156–90 in Georges Lukács, *La Théorie du roman*, trans. Jean Clairevoye. Geneva: Éditions Gonthier, 1963, pp.156–90.

—— *Structures mentales et création culturelle*. Paris: Éditions Anthropos, 1970.

Gombrich, E.H., 'Tradition and Expression in Western Still Life' in *Meditations on a Hobby Horse*. London: Phaidon, 1963.

Goumarre, Pierre J., 'Montaigne et Machiavel et les grands capitaines de l'antiquité', *Les Lettres romanes*, vol. XXVI, no. 1 (February 1973): 3–15.

—— '*Rabelais*: les possibilités de l'écriture, et celles de la nature', *Rivista di litterature moderne*, vol. 28 (December 1975): 245–51.

Grabes, Herbert, *Speculum, Mirror and Looking-glass*. Tübingen: Max Niemeyer Verlag, 1973.

Gracey, Phyllis, *Montaigne et la poésie*. Paris: Les Presses Universitaires de France, 1935.

Gray, Floyd, 'Montaigne and the *Memorabilia*', *Studies in Philology*, vol. 58 (1961): 130–9.

—— 'Montaigne's Friends', *French Studies*, vol. XV, no. 3 (July 1961): 203–12.

—— 'Montaigne's Pyrrhonism'. pp.119–136 in *O Un Amy! Essays on Montaigne in Honor of Donald M. Frame*, ed. Raymond C. La Charité. Lexington: French Forum, 1977.

Green, Thomas M., 'Petrarch and the Humanist Hermeneutic', pp.201–24 in *Italian Literature: Roots and Branches, Essays in Honor of Thomas Goddard Bergin*, ed. Giose Rimanelli and Kenneth John Atchity. New Haven: Yale University Press, 1976.

—— 'The Flexibility of the Self in Renaissance Literature' in *The Disciplines of Criticism: Essays in Literary Theory, Interpretation and History*, ed. Peter Demetz, Thomas Greene and Lowry Nelson, Jr. New Haven: Yale University Press, 1968.

Grene, Marjorie, *Approaches to a Philosophical Biology*. New York: Basic Books, 1968.

Griffin, Robert, *Coronation of the Poet: Joachim Du Bellay's Debt to the Trivium*. Berkeley: University of California Press, 1969.

Guelley, R., 'L'Évolution des méthodes théologiques à Louvain d'Erasme à Jansénius', *Revue d'histoire ecclésiastique*, vol. 37 (1941): 31–141.

Guggenheim, Michel, 'Gide and Montaigne', *Yale French Studies*, no. 7 (1951): 107–14.

Guillen, Claudio, *Literature as System, Essays Towards the Theory of Literary History.* Princeton: Princeton University Press, 1971.

Gusdorf, Georges, 'Conditions et limites de l'autobiographie', pp.105–23 in *Formen der Selbstdarstellung*, ed. Günter Reichenkron and Erich Haase, Berlin, Dunker & Humbolt (1956): 105–23.

Gutwirth, Marcel, '*Des Coches:* ou la structuration d'une absence', *L'Esprit créateur*, vol. XV, nos 1–2 (Spring–Summer 1975): 8–20.

Gutwirth, Marcel, *Michel de Montaigne, ou le pari d'exemplarité.* Montréal: Les Presses de l'Université de Montréal, 1977.

Habermas, Jürgen, *Between Facts And Norms: Contributions to a Discourse Theory of Law and Democracy.* Cambridge, MA.: The MIT Press, 1966.

Hallie, Philip P., *The Scar of Montaigne, An Essay in Personal Philosophy.* Middletown: Wesleyan University Press, 1966.

Hamel, S., 'Expérience-Essai: contribution à l'étude du vocabulaire de Montaigne', *Bulletin de la Société des Amis de Montaigne*, Third Series, nos. 11–12 (1959): 23–32.

Hart, Francis R., 'Notes for an Anatomy of Modern Autobiography', *New Literary History*, no. I (1970): 485–511.

Hartman, Geoffrey H., *The Fate of Reading and Other Essays.* Chicago:University of Chicago Press, 1975.

Hay, Camilla Hill, *Montaigne: lecteur et imitateur de Sénèque.* Poitiers: Société Française d'Imprimerie, 1938.

Hegel, G.W.F., *The Phenomenology of Mind*, translated with an Introduction and Notes by J.B. Baillie. London: George Allen & Unwin, 1949.

Heitmann, Klaus, *Fortuna and Virtus, Eine Studie zu Petrarcas Lebensweisheit.* Cologne: Böhlau Verlag, 1958.

Heller, Agnes, *Renaissance Man.* London: Routledge & Kegan Paul, 1978.

Henry, Patrick, 'Les Titres Façades, la censure et l'écriture défensive chez Montaigne', *Bulletin de la Société des Amis de Montaigne*, Fifth Series, no. 24 (October–December 1977): 11–28.

Holyoake, S. John, 'How to Read Montaigne', *Kentucky Romance Quarterly*, vol. XIX, no. 3, 1972, pp.337–45.

—— 'The Idea of *Jugement* in Montaigne', *Modern Language Review*, vol. LXIII (1968): 340–51.

Horace, *Satires, Epistles and Ars Poetica*, trans. H. Rushton Fairclough. London: Heinemann, 1978.

Horkheimer, Max, 'Montaigne und die Funktion der Skepsis', *Zeitschrift für Sozialforschung*, vol. 1/2 (1938): 1–54.

Huppert, Horst, *Les Bourgeois Gentilshommes: An Essay on the Definition of Elites in Renaissance France.* Chicago: University of Chicago Press, 1977.

Hutter, Horst, *Politics as Friendship: The Origins of Classical Notions of Politics in the Theory and Practice of Friendship.* Waterloo: Wilfrid Laurier University Press, 1978.

Hyppolite, Jean, 'The Structure of Philosophic Language According to the 'Preface' to Hegel's *Phenomenology of Mind*', pp.157–185 in *The Languages of Criticism and the Sciences of Man: The Structuralist Controversy*, ed. Richard Macksey and Eugenio Donato. Baltimore: Johns Hopkins University Press, 1970.

Iser, Wolfgang, 'Indeterminacy and the Reader's Response in Prose Fiction', pp.1–45 in *Aspects of Narrative*, ed. J. Hillis Miller. New York: Columbia University Press, 1971.

—— 'The Reading Process: A Phenomenological Approach', *New Literary History*, vol. III, no. 2 (Winter 1972): 279–89.

Jamieson, I.W.A., 'Augustine's Confessions: The Structure of Humility', *Augustiniana*, vol. 24 (1974): 234–46.

Jansen, J.B., *Sources vives de la Pensée de Montaigne, études sur les fondements psychologiques et biographies des 'Essais'*. Copenhagen: Levin & Muskgaard, 1935.

Jasinski, René, 'Sur la composition chez Montaigne'. pp.257–67 in *Mélanges d'histoire littéraire offerts à Henri Chamard*. Paris: Librairie Nizet, 1951.

Joly, Robert, *Le Thème philosophique des genres de vie dans l'antiquité classique*. Brussels: Palais des Académies, 1956.

Jones, Robert F., 'On the Dialogic Impulse in the Genesis of Montaigne's *Essais*', *Renaissance Quarterly*, vol. XXX, no. 2 (Summer 1977): 172–80.

Jost, François, 'La Tradition du Bildungsroman', *Comparative Literature*, vol. XXI, no. 2 (Spring 1969): 97–115.

Joukovsky, F., *Montaigne et le problème du temps*. Paris: A.G. Nizet, 1972.

Joyce, James, *Ulysses*. Harmondsworth: Penguin Books, 1968.

Judrin, Roger, *Montaigne et son œuvre*. Paris: Éditions, Seghers, 1971.

Keller, Abraham C., 'Anti-War Writing in France 1500–1600, *PMLA*, no. LXVII (1952): 240–50.

—— 'Optimism in the Essays of Montaigne', *Studies in Philology*, vol. 54 (1957): 408–28.

Kellerman, Frederick, 'The *Essais* and Socrates', *Symposium*, vol. 10 (1956): 204–16.

—— 'Montaigne's Socrates, *Romantic Review*, vol. XLV, no. 3 (October 1954): 170–7.

Kelley, Donald R., 'Guillaume Budé and the First Historical School of Law', *American Historical Review*, no. LXIII (1967): 807–34.

Keohane, Nannerl O., 'Montaigne's Individualism', *Political Theory*, vol. 5, no. 3, (August 1977): 363–90.

Kerr, W.A.R., 'The Pléiade and Platonism', *Modern Philology*, vol. 5 (1907–8): 1–15.

Kilbansky, Raymond, Panofsky, Erwin, and Saxl, Fritz, *Saturn and Melancholy, Studies in the History of Natural Philosophy, Religion and Art*. London: Thomas Nelson, 1964.

Kölsch, Manfred, *Recht und Macht bei Montaigne, Ein Beitrag zur Erforschung der Grundlagen von Staat und Recht*. Berlin: Dunker & Humbolt, 1974.

Kritzman, Lawrence, 'Montaigne's Fantastic Monsters and the Construction of Gender' in *Writing the Renaissance: Essays in Sixteenth Century Literature in Honor of Floyd Gray*, ed. Raymond C. La Charité. Lexington: French Forum, 1992.

Lablénie, E., *Essai sur Montaigne*. Paris: Gallimard, 1968.

La Boétie, Étienne de, *Le Discours de la servitude volontaire*, texte établi par P. Léonard, avec *La Boétie et la question du politique*, textes de Lammenais, P. Leroux, A. Vermonel, G. Landauer, S. Weit, et de Pierre Clastres et Claude Lefort. Paris: Payot, 1976.

—— *The Politics of Obedience: The Discourse of Voluntary Servitude*, trans. Harry Kurz, Introduction by Murray N. Rothbard. New York: Free Life Editions, 1975.

Lacan, Jacques, 'The Mirror-Phase', trans. Jean Roussel in *New Left Review*, no 51 (1968): 71–77.

La Drière, Craig, 'Horace and the Theory of Imitation', *American Journal of Philology*, vol. LX (1939): 288–300.

Lapp, John C., *The Esthetics of Negligence: La Fontaine's 'Contes'*. Cambridge: Cambridge University Press, 1971.

—— 'Montaigne's '"negligence" and some lines from *Virgil*', *Romantic Review*, no. LXI (1970): 167–81.

Larkin, Neil M., 'Montaigne's Last Words', *L'Esprit créateur*, vol. 15, no. 1 (Spring 1975): 21–38.

Lebèque, Raymond, 'Montaigne et le paradoxe des cannibales', pp.359–63 in *Studi di letteratura storia e filosofia in onore di Bruno Revel*, Florence, Leo S. Olschki Editore, 1965.

Lee, Rensselaer W., 'Ut pictura poesis: The Humanistic Theory of Painting', *Art Bulletin*, no. XXII (December 1940): 197–269.

Lejeune, Philippe, *Le Pacte autobiographique*. Paris: Éditions du Seuil, 1975.

Limbrick, Elaine, 'Montaigne and Socrates', *Renaissance and Reformation*, vol. IX, no. 2 (1973): 46–57.

Livius, Titus, *The History of Rome*, trans. George Baker. London: Jones, 1830, vol. 1.

Locher, Caroline, 'Primary and Secondary Themes in Montaigne's "Des Cannibales" (I, 31)', *French Forum*, vol. I (1976): 119–26.

Lofberg, John Oscar, *Sycophancy in Athens*. Chicago: University of Chicago Press, 1917.

Lowenthal, Marvin, *The Autobiography of Michel de Montaigne*. Boston: Houghton Mifflin, 1935.

Lowinsky, Edward E., *Secret Chromatic Art in The Netherlands Motet*. New York: Russell & Russell, 1946.

Lukács, Georg, 'On the Nature and Form of the Essay' in his *Soul and Form*, trans. Anna Bostock. Cambridge, MA.: The MIT Press, 1971.

Macherey, Pierre, *A Theory of Literary Production*, trans. Geoffrey Wall. London: Routledge & Kegan Paul, 1978.

Macksey, Richard, and Donato, Eugenio (eds), *The Languages of Criticism and the Sciences of Man, The Structuralist Controversy*. Baltimore: Johns Hopkins University Press, 1970.

MacPhail, Eric , 'Friendship as a Political Ideal in Montaigne's *Essais*', *Montaigne Studies* 1 (1989): 177–87.

Mahieu, Isabelle, 'Fetishism and Beyond: Notes of Reading and Pleasure', *Cambridge Review*, vol. 95, no. 2219 (March 1974).

Malloch, A.E., 'The Techniques and Function of the Renaissance Paradox', *Studies in Philology*, vol. LIII (1956): 191–203.

Marchand, Ernest, 'Montaigne and the Cult of Ignorance', *Romantic Review*, vol. XXXVI, no. 4 (December 1945): 275–82.

Martin, Daniel, *L'Architecture Des Essais De Montaigne: Mémoire Artificielle Et Mythologique*. Paris: Librairie Nizet, 1992.

Masters, G. Mallory, *Rabelaisian Dialectic and the Platonic–Hermetic Tradition*. Albany: State University of New York Press, 1969.

Mayer, Gilbert, 'Les Images dans Montaigne, d'après le chapitre de l'institution des enfants', pp.110–18 in *Mélanges de philologie et d'histoire littéraire offerts à Edmond Huguet*. Paris: Bovin, 1940.

McGowan, Margaret, *Montaigne's Deceits, The Art of Persuasion in the Essais*. London: University of London Press, 1974.

McKeon, Richard, 'Literary Criticism and the Concept of Imitation in Antiquity', *Modern Philology*, vol. XXXIV, no. 1 (August 1936): 1–35.

Medina, Angel, *Reflection, Time, and the Novel: Toward a Communicative Theory of the Novel*. London: Routledge & Kegan Paul, 1979.

Mehlman, Jeffrey, *A Structural Study of Autobiography: Proust, Leiris, Sartre, Lévi-Strauss*. Ithaca: Cornell University Press, 1974.

Meijer, Marianne S., 'Montaigne et la Bible', *Bulletin de la Société des Amis de Montaigne*, Fifth Series, no. 20 (October–December 1976): 23–57.

Menut, Albert D., 'Montaigne and the Nicomachean Ethics', *Modern Philology*, vol. XXXI, no. 3 (February 1934): 225–42.

Merleau-Ponty, Maurice, *Phenomenology, Language and Sociology, Selected Essays*, edited and with an Introduction by John O'Neill. London: Heinemann Educational, 1974.

—— *Sign*, trans. Richard C. McCleary. Evanston: Northwestern University Press, 1964.

Mermier, Guy, 'L'Essai "Des Cannibales" de Montaigne', *Bulletin de la Société des Amis de Montaigne*, nos 7–8 (July–December 1973): 27–38.

Montaigne, Michel de, *The Complete Works of Montaigne, Essays, Travel Journal, Letters*, newly translated by Donald M. Frame. Stanford: Stanford University Press, 1948.

—— *The Essays of Michel de Montaigne*, translated and edited by Jacob Zeitlin. New York: Alfred Knopf, 1935.

Musil, Robert, *The Man Without Qualities*, trans. Eithne Wilkins and Ernst Kaiser. New York: Capricorn Books, 1965.

Nadal, Octave, 'L'Ethique de la gloire au dix-septième siécle', *Mercure de France*, vol. 308 (1950): 22–34.

Nelson, Cary, 'Reading Criticism', *PMLA*, vol. 91, no. 5 (October 1976): 801–15.

Nelson, Lowry, Jr, 'The Fictive Reader and Literary Self-Reflexiveness', pp.173–91 in *The Disciplines of Criticism, Essays in Literary Theory, Interpretation and History*, ed. Peter Demetz, Thomas Greene and Lowry Nelson, Jr. New Haven: Yale University Press, 1968.

Neuschel, Kristen B., *Word of Honor: Interpreting Noble Culture in Sixteenth-Century France*. Ithaca: Cornell University Press, 1989.

Newton-De Molina, David (ed.), *On Literary Intention: Critical Essays*. Edinburgh:

Edinburgh University Press, 1976.

Norton, Glyn P., 'Translation Theory in Renaissance France: Étienne Dolet and the Rhetorical Tradition', *Renaissance and Reformation*, vol. X, no. 1 (1974): 30–44.

O'Neill, John, 'Can Phenomenology be Critical?' pp.200–16 in *Phenomenology and Sociology*, ed. Thomas Luckmann. Harmondsworth: Penguin Books, 1978.

—— 'The Concept of Estrangement in the Early and Later Writings of Karl Marx', *Philosophy and Phenomenological Research*, no. XXV (September 1964): 69–84.

—— 'Critique and Remembrance'. pp.1–11 in *On Critical Theory*, ed. John O'Neill. New York: Seabury Press, 1976.

—— 'Hegel and Marx on History as Human History'. pp.xi–xx in Jean Hyppolite, *Studies on Marx and Hegel*, edited and translated by John O'Neill. New York: Basic Books, 1969.

—— 'Le Langage et la décolonisation: Fanon et Freire', *Sociologie et Sociétés*, vol. 2 (November 1974): 53–65.

—— 'Language and the Legitimation Problem', *Sociology*, vol. 11, no. 2 (May 1977): 351–8.

—— 'Language and the Voice of Philosophy', pp.xi–xvi in Maurice Merleau-Ponty, *The Prose of the World*, trans. John O'Neill. Evanston: Northwestern University Press, 1973.

—— 'The Literary Production of Natural and Social Science Inquiry', *Canadian Journal of Sociology*, vol. 6, no. 2 (Spring 1981): 105–120.

—— *Making Sense Together: An Introduction to Wild Sociology.* New York: Harper & Row, 1974.

—— 'On Body Politics', pp.251–67 in *Recent Sociology, No. 4, Family, Marriage and the Struggle of the Sexes*, ed. Hans Peter Dreitzel. New York: Macmillan, 1972.

—— 'On Simmel's "Sociological Apriorities"', pp.91–106 in *Phenomenological Sociology, Issues and Applications.* New York: John Wiley, 1973.

—— *Perception, Expression and History: The Social Phenomenology of Maurice Merleau-Ponty.* Evanston: Northwestern University Press, 1970.

—— 'Self-Prescription and Social Machiavellianism', pp.11–19 in his *Sociology as a Skin Trade: Essays Towards a Reflexive Sociology.* New York: Harper & Row, 1972.

—— 'Situation, Action and Language'. pp.81–95 in his *Sociology as a Skin Trade: Essays Towards a Reflexive Sociology*, New York, Harper & Row, 1972.

—— 'Time's Body: Vico on the Love of Language and Institution', pp.333–9 in *Giambattista Vico's Science of Humanity*, ed. Giorgio Tagliacozzo and Donald Phillip Verene. Baltimore: Johns Hopkins University Press, 1976.

Ornstein, Robert M., Donne, 'Montaigne and Natural Law', *JEGP*, no. LV (1956): 213–29.

Panofsky, Erwin, *Early Netherlandish Painting: Its Origins and Character.* New York: Harper & Row, 1971.

—— *Renaissance and Renascences in Western Art.* Stockholm: Almqvist Wiksell, 1960.

Paris, Jean, 'Tel qu'en leu-même il se voit'. pp.97–121 in his *Rembrandt.* Paris: Librairie Hachette, 1965.

Pascal, *Pensées*, translated with an Introduction by A.J. Krailsheimer. Harmondsworth: Penguin Books, 1966.

Pearson, Lionel, *Popular Ethics in Ancient Greece*. Stanford: Stanford University Press, 1962.

Pease, A.S., 'Things Without Honor', *Classical Philology*, no. XXI (1926): 27–42.

Perelman, Chaim, 'La Méthode dialectique et le rôle d'interlocuteur dans le dialogue', *Revue de métaphysique et de morale*, vols 60–1 (1955–6): 26–31.

Pertile, Lino, 'Paper and Ink: The Structure of Unpredictability'. pp.190–218 in *O Un Amy! Essays on Montaigne in Honor of Donald M. Frame*, ed. Raymond C. La Charité. Lexington: French Forum, 1977.

Petrarca, Francesco, *Sonnets and Songs*, trans. Anna Maria Armi. New York: Pantheon, 1946.

Petrarch, *De ignorantia*, trans. Hans Nachod, in Ernst Cassirer, *The Renaissance Philosophy of Man*. Chicago: University of Chicago Press, 1948.

—— *Familiariam rerum libri*, ed. V. Rossi, *Le Familiari*. Florence, 1923–42, I.

—— *Four Dialogues for Scholars*, from *De remediis utriusque fortunae*, edited and newly translated into English by Confrad H. Rawski. Cleveland: Western Reserve University Press, 1967.

Pfeiffer, Rudolf, *History of Classical Scholarship, from 1300 to 1850*. Oxford: Clarendon Press, 1976.

Pico della Mirandola, Giovanni, *De hominis dignitate, Heptaplus, De Ente et uno, e scritti vari*, ed. Eugenio Garin. Florence, 1942.

Plato, *Ion*, trans. Jowett, *The Dialogues of Plato*. Oxford: Clarendon Press, 1953, vol. I.

—— *Phaedrus*, trans. B. Jowett, *The Dialogues of Plato*. Oxford: Clarendon Press, 1953, vol. III.

—— *Symposium*, trans. B. Jowett, *The Dialogues of Plato*. Oxford: Clarendon Press, 1953, vol. I.

Pouilloux, Jean-Yves, 'Deux discours de Montaigne: du manque d'espace à l'espace du manque', *Scolies*, Fasc, 3–4 (1973–4).

—— *Lire les 'essais' de Montaigne*. Paris: François Maspero, 1970.

Poulet, Georges, 'Criticism and the Experience of Interiority', pp.56–73 in *The Languages of Criticism and the Sciences of Man: The Structuralist Controversy*, ed. Richard Macksey and Eugenio Donato. Baltimore: Johns Hopkins University Press, 1970.

—— 'Phenomenology of Reading', *New Literary History*, no. 1, 1969–70, pp.53–68.

Preston, John, *The Created Self: The Reader's Role in Eighteenth Century Fiction*. New York: Barnes & Noble, 1970.

Quint, David, *Montaigne and the Quality of Mercy: Ethical and Political Themes in the Essais*. Princeton: Princeton University Press, 1998.

Rabelais, *Gargantua and Pantagruel*, trans. Jacques Le Clercq. New York: Modern Library, 1944.

Rathé, C.E., 'The Theatricality of Montaigne and the Problem of Self-Knowledge'. pp.83–98 in *Historical and Literary Perspectives, Essays and Studies in Honor of Albert D. Menut*, ed. by Sandoro Sticca, Lawrence. Kansas City: Coronada Press, 1973.

Raymond, Marcel, 'Montaigne devant les sauvages d'Amérique', pp.13–37 in his

Être et dire, Études, Neuchâtel, Éditions de la Baconnière, 1970.

Rawls, John, *Political Liberalism*. New York: Columbia University Press, 1996.

Recksieck, Margot, 'Montaignes Verhältnis zu Klassik und Manierismus'. Bonn thesis, 1966.

Regosin, Richard L., 'Conceptions of the Text and the Generation(s) of Meaning: Monatigne's *Essais* and the Place(s) of the Reader', *Journal of Medieval and Renaissance Studies*, 15 no.1 (Spring 1985): 101–14

—— *The Matter of My Book: Montaigne's 'Essays' as the Book of the Self*. Berkeley: University of California Press, 1977.

—— *Montaigne's Unruly Brood: Textual Engendering and Challenge to Paternal Authority*. Berkeley: University of California Press, 1996.

Rendall, Steven, 'Dialectical Structure and Tactics in Montaigne's "Of Cannibals"', *Pacific Coast Philology*, no. XII (1977): 56–63.

Richmond, Hugh M., 'Personal Identity and Literary Personae: A Study in Historical Psychology', *PMLA*, vol. 90, no. 2 (1975): 209–21.

Rigolot, François, *Poétique et onomastique, L'exemple de la Renaissance*. Geneva: Librairie Droz, 1977.

Rimanelli, Giose, and Atchity, Kenneth John (eds), *Italian Literature: Root and Branches, Essays in Honor of Thomas Goddard Bergin*. New Haven: Yale University Press, 1976.

Riveline, Maurice, *Montaigne et l'amitié*. Paris: Librairie Alcan, 1939.

Roubichou-Stretz, Antoinette, *La Vision de l'histoire dans L'œuvre de la Pléiade, thèmes et structures*. Paris: Librairie A.G. Nizet, 1973.

Rousset, Jean, *La Littérature de l'âge baroque en France, Circé et Paon*. Paris: Librairie Jose Corti, 1953.

Russell, H.K., 'Elizabethan Dramatic Poetry in The Light of Natural and Moral Philosophy', *Philological Quarterly*, vol. XII, no. 2 (April 1933): 187–93.

Saccone, Eduardo, *'Grazia, Sprezzatura*, and *Affettazione* in Castiglione's *Book of the Courtier'*, pp.34–54 in *Glyph 5*, Johns Hopkins Textual Studies. Baltimore: Johns Hopkins University Press, 1979.

Sacy, S.de, 'Montaigne essaie ses facultés naturelles', *Mercure de France*, vol. 1, no. VI (1952): 285–306.

Said, Edward W., *Beginnings, Intention and Method*. New York: Basic Books, 1975.

Sanders, Sylvia G., 'Montaigne et les idées politiques de Machiavel', *Bulletin de la Société des Amis de Montaigne*, Fifth Series, nos 18–19 (April–September 1976): 85–98.

Sartre, Jean-Paul, *What is Literature?*, trans. Wallace Fowlie. New York: Harper & Row, 1967.

Sayce, R.A., 'Baroque Elements in Montaigne', *French Studies*, vol. 8 (1954): 1–15.

—— *The Essays of Montaigne, A Critical Exploration*. London: Weidenfeld & Nicolson, 1972.

Sayre, Robert, *Solitude in Society: A Sociological Study in French Literature*. Cambridge, MA.: Harvard University Press, 1979.

Schellhase, Kenneth C., *Tacitus in Renaissance Political Thought*. Chicago: University of Chicago Press, 1976.

Screech, M.A., 'Medicine and Literature: Aspects of Rabelais and Montaigne (with a Glance at the Law)', pp.156–69 in *French Renaissance Studies 1540–70:*

Humanism and the Encyclopaedia, ed. Peter Sharrat. Edinburgh: University Press, 1976.

—— *Montaigne and Melancholy: The Wisdom of the 'Essays'*. London: Duckworth, 1983.

Segers, Rien, Readers, 'Text, and Author: Some Implications of Rezeption-aesthetik', *Yearbook of Comparative and General Literature*, no. 24 (1975): 15–23.

Seigel, Jerold E., 'Ideals of Eloquence and Silence in Petrarch', *Journal of the History of Ideas*, vol. XXVI, no. 2 (April–June 1965): 147–74.

Selzer, Richard, 'Kidney Stone', *Esquire*, vol. 82 (August 1974): 100–1, 118–20.

Seneca, *Moral Essays*, trans. John W. Basore. London: Heinemann, 1965.

Sinaiko, Herman L., *Love, Knowledge and Discourse in Plato: Dialogue and Dialectic in Phaedrus, Republic, Parmenides*. Chicago: University of Chicago Press, 1965.

Sixel, Friedrich W., 'The Problem of Sense: Habermas v. Luhmann', pp.184–204 in *On Critical Theory*, ed. John O'Neill. New York: Seabury Press, 1976.

Stackelberg, Jurgen von, 'Das Bienengleichnis: ein Beitrag zur Geschichte der literarischen Imitatio', *Romanische Forschungen*, no. 68 (1956): 271–93.

Stanton, Donn C., 'Woman as Object and Subject of Exchange: Marie Le Gournay's *Le Proumenour* (1594)', *L'Esprit Createur*, Vol. XXII, No 2 (1983): 9–25.

—— 'Autobiography: The Case of Marie de Gournay's *Apologie pour celle qui escrit*', French Literature Series, Vol. XII (1985): 18–34.

Starobinski, Jean, 'Distance et plénitude', *Mercure de France*, no. 348 (1963): 400–9.

—— 'Montaigne: des morts exemplaires à la vie sans exemple', *Critique*, no. 258 (November 1968): 923–35.

—— 'Montaigne en mouvement', *Nouvelle Revue française*, vol. 15 (1960):16–22, 254–66.

—— *L'Œil vivant II, La Relation critique*. Paris: Gallimard, 1970.

Starowski, F., 'Une Source italienne des *Essais* de Montaigne: 'L'Examen Vanitatis Doctrinae Gentium' de François Pic de la Mirandole', *Bulletin Italien*, vol. V, no. 4 (October–December 1905): 309–13.

Struever, Nancy S., *The Language of History in the Renaissance: Rhetoric and Historical Consciousness in Florentine Humanism*. Princeton: Princeton University Press, 1970.

Sturtz, Edward L., 'The Defence of Pleasure in More's Utopia', *Studies in Philology*, vol. XLVI, no. 2 (April 1949): 99–112.

Supple, J.J., 'Montaigne's "De la Gloire": Structure and Method', *French Studies*, vol. XXVII, no. 4 (October 1973): 385–94.

Taffon, Dain A., 'Ancients and Indians in Montaigne's "Des Coches"', *Symposium* (Spring 1973): 76–90.

Tetel, Marcel, 'Montaigne et Pétrarque: irrésolution et solitude', *Journal of Medieval and Renaissance Studies*, vol. 4, no. 2 (Autumn 1974): 203–20.

Thibaudet, Albert, 'Langage, littérature et sensualité', *Nouvelle Revue franéaise*, no. 38 (1932): 716–26.

Tigerstedt, E.N., 'The Poet as Creator: Origins of a Metaphor', *Comparative Literature Studies*, no. 5 (1968): 455–88.

Toldo, Pietro, 'L'Homme sage de Montaigne', pp.132–53 in *Mélanges offerts par ses amis et ses elèves à M. Gustave Lanson*. Paris: Librairie Hachette, 1922.

Traeger, Wolf Eberhard, *Aufbau und Gedankenführung in Montaignes Essays*. Heidelberg: Carl Winter Universität Verlag, 1961.

Trilling, Lionel, *Sincerity and Authenticity*. Cambridge, MA.: Harvard University Press, 1974.

Trinkhaus, Charles, *In Our Image and Likeness: Humanity and Divinity in Italian Humanist Thought*. London, Constable, 1970.

Tronquart, Georges, 'Montaigne à la recherche des Essais', *Bulletin de la Société des Amis de Montaigne*, Third Series, nos. 11–12 (1959): 16–22.

Ullmann, Walter, *Medieval Political Thought*. Harmondsworth: Penguin Books, 1975, pp.200–14.

Vance, Eugene, 'Augustine's "Confessions" and the Grammar of Selfhood', *Genre*, vol. 6 (1973): 1–28.

—— 'Le Moi comme langage: Saint Augstin et l'autobiographie', *Poétique*, vol. 14 (1973): 163–77.

Vernon, John, *The Garden and the Map: Schizophrenia in Twentieth Century Literature and Culture*. Urbana: University of Illinois Press, 1973.

Villey, Pierre, *Les Sources et l'évolution des Essais de Montaigne*. Paris: Librairie Hachette, 1908, vol. I.

Wadsworth, Philip A., 'Montaigne's Conclusion to Book II of His *Essais*'. pp.249–60 in *Renaissance and Other Studies in Honor of William Leon Wiley*. Chapel Hill: University of North Carolina Press, 1968, pp.249–60.

Weber, Max, *The Protestant Ethic and the Spirit of Capitalism*, trans. Talcott Parsons, with a foreword by R.H. Tawney. New York: Scribner, 1958.

Weinberg, Bernard, 'Montaigne's Readings for "Des Cannibales"', *Renaissance and Other Studies in Honor of William Leon Wiley*, ed. George Bernard Daniel, Jr. Chapel Hill: University of North Carolina Press, 1968, pp.261–79.

Wellek, René, *Concepts of Criticism*, ed. Stephen G. Nichols, Jr. New Haven: Yale University Press, 1963.

Weller, Barry, 'The Rhetoric of Friendship in Montaigne's *Essais*', *New Literary History*, vol. IX, no. 3 (Spring 1978): 503–23.

Welter, J.-Th., *L'Exemplum dans la littérature religieuse et didactique du Moyen Age*. Paris: Occitania, 1927.

Wenzel, Siegfried, 'Petrarch's *Accidia*', *Studies in the Renaissance*, vol. 8 (1961): 36–48.

White, Hayden, 'The Forms of Wildness: Archeology of an Idea' in *The Wild Man Within, An Image in Western Thought from the Renaissance to Romanticism*, ed. Edward Dodley and Maximillian E. Novak. Pittsburgh: University of Pittsburgh Press, 1972.

Wijngaarden, N. van, *Les Odyssées philosophiques en France entre 1616 et 1789*. Haarlem: Drukkerij Vijlbriet, 1932.

Wilden, Anthony, '*Pars divers moyens on arrive à pareille fin*: A Reading of Montaigne', *Modern Language Notes*, vol. 83 (1968): 577–97.

—— *System and Structure: Essays in Communication and Exchange*. London: Tavistock, 1972.

Wiley, Karen F., 'Montaigne's Artful Praise of Artlessness', *Modern Language Studies*, vol. V, no. 2 (Autumn 1975): 78–84.

259

Wilkins, Ernest Hatch, *Life of Petrarch*. Chicago:University of Chicago Press, 1961.

—— *Petrarch's Correspondence*. Padua: Editrice Antenore, 1960.

Willetts, R.F., *Aristocratic Society in Ancient Crete*. London: Routledge & Kegan Paul, 1955.

Williamson, Edward, 'On the Liberalizing of Montaigne: A Remonstrance', *French Review*, vol. XXIII (October 1949): 92–100.

Winter, Ian J., 'From Self-Concept to Self-Knowledge: Death and Nature in Montaigne's "De la Phisionomie"', *Kentucky Romance Quarterly*, vol. XXI, Supplement no. 2 (1974): 351–65.

—— *Montaigne's Self-Portrait, and its Influence in France, 1580–1630*. Lexington: French Forum, 1976.

Wittkower, Elly, 'Die Form der Essais von Montaigne'. Basle thesis, 1935.

Wolff, Kurt H., 'Beginning: In Hegel and Today', pp.72–105 in *The Critical Spirit: Essays in Honor of Herbert Marcuse*, ed. Kurt H. Wolff and Barrington Moore, Jr. Boston: Beacon Press, 1967.

Yale French Studies, nos. 55–6 (1977), 'Literature and Psychoanalysis, The Question of Reading: Otherwise'.

Index

Index

Index